Simone Signoret

Also available from Continuum:

Bondanella: Italian Cinema, 3rd edition
Jones: The Guerilla Film Makers Movie Blueprint
Jones and Jolliffe: The Guerilla Film Makers Handbook
Kagan: The Cinema of Stanley Kubrick
Lanzoni: French Cinema
McMahan: Alice Guy Blaché: Lost Visionary of the Cinema
Rayner: The Films of Peter Weir
Schroeder: Cinema's Illusions, Opera's Allure
Vincendeau: Stars and Stardom in French Cinema

Forthcoming:

Kickasola: The Films of Kryzstof Kieslowski
McMahan: The Films of Tim Burton

Simone Signoret

The Star as Cultural Sign

Susan Hayward

continuum
NEW YORK • LONDON

2004

The Continuum International Publishing Group Inc
15 E 26 Street, New York, NY 10010

The Continuum International Publishing Group Ltd
The Tower Building, 11 York Road, London SE1 7NX

www.continuumbooks.com

Printed in the United States of America

Library of Congress Cataloging-in-Publication Data

Hayward, Susan, 1945-
    Simone Signoret : the star as cultural sign / Susan Hayward.
        p.   cm.
    Includes filmography.
    Includes bibliographical references and index.
    ISBN 0-8264-1393-5 (alk. paper)—ISBN 0-8264-1394-3 (pbk. : alk.
paper)
    1. Signoret, Simone, 1921—Criticism and interpretation.   I. Title.
PN2638.S47H39   2004
791.4302'8'092—dc22   2004001220

This book is dedicated to the memory of four extraordinary women, all of whom died too early from cancer. They were good friends and brilliant academics.

Lammy Betten

Claire Duchen

Jill Forbes

Fee Wellhofer

Contents

Acknowledgments

I WISH to thank the following institutional bodies for their very great help in getting this project off the ground and written: the British Academy and the University of Exeter Research Committee, which funded my primary research in 1998; the Arts and Humanities Research Board for the Research Leave Scheme Grant, which enabled me to complete the writing of the book; the British Film Institute Film Archives and Library, for their invaluable resources and in particular the library staff for their tremendous help; the Centre National de la Cinématographie (CNC) and the Cinémathèque Française, for the films I was able to view there; and the Bibliothèque Nationale Française François Mitterrand (BNF), where the television archives of the Inathèque are held, as well as a bountiful number of films on video in the Audiovisual Section. I am grateful also to the Maison Suger (part of the Centre National de la Recherche Sociale [CNRS]), for being so welcoming during my research sojourns in Paris.

On a more personal level, I would like to thank the following individuals for their considerable help. First, I must thank Ginette Vincendeau and Pam Cook for initially inviting me to write this book. I thank David Barker, my editor, for his patience and forbearance; Flo Martin, whose willingness to read all my chapters and comment upon them has been of tremendous help and support; and my mother, Kathleen Hayward, for proofreading and other forms of invaluable input. For helpful suggestions on archival and video material, I wish to thank Claire Duchen, Chantal Duchet, Michèle Lagny, Mifa Martin, and Geneviève Sellier. Technicians who were so helpful include Laure Boissou (Cinémathèque Française), Daniel Courbet (CNC), Mark Desrues (BNF), and Arzura Flornoy Bibliothèque du Film [BIFI]. For facilitating my access to archival material, I wish to thank Christine Barbier-Bouvet (Inathèque), Jacqueline Mathey (Inathèque), Martine Delcambre (BNF), Eric Leroy (CNC), and Bernard Benoliel (Cinémathèque Française). I wish to acknowledge my debt to my close friends for their moral support and interest. And, finally, I thank my cat Ibubese.

Chapter One

Signoret, a Life—Chronotopes or Topographies of Space and Time

*T*HIS BOOK is not intended to be a biography of Simone Signoret. However, it does seem crucial to place this important icon of Frenchness and French cinema—who was not just a star but also a significant political personage and an author—within the contexts and locations of her times. To this effect, the sections that follow are called chronotopes. *Chronotope* (literally "time-space") is a term coined by the critical theorist Mikhail Bakhtin to refer to the idea of the spatiotemporal structures of the novel. Bakhtin, influenced by Albert Einstein's theory of relativity, defines the chronotope as "the intrinsic connectedness of temporal and spatial relations that are artistically expressed in literature" (Bakhtin 1981, 84).[1] Here, I will use it to refer to the intrinsic connection between time and space and the structures of Signoret's own life. The chronotope is a means whereby we can roam through time and space, see the past in the present, read a person's life, and give it material substance. The chronotope is richer than the concept of topography (a placing of a subject), because it refers to space (which includes the concept of place) and time. It seems a very apt term to use, therefore, when studying the density, historically and politically, of Signoret's star persona. Thus, the chronotopes that follow are time-space discursive images that textualize Signoret and function to evoke her existence. But, because a life is a series of overlapping time-space narratives, the reader will notice that some of the chronotopes in this chapter, for example, chronotopes 2 and 3, come back on themselves.

CHRONOTOPE 1
1921–1944

Simone Signoret (given name Simone Henriette Charlotte Kaminker) was born in 1921 in Wiesbaden, Germany, the daughter of Georgette and André Kaminker. Her father, a French citizen, was the son of a Polish Jew who had emigrated to France. Signoret's mother, who was born in Paris, was the daughter of a milliner and an obscure artist from Marseille (Signoret 1978, 14). André Kaminker had been stationed in Wiesbaden as part of the French occupying troops in the Rhineland following World War I.

The family lived in Wiesbaden until 1923, when they moved to Neuilly-sur-Seine, a suburb of Paris, residing at first on rue Jacques Dulud. The street, which runs parallel to the rather grand avenue du Roule, is modest. Residences run from two- and three-story eighteenth-century houses to late-nineteenth-century apartment buildings. Signoret attended nursery school at the cours Lafayette, near rue Jacques Dulud. A small synagogue on the street indicates that there was a significant Jewish presence in this very bourgeois enclave. It is doubtful that Signoret ever attended the synagogue, however, being brought up, as she readily admitted, in blissful agnosticism. Furthermore, her father, if he had any aspirations at all, was fully committed to becoming assimilated into the Parisian bourgeoisie (Signoret 1978, 30). By the early 1930s, the Kaminkers had moved to a sixth-floor apartment on the corner of avenue du Roule and the rue d'Orléans. This eight-story Haussman-style building was, with its seven rooms, a far more prestigious affair than their modest apartment on rue Jacques Dulud.

Signoret's parents had two more children, Alain (1930) and Jean-Pierre (1932). Signoret's primary education was at the Lycée Pasteur in Neuilly, near her home, where, up until the secondary level, education was coeducational. However, because there was no secondary school for girls in Neuilly, she and the other girls were obliged to take lessons in a building across the street from the Lycée Pasteur (on the corner of rue Borghèse and boulevard d'Inkermann), although they had the same teachers as the boys. She remained friends with a number of her schoolmates. The filmmaker Chris Marker was a close friend for life, as well as the actor Jean Carmet. Carmet appeared with Signoret in one of her early films, *Les démons de l'aube/The Dawn Devils* (Yves Allégret, 1946). Later, in the 1960s and 1970s, she worked with Marker on a number of his documentaries. Intellectual culture resonated around Signoret even at this early stage in her life. She and Marker worked on a student newspaper called the *Trait-d'union*. In her teens, Jean-Paul Sartre taught philosophy at the Lycée Pasteur, and although Signoret was not taught by him (because she was not yet at baccalaureate level), she certainly heard all about him from the boys. She would get to meet him later (in the 1940s) in the Café de Flore on boulevard St.-Germain.[2]

In the late summer of 1939, Signoret had reached the stage of preparing for her baccalaureate examinations. The Kaminker family were on their annual holiday in Brittany, but France was now at war with Germany. World War II had begun. Paris, threatened by invasion, had become unsafe, and André Kaminker instructed his wife and children to remain in Saint-Gildas-de-Rhuys (Morbihan), where they regularly spent their summer holidays. Signoret enrolled at a lycée in Vannes and sat for her baccalaureate in the spring of 1940. Among her instructors was the history teacher Madame Samuel, better known to us as the Resistance fighter Lucie Aubrac. Signoret remained unaware of her teacher's true identity until 1947. Aubrac would reappear in her life some twenty years later when her daring and courage acted partly as a source for Signoret's role in *L'armée des ombres/Army in the Shadows* (Jean-Pierre Melville, 1969). By June 1940, Saint-Gildas-de-Rhuys was occupied by the Germans. The Kaminker children were denounced by someone in the village as having a Jewish father, and the family was given twenty-four hours to leave. They returned to Paris. In the meantime, Signoret's father, who had remade his career as a simultaneous translator, escaped to England, where he joined up with General Charles de Gaulle and broadcast on BBC radio for the Free French.

Upon the Kaminkers' return from Brittany to Paris, Signoret became the only viable breadwinner and sought out work. Although she hoped to land a bilingual secretarial job with the famous photography agency Harcourt, she ended up working for the notorious collaborator Jean Luchaire as a secretary on his newly founded newspaper, *Les nouveaux temps*. Luchaire was the father of a former schoolmate, the film starlet Corinne Luchaire, and it was this link that got Signoret the all too precious commodity of a full-time job, which paid 1,400 francs a month.[3] However, the major drawback of the job for Signoret was the nature of the newspaper, an overtly collaborationist publication. Signoret stuck it out for nine months (September 1940 to June 1941). In the meantime, her mother, increasingly anxious for the safety of her children, had the boys baptized as Protestants, something her daughter refused to do. When, in June 1941, Signoret gave her notice to Jean Luchaire, there was no more money coming into the household. Her mother was obliged to leave the Neuilly apartment and take work as a laundress in the free zone of France (in Valréas, 65 kilometers from Avignon), where she spent the duration of the Occupation with her two sons.[4]

Signoret (1978, 27) summed up her experience of the first twenty years of her life as one of displacement, of never feeling settled, as occupying either a space where she did not belong (Wiesbaden) or an environment that was not right for her (especially in the more sumptuous apartment in Neuilly), as sensing herself as "other" and not belonging in these different sets of worlds. The fact also that very early in life (at the age of nine) she found herself being responsible for her brother Alain meant that she bypassed to a degree her own childhood (1978, 25). In the early part of the Occupation, she again found herself in a position that was not naturally hers—as "father" of the family and breadwinner.[5] Finally, twice during this harrowing period, Signoret was in danger of having her Jewish background "discovered": in 1943, during a check of identity papers on a train returning to Paris from Dax, where she had played a bit part in Pierre Prévert's *Adieu Léonard/Goodbye Leonard* (1943), and in 1944, when she and Yves Allégret, her then lover, were rounded up in a *rafle* (police raid) in Paris and taken to the *commissariat de police* of the sixth arrondissement. Although she herself maintained that she was not heroic during this period (Signoret 1978, 78), she lived with danger.

In March 1941, a few months before the Kaminkers had to give up their flat in Neuilly, Signoret's life took a turn that was to change it forever. A young man she had met at the Théâtre des Mathurins, Claude Jaeger, arranged to meet her at the Café de Flore, and in so doing introduced her to the world she had, as she herself admitted, been looking for unconsciously for a very long time (Signoret 1978, 51). This unconventional world, made up of artists, actors, intellectuals, refugees, writers, poets, Communists, Trotskyists, and members of the anarchist Groupe Octobre, was the one that became her family (Signoret 1978, 54–55). People were on a first-name basis—unless their surname *was* their name—and they used the familiar *tu* form of address. Among these friends were the Prévert brothers, Pierre and Jacques,[6] Pablo Picasso, Dora Maar, Alberto Giacometti,

Raymond Rouleau, Raymond Bussières, Serge Reggiani, Roger Blin, Mouloudji, Crolla, Sonia Mossé, Marcel Duhamel, and, later, Yves Allégret.

It was this new family who helped her realize that she could no longer accept the contradiction between her own political conscience and the politics espoused by the paper she worked for. In June 1941, she handed in her notice and announced her decision to all around her (Luchaire, her mother, and her friends at the Flore) that she was going to become an actor—something that, up until that moment, she had longed for, but for which she was now prepared to fight (Signoret 1978, 54–55). Kiki Kaminker (her nickname) became Simone Signoret. By adopting her mother's maiden name, Signoret, she figured she might at least be able to obtain walk-on parts in films.[7] Despite having changed her name to Signoret, however, her identity card was still in her father's name, and she thus retained her half-Jewish identity, which meant she could not get the actor's card issued by the German-controlled Comité d'Organisation de l'Industrie Cinématographique (COIC).[8] However, her new name did mean she could "pass" as Aryan for small walk-on parts, for which the presentation of the card seemed less necessary. Apart from *Le Prince Charmant/Prince Charming* and *Boléro,* in which she landed tiny parts thanks to a recommendation, it was also the case that, during this period, most of those films in which she appeared were made by or were with people she had befriended at the Café de Flore.[9] Alternatively, they were made by associates of the Café de Flore crowd—or by someone closer still, her lover, as in the case of her film with Yves Allégret, *La boîte aux rêves/The House of Dreams* (1945), based on the Café de Flore's "inhabitants," with Signoret in a speaking role. In 1942, she appeared in four films: two by Jean Boyer (*Le Prince Charmant* and *Boléro,* Marcel Carné's *Les visiteurs du soir/Night Visitors,* Louis Daquin's *Le voyageur de Toussaint/The Visitor on All Saints' Day,* and André Berthomieu's *L'ange de la nuit/Night Angel* (which was not released until 1944). In 1943, she was in five films: Pierre Prévert's *Adieu Léonard,* Jean Faurez' *Service de nuit/Night Service,* Jean Tarride's *La mort ne reçoit plus/Death No Longer Awaits,* and Jean de Marguenat's *Béatrice devant le désir/Beatrice's Temptation* (all released in 1944), and Allégret's *La boîte aux rêves* (which was not released until 1945).

CHRONOTOPE 2
1941–1985

Once Signoret had left Neuilly and gone to Paris (and her new family of friends), the locations of her living spaces were interestingly limited, first, to the Left Bank and, subsequently, to the Ile de la Cité—number 15 place Dauphine. She first came alive, as we know, on that memorable entry into the Café de Flore, on the boulevard St.-Germain, in 1941. This was the café of the intellectuals and artists, where the Groupe Octobre met, led by the Prévert brothers. Just down the road from this now famous café, down the rue St.-Benoît, is the Impasse des Deux Anges, the real location of Signoret's 1948 film *Impasse des deux anges* (Maurice Tourneur, shot in the Neuilly studios and costarring Paul Meurisse, with whom she made three other films of note (*Macadam,* Marcel Blistène, 1946; *Les diaboliques/The Fiends* [alternative title, *Diabolique*], Henri-Georges Clouzot, 1955; and *L'armée des ombres*). Prior to her full entry into a film career, she lived on the rue du Cherche-Midi, and, during that brief period (1941–1942), she was first involved with Daniel Gélin (a rising star in his own right) and subsequently Marcel Duhamel, who would go on, in 1946, to launch the Série noire (detective pulp fiction series), which would render him a household name. By the time Signoret was established in her relationship with Yves Allégret, she was living on the rue du Dragon, just one street down from Cherche-Midi and a stone's throw from the major meeting places of the Paris intelligentsia of the mid- to late-1940s: the Café de Flore, Les Deux Magots, and the Brasserie Lipp. This was a heady atmosphere to be in. Here is how Jean-Paul Sartre described the atmosphere at the Flore:

> The unchanging clientèle gathered in small, completely closed groups: if, one day, a pretty woman whom one did not recognise arrived, every member in the group would say to each other: 'there's a new one'. When Sylvia Montfort began to frequent the Flore, everyone talked about her for ages. It was like an English Club. People coming in knew everyone; everyone knew everybody else's business, even their private affairs; but people did not say hello to each other from group to group. . . . [10]

Sartre compartimentalized the famous cafés as follows: Flore, young literature; Deux Magots, old men of letters; Lipp, politics.[11] Boris Vian (1997, 117–120) also gives an eloquent evocation of this quarter during the Occupation. It was an intellectual ghetto, vibrant and exciting, although it was not without danger, despite the fact, as Signoret herself stated, that the Latin Quarter was the least occupied part of Paris.[12] This, then, was the Saint-Germain-des-Prés in its first major embodiment as the intellectual and artistic hot spot, primarily, of left-wing thinkers. This was Saint-Germain-des-Prés prior to its explosion in the 1950s, when it became a *mise-en-spectacle* of what had preceded it, with its existentialist cachet, its jazz singers and clubs, its rendezvous of the bohemian and intellectual *tout Paris*.

After the Occupation, Signoret and Allégret (with their daughter Catherine, born 1946) went to live on the rue Vaneau, in the more bourgeois and respectable seventh arrondissement. Finally, shortly after Signoret met Yves Montand, she moved to the Place Dauphine (1950), a mere ten to fifteen minutes' walk from her earlier haunts, which she continued to frequent.[13] Succinctly put, Signoret lived all her adult life within a small rectangle of Paris, the corners of which are the rues Vaneau, Cherche-Midi, Monsieur-le-Prince, and place Dauphine.[14]

What do we make of these different spaces, and how do they help locate Signoret for us in our own imagination? Our starting point here is that where a person lives is part of his or her body's meaning, in this case the star body, Simone Signoret.

Saint-Germain-des-Prés

The Saint-Germain-des-Prés that Signoret came to know first was that of the Occupation years. In his novel *Drôle de jeu* (1945), the author and, at the time, Resistance fighter Roger Vailland vividly described what it was like to live and breathe in this Paris quarter, during that period. Not only were you uncertain how you would survive, if you were part of or even loosely associated with the Resistance, you were not even sure you would live to see the next day. Denunciation was rife. According to recent documentation, throughout France, there were over three million people who denounced others to the Nazi authorities.

Not all denunciations were war related, however. People denounced former friends; it was a means of settling old scores. Officially, denunciation was justified as a way of cleansing decadent France—particularly of Jews, Communists, Masons, and strangers (the so-called anti-France).[15]

Because of her Jewish background, Signoret's life was in danger (technically, she was part of the "anti-France"). If denounced and believed to be part of the anti-France, a person faced immediate arrest, and there would be no trial. In most instances, torture was followed by death. Beyond Signoret's two skirmishes with identity controls mentioned above, her actual living quarters were also a threat to her security. Indeed, the rooms she was sharing with Allégret at 7 rue du Dragon were in a house that was used as what was euphemistically termed a *boîte aux lettres* (mail box)—a place for dropping off and receiving messages—for one of the largest Resistance networks (Signoret 1978, 85). At that same address, she put up her friend Claude Jaeger, who had introduced her to the Flore crowd. Unbeknown to her, Jaeger was a colonel in the Francs Tireurs Partisans (FTP), a Communist-organized branch of the French Resistance. As Signoret noted, she was not involved in the Resistance even though she may have rubbed up against it: "Personally I never acted heroically. I didn't act badly, which was already quite something." (1978, 78) As to the effect of the Occupation years on her generation, she said, "We belonged to a different generation which has never recovered. It is impossible to speak about it."[16] She admitted that it enriched her life,[17] but we get a measure of how it felt for her as a lived experience when she described it as "that long four-year night"[18] and as a period that, mentally at least, seemed to last twenty years (1978, 83). Signoret would relive some of this life of complete uncertainty, with its inherent danger of denunciation and betrayal, in several Resistance films that she made. There are three major titles in which she starred as a Resistance fighter: *Against the Wind* (Charles Crichton, 1948), *Le jour et l'heure/The Day and the Hour* (René Clément, 1963), and *L'armée des ombres*.

In his autobiography, Daniel Gélin (1977, 55) recorded the terrible cold of the winters in occupied Paris, the lack of food, and the making do where clothing and shoes were concerned (1977, 62–63).[19] Indeed, Signoret, who was never to become a great follower of fashion,[20] nonetheless described her elation when, for the first time, after the war she was dressed in stylish couturier clothes (by Jacques Heim for her roles in *Macadam* and *Impasse des deux anges*).[21] Gélin also recorded the cultural excitement of the Occupation period, the Latin Quarter clubs that were meeting places for all and sundry in the artistic and cultural spheres (such as the Saint-Yves on rue de l'Université), and the music, especially of Django Reinhardt. It was, he declared, like living in a *"happening permanent"* (1977, 37).[22] Theaters continued to put on plays. That was how, in 1942, Gélin met Signoret. Both were performing at the Théâtre des Mathurins.[23] Unfortunately, she got kicked out of the play for laughing too much, but their love affair gathered in strength. Here is how Gélin described Signoret: "I had never met anyone so alive. Simone Signoret dominated everything with her culture, her intelligence, her brio and her love of laughter (ah! that wonderful clear laughter, so sensual and infectious), her startling beauty and plain speaking" (1977, 61). They lived together briefly on the fifth floor of a small hotel on the rue Monsieur-le-Prince (just off the boulevard St.-Michel), even though Signoret kept her room on the rue du Cherche-Midi. It was her first love affair: "for the first time, I was living my life as a woman" (Signoret 1978, 69). But, as Gélin acknowledged, he was no match for her strong personality (1977, 61–62).[24] He was too young and immature for Signoret and, during one of his absences on tour making a film, in 1942, she fell for the considerably older Marcel Duhamel, some twenty years her senior. An extremely cultured man, he was, as a founding member of the Groupe Octobre, a staunch leftist. He offered Signoret what she called much-needed fatherly protection (Signoret 1978, 70). Duhamel was married. His wife, Germaine, was in the free zone of France, and all three accepted this rather curious, if brief, ménage à trois.

Yves Allégret was also an older man, some fourteen years her senior. He too was a committed leftist. A member of the Groupe Octobre, he had been one of Leon Trotsky's secretaries (Signoret 1978, 73). Signoret met Allégret at the Café de Flore, and their love dates from 1943. That same year coincides with the first film she made with him, *La boîte aux rêves* (released in 1945). She would go on to make three other films with Allégret, all of which got her noticed and contributed to her rise to star status (*Les démons de l'aube*, *Dédée d'Anvers*, 1948, and *Manèges/The Wanton*, 1950). In their six-year relationship, they had two children. The first, a son, born in 1945, died nine days later due to hospital negligence (Durant 1988, 51). The second, a daughter, Catherine, born in 1946, survived. Catherine was to remain Signoret's only child despite three other pregnancies with Yves Montand, whom she was soon to fall completely and passionately in love with. All of these ended in a late miscarriage.[25] Catherine was born out of wedlock. Yves Allégret was still married, though separated from his wife, and he already had a son, Gilles, from this marriage. The fact of having a legally conceived child meant that he could not, by law, recognize his illegitimate daughter (Signoret 1978, 75). Thus, legally, Signoret was registered as a *fille-mère* (single mother) and Catherine as a child *née d'un père inconnu* (father unknown) (1978, 74). Bearing an illegitimate child had a considerable stigma attached to it in the 1940s, and not just within "polite society." Allégret's very bourgeois family kept their distance. But Signoret also bore the brunt of intended insults from the local officials, who were ostensibly there to hand out extra rations to pregnant women. Signoret related with humor how she dealt with the prejudices she encountered (1978, 74). By accepting the injunctions with a smile, she was able to show to herself how little she cared for their good opinion. By the time she and Allégret were married, in 1949, Catherine was three years old.

After the Occupation, Signoret and Allégret moved to rue Vaneau, living in inexpensive furnished apartments at numbers 54, 52, and finally 56. Immediately behind their street is the prime minister's residency: the Hôtel Matignon. This chic area of Paris (the seventh arrondissement) is reminiscent of Neuilly in its upper middle classness. Buildings are predominantly nineteenth century, and among the illustrious people who lived on that street one can count André Gide. There is no scent of bohemian life here; indeed, after the intellectual vibrancy and bustle of rue du Dragon and the Flore nearby, this road seems dull and empty of life. The street is wide and long yet has very few cafés or food shops (a couple on the corner with the rue de Baylone and one right at the far end near rue de Sèvres). Farther down from number 56 is the rather grim-looking building of the Hôpital Laennec, which specializes in cancer treatment.[26] Signoret and Allégret continued to frequent Saint-Germain-des-Prés, however—he drove her around in a Morgan (Signoret never learned to drive). In particular, they visited the newly opened *caves*, or jazz and dance clubs, most famously Le Tabou, and the cafés of their past.

In 1949, this life came to an end. Signoret had fallen irrevocably in love with Yves Montand, whom she met while on vacation in Saint-Paul-de-Vence. In her autobiography, Signoret recorded this simultaneously exhilarating and painful moment in her life, acknowledging the hurt she caused Allégret, with whom she remained friends (1978, 91–94). She divorced Allégret and was subsequently married to Montand in December 1951. By that time, they were already living in the building that was to be Signoret's Paris home for the rest of her life: 15 place Dauphine.

Place Dauphine

The architectural importance of Place Dauphine is a first point to be made. This square was designed at the time of Henri IV, which is why his statue adorns the Pont Neuf. Indeed, the Pont Neuf and the square were all part of a political statement being delivered by the king: that of a France that was modernizing itself. The Pont Neuf (1605) is now the oldest bridge in Paris, but it was the first to be built without houses on it. The Place Dauphine was the first in a series of three piazzas Henri IV wanted to develop as commercial centers. Launched in 1607, Place Dauphine was linked to the busy Pont Neuf, the Louvre, and the old palace on the Ile de la Cité, which contained most of the royal administration. The arcades were filled with shops, workshops, and restaurants, much like today. Later, in the nineteenth century, the Palais de Justice was built opening onto the Place Dauphine and extending along the Quai des Orfèvres. Right next to the Palais de Justice is the Prefecture de Police. In other words, this part of the Ile de la Cité is the nerve center of the French judiciary—a very masculine space therefore. In terms of urban geography, the Ile de la Cité is the bridge between the Left and Right Banks of Paris; metaphorically, it is a median/mediator between the intellectuals of the Left (Bank) and the technocrats (the ministries) of the Right (Bank). But this place, which was an important meeting space for the surrealists, has also been described, given its triangular shape, as the beginning of Paris, as its sex—that is to say, as feminine.[27] With its complex connotative combination of the masculine, the feminine, and the mediating, Place Dauphine was undoubtedly an appropriate place for a person such as Simone Signoret.

During the Occupation, Signoret had declared that one day she would live in one of the houses that gave onto both the Quai des Orfèvres and the Place Dauphine (1978, 95). In its former life, number 15 was a bookshop, and it was to become Signoret and Montand's permanent Paris home (Autheuil, their country home some 90 kilometers outside Paris, was Montand's property). They lived in a small ground-floor mezzanine apartment that Signoret affectionately called *la Roulotte*, (the caravan)—a term used in general by actors, artists, and intellectuals to refer to their somewhat exiguous living arrangements—with her daughter, Catherine Allégret. Curiously, given its connotative status, as described in the previous section, what is striking is just how out of place, or rather, time, the actual square is in relation to what surrounds it. It feels more like a small provincial town square, with its chalky triangular park around which six-story seventeenth-century apartment buildings coexist with small restaurants down below at street level. Signoret (1988, 377) described this square as follows in her novel *Adieu Volodia*: "In discovering the Place Dauphine, he also discovered the doors of justice which opened majestically onto this most peaceful of provincial small squares." A place of contradictions, then—a space that, as we will see in Chapter Two, is one that is equally occupied by Signoret herself.

Right next door to Signoret's is Chez Paul, the restaurant she most frequented, and where she met up with her friends to eat, drink, and discuss. At times, the other floors of 15 place Dauphine were inhabited by the great majority of Montand's immediate family, the Livis, who had left their native Italy to be close to their now famous son. Catherine Allégret fully described how this extended family of grandparents, aunts, and cousins greatly enriched her own life and how, when Signoret and Montand had to be away, she would be in the care of the Livi family (Allégret 1994, 41–44).

But what really surprises is the coexistence, within this small pocket of Paris, between, on the one hand, this very visible couple and their known political views—which could only be read as antiestablishment and espousing the politics of the Left, especially during the 1950s and 1960s—and, on the other, the many hands of justice (police headquarters, courts, etc.). A brief survey of their activities makes this point clear. In 1950, at the height of the cold war, Signoret and Montand had signed the *Appel de Stockholm* (Stockholm Agreement), which called for a ban on nuclear weapons—a petition that the American government (rightly, as it transpired) saw as Soviet-inspired. Even though neither Signoret nor Montand were card-carrying Communists,[28] their sympathy with the socialist revolution was common knowledge and made them undesirables in the United States. Their signing of the petition was a major reason why, during the 1950s, neither of them could obtain visas to the United States to work out their contracts. Nor did their sympathies with the Parti Communiste Français/French Communist party (PCF) particularly endear them to the successive French governments of the time. We must recall that by 1947, at the beginning of the cold war, the PCF was effectively pushed out of governmental office. Thus, the PCF found itself in the political wilderness even though its workers' union, the Confédération Générale du Travail/General Workers Union (CGT), remained extremely active. Within the French political arena, the PCF was perceived (correctly) as toeing the Kremlin line. So when, in 1956–1957, Signoret and Montand went on their tour of Eastern Europe, just after the Soviet Union had invaded Hungary, this did little to change their image as defenders of communism. In fact, this tour represented a terrible dilemma for Montand and Signoret: whether to go on Montand's prearranged singing tour to Soviet Russia and its satellites or to cancel—neither decision felt right.

The controversies surrounding Signoret continued. During the 1950s, she was active in relation to the Algerian crisis. And in 1960, when the situation was truly critical, Signoret signed the 121 Manifesto, which called for soldiers not to go to Algeria to fight the war. As a result of this, she was banned from appearing on state radio or in state theaters (the ban lasted eight months). Funds were withheld from a film she was starring in (*Les mauvais coups*/*Naked Autumn*, François Leterrier, 1961) by the state funding body, the Centre National de la Cinématographie (CNC) because she had signed the manifesto.[29] Finally, in this brief enumeration of her activities, in the 1970s, Signoret had reason to enter the courts of justice on two separate occasions. The first time was in 1974, when she was almost a daily presence at the first trial of Pierre Goldman, a supposed anarchist accused of murdering a pharmacist and his wife and attempting to kill a policeman in the failed holdup. Literally, she just had to cross the road and walk up the steps to the court. The second was in 1977, and her own court case this time: a libel action against radio journalists from France-Inter who had intimated that she was not the author of her autobiography, *La nostalgie n'est plus ce qu'elle était* (first published in 1976). In the Goldman court case, she fought for a retrial on the basis that evidence was severely flawed. There eventually was a retrial, and Goldman was acquitted.[30] As for the second case, she also won. This fighting for a principle was a trademark of Signoret and one that was present in her performances throughout her life, on whichever side of the law or moral code she might find herself. Doubtless her experience in the courts in 1974 during the Goldman trial and her role in the appeal gave her material that she was able to exploit later for her role as Madame le Juge in the television series of the same name (made in 1976). She played a judge with a difference: a judge with compassion and strength who attempts to understand the perpetrator of the crime and the circumstances that led up to it; a judge who refuses to be guided by circumstantial evidence and duped by weak testimonies.

In all these instances, what is striking is the interface between Signoret's geographical location and her political location. There is an audacity to it in a very fundamental sense. In fact, Signoret (1978, 96) commented on the fact that there was something profoundly moral about choosing to live there.[31] She stood, as a woman, for political positions that challenged the establishment (the feminine takes on the masculine). Thus, she stood, morally, as a feminine body against part of the connotative symbolism of Place Dauphine, namely, as an institution reflecting the rule of law/father (first of the monarch, then of the judiciary). We have seen for example that, although she was not against the law per se, she was certainly against the miscarriage of justice (such as she had witnessed for herself in the case of Goldman's first trial). She spread, then, her femininity across that space, and did so in an authentic manner, through voicing and inscribing her concerns (speaking out for human rights and signing petitions). As part of that authenticity, she remained, until her death, a committed woman of the Left.

Her immediate entourage of friends and family were, for the most part, of a similar disposition. The building in which she lived housed members of her family (albeit in-laws) who were card-carrying Communists. Friends who came on a regular basis to visit were primarily of the Left and included Claude Roy, a journalist and subsequent editor of the Communist paper *L'Humanité*; the philosopher Michel Foucault; the actors Raymond Rouleau, François Périer, René Pigaud, Danièle Delorme (Signoret's closest woman friend), Yves Robert, Serge Reggiani, and Gérard Philipe; the filmmaker Chris Marker; and Lila de Nobili, a set and costume designer.

In keeping with this admixture of left-wing culture and very real symbols of law and order, just down the road from her, were Louis Aragon's publishers, Martin and Karl Flinker, nearby on the Quai des Orfèvres (number 68). Aragon was a man with whom Signoret had shared a deep political affinity and friendship until the Hungarian uprising of 1956 and Montand's controversial decision to go ahead with his singing tour of the Communist bloc. Montand had been committed to this tour a year before the uprising. If he canceled, it would have looked as if he were condemning communism and the cause of the Left. If he went, it would have seemed as if he were condoning the Soviet repression of the uprising. A real catch-22 situation: whichever way he decided, he would give grist to one section of the political class and press or the other. Aragon first persuaded Montand and Signoret that they must still go. But then, just a few days before they were due to leave, he let slip at a dinner party that he thought the trip was "inopportune." When Signoret found this out (Claude Roy, who was present at the dinner party, told her), she refused to forgive Aragon for what she considered to be a totally disloyal act—literally disassociating himself from any pressure he had put on Montand to go—and she closed the famous *Roulotte* door on him forever.[32]

CHRONOTOPE 3
1944–1958

This fourteen-year period represents the most turbulent era of France's history postwar. The choice of this slot of history for our third chronotope is not just its fortuitous coincidence with the life and span of the Fourth Republic, although that is part of it. What also motivates the choice is Signoret's own statement that 1958 represented a frontier date for her (Signoret 1978, 229). On 10 December 1958, her brother Alain was drowned while making a documentary about the dangerous lives led by fishermen—Alain, whom she had requested as a Christmas present from her parents and whom she mothered when her second brother, Jean-Pierre, was born and whom she had helped to bring up until 1941, when her mother left Paris with her two sons. As Signoret herself said, 1958 acted as a marker to her own life: her memory aligned her life by what happened before and after that year.

During this period, France went through one of the most censured moments of its republican tradition, one, in fact, that would perdure until the abolition of censorship in 1974. From the Occupation to the arrival of General de Gaulle to power in 1958, France's citizenry was subjected to wave after wave of interdiction. In 1944, France had just emerged from the Occupation, which had curtailed the freedom of most, imprisoned many, and sent others to their death (Jews, Resistance fighters, Communists, and other "undesirables"). The post-Occupation period witnessed different styles of reprisals. Women who had slept with the enemy were publicly humiliated by having their hair shorn (they were known as *les tondues/les tontes,* the shaved ones); often they were stripped to the waist or completely naked while they endured this humiliation. The more official reprisals took the form of *comités d'épuration* (cleansing committees), which, over a five-year period, sentenced collaborators according to the deemed severity of their crimes. Sentences ranged from the death penalty to years or months of emprisonment. Jean Luchaire, Signoret's former boss, was one of those who were executed. In the entertainment industry, 272 artists were brought before the committee, along with 1,032 film technicians (a term that covered all film practitioners behind the camera).[33]

Then came the cold war. The Communists, formerly the heroes of the Resistance, now found themselves banned from the political arena. In 1950, the Korean War began. In that same year, U.S. Senator Joseph McCarthy was appointed head of the House of Un-American Activities Committee (HUAC). The witch-hunts instigated by this notorious committee lasted from 1950 to 1954, although their effects lasted for a great deal longer. At the same time, France's colonies, Indochina and North Africa, in particular, were fighting for independence. The Algerian crisis had led to the imposition of extreme censor-ship on the media and cinema. France was seemingly so totally divided on its future that there was a very real threat of civil war. The successive governments argued that the only way to contain this threat was to impose a virtual blackout as to what was going on in Algeria. Anyone who transgressed this censorship was immediately punished. For example, films about the Algerian or colonial question were banned, as was the case for *Les statues meurent aussi/Statues also Die* (1953), made by Chris Marker and Alain Resnais. Some directors were even imprisoned, for example, René Vautier for his film *Afrique 50* (1955). His later film, *Algérie en flammes/Algeria in Flames* (1958), was also banned. Equally, Indochina was off-limits. Paul Carpita's film *Le rendez-vous sur les quais/ Rendez-vous on the Quayside* (1953) was banned because it showed the hostil-ity of the dockworkers in Marseille toward sending arms to Indochina. In other words this period was lived in an atmosphere in which the body was surrounded by interdiction.

During this same period, Signoret established herself as an international star—an extraordinary feat when one considers the level of interdiction sur-rounding her own person. Indeed, one could argue that her adult life was stamped from the beginning by interdiction if we recall that, during the Occupa-tion, she was banned from being an actor because of her Jewish background (under Nazi and Vichy law, being half-Jewish meant you could not get papers to work anymore than if you were entirely Jewish). By the early 1950s, her con-dition of interdiction expanded internationally and shifted continents. Having signed a film contract with the American millionaire Howard Hughes, Signoret was due to go to Hollywood to make some films.[34] However, she was banned from entry into the United States because she was perceived as a Communist, which, despite her sympathies, she was not. Indeed, soon after the Hungarian repression of 1956 and her tour of Eastern bloc countries with Yves Montand, she distanced herself from the party. Nonetheless, her exclusion from the United States dates from 1950 and lasted until 1959, when she was allowed entry for the Oscar ceremonies.[35] Not only had she signed the Stockholm Agreement, she had also (in February 1953) signed the petition appealing the death sentences for Ethel and Julius Rosenberg, who were accused of espionage for the Soviets, found guilty on the thinnest of evidence, and executed in 1953. She had also spoken out in support of North Vietnamese and North Korean women at a rally in Paris at the Vel'd'Hiv in March 1953, a clear anti–cold war stance if ever there was one.[36] And in the mid-1950s, she went twice to the East German film studios Deutsche Film AG (DEFA) to shoot, first, *Mother Courage* (a project that was never finished) and, later, *Les sorcières de Salem/The Witches of Salem* (Raymond Rouleau, 1957). All of these actions continued to preclude her from obtaining a visa for the United States.

During this same period, France went through a period of tremendous mod-ernization. This was the beginning of what became known as the *"trente glori-euses"* (the thirty glorious years of economic revival and expansion, which ended with the second oil crisis in 1974). In 1944, women, at last, got the vote. In the first election in which they were to vote, the general election of 1945, more women than men voted (2 percent more). Women also went to universities in greater numbers than ever before. In 1947, Christian Dior launched the New Look, with its long skirts and tight waists—a tremendously defiant style given that commodities including cloth, were rare and often still rationed. In 1948, Le

Corbusier's *Cité Radieuse* was inaugurated at sites in Marseille, Briey-en-Forêt, Nantes-Rezé, and Firminy. His conception of dwellings as *machines à habiter* (machines to live in) gained recognition for its modernity and constructive use of reinforced concrete. In the car industry, first the Renault 4CV (1946–1947) and then the even cheaper Citroën 2CV (1948) came on the market.[37]

A major contribution to the modernization plan was, of course, the American-funded European Recovery Program, proposed by U.S. Secretary of State George Marshall, which began in 1948 and is better known as the Marshall Plan. France received $2.8 billion. Along with the aid came a massive influx of American goods—not just Coca-Cola, but clothing and domestic appliances, among other consumer products. Interestingly, in Signoret's first major film, Allégret's *Démons de l'aube*, posters advertising Coca-Cola hang on the walls of the soldiers' mess. This kind of product placement is not without its significance, particularly given the French commandos reaction to it, calling it "an offensive poster" where "the colors are terrible." There were already, therefore, resistances to this invasion of American products, even before it had properly begun. Within a year of this film's release, Signoret and others were protesting even more fulsomely—in street rallies and marches—against other forms of American cultural imperialism, in particular Hollywood. Postwar, France's cinema was in a parlous state. France had to build up its industry again. There was a dearth of producers, studios were shutting down, and consequently too few films were being made. It was in these circumstances that the Blum-Byrnes agreements were signed, lifting the quota system on film imports from the United States and imposing in its stead a screen quota. This meant that nine out of every thirteen weeks American products were screened leaving a mere four for the French. American films flooded the market—70 percent of the films shown in France were American.[38] Film stars and related personnel protested against these agreements by demonstrating in the streets of Paris. Simone Signoret can be seen in news footage on one of these marches from the Madeleine to the Place de la République (5 January 1948). She is arm in arm with Jean Marais and looking over to her left at Yves Allégret.[39]

One of the ways in which France did hit back against its unwelcome competitor was through fashion. The 1950s saw a resurgence of fashion *à la française*. From the wartime fashion of "make do," France's fashion houses now went for opulence. Dior—the uncontested leader—has already been mentioned. But Fath, Griffe, Givenchy, Balenciaga, Laroche, Heim, Carven, and Balmain were also all top names. Coco Chanel made her comeback in 1954 after a few years on the sidelines because of her collaboration with the Germans. Numerous designers dressed stars for their screen roles and their private life. Carven dressed Vera Clouzot. Jacques Heim did Signoret's costumes for *Macadam*, her breakthrough film (he also designed her clothes for *Impasse des deux anges*). Balmain did her outfits for *Ombre et Lumière/Shadow and Light* (Henri Calef, 1951). Signoret's private couturier was Givenchy, the enfant terrible of design;[40] he mixed colors that were not supposed to go together, and he saw clothes as the *mise-en-style* of women's beauty. Following in the wake of his mentor, Balenciaga, he too was the master of the cut and believed in smooth lines (Chapsal 1986, 19).

Fashion during the 1950s was one of extreme femininity—a backlash against the Occupation years, when fashion, according to Madeleine Chapsal (1986, 11), "had over-masculinised women: square shoulders, male jackets, short skirts so they could pedal freely." Fashion in the 1950s was also one of excess—length upon length of material was used to create fluid clothes that spoke of value; cost was not an issue.[41] Fashion during the Occupation had been about recycling what at first seemed unusable: cork and wood for soles of shoes; tulle, gauze, and paper for clothes. Françoise Giroud complained that the French woman of the Occupation looked like an asexual gray mouse.[42] Sartre, in contrast, saw this period in fashion as the height of freedom (*morale de la liberté* is the phrase he coined), when women no longer dressed like their mothers.[43]

To some, Dior's New Look seemed like a retrograde step, with women becoming, once more, luxury objects. Chapsal (1986, 12) argues, however, that Dior understood that the true modernization of women was not to reject what symbolized femininity, but to play with it. This notion of containment and play is a useful key when studying Signoret's performativity (body as performance) in her films of this era. A good example would be her film *Ombre et Lumière*. Two different designers were employed for the costumes: Balmain for Signoret and Drécoll for Maria Casarès. Balmain was a contemporary, opening his house in 1945. Drécoll's origins are Viennese; his first house was launched in 1902. By 1951 (the year of the release of this film), Balmain had set up his own ready-to-wear branches in the United States (predating prêt-à-porter in France by some five years).[44] In this film, Signoret plays Isabelle Leritz, a famous international pianist who has just suffered a nervous breakdown. The film opens with her returning home after a two-year absence (in an asylum). As if to mark this new emergence of her self, she wears clothes that are light and modern. Conversely, the spectator is struck by the severity and traditional tailoring of Casarès' suit (and clothes in general). Her suit is dark and tight-fitting, as if corseting her upper torso, befitting the persona she plays on screen: the jealous, controlling older sister (Caroline) who, incidentally, is a couturier. Signoret, however, does not look as if she is corseted. Indeed, the skirts she wears are simple in line (bell-shaped or sheathed), and she wears simple silk blouses. Her evening gown, which she wears for her comeback performance, has the same slender, supple, and elegant line so associated with Balmain. Finally, the cut of the three-quarter coat she wears is generous, with a full back and leopard trim on the cuffs and collar. In this female Cain-and-Abel narrative of sibling rivalry, Casarès is cruel and spiteful. Thwarted in love (because her lover has fallen for Signoret), she will go to any lengths to hurt her sister. Signoret thrives on this new love, but she is not without her darker side either, nor is she as naive and angelic as her city Balmain designer clothes might lead one to suspect. She disguises truth, hiding her true identity from her lover. It is only once she has gone to the country and adopted a completely new casual attire (slacks and sweaters, pajamas, also created by Balmain[45]) that the truth about her is allowed to emerge. Caroline arrives, still in her tight-fitting, black, tailored city suit, intending to expose her sister. But Isabelle, in these natural environments and her unadorned clothing, is ready to admit the truth herself.

France's fashion and perfume industries were but a small sector of its national assets that film stars and fashion models helped to promote abroad as part of France's much needed export drive. Modernization also meant streamlining the automobile industry, running it efficiently along American production lines and producing cars that were affordable (as with Renault's 4CV). Modernization crept into the agricultural sphere in the form of tractors and combine harvesters (imported from the United States). Finally, but significantly, modernization meant a form of privatization of the industrial sphere, in the shape of household appliances.[46] Technology came into the domestic front in the form of stoves, refrigerators, and vacuums (Ross 1995, 97–103). The all-electric home was advertised as the supreme dream (89). Bathrooms were the emblem of a modern France (24).

It is here that we need to take a closer look at the 1950s and take readings of Signoret's performances during it. In her book *Fast Cars, Clean Bodies*, Kristin Ross (1995, 80–92) argues that the emphasis in France on the modernization and cleansing of cities and households during the postwar period, more especially the 1950s, is far more complex than a mere drive to appear a modern European society. Ross explains how France underwent a massive desire to be clean, starting, as we have seen, with the work of the cleansing committees (*comités d'épuration*) in the immediate aftermath of the war. This cleansing went further than these judicial committees. It included social hygiene in the form of closing down brothels (the loi Marthe Richard, 1947). But it was not just the immediate unclean past that was being expunged.

By the mid-1950s, the drive for cleanliness and modernization within the nation masked another dirtiness, this time the dirtiness of the Algerian war—the so-called *sale guerre* (dirty war). This dirty war was one of rape and torture of the Algerian community by the French army, one of guerrilla tactics on both sides, with vicious bomb attacks on civilians. The torture itself often left no traces, and so was called clean torture. In this clean torture, the French army employed electricity attached to genitals and used water-filled bathtubs to submerge prisoners and force them to confess. Meantime, back in France, in the home, the stress was continuously on the need for the French woman to be clean, to have clean children, and to run a clean home (advertisement after advertisement insists upon this). Ross (1995, 77–78) interprets this stress on cleanliness as follows:

> In the roughly ten-year period of the mid-1950s to the mid-1960s—the decade that saw both the end of the empire and the surge in French consumption and modernization—the colonies are in some sense 'replaced', and the effort that once went into maintaining and disciplining a colonial people and situation becomes instead concentrated on a particular 'level' of metropolitan existence: everyday life. And women of course . . . *are* the everyday: its managers, its embodiment. The transfer of a colonial political economy to a domestic one involved a new emphasis on controlling *domesticity*, a new concentration on the political economy of the household. An efficient, well-run harmonious home is a national asset: the quality of the domestic environment has a major influence on the physique and health of the nation. A chain of equivalences is at work here; the prevailing logic runs something like this: If woman is clean, the family is clean, the nation is clean.

As we know, reference to the Algerian war could not be made in film, on TV, or on radio. Films alluding to it were banned. The period was, after all, one of the severest in censorship ever. So the question for us is, where and how do we locate Signoret's performing body in all of this? Given her political engagement, are there, within her films, pockets of resistance to this climate of interdiction? Later chapters will look in detail at this issue, but, by way of an answer, I will refer for now to two films in particular, *Les sorcières de Salem,* based on Arthur Miller's play *The Crucible*, and *Les diaboliques,* a popular thriller. Miller's play is a plea against intolerance, the kind of intolerance shown in the United States during the McCarthy/HUAC era. More specifically, it was read at the time as a denunciation of the execution of the Rosenbergs. Signoret and Montand had played the roles of the Proctors (the central protagonists of the play, who are loosely identified with the Rosenbergs) for a year (1954) on stage in Paris, at the Théâtre Sarah Bernhardt, and were well aware of its political connotations. Signoret and Montand then went on to make the film of the play. The play, with its barely disguised appeal for political tolerance, was rescripted for the cinema by Jean-Paul Sartre. The film, therefore, is heavily layered with political meanings and intertexts (associated with tolerance, openness, and the Left) and stands as a remarkable piece of cinema, given its time of release. The allegorical value of this film—as a manifesto against the abuse of human rights, indiscriminate torture and irrational sentencings to death based on the say-so of hysterical young girls and greedy profiteers—stands out just as clearly as a political message about the times being endured by France and the United States during this period. Signoret as Elizabeth Proctor, in her refusal to compromise, embodies a courage that inspires others, including Elizabeth's husband, John, to stand up to the hypocrisy and dangers of intolerance. Above all, she and her husband (the Proctors and Signoret/Montand, both) stand for the exercise of free speech.

In the other film mentioned, *Les diaboliques* (which, won the Prix Louis Delluc in 1955), the references to the Algerian situation and infringements of civil liberties are more oblique but nonetheless present. In this film, two women plot to murder the central male character (played by Paul Meurisse), who is the abusive husband of one and the sadistic lover of the other. The two women (Signoret and Vera Clouzet) scheme to entrap him, drug him, and, finally, drown him in a bathtub. The drowning of the man is graphically represented on screen, with Signoret forcing, pushing him down under the water, and holding him there to drown. She even resorts to placing a bronze statue of a lion on his chest to ensure that he will remain submerged. Signoret embodies the scheming murderess. Her partner in crime, the wife, is but a weak shadow who merely follows Signoret's orders. There are two, related, readings we can make of this scene. Clearly, in conducting this dirty murder, albeit through a "clean" torture, Signoret completely subverts the sanctioned myth of woman as clean, as the harbinger of the modern French woman (that is, being in her home, making babies, and keeping everyone and everything clean). Second, a subtextual reading allows us to see how, even though censorship proscribed talking truthfully about the past (the complicities and connivances of the Occupation) or the present (the torture in Algeria), such a mise-en-scène can be read as a counterimage to the monumental self-deception behind the postwar mythology of heroism, created via the overemphasis on the Resistance, and the triumphant rebirth into a morally pure modernity, in the form of privatization of the industrial sphere.

CHRONOTOPE 4
1950–1960

Simone Signoret built her career and international reputation on the seventeen films she made between 1945 and 1958, culminating in *Room at the Top* (Jack Clayton, 1959), for which she won the 1960 Oscar for best actress (she also won the British Academy Award and the Cannes Palme d'Or for this film). Prior to her performance in this film as Alice Aisgill, she had also mustered two earlier

British Academy Awards (in 1952, for her role as Marie in Jacques Becker's *Casque d'or/Golden Helmet*, and in 1957, for her role as Elizabeth Proctor in *Les sorcières de Salem*) and a Silver Lion (Venice Film Festival, 1954, for her eponymous role in Marcel Carné's *Thérèse Raquin*[47]). From 1959 until her death in 1985, she appeared as a central character or in a major cameo role in an additional twenty-seven films. However, she won only two other international prizes for her performances. In 1963, she won the Moscow Film Festival Popularity Award for her role in *Le jour et l'heure*. In 1972, she won best actress at the Berlin Festival and the San Francisco Film Festival for her role as Clémence in *Le chat/The Cat* (Pierre Granier-Deferre, 1971).[48] What is intriguing, however, is the inversion here of a typical female star trajectory. In the first thirteen years of her career—during which she produced, in crude statistical terms, 28 percent of her output—she was a beautiful woman, five times crowned for her roles, and yet was only moderately in demand. Paradoxically, it was from the 1960s onward, when her looks began to decline significantly, that she was in greater demand and produced most of her output (62 percent).

There are three major reasons why Signoret's earlier career was not as extensive as her later one. And there is one personal reason that she readily supplied. In the period after the war, Signoret worked extremely hard to get herself established as an actor of substance (in 1947, she won the Suzanne Bianchetti award for most promising female actor for her roles in *Les démons de l'aube* and *Macadam*). But once she met Montand in 1949, she no longer felt so driven—even to the point of giving up her career (Signoret 1978, 120–121). For eighteen months, from 1951 to 1953, between shooting *Casque d'Or* and *Thérèse Raquin*, she did not work, but was content to be Montand's "groupie" (1978, 120). Indeed, she would not have gone for the role of Thérèse Raquin had Montand, who was less than content with her new role, not challenged her to land the part. Once she did decide to continue, she readily found herself in the privileged position, economically speaking, of being able to pick and choose her roles even if they did not come pouring in (1978, 330).[49]

To turn to the ostensibly "professional" reasons, the first two are interlinked. If we consider the roles that Signoret played for the first ten years of her full acting career (1945–1955), most of them, on the surface, appear to be redolent with the legacy of the 1930s cinematic tradition of poetic realism. Nearly all are dark and pessimistic films, and Signoret—despite her tough, sexy, and disruptive performances—is nonetheless most often the victim of fate or circumstances. Signoret was aware of the problems of being associated with the poetic realist archetype and strove very hard not to be like the prewar actors (Durant 1988, 159). Unsuccessfully, as far as French critics were concerned. Even her internationally successful film *Casque d'Or* was dismissed as stylistically too embedded in a past tradition of cinema.[50] Not even the new postwar tradition of "black realism," with which she was also closely associated because of her two very successful films with Yves Allégret (*Dédée d'Anvers* and *Manèges*), could shift this image in some critics minds. Thus, Signoret was associated with a film style that ran counter to a France that was trying to modernize itself. Furthermore, she played, almost without exception, the role of a tart or a scheming woman (*garce*)—a role that made its appearance in the mid-1930s and lasted through the Occupation years (Burch and Sellier 1996, 52–53), but which was deemed out of touch with the times of the late 1940s and early 1950s, particularly in light of France's drive toward purity and modernity. Interestingly, Signoret is on record as believing that her encounter with the Café de Flore "family" saved her, given how poor she was, from ending up as a prostitute herself (Durant 1988, 32–35).

As a body type, she was also associated with an earlier, prewar cinema. Although critics spoke of her incendiary eyes and long slim legs and the rich sensuality of her performances, she did not possess the *"look de l'époque."*[51] She was not tiny waisted (as in Dior's *taille de guêpe*). She was reasonably tall (1 m., 69, or 5 ft. 6 in.), often as tall as, if not taller than, her leading man. Her walk was neither that of a model's nor a dancer's. She had more of a stride and, occasionally, a precipitous rushing forward, as if she were in a purposeful hurry to get somewhere. It is instructive to compare Signoret with other actresses in French cinema in the 1950s. In terms of female stars, there was the voluptuous Martine Carol and the classy Michèle Morgan. There was the "woman-child" Danièle Delorme. But primarily there was Brigitte Bardot and the cleanliness and blondness of her body—BB the Body Beautiful, BB the dancer, the sexy undulating mover. It was not Signoret who was groomed for export as the sex symbol, but BB (it is also extremely doubtful whether Signoret would have allowed this grooming to happen).[52] Signoret herself commented on this as always coming in "second" to Carol in the early 1950s and then, a bit later, Bardot (David 1992, 129). However, it was not just a case of looks and body type, but of perfomativity (body as performance) and performance style that kept her second. From 1951 on, Signoret exudes mature sensuality and sexuality on the screen, not the infantilo-eroticism of Bardot. Nor did she agree to play parts she could not be proud of. Thus, she rejected scripts depicting weak and stupid characters, many of which poor Martine Carol felt forced to accept in her ambition to remain at the top (by being visible all the time) and be France's most popular female actor (against the likes of Morgan and Bardot).[53]

Linked to this point is the second reason, which in itself appears to contradict the first, and which has to do with Signoret's extreme modernity. In all of her performances, she is ineluctably the subject of her own desire, not the object. Furthermore, she brings an intelligence to her performances—one that is regularly commented upon.[54] In this respect, she goes against the grain. Although, in more liberal critical quarters, she was admired as a "woman's woman as much as a man's,"[55] strength and independence in a woman were, in the 1950s, threatening, particularly to a patriarchal order, such as the one that so strongly prevailed in France at that time. Indeed, the right-wing press made this all too clear in its vociferous attacks on her.[56] Signoret was the intelligent woman in a period when the focus was the body beautiful and not the mind, a time when the nation's (female) body was to be clean and domesticated. We recall that, while Signoret was at the height of her beauty and renown, this was the most repressive decade in postwar France. The post-Occupation period demonized women collaborators; the women's new vote was considered untrustworthy (the fear was that women would vote for the more conservative deputies and not for de Gaulle's new vision of France, thus empowering the Catholic lobby); and the Algerian war, the dirty, unspeakable war, raged on with its torture, including the rape and torture of women. In this repressive context, the female star was her body, not her mind, almost as though to say: even if her body can no longer be controlled as a minor (because she is now enfranchised), then, at least, her mind can be kept under wraps. The female star's body was supposed to be the sight and site of sexual beauty. She could be in excess, yes, but only in the sense of the body as spectacle. Small wonder BB was so timely as *the* spectacle of Beauty—that is, that there was lots to see: the breasts and buttocks of the great BB, and her huge mane of golden blond hair. Thus, not only did Signoret not match the political climate of the times, she fell short, to a certain degree, of the film industry's perceived needs.

So how did a star like Signoret survive in this arena? How did she make sense? How did her body get read? Despite all the above explanations for her undervalued status within the industry, she was consistently appreciated by audiences, with an average of two million spectators per film. Furthermore, even if critics did not always like the films she starred in, nonetheless, they were fairly unanimous in applauding the intelligence of her performances. Moreover, she was readily recognized internationally as a sexy performer. An American studio press release spoke of her as an actor who "as sheer woman both excites men and magnetizes the curiosity of women."[57] BB might well have elicited excitement and prurience but never curiosity, a term that suggests that there is an enigma to be understood and an intellectual challenge to be met with Signoret. Thus, a part answer to these questions as to how we read Signoret is the overriding perception of her as different. Her attraction was her difference. In that she had intellectual characteristics attributed to her, she stood out. She was part of a rare class of women of that period (which included Simone de Beauvoir) who had, within a very male-centered society, equal status to men. Of course, today this sort of "status qualifying" in relation to a patriarchal system of values is problematic, but within the context of the 1950s, this was a remarkable feature of Signoret's star persona. What Signoret offered her audience, therefore, was the watchable intelligent woman, that is to say, another possibility within the realm of performativities of the feminine. Through her intelligent performances, she reached her audience through her body as the site of performance, not of display—as opposed to BB or Martine Carol, for whom the body was more or less all they were allowed to be. In Signoret's case, it is the performance, the full presence, that is watched, not merely the bodily contour.

A third reason for her undervalued status in her own country, particularly with regard to the film industry, concerns her political positioning, which she had held ever since her awakening at the Café de Flore and which became reinforced after her marriage to Yves Montand. This lack of appreciation became particularly accentuated after her visit with Yves Montand in 1956–1957 to the Communist bloc countries. Not only did it bring her considerable opprobrium in the right-wing press, it also silenced her telephone for nine months where the film industry was concerned (Signoret 1978, 215). She was perceived as a Communist party member, something that at the time, out of a sense of political and personal integrity, she would neither confirm nor deny.[58] Meantime, of course, the Communist press in France capitalized on the couple's visit to the Soviet bloc countries.[59] Ironically, as it turned out, it was the French film industry's neglect that left her free to accept the role of Alice Aisgill in *Room at the Top*, a role that consecrated her as an international star. This irony is compounded by the fact that, although she was overlooked by the French New Wave filmmakers, who saw her as too asssociated with the *cinéma de papa*, she went on to star in the film that launched the British New Wave (Signoret 1978, 215).

In terms of her image among the general public during the 1950s, she was held in considerable esteem, both in her own right and as part of the dream love match with Montand. Curiously though, she appeared only intermittently in the popular film fanzines—certainly nowhere near the level of her contemporaries (Carol, Morgan, and Bardot). In the popular film magazine *Cinémonde,* she appeared on average nine times a year during the period 1950–1955, which is quite low. In the next four years, it was even lower, averaging three to four a year (dropping to just one in 1958). Partly this is from personal choice. She disliked interviews (indeed, she was awarded the *Prix Citron,* the Lemon Award, by journalists for being a disagreeable interviewee),[60] and she hated to pose for photographs—primarily, she said, because underneath her assertive exterior she was quite shy.[61] Unlike the other female stars of the 1950s, she would not pose *en déshabillé* (in slips, swimsuits, etc.), nor were her vital statistics disclosed.[62] Interviews had to be on her terms. Photographs of her daughter were not allowed. In other words, outside the confines of her screen performance, she refused the spectacularization of her body and life. But the other reason for the low popular press coverage she received has to be ascribed to her political persona. It is instructive that after winning the Cannes Palme d'Or and the Oscar for best actress, she did not get top coverage in her own country's major popular magazines. *Cinémonde* had a brief article on her Cannes victory, but devoted a great deal of the rest of the issue to Brigitte Bardot.[63] Yet, paradoxically, a few months earlier it had bemoaned the fact that Signoret was undervalued in her own country.[64] As for the Oscar, admittedly *Cinémonde* ran a four-page spread inside, but the front cover was again given to Brigitte Bardot.[65] *Paris Match* virtually "lost" Signoret's name in the list of Cannes winners, and where the Oscar is concerned, published a photograph of Signoret taken from the back.[66]

CHRONOTOPE 5
1960–1985

In the 1960s, however, the mood in the press swung, and Signoret became almost a national icon of French femininity. Articles and interviews with *Cinémonde* "soared" to the earlier all-time high (an average of 9 a year). Signoret engaged directly with the *Cinémonde* readers by writing them a letter.[67] In 1960, she was at long last consecrated a star by this magazine. Up until then she had only been a *vedette*—a second-order star—even though she had won five major international awards.[68] It was also the year she was finally nominated for *Cinémonde*'s popular fanzine award, the Victorine,[69] an award she would not win actually until 1965.[70] Undoubtedly, the Oscar played a large role in this increased popularity (but, as we shall see, other factors of a more personal nature also fed into this shift of opinion). At the Oscar cermeony, Signoret declared in her acceptance speech, "I wanted to be very dignified and all that, I can't. You cannot imagine what it is like for me, being French."[71] Much of her happiness and pride in accepting the Oscar was her sense of her Frenchness. "I was so proud to be French," she said.[72] Later in interviews she modestly stated that winning the prize was above all "a victory for French cinema"[73]—a slightly bizarre interpretation, since it was a British film. Nevertheless, in her victory, she flew the national colors. France had cause to be proud because it was the very first time that the Best Actress award went to a "foreigner," that is, a non–native English speaker (Claudette Colbert had won it in 1934, but she was a naturalized American). It would taken seven more years, however, before she was elevated by *Cinémonde* to the supreme status of superstar,[74] the same year that she was recognized as "the greatest personality in French cinema" and a *"monstre sacré."*[75]

In the early 1960s, Signoret also flew the national colors on another count: the superiority of French women in matters of love. During their stay in Hollywood, Montand and Signoret had met and befriended Arthur Miller (the author of *The Crucible*) and Marilyn Monroe. Signoret had a contract to fulfill in Italy with Antonio Pietrangeli for *Adua e le compagne/Adua and Her Friends* (1960). Montand was held on in Hollywood to make George Cukor's *Let's Make Love* (1960), starring opposite Marilyn Monroe. Montand and Monroe had a much publicized affair. Signoret's marriage, as far as the French nation was concerned, was under threat. It was a national issue; French pride was at stake. *Cinémonde* began a new column on astrology, and its first stellar bodies were Signoret, Montand, and Monroe. Monroe, it declared, did not stand a chance against Signoret.[76] Journalists hounded Signoret in Italy. She steadfastly assured them that she awaited Montand's return.[77] Uncharacteristically for her, however, she turned up two days late on the set for *Adua*. She tried to break the contract; she was rude. She was, in short, showing all the signs of being extremely angry from the deep hurt.[78] In her autobiography, Signoret herself was very discreet on the whole matter (1978, 279–294). However, scars were left. In the five years following this incident, Signoret's looks took a marked decline, and she continued thereafter to age rapidly, a decline not helped by heavy drinking and smoking.[79]

I have discussed elsewhere (Hayward 1995) this spectacle of Signoret's suffering and only want to mention here what Signoret herself had to say about the emotional scars she endured and their effect: "exterior wounds are far more visible, but it is the inner ones that are more serious."[80] What is important in the context of this study is that Signoret took responsibility for her decline and decided to turn it to her advantage. Let us compare what press coverage of her decline had to say with her own account. The first two quotes are from publications some eleven years apart (the first is *Queen* in 1966, the second from *The Evening Standard* in 1977):

> Ever since devotees of French film saw Signoret long ago in *Dédée d'Anvers* playing a young waterfront whore with incendiary eyes and long slim legs, she has maintained her impact not only as an actress of conviction but as a luscious example of sensual woman in full bloom. . . . Although Signoret is today a mature woman of 45 with a full face and a ripe indeed matronly figure she is still a past mistress of the slow sulphorous look and the throaty purr of invitation.[81]

> The tender qualities she showed in her early films . . . are only memories now. Her manner is tough. There's a rough, fruit peel texture to her skin. A hard smile braces the edges of her mouth. She has broad fullback shoulders and short masculine hands.[82]

Signoret, speaking in 1964, said that, when she looked at her face and its rugged lines, it left her indifferent and that she would not consider a facelift (quoted in Monserrat 1983a, 164). Nearly ten years later, in 1973, she went on to say:

> I think there is nothing sadder than an actress of my age trying, through artifice, to appear thirty years old. What a pain it must be to have to constantly struggle against lines and bags under your eyes. Especially since actresses who refuse to

grow old miss out on some very good roles. . . . If I have changed, then I only have myself to blame. Out of laziness I let myself go. . . . But in the end I wonder if this letting-go hasn't helped me. I haven't lost the hours I could have spent looking after my figure, I have spent them living. And it's from having lived that an actor can evolve. It's in ageing that one learns to act better and better, because experience helps you to draw in depth upon what you have known, be they moments of sorrow or joy.[83]

Some women, said Signoret, do not want to let go of their physical prestige. They want it suspended for eternity, so they disappear. The example she gave was Greta Garbo:

[Garbo] wanted to stay as Garbo. That's now forty years! I hope she is happy in life, got lots of friends, does interesting things. . . . At the same time, I realise that it shocks people and upsets them that we age at the same rate as they do. . . . In the end, that's what really upsets them: that we age alongside them.[84]

It is this last point that is central to the railings of *The Evening Standard*. Beautiful women must not be seen to grow old and, presumably, ugly. The point is, of course, that ugliness is a state of mind and as Signoret herself asserted, by acknowledging that she was fat and ugly, she had the very alibi that would enable her to play fat, old, ugly but interesting women as she did in *La vie devant soi/Mme Rosa* (Moshe Mizrahi, 1977), in her role as the aged prostitute Madame Rosa.[85] Thus, during the 1970s in particular, she used her loss of looks to her advantage, taking on roles as older women.[86] In fact, she starred in thirteen films (nearly a third of her star performances) as a mature, even old, woman who had lost her looks.

Signoret assumed her changing. She asserted her agency over her decline. There is no outside other/otherness that is responsible (no matter how much some might like to finger Montand). This is part of Signoret's seductiveness as star. Her authenticity was unquestionable. In effect she was saying: "I have made me what I am." Furthermore, even in her decline, she never relinquished being the subject of desire, of sharing mutually in the exchange of gazes between man and woman. From *Dédée d'Anvers* right up to her very last film, *L'Étoile du Nord/The Northern Star* (Pierre Granier-Deferre, 1982), Signoret remained forthright in agencing her subjectivity. In the former film, she looks on the man of her desire, a gaze that is fulsomely returned. In the latter film, she fulfills her desire to befriend a middle-aged man who is as much lost in his own despair as she is in hers. They exchange knowing looks and silently observe each other, she coquettishly touches her hair in response to his flattering comments and never hesitates to look him straight in the eye over the most difficult of home truths (his and hers).

To return to 1960: this was a significant year for Signoret. She struck out on her own, not against Montand, but for herself, and thereafter became increasingly involved in sociopolitical and human rights issues. She signed the 121 Manifesto before Montand returned from the United States. During the 1960s, de Gaulle's presidential style increasingly took the form of dictatorship by consent. State control of the radio and television networks was total—both were seen as the voice of the state. Furthermore, the civil liberties of many, especially minorities, were under continuous erosion—all of which explains why the events of May 1968 represented such an explosion within the political culture of France. Having been denied a voice for so long, much of France's citizenry, especially the young, spoke out in their frustration at so much legitimated repression. Then came the women's movement, the legalization of abortion, and, by 1974, the end of censorship.

Signoret is on record as stating that she was not a feminist but that if signing petitions in support of rights to abortion and birth control made her a supporter of the feminist cause, then so be it. In 1973, she signed the Manifesto of the 343 on abortion (a petition signed by renowned French women who had had "illegal" abortions). In two interviews in 1973 she staunchly supported the Mouvement pour la Libération de la Femme (MLF), the leading radical women's movement group and its stance on abortion.[87] She generously made public her own miscarriages to support the MLF cause: "Let she who has never had a miscarriage shut up, I've had them, and the MLF protestors deserve everybody's thanks."[88] But equally, disassociating herself from the MLF, she stated: "I didn't wait for these ladies of the MLF in order to become emancipated. . . . I don't like the MLF racism against men. . . . I leave them entirely . . . when they reject men."[89] In this same interview she readily admitted that she was not a "woman's woman" but is far more readily moved by a man's sorrow than a woman's tears. A few years later, in an interview with Jacques Chancel (*Radioscopie*, 11 November 1976), she again admitted she was not a feminist, but added that she had nothing against the MLF and supported their struggle for equal pay and free abortion. She had never been a victim of men, she maintained, and ascribed her lack of feminist tendencies to the fact that "I am deeply Mediterranean and instinctively submitted to the man I love."

Although Signoret was frequently out of the country during the 1960s, she kept an eye on the political pulse, even though she purposefully stayed away during May 1968. She had been present in Paris campaigning for the reinstatement of Henri Langlois at the Cinémathèque in April 1968, which arguably marked a first strong demonstration of public outrage against the state's overarching powers. (Langlois had been sacked as director of the Cinémathèque for incompetence—not necessarily untrue—but it was read by the public and film people as a politically motivated sacking of someone who would not obey state orders.) Of the actual revolt in May, she said she did not participate because it was a young people's revolution. Furthermore, among their demands and protesting behavior there were things that she could not support, such as the hounding of the theater director of the Théâtre National de Paris, Jean Vilar, a dedicated man of the Left. Nor did she like the fact that people who had not taken a position during the Occupation were now prepared to demonstrate in what to her mind were safe circumstances (Signoret 1978, 341–345).

During the 1970s, however, she became extremely active and was always prepared to take up the cause for someone whose civil liberties had been infringed upon. Thus, in 1971, she used her contact with Pierre Lazareff, a friend of her father's and the editor-in-chief of *France-Soir* and *France-Dimanche*, to help expose the dreadful conditions in French prisons by bringing it to the attention of the press (Signoret 1978, 346–348). She also was involved in the Renault car factory hunger strike of 1972. The three-man hunger strike was completely ignored by the press. In order to give it some oxygen of publicity, Signoret was asked if she could help. In response, she visited the three men on a daily basis. But that still brought no results. It would take the fatal shooting of Pierre Overney by a Renault security guard to bring the press in (Signoret 1978,

349–353). In that same year, she campaigned with other intellectuals of the Left for the release of Alain Krivine, leader of the Trotskyite Revolutionary Communist Front, who was placed under arrest for civil unrest. In 1974, she worked on the successful appeal for a retrial in the Pierre Goldman case. Once she became an author and was invited onto television programs (from 1975 until her death), she used that medium as a platform to put forward causes that were being "ignored" by the political arena or that needed a voice that carried weight with the general public. Thus, in the 1980s, she spoke up against the arrest of Polish Solidarity leader Lech Walesa and the kidnapping of Jean-Paul Kauffmann by the Islamic Jihad. She helped to promote the antiracism campaign SOS Racisme (without her voice, Harlem Désir, the leader of the campaign, is on record as saying, it would never have got the media exposure it did).[90] It was thanks to her that Mosco's television documentary on a purported betrayal within the Resistance, *Des terroristes à la retraite*, was not left on the shelf.[91] She called such interventions *"des coups de coeur"* (matters of the heart).[92] She was always saying "something must be done." For all these actions, she was recognized as a great defender of human rights.[93]

Signoret was also a champion of young talent and helped numerous aspiring filmmakers in their debuts. Signoret and Montand, for example, produced Raymond Rouleau's *Les sorcières de Salem*. Constantin Costa-Gavras got his lucky break when the couple agreed to star in his film *Compartiment tueurs/Sleeping Car Murders* (1965). They helped to finance his project by taking out shares in the film and forgoing a fee. In a similar vein, Signoret helped unlikely projects to get off the ground by agreeing to star in them for a small percentage of the takings (12.5 percent).[94] Thus, for example, in the 1970s, she regularly performed in a number of films that were far from box office hits but whose scripts she believed in. She did two Patrice Chéreau films (*La chair de l'orchidée/The Flesh of the Orchid*, 1975, and *Judith Therpauve*, 1978), René Allio's *Rude journée pour la reine/Rough Day for the Queen* (1973), Marcel Bozzuffi's *L'Américain/The American* (1969), Roger Pigaut's *Comptes à rebours/Countdown* (1971). Although she made little money on these performances, the essential point for her was to give help and to be supportive of people she counted among her friends.

CHRONOTOPE 6
1975–1985

During the last decade of her life, Signoret turned toward what became another of her personal goals, to be a writer. In the 1960s she had already translated and adapted texts into French (Lillian Hellman's *The Little Foxes*, 1962, and Peter Feibelmann's *Fever*, 1967). In 1975, based on a series of recorded interviews with Maurice Pons about her life, she worked them up into her autobiography, *La nostalgie n'est plus ce qu'elle était* (first published in 1976 by Seuil). This experience, and the success of her book, gave her the incentive to do more. There were two more texts to come: *Le lendemain elle était souriante* (1979), which picked up from where her earlier autobiography left off, in 1975, and her novel *Adieu Volodia* (Fayard, 1985).

Signoret was always afraid she would be considered a lightweight by the literary circles (Josselin 1995, 47). But that did not diminish the popularity of her writing with the general public (all three books did very well), nor with the presenters of literary programs on television. Her first book, *La nostalgie*, was well received by the press. *Libération* remarked that the book is a "generous chronicle that zigzags through history from the end of the Second World War."[95] *Le Parisien* applauded it as a book that was committed to truth and yet remained extremely discreet.[96] From the opposite ends of the spectrum, *France Catholique* and *Libération* took delight in the book, which they both saw as a kind of written oral history.[97] Signoret's second book, *Le lendemain*, covers three aspects of the short time that elapsed between her two autobiographies. First, in reaction to the libel suit she took against France-Inter and won, she established her own authorial voice over the first text and explained how she came to write the book. Second, she revealed her involvement in the Pierre Goldman trial. Third, she talked about her work on several of her 1970s films and the importance to her of her makeup artist Maud Begon, to whom she dedicates the book. As for her novel, *Adieu Volodia*, which she began writing in the early 1980s, it spans a twenty year period (1925–1945) and traces the lives of an extended family and friends through the early part of their life in France, when they arrived as Jewish refugees and became naturalized French, only to find themselves victims of yet another wave of anti-Semitism that would lead some of them to be deported to concentration camps. It is the story that Signoret could have experienced herself. Her paternal roots were from Poland, a Jewish shtetl. During the Occupation, her own aunt was deported to Ravensbrück, her father had to leave France, and her mother and brothers went into hiding. It is an amazingly complex novel, with many threads woven together. What is equally amazing is that it was written by Signoret as she was going completely blind. Retina failure had begun to set in by 1980. By 1985, she could no longer see.

Illness did indeed shadow Signoret for a considerable part of her last twenty years.[98] In 1969, while in the United States, she was rushed to a hospital for tests. She thought she was doomed and that cancer would be diagnosed. In fact, she was given a clean bill of health.[99] Throughout the 1970s she suffered severe bouts of chronic alcoholism. In 1972, while on the set for the film *Les granges brûlées/The Burned Barns* (Jean Chapot, 1973), she was consuming a bottle of whiskey a day.[100] She spoke of her loneliness, which—when she became an author—she believed she might fill: "When one writes one knows that one will never ever feel alone again," she declared.[101] However, she kept on drinking. Montand left her increasingly on her own.[102] They fought and quarreled.[103] She wrote to him, in 1978, telling him he was "the most selfish person" she had ever known and that because he hated "being attached to this too old, too fat, too contemporary" woman, he should unattach himself.[104] Their love-hate relationship perdured, along with her drinking. Then, in 1981, she was rushed off the set of *L'Étoile du Nord*, her last film, to be operated on for gallstones. She was forced to convalesce and give up drinking. This delayed the shooting of the film, but she came back rejuvenated (Durant 1988, 267–268). She went on to work for television, making two programs: the four-part series *Thérèse Humbert* (1982) and the two-part *Music Hall* (1985). By the time she was working on *Music Hall*, however, she knew she was dying of cancer. Yet she forced herself to see the scheduled shooting of the program through. In August 1985, she was operated on for cancer, but to no avail. She died on 30 September 1985 in Autheuil. Her daughter, Catherine Allégret, nursed her through the last three weeks of her life.[105]

Chapter Two

The Actorly Body and
the Body Political

SIGNORET'S FILM acting career has known equal amounts of highs and lows. Of the thirty-two films (out of forty-five) in which she is one of the central protagonists, fourteen were hits or highly acclaimed, and an equal number were flops. The remaining four were modest successes at the box office. What is of primary interest, however, is the fact that this pattern was repeated throughout her career, even though, as we noted in Chapter One, she made more films in the post-1960 stage of her career, when she was progressively losing her looks. Her smaller output pre-1960 was, as we saw, partly from personal choice, partly because her body type and performance style represented a challenge to the predominant image of femininity, and partly because, in the 1950s, there were times when, for political reasons, she was commercially unviable. In the post-1960 period, Signoret did not change in terms of her political persona; thus, a paradox remains as to why she was more present, more in demand, in this later period. It should be added, though, that in the 1960s, she was more active on the international scene than at home (where she mostly played cameo roles). Only after she had starred in Jean-Pierre Melville's *L'armée des ombres* did her film career really gain ascendancy in France once more. The point remains, however, that despite box office flops, despite her loss of looks, and despite her continued political leanings, filmmakers nonetheless managed to persuade producers to back projects that had her name attached to them. More than this even, some projects, in particular, the first films by Costa-Gavras, Chéreau, and Allio, would probably not have got off the ground without her presence or her willingness to be a stakeholder in the film.

When we look to why she remained a viable star body, a major reason to emerge is her commanding persona. Certainly, from the 1960s onward, filmmakers speak of "La Signoret" and of Signoret as a woman with "presence"—clearly, that is what they were buying into when selecting her for their films.[1] This presence was one that she could always muster for the screen but not for the theater, as we shall see in the next chapter. This presence was what made her stand out as different throughout her career. A presence that was seductive and sensual, but that was also strong, even hard-edged. A presence of counterpoints: one in which her visible or suggested sensuality was balanced by a wide-ranging economy of movement—wide ranging because a single, minimalist gesture could express anything from desire to hatred, irony to contempt, malice to terror, fear to surprise. The terms critics used at the time of her earliest performances have seemingly already pinpointed this "presence of counterpoints." For example, Georges Baume, who later became her agent, saw the kiss scene in *Les démons de l'aube* as the revelation of Signoret. He said that "she turned this kiss into one of the most healthily clean erotic moments of the cinema of that period."[2] Speaking of her role as Dédée in *Dédee d'Anvers*, *Paris-Presse* described the "sobriety and intensity" of her acting.[3] She was "sensually contemptuous" in *Macadam*.[4] In fact, it was the strength of her performance in this film and the producers' response to it that made its director, Marcel Blistène, review his earlier opinion of Signoret (he did not like her and did not want her for the role). Once the film was edited, he was obliged to agree with the producers that the publicity should be focused around her. This effectively gave her top billing in the film with Françoise Rosay and Paul Meurisse.

THE STAR TEXT, THE ACTORLY BODY: A "PRESENCE OF COUNTERPOINTS"

Signoret consistently rejected the idea of being a star, as well as the epithet *monstre sacré*.[5] However, she obtained enough international distinctions (Oscar, British Academy, Silver Lion awards, etc.) to consecrate her as a star, and her strong persona was so much a sum of all its parts that she could not help but be a *monstre sacré*. Furthermore, a *monstre sacré* connotes the idea of perdurabilty. The longevity of Signoret's career (forty years), plus the fact that a good number of her films are still regularly screened on television or in art houses, means that she lives on within the national, and indeed, international, consciousness (for example, *Les diaboliques* is regularly shown on British television).

In the forty years of her career, Signoret embodied four different but complementary types of star texts. First, she was the beautiful star body-text, the woman with incendiary eyes and long, slim legs. Second, after her marriage to Montand, to this first star body-text was added another; she became the political star body-text, which both detracted from and enhanced her 1950s star status. Interestingly, prior to Montand, she was in fact already a politicized persona, as evidenced by her association with the people of the Left at the Café de Flore and her not infrequent appearance (mid- to late-1940s and early 1950s) in *L'Ecran français* and *Heures claires des femmes françaises* (both Communist-based publications). Thus, she was in fact already both these star body-texts: the beautiful and the political. However, it would take the linking of her name to Montand's to bring that persona more fully into the public domain—in a peculiar way, as if to give it full legitimacy. Paradoxically, however, this persona worked against her star status in certain quarters within the film industry and parts of the general public. Third, her standing as an international star body-text was confirmed by her Oscar win in 1960, although, again, she already occupied this place: in the 1950s, the British Academy had three times acclaimed her as an international star. Fourth, she evolved into the aging star body-text: the sum of all her parts. Perhaps it is truer to say that she was in some respects both more and less than those parts: less, insofar as she had lost her looks and become ugly; and more, insofar as she now inhabited a new body type, one that was in excess of her former self (a body swollen from abuse of alcohol).

Signoret mostly appeared in popular, mainstream cinema, even though the tendency now is to see her work as more immediately associated with art films. This association probably results from the fact that, although many of the movies in which she appeared were made by filmmakers who are not most readily linked with mainstream films, nonetheless, the particular films in which she starred were popularly received. For example, she made the very popular *L'armée des ombres* with the auteur filmmaker Jean-Pierre Melville. Of her forty-five films, a quarter were made with auteurs (Jacques Becker, Luis Buñuel, Marcel Carné, Melville, Max Ophuls). The list of other filmmakers she worked with is long, illlustrious, and international. Among them are René Allio, Marcel Bozzuffi, Patrice Chéreau, Jack Clayton, René Clément, Alain Corneau, Constantin Costa-Gavras, Peter Glenville, Stanley Kramer, Sidney Lumet, Jeanne Moreau, Moshe Mizrahi, Antonio Pietrangeli, Roger Pigaut, and Raymond Rouleau.

Signoret had to work very hard at the beginning of her career to get into films. She learned her craft the tough way, almost as though she went through an apprenticeship with her small roles. Her early work, however, formed the foundation for her ethics and method of acting. Acting was the one area of her life (the only one, she readily admitted) where she was truly disciplined.[6] Her years as a *figurante* taught her punctuality and shaped her professionalism for life (Durant 1988, 49).[7] If, after *Manèges*, she no longer strove to secure roles, it was not a question of whether she was much in demand or not but the result of a change in ambition. As a result of her marriage to Montand, she no longer felt driven by the need to succeed, and, furthermore, she wanted to be chosen on her own merits. Thus, she waited for people to approach her for a role, for someone else to imagine her in the role (Signoret 1978, 117).

Part of her humility as an actor lay in her willingness to be guided by the director. Only once did she meet with difficulties in this respect, when making *Les diaboliques* with Henri-Georges Clouzot. She knew the ending of the film and kept playing her role as if she were guilty. Clouzot had to work extremely hard to undo this; otherwise, obviously the suspense of the film would have been ruined (Signoret 1978, 129). Signoret believed that the ultimate arbiter where filmmaking was concerned was the director. She would put herself completely into his hands. The director appeared to embody a father figure for her.[8] It was thanks to his direction, Signoret believed, that she was good or not (Durant 1988, 161). For this reason, with the remarkable exception of one or two films, she made no attempt to "improve" on the script but endeavored always to remain fresh—even naive—in relation to it (Durant 1988, 153).[9] She brought only herself to the role in a completely unprescriptive way, but with high hopes of what she could achieve (Signoret 1978, 117). For example, when she made *Judith Therpauve* with Patrice Chéreau, he made her do things she would never normally do (like being a grumpy old granny), but she played it with utter conviction, as she did her overall performance as a combative, unyielding newspaper proprietor. The film was not a success, and Chéreau readily admitted that he had not thought through the scenario well enough—Signoret, with all her years of experience might well have intervened, but she had willingly accepted the role and followed Chéreau's direction without fail.

Commenting on her improvisational approach, Moshe Mizrahi said "She is a purely intuitive actress, relying on her instinct. . . . The less you talk about her role, the better she is." For this reason, he went on to argue, it was better not to do too many takes with her because it would kill that spontaneity and life she brought to her perfomance.[10] Yet Signoret at one point expressed her concern that she might only be copying herself because of this spontaneity and improvisation.[11] Although she played instinctually, she invested a great deal of energy in finding out about the persona who was about to inhabit her. She paid huge attention to detail (Durant 1988, 128–129). As viewers, we feel the character she plays existed before the film began, such is her knowledge of that persona. As such, her ability to empty herself out and ingest the new persona was part of what made her perpetually different and her performance always redolent with authenticity. To take her late roles by way of illustration, she is a convincing peasant in *La veuve Couderc/The Widow Couderc* (Pierre Granier-Deferre, 1971) thanks to the hardness of her gestures that bespeak her stubborn defiance; it is her hard-edged performance in *La vie devant soi* that injects the film with a social realism that prevents it from falling into total sentimentality; she convinces as the frumpy cleaner in *Rude journée pour la reine*; twice she is an ex-circus artist (*Le chat* and *La chair de l'orchidée*) whose body has gone to seed but whose persona Signoret interprets with such dry intensity that we admire the moral and corporeal density that she embodies; finally, in *L'Étoile du Nord*, it is Signoret's hands that tell us everything about the enduring daily labor of the guesthouse proprietor, Madame Baron (as she sews, prepares meals, in short maintains a household).

Signoret provides a performance where everything fits. The clothes she wears and the way in which she inhabits them produce a series of gestural signs by which we can read her persona. Thus, in *Rude journée pour la reine*, the old housecoat she wears for cleaning is molded to her body. In its solid materiality (body and cloth), it functions as an act of defiance to the oppressive nature of her daily chores at home and at work. As if to say "Here I am and here I stay," it constantly refers to her function and the longevity of that function. Furthermore, as if to compound that defiance, it is a uniform she can change at will in her mind by adorning herself, in her fantasies, in the regalia of the aristocracy. In *Le chat*, we can measure Clémence's defiance against her husband, Julien, (played by Jean Gabin), who has banished her to silence for killing his cat, through the extravagant tops with their huge sleeves that she wears indoors— impractical for cooking, but which hark back in their coding to her days as a trapeze artist. She insists on her exotic past and persists with it in her consumption of extravagant goods, such as oysters and rum for lunch.

Signoret uses movement and nonmovement, respectively, to reveal and keep private the inner persona. Simone Benmussa (1993) provides an intriguing analysis of gesture in acting that can assist our understanding of the depth of Signoret's performance style. Benmussa (151) argues that movement creates the body, not the reverse. Gestures bespeak an emotional state, make public our inner being (152). Immobility silences that emotional state, keeps it within. Thus, when the body is inert, it is close to the unconscious, and, as such, immobility is an intense state of being. But, says Benmussa (151), the nonexistence of sound in a performance is closely linked to femininity (the silent and silenced one), which suggests that silence, nonmovement, and the unconscious are all closely interlinked. It is here that we can again find a key to Signoret's "presence," particularly when we consider the following statement from Benmussa (153):

> In immobility and silence, the vibrations of one's breath, the intensity of one's look are just as much minuscule movements. The image of a suspended gesture, of a non-movement is like a very fine transparent skin that is adhered to a secret emotion.

That secret emotion is just a skin layer away, so close to secretion. It is a breath away, close to exhalation. We sense its presence but cannot quite seize it. Beneath that, we equally sense but cannot quite seize the persona's "in-touchness" with the unconscious. It makes sense, therefore, in *Le chat*, in which silence has such a deafening role, that Clémence has intermittent flashbacks to earlier, happier times in the relationship—occasionally the thin layer gives way, and images of desire, which had been repressed into the unconscious, secrete their way through.

Benmussa's study makes it possible to suggest that there is a structuring absence to a Signoret performance that is different than that other aspect mentioned above, namely, the sense that the character she embodies had a life before coming on-screen. It allows us to grasp at what could be termed a geology of performance style, of which this structuring absence, this contiguity between the conscious being and the unconscious state, is an important factor. It is a key to what informs her work: we do not just watch the surface, nor for that matter are we merely aware of a past. There is also this deep-rooted element. Thus, we are aware that there is a style, but there is also more: a geology of performance style that creates room for more in all domains of her performance. It is from this geology that Signoret managed to hone her own remarkable minimalist style, a style that is redolent with meaning. Her performances throughout her career were marked by their minimalism and restraint, relying on small gestures (a shrug of the shoulders, dismissive hands), a few words (marked by a slight lisp), eyes and lips to say it all. These gestures and looks can range from soft and sensual to hard and threatening. Indeed, more minimalist still, Signoret could express the whole gamut from hatred to love through her eyes and lips. From early on in her career, her gaze was often described as ironic, volcanic, cruel, and disturbing,[12] her lips as redolent with an erotic sensuality.[13] These descriptors did not fade away as her looks disappeared. Her eyes and full, sensual mouth continued to be commented upon, as well as her fierceness.[14] It has been said that she was her eyes and lips (De Vorges 1986, 60). A flicker from her eyes, a narrowing of the lids—nothing more needed to be said. A pout and you knew exactly where you stood. She could seethe without moving, and she could seduce with only so much as a look. This represents a lot of power for so little movement and such a limited part of the body. An interesting economy in one sense, but also an intimation of enormous value—that is, of the rest of the body to come. In other words, Signoret's eyes and lips functioned metonymically in her performances for the body. This is one reason why she had such durability. Spectators were drawn, magnetized by the less, because it stood for so much more.

What I am suggesting here is that because of this metonymic power of her eyes and lips, Signoret's body was not—when she was at her most beautiful (1945–1960)—fetishized in the way that Martine Carol's and Brigitte Bardot's were. Signoret was never shot in the nude (Carol and Bardot both were). However, in her intimist moments—where she is simply dressed in a negligee or silken slip—she is so erotically charged because of all the visual information that came before this shot that she does not need to be "seen." We know more than enough, and that enough is more. Signoret represented strength and power, including mental power, attributes she never lost in her performances. Certainly, in the first part of her career, her beauty allowed her to be a presence when she came on screen. But there had to be more to explain why she could still be a commanding screen presence in her later films.

If Signoret was the beauty she was in the 1940s and 1950s, she also gave every evidence of great intelligence, lucidity, and especially insolence. Her beauty was not that of Martine Carol, a female matinee idol in terms of star construction, nor that of Brigitte Bardot. If Bardot embodied "total" beauty, then Signoret transcended beauty and was more than "it." Signoret was well aware that beauty irritates (Durant 1988, 166). It can also cause one to get typecast. To a degree this was true for Bardot. It was a danger for Signoret as well, as she was only too aware, especially given that in the heyday of her beauty she was typically offered roles as a prostitute or a scheming woman. Early in her career (1951), she was on record as wanting to get out of these typecast roles.[15] Signoret realized that the body-text, once on display, was potentially an unliberating place to inhabit. The challenge was to make it work as a system of signs that communicated, not a series of essentializing myths, but a set of flexible truths. This indeed was Signoret's trajectory since her earliest triumphs to her very last film. Signoret gave us to believe that she was always more than her sex, and she consistently resisted the ideological construction of the gendered subject. Thus, she always had agency over her erotic, desiring being and gave full evidence of an intelligence and purpose in her comportment and role play. Even as late as her last film, *L'Étoile du Nord*, and last piece for television, *Music Hall*, she is revealed as a desiring subject (she is coquettish with one of her lodgers in the former and has a younger lover in the latter). More than that, she also had agency over her own outcome within the narrative, the rare exception being Buñuel's *La mort en ce jardin/Evil Eden* (1956), where she is shot dead by a madman. Her endings may be tragic (her own death or the loss of a lover), but whatever the ending, she has power over that closure. What allowed her to be a presence throughout her career, therefore, was her sense of agency (her subjectivity is never in doubt) and her lack of fixity.

This notion of a performance style that is *more* in its minimalism is also supported by the way in which Signoret spoke of the roles "inhabiting" her (rather than the other way around as in method acting), to the point that what occurs is a doubling of personas—*"un dédoublement,"* as she termed it, referring to Denis Diderot's famous treatise on the actor and his double (Simone 1978, 115–116). She became the "other/*l'autre*," as she put it.[16] There are two people in the same body: hers and the character's (Durant 1988, 156). This other person becomes her lodger and cohabits with her the duration of the role and even beyond (Monserrat 1983a, 267). Before she actually played the part, she lived it, was inhabited by it, did what that person would do, instinctively, without thinking—as she did for Jeanne in *Rude journée pour la reine*.[17] She was so much inhabited by the role, that the separation after the film was over was like a death, in which she, Signoret, became the orphan. Again, in the context of Allio's film, she talked of how she had a terrible time getting out of the character because she had fallen in love with it.[18] It was like a divorce and nearly killed her.[19] Strong terms—but a measure of the depth of cohabitation and invasion of her own person by the character. As Durant (1988, 165) so aptly put it, Signoret could totally disengage from her self as a woman and give her body over to the other role. This allowed her in later years to embody roles that portrayed her as even more ugly than she had become (Jeanne, Lady Vamos, and Madame Rosa, to name but three roles). Signoret firmly believed that by accepting her aging, she could play someone entirely different from herself, as a result of which her later roles had greater substance in her view (Durant 1988, 165): "I have more pleasure now . . . because I can go deeper. It is not the experience of acting that counts but the experience of life. It gives you a wider scale of feelings."[20]

Apart from the fact that Signoret wished to acknowledge that gaining in life experience helped to deepen her performances, counternostalgia and counter-narcissism appear to be at work here. This belief is belied by her earlier performances. She was always able to transform herself and become the person she embodied. Furthermore, and rather self-evidentially, as she matured, she played roles consonant with her real age and never tried to pass as younger. These are roles in which spectators might well expect to find a greater range of feelings, based on knowledge of life. However, in her early career, beginning in particular with *Casque d'Or*, there is already great depth to her performance (the geology referred to above). She is on record as claiming this film as one of her favorites, as well as considering it the only film she appeared in that was a masterpiece.[21] If anything, this film marks the moment when she was able to bring greater strength and substance to her persona and thereby constitute a formidable presence that was only hinted at in earlier roles. Finally, this film acts as something of a watershed. For what also adds stature to her performance here is the noticeable ease of movement—here, she has lost the earlier, slightly ungainly steps that characterized many of her previous roles.

This idea of substance raises a final area of Signoret's performance style not yet discussed, namely, her cachet of authenticity. Signoret's performances strike us through their veracity; we believe her to be that person she enacts. And we believe in the characterization, because Signoret makes us forget it is her playing the role. She has the right touch and gesture. For example, in *Thérèse Raquin*, she begins with bitter, hard gestures. Her face, too, is hard and unyielding, as she stands, stifled, in the drapery store that belongs to her husband and mother-in-law. But once she finds love, her gestures soften, her face lights up, her body becomes sensuous. We feel the transformation as much as she embodies it. Signoret's voice is also a marker of this authenticity. As she grew older, her throaty voice and tender lisp evolved into a voice that now sounds bruised, wounded by life, but which also kept its earlier moist and inviting sound. The lisp remains but has evolved to suggest a new and different intimacy, one that is not just purely erotic, but that invites interlocutor and spectator alike into a set of confidences. Her voice excites the ear and the other senses. Her manner of speaking and gesturing has a way of leaving life in the air, as if offering a history to which we are privy. Her authenticity further lies in her being available to us, the spectators, in her ordinariness. Her understated clothing, her roles—nearly all of them those of ordinary women (whether proletarian or middle class)—her weaving of her own pastimes into her characterization (such as knitting, cross-words, petit point, and crocheting), her insolence, her vulgarity (particularly the way she holds cigarettes and stamps them out), her vulnerability (her lisp): all of this makes her ordinary, accessible. But so too does the authenticity of the real persona: the politicized, active, and intelligent woman. This Signoret also felt very accessible and undoubtedly fed the imagination of the spectators who thought they knew this woman up there on screen even as she, through her performance, made them forget who she was. She did not create characters, she created existences. Signoret summed up this experience quite clearly when speaking about her role in *Rude journée pour la reine*. She said she felt that because she always stayed in touch with what went on in the outside world, she was able to play the role; without it, she would not, she declared, have had the same understanding of Jeanne.[22] Unlike many stars, then, she felt substantial; she had matter and could be touched. Yet she still kept her star aura, undiminished in her ordinariness, an ordinariness counterpointed by an aura that allowed her to continue to star in films years after she stopped being a beauty— because being a beauty was not the issue; being able to perform was. Therein also lies her specialness: she was never commodified, thus never fixed. She created a freedom for herself that allowed her to go through the three ages of womanhood in spectacular form.

THREE FILM CAREERS

Just as we spoke earlier of Signoret's four different star body-types, so too we can demarcate her career into definite eras. Only, this time, it breaks down into three logical periods: the early days of her ascendancy to stardom (1945–1957), the middle career (late 1950s to late 1960s), and her late career (1970s–1982). In all three periods she worked with a wide spectrum of filmmakers, sometimes making two or three films with one in particular. However, she never became a fetish star of any particular filmmaker, nor did she become identified with any one director. Let us now take a look at the roles she played and embodied during these periods.

Part One: 1945–1957

In the first period of her career, Signoret's roles have a fairly limited range. With the exception of four films from this period—*Fantômas* (Jean Sacha, 1947), *Against the Wind*, *Ombre et Lumière*, and *Les sorcières de Salem*—she is, in turn, the golden-hearted tart (*Macadam*, *Dédée d'Anvers*, and *Casque d'Or*, the treacherous, scheming female (*Four Days' Leave*, Leopold Lindtberg, 1948, *Manèges*, and *La mort en ce jardin*), and even a murderer (*Thérèse Raquin* and *Les diaboliques*). Despite the limitations of these roles, in which she nearly always ends up losing everything, she consistently embodied the role of a woman with a mind of her own. Her strength and independence come through in at least three ways. First, her very corporeality evokes and exudes an independent air: when she walks, she strides purposefully forward, she smokes and stamps out cigarettes with a wonderfully insouciant vulgarity, and, to show her determination, she firmly but sensuously plants her hands on her hips as if to dare anyone to oppose her. Second, her gestures are at a bare minimum yet speak volumes: a glance, a lifting of an eyebrow, a moue from her very full lips, a shrug of the shoulders, her dismissive hands—these constitute a formidable repertoire of expressivity that requires no speech, or very little. Finally, she embodies a strong sense of the everyday, of being a part of the "real" world.

The rough, even wounded and seemingly untrained edge of her voice reinforces this, inviting audiences to identify with her apparent ordinariness.

This strength, however, is countered by two facts: first, the fact that most of these roles have been described as having more in common with earlier cinematic traditions in France, most specifically the poetic realist cinema of the 1930s, with its pessimistic fatalism, and more generally the popular cinema of that same decade, in which women were often represented as being on the seamier side of life (Durant 1988, 159);[23] second, the fact that many narratives of the postwar period and well into the 1950s were imbued with a strong sense of retribution and revenge, in which the woman is often the site upon which this vengeance is wreaked. In either case, the woman is represented as untrustworthy, as manipulative, and therefore as dangerous (she can stoop to murder, after all). The construction of femininity within these films of the transgressive woman who must be punished for her misdemeanors acts as a powerful tool to undermine any idea of feminine agency. Thus, within any Signoret film of this period, there is a tension between her modernity (her strong sense of self, as discussed in Chapter One) and the apparent retrorole casting, which has her embodying a past—or seemingly looking to the past. But one wonders at this perceived need to qualify her work as *passéiste* (old hat) because at the same time she was saluted as being "devilishly seductive," "disconcerting," and "intelligent," and her acting as "natural."[24] This points to a perception of her femininity that, to all appearances, is based on contradiction (as retrograde, yet challenging). However, a study of her performances simply does not justify this perception. What I want to suggest is that the term *passéiste* represents an inability to recognize that the films, for all that they might appear to be harking back to a past, were in fact perpetuating an earlier perception of women (by way of a convenient essentializing shorthand) and relocating it into a new contemporary, that of postwar France.

Indeed, this new contemporary was a time of paradox. On the one hand, France was attempting to rebuild its sense of national identity after its humiliating defeat and subsequent occupation by the Germans. On the other, it was busily looking for scapegoats for the national shame and guilt over the acts of collusion and collaboration with the enemy during that same period. Reconstruction of the image of France came in the form of a heroization of France's resistance to the enemy. Retribution took the form of cleansing committees, which dispensed sentences, including the death sentence, to those who served as embodiments of France's shame. Retribution also took the wider form of a nationwide punishing of women who were accused of horizontal collaboration with the enemy; they came to embody the whoring France that had given itself over so passively to the enemy.

The hypocrisy latent in these strategies of rebuilding and retribution finds a ready reflection in postwar films that either offered images of a resisting, honorable France or proffered a dark social realism (*réalisme noir*) in which the woman was represented as a whore and a femme fatale. The dark pessimism of the cinema of the late 1930s now gave way to a new cynicism that was distinctly darker in its bitterness from its earlier prototype. Whereas, before, in the poetic realist cinema, in particular, the hopelessness in the face of economic hardship and the inevitability of war was collectively shared, the characters now remained isolated as they face yet more economic hardship and an ever greater sense of a lack of identity. Theirs was an individuated, bleak, no-exit reality. In much of the social realist cinema of this period, the impossibility of dealing with the meaning of the Occupation and the impossibility of coping with present hardships led to the rise in images demonizing women. That is, the representation of women became the site upon which the repressed guilt of a nation humiliated in defeat got played out. Indeed, the punishment and vengeance wrought on women in films during the postwar period were clear indications of a masculinity and a nation in crisis (Allégret's *Manèges* is but one example of this).[25] It is in this light that we must consider the contemporary perception of Signoret's film roles and the apparent contradictory reading of her femininity.

Jacques Doniol-Valcroze (1954) conducted a survey of films over the years 1945–1953 with a specific view to analyzing the construction of femininity during that period. He selected sixty-three films for this representative study. What emerges is indeed revelatory of a nation that is unwilling to rethink its view of the role of women. Three types of women emerge from this survey, and the first and second types are the ones that predominate. The first type to emerge, but only by a small margin, is the young *petite-bourgeoise* who is characterized as standing for love, honesty, purity, and the Christian ethic and for whom the essential goal is marriage into the bourgeoisie. Symbolically, argued Doniol-Valcroze (1954, 12), this type embodies a society that confounds material well-being with moral value and equates progress with social success. The second type to emerge is the proletarian woman (she appears in twenty-six films to the *petite-bourgeoise*'s twenty-eight). She is a prostitute in over a third of these films. Often she is in pursuit of true love, but fate generally plays against her. At times she is driven by ambition, at others by a destructive passion, or finally by a desire to betray. This second category reveals a more complex representation of the female, however. Within the narrative, her desire to fulfill the social order of things in the form of marriage is ostensibly thwarted either by fate conjuring against her or her own behavior dooming her to fail. Even the aristocratic women (who make up the last type, nine in all) fare badly. Their pursuit of love is full of danger or leads to death. They are often treated as no more than objects—as indeed, noted Doniol-Valcroze, are their *petite-bourgeoise*'s counterparts. The least objectified are the proletarian women, perhaps because their representation is more complex, even though their outcomes are no less extreme than the two other types.

What I want to suggest is that this overall negative representation of women, which breaks down into several constructions of femininities (across class, for a start), can be examined against the backdrop of a series of oppositional debates that held currency within the sociopolitical scene of the times and which begin with postwar France's rejection of the Third Republic. Immediately after the war, a series of referenda were held, beginning with the decisive vote to reject the constitution of the Third Republic (referendum of 21 October 1945). The Third Republic became the scapegoat for all that had ailed France. The perception of this republic as weak and degenerate remained unchanged from the one put forward by Marshal Philippe Pétain when he took over as head of state during the Occupation. This weak, emasculated republic had to be revitalized, remasculinized, part of which entailed a complete reform of its institutions. It is in light of this rejection that we must read the masculinist cult that grew up after the war in the form of a totally false exaggeration of the importance of the French Resistance and a cultification of the personage of General de Gaulle. Women in this context provided a safe locus for the rechanneling of political anxieties during this period, which were many. I have already mentioned the repressed guilt and humiliation that was played out on the female body; I want now to suggest that the constructions of femininity also created the woman as the embodiment, even object, of social disorder. We must recall that women were given the vote in 1944, that by 1947 the Fourth Republic was only in its second year, and yet there were thirty-five women *députés*, one of whom was the minister of health. This increase in the visible and voiced woman and her presence within the very institutions that postwar France was attempting to masculinize and modernize clearly constituted a threat. History reveals that when women get too close to power, when they control institutions or have a say in their running, they become demonized. Thus, for example, in certain counterrevolutionary allegorizations, the fighting proletarian woman of the French Revolution was the whore on the barricades. In the commune of 1871, she was the caricatural masculine *pétroleuse* (gasoline bomber) on the barricades. Male hysteria under political pressure leads patriarchal discourse to represent the female as unnatural or as Medusa-like, as castrating and as the antithesis to the maternal ideal.[26]

What is so interesting, then, is that this so-called *passéiste* cinema, in which Signoret figures so heavily, should give such a true reflection, through its constructions of femininities, of the anxieties that postwar France was facing. Given the stress, where women were concerned, within ideological discourses on the reconstruction of France, on domesticity and reproduction, it seems strange that so many films of this period show marriage, let alone procreation, as an impossibility. Why is it virtually absent from the social realist films? Curiously, the only generic arena in which the myth of marital bliss makes any appearance is the comedy costume drama (such as *Fanfan la Tulipe*, Christian-Jaque, 1951), the most unrealistic of all the types of films being produced at that time. What makes woman so fearful within the context of realist cinema—so much so that she must be repeatedly punished in narrative after narrative? Ostensibly, if we are to believe the above analysis, it comes down to a fear that she would undermine the reconstruction of postwar France

Furthermore, even though these very images of woman as whore or gold digger most assuredly flew in the face of France's desire to position itself as a modern society, nonetheless they endured. And it is here perhaps that we can find some answers to the above questions. Fear of the new, the unknown very quickly turns into fear of the unfamiliar, the uncanny. Science fiction creates monsters, even robots, onto which we project our worst fears of the future that technology holds for us. It is not unreasonable to read this same process of containment and displacement of fear onto the female body in the films we are talking about. If woman is represented as the usurper of the social order of things for which she must be punished, it is because in the new republican consciousness she is perceived as both holding France back and representing a reality that France would just as soon deny equal rights with men. In the postwar period, women—who had "enjoyed" a measure of economic independence during the war and who had held positions in the workforce formerly occupied by men— had now to return to a nonpaying or less remunerative situation. Clearly, this drive to return women to the home meant they were not truly equal before the law, nor were they equal in terms of economies of scale. Thus, the construction of femininity as a corporeal entity that must be punished comes down to the fear that they will refuse to conform to their predetermined role as a maternal ideal. Such a refusal is a refusal to a rebirthing of France.

Finally, this demonization of women can be attributed to the desire to repress the fact that many women postwar found themselves caught in the poverty trap and had to turn to prostitution or gold digging in order to survive.[27] We need to recall that, in 1946, the government had passed a law closing all brothels. Under the guise of cleaning up France, this law was part of a concerted effort to legislate the female body, restrict women's earning power, and force them back into the domestic sphere. Despite these measures, illicit prostitution continued, because the poverty trap did not miraculously disappear overnight. Political exigency was undoubtedly at variance with social practice (and reality). Thus, even if the brothels were closed, other ways were found to keep this economy going. But as far as the desired projected image of France was concerned, there was clearly a felt need to be seen to be cleaning up this very real underbelly of the economy. If, therefore, women are so consistently punished in film narratives where they are prostitutes or gold diggers, there must surely be some moral intention behind that punishment. The audiences may feel sorry for these women, or, conversely, disdain. But they will also feel comforted that they are not part of a degenerate society of fallen women and that their own values are entirely secure.

Signoret's roles in this period provide us with a wide set of variations on this theme of the fallen woman, particularly when she embodies a proletarian role. Of the sixteen films in which she appears, she is either a prostitute or a woman on the make in twelve of them.[28] Her first and her last incarnations of this role during this period—Lili in *Les démons de l'aube* and Djin in *La mort en ce jardin*—serve as apt reminders of the breadth of her repertoire. Lili is the first in a line of Signoret's warmhearted, generous tarts—a type that dominates; Djin, the last in a line of greedy, manipulative tarts who, in this case, comes to some kind of awareness only to die, the victim of a stray bullet. Signoret played to different economies of desire in these two films, as she did in all her roles of this nature. In the first film, as Lili, she is free with her favors, and there is no indication of economic exchange. In the second, nothing is free, everything is negotiated by Djin before the sexual exchange. In both instances, however, the two women control their laboring and desiring bodies—there is no pimp involved, and they choose whether they are willing to offer or sell their services. Interestingly, in the two films where there is a pimp who tries to capitalize on Signoret's prostitute (*Dédée* and *Casque d'Or*), he is eventually eliminated (murdered).

There is, therefore, a consistency of sorts in the representation of prostitution through Signoret's body that is quite intriguing in view of my comments above about the postwar period. To all intents and purposes, Signoret's prostitute has the ability to work for a particular period of time at a particular level of intensity—in other words, she controls the services she provides. This prostitute, though she may well be the embodiment of a social disorder that society so fears, is also in control of her own means of production: *she* sells her labor. In *La ronde* (Max Ophuls, 1950), for example, she certainly acts as a fully independent prostitute, giving freebies to men she finds attractive and spending the entire night with her handsome count.[29] In *Dédée d'Anvers* and *Casque d'Or*, she eventually frees herself from being a form of commodification. Signoret as Marie stops being "the object" (as she is referred to in *Casque d'Or*), that is, being another man's commodity to sell, and occupies a completely different space. Even before her pimp, Roland (played by William Sabatier), is killed, she has made it very clear that she intends to seduce Manda (played by Serge Reggiani), the carpenter she has just met. She leaves the community of prostitutes and goes in search of a freer life with her new lover—for however long it will last. In *Dédée*, the eponymous heroine is the most classy and expensive tart on the block. At first, Marco, her pimp (played by Marcel Dalio), is able to exploit her absolute surplus value and force her to work more than any of the others. If she refuses, he beats her or burns her with his cigarettes. As such, she is enslaved. Marco's economies of desire work, or so he believes, to erase her identity. But this is to underestimate her own economies of desire. When the film opens, we are made aware almost immediately of her desiring subjectivity. She meets a man with whom she falls in love. She signals her desire for him, and in so doing effectively begins the process of breaking the relations of power between Marco and herself. At the end of this film and *Casque d'Or*, both Dédée and Marie lose their lovers (one is murdered, the other guillotined), and it is clear that they will have to resume their profession. But what is made equally clear is that they will be in charge of selling their labor. The films' endings could be read as a "tragic outcome," and this was doubtless the intended reading of the time. However, the Marxist reading that we have just provided—and that allows us to read against the grain—suggests that these portrayals, far from diminishing the power of women, through a series of stereotypes about their class and profession, point to a diversity of economies of desire in relation to their sexuality (free exchange, variable rather than fixed price exchange, and so on), a different market economy that is not alienating to the worker because she is in charge of the means and the ends of production. Small wonder that Signoret's performances were seen as troubling and disruptive.[30] Later on, in the film *Adua e le compagne*, in which Signoret as the protagonist sets up a women's collective of "ex"-prostitutes to run a restaurant (precisely to be economically free of pimps and middle men), she is still embodying the same political message about sexual freedom and the right for women to determine their own lives, irrespective of the economic frameworks put in place by capitalism.[31]

In these roles, as in all her films of this period, Signoret embodies female agency and empowerment, economic or otherwise. In this embodiment, she can be soft and she can be hard. She can use her lisp and sensual mouth to seduce and to mortify. Her eyes can be on fire, but they can also be on ice and full of malice—literally, they change color from green to gray when anger is on its way (Durant 1988, 39). A man caught in the cross-fire of Signoret's gaze will know exactly what she feels, no ambiguity, no messing. What makes Signoret stand out, have presence, therefore, is her refusal—through both her strength of performance and her agencing of desire—to allow her subjectivity to be erased.

Part Two: 1958–1969

In her middle career, starting with her Oscar-winning performance in *Room at the Top*, Signoret embodies the roles of intelligent, often politically engaged, women who are also sexually mature. But, as with the previous phase, she still loses out, either her own life or her happiness. Signoret made fifteen films during this eleven-year period, seven of which were produced outside France with American, British, and Italian filmmakers and production companies. Of the eight remaining, only two cast her in a central role: *Les mauvais coups* and *Le jour et l'heure*). A third film gave her a significant and pivotal role: *L'armée des ombres*. However, there were major time gaps between these three films (1961, 1963, 1969). The other five roles were small cameo parts. If *Room at the Top* had consecrated her standing as an international star, then her home output does not give great evidence of production companies rushing to cash in on her as a bankable star (this would not happen until the 1970s). In fact, the whole picture is rather strange, given the normal trajectory of a post-Oscar-winning performance. On the American side, she worked with non-Hollywood, independent directors (Stanley Kramer, Sidney Lumet, and Curtis Harrington), and she was nominated for an Oscar for her role in Kramer's *Ship of Fools*. On the British side, she worked with the independent producers John and James Woolf and their company, Romulus Films (*Room at the Top* and *Term of Trial*, Peter Glenville, 1962). The Woolf brothers were highly respected producers, but their output was varied and eclectic and often challenged the establishment (as, for example, their production of *I Am a Camera*, 1955, with its less than covert homosexual theme). As for her cameo roles in the French films, these were parts she took on to help young filmmakers get a start. Of her three major roles, only two were in films with established filmmakers (Clément and Melville). In other words, she did not move in the heady circles one might expect after her Oscar success. She did, however, get to work within the more radical arena abroad and the less establishment domain at home.

In Chapter One, I explained the various levels of interdiction surrounding Signoret's persona. The ban imposed by the French government in 1960 as a result of her signing the 121 Manifesto certainly placed her on the margins of French cinema for quite a while (and not for the first time). Because of this ban, her film with François Leterrier, *Les mauvais coups*, which should have come out in 1960, suffered delays by having its government subsidies withdrawn during the last stages of shooting and was not released until the following year. In a broader context, she was virtually absent from French cinema for this whole decade. She was spurned by French New Wave filmmakers and politically was considered difficult to produce. In the early 1960s, *Cinémonde* regularly commented on how underused she was.[32] This situation is not without its irony given that Signoret was on record, during this period, as wanting to put her career first.[33] This proved a double irony in that, if she was finally able to do so, it had to be within the international context and not that of her own country.

However, her internationally acclaimed role in *Room at the Top* opened up another set of issues around the question of interdiction, this time related very specifically to the body, the body as performance, and the question of censorship. According to John Trevelyan, then secretary of the British Board of Film Censors (BBFC), *Room at the Top* was "a milestone in the history of British film and . . . in the history of British film censorship,"[34] and for the following reasons. In January 1951, the X certificate was introduced by the BBFC. Up until then, censorship in the United Kingdom had to be geared to the susceptibilities of a family-centered audience, which effectively meant to those under sixteen years of age (no film could be passed that was not suitable for accompanied children). This strange guideline reposed in the idea that film was above all family entertainment. The introduction, in 1951, of the X certificate for adult-only films represented a breakthrough in that it recognized that intelligent films could be made even though they would exclude young audiences by virtue of their content. Thus, films with adult themes and those that forefronted sexuality, adulterous relationships, hooliganism or violence, and poor morals all received an X, whereas before they might have been severely cut or not passed at all by the BBFC. In the early 1950s, very little advantage was taken of this break-through by the British film industry because it feared that it would lose its pre-dominantly family-based audience. In general, then, it was a case of films coming from Europe obtaining the X certification. In particular, given the con-text of this study, all of the films starring Simone Signoret that were exported from France were given an X rating. Thus, none of her early films (*Dédée*, *Manèges*, *La ronde*, *Casque d'Or*) were released in the United Kingdom until after the X-rating system had been instituted. In a way, it is thanks to this new system of certification that a broader British public got to see and know Signo-ret—in a bumper bundle (1951–1952) and without any cuts. But what is also fascinating is that Signoret's body, outside of its own national context, was pri-marily associated with X-rated films, which at this point in the 1950s primarily became associated in the public's mind with daring foreign films and sex. As Trevelyan, writing in 1959, stated: "I think the shock appeal of the film [*Room at the Top*] rests mainly on the personality of Simone Signoret, who always car-ries about with her the climate of a sultry foreign 'X', to which patrons of English-speaking 'X''s are not accustomed."[35]

By the late 1950s, movie audiences were on the decrease. Thus, the moral censorship argument that British producers and distributors had earlier invoked for not making and showing "adult subject" films no longer seemed so perti-nent, and production became more widespread. But, having earlier refused to take advantage of the new rating, they now argued that the X certificate, and censorship in general, actively worked against them. For example, television—which in part was stealing audiences away from cinema—was not subject to the same prescriptive system of certificate rating as films. Furthermore, the expecta-tion was that producers would submit their script to the BBFC for advance scru-tiny. Effectively they were subjected to a precensorship examination. In order to get more audiences into theaters, they argued, they had to be able to address adult issues freely. It was in this respect that *Room at the Top* was a landmark film. The Woolf brothers did not put in their script for advance scrutiny but submitted instead the near final cut of the film (Aldgate 1995, 43). Faced with this *fait accompli*, Trevelyan had to tread carefully, first, so as not to lose credi-bility by sanctioning the Woolf brothers' lack of regard for due procedure, and, second, so as not to cause a public outcry by censoring it. In the end, only minor amendments were made to the soundtrack; the images were left intact (Aldgate 1995, 44). As Trevelyan noted: "At the time its sex scenes were regarded as sen-sational, and some of the critics who praised the film congratulated the Board on having the courage to pass it."[36] Indeed, at the time, the American film indus-try weekly *Motion Picture Herald* issued a warning to exhibitors to the effect that "the love scenes in *Room at the Top* are extraordinarily frank and explicit."[37] But Trevelyan was clear. Noting that "this film dealt with real people and real problems," he went on to say, "There was no nudity or simulated copu-lation, but there was rather more frankness about sexual relations in the dia-logue than people had been used to."[38]

It is difficult to recall that *Brief Encounter* (David Lean, 1945) remained, until *Room at the Top*, Britain's most serious and realistic treatment of adulter-ous relations. So film critic Penelope Huston was right to declare that "some-thing controversial had arrived."[39] Indeed, she saw this film, in its realism, as a

potential turning point for British cinema. For his part, what Trevelyan was trying to achieve was a way forward to help the ailing British film industry and get
audiences back into the movie theaters. He saw *Room at the Top* as a way of
rehabilitating the X certificate, of clearing it of its scurrilous associations, and
of making going to X-rated films a perfectly respectable practice (Aldgate 1995,
60, 24n). For Britain, this was a vanguard film, heralding a new kind of realism
so readily associated with the British New Wave cinema that followed in its
wake. The film was a success (fourth biggest hit in 1959 in the United Kingdom)
and "according to most reviewers [the] British 'adult' films had arrived" (Aldgate 1995, 50).

Maurice Elvey is right to argue that this film reflects the rapidly "changing
social patterns' of late-1950s Britain."[40] It exposes petty class consciousness and
snobbery. But this film is about both class and sex, and it took a French body to
help British cinema move forward and shift its thinking around censorship. Jack
Clayton was extremely astute when he suggested bringing in Simone Signoret to
play the role of Alice Aisgill, who, in the John Braine novel, was English. At
first, the Woolf brothers wanted Jean Simmons for the part (Aldgate 1995, 43).
In one respect, Clayton may well have realized that it would make it a great deal
easier for the strong sexuality of the film to be passed (not unnoticed) by the
BBFC, and for British audiences to accept, if the role were played by a foreigner,
in particular, by Simone Signoret, who by now was associated in the British
filmgoing public's mind with the image of a strong, earthy, and very sexy French
woman. It also allowed for a passionate interpretation of the role, which one is
hard pressed to imagine in a Jean Simmons performance.

Thus, in terms of censorship, Signoret's body shifted in meaning in this film
and stands differently in the arena of interdiction from her earlier period. This
time, the context is that of sexual rather than political censorship. Certainly, the
body still remains political, but with this film, it resides within a different realm
of sexual politics, namely, sexuality. Signoret continues to challenge class- and
gender-based assumptions of power and to assert her own economies of desire.
However, as the mature woman, she no longer represents the defiant, non-
maternal body of her earlier whores and schemers. Rather, she suggests a greater
range of femininities, which her earlier films only hinted at but which her subsequent films of the 1960s would go on to develop. Finally, for the puritan British,
she lifts the curtain of respectability, lays down sexual desire untrammeled in
the domain of free expression. As a critic in *The Daily Cinema* put it at the time,
the "intensity and truthfulness [of this film] is, indeed, partly due to the presence
of a Continental star—Simone Signoret—who, as the married woman, gives a
performance of extraordinary intensity."[41]

That intensity is a constant of Signoret's performances and is one that emanates both from her ability to convey a whole life behind a character and from
her use of silence and non-movement to suggest the structuring absence of her
unconscious. We are convinced that Alice Aisgill lived, which is why we feel
such compassion for her when she is abandoned by Joe Lampton (played by
Laurence Harvey). In her silence we sense her unconscious warning her that the
affair will end badly, yet her conscious self drives her on—and in the end she
drives herself to her death. In *Ship of Fools* (Stanley Kramer, 1964), the loneliness of the drug-addicted countess that Signoret plays is palpable even though
her performance is completely understated—contrasting with Vivien Leigh's
role as the hysterical divorcee. We feel and hurt with her, just as we did with

Alice before. Deep down, we again sense her inner understanding that love cannot offer her hope. As *Variety* remarked, she gave a finely balanced performance between pathos and lust for life.[42] It is that balance of opposites, or two ways of being, performed with such an economy of means, that is the striking feature of her actorly style and stands as a fundamental marker of her authenticity. It is a balance that I referred to above as a presence of counterpoints and that Signoret achieved through her ability to project a contiguity between the conscious and the unconscious states. This was her strength as a performer, it is the kernel of her art and what gave her such commanding presence.

By the middle period of Signoret's career, this penetrating depth of her performance style allowed her to suggest a complexity that was psychological as well as physical. There is increasingly more for us to observe as our fascination with her is no longer impelled, in the first instance, by her former beauty. The audience was intrigued by her as she displayed different types of femininities that were not normally privileged by movie screens. Thus, she played the aging coquette in *Les amours célèbres* (Michel Boisrond, 1961), *Games* (Curtis Harrington, 1967), and *The Seagull* (Sidney Lumet, 1968), but not any ordinary aging coquette. In the first, she is pitiful as the rejected woman, and also extremely dangerous, because she discreetly murders her lover. In the second, she is a ruthless bounty hunter who seduces her way into the home and heart of a young couple and gets away with their fortune, having institutionalized the one and murdered the other. In the third, she is a monstrous mother and aging actor whose lack of caring for her son, a playwright, helps to precipitate his suicide. But the monstrosity of these various characters is not caricatured, as we might expect from a Bette Davis interpretation; rather, it is understated, utterly banal, and real—hence its force. In *Les mauvais coups*, she again reveals her power to combine pathos with danger. This time, in an attempt to rekindle her husband's passion for her, she gradually seduces a young woman (played by Alexandra Stewart) by sucking her into her life story. She then attempts to make this woman over into her former self in the hopes that it will remind her husband of their own earlier happiness together. She does not persuade her husband, who leaves her, but she has awoken the younger woman to the greater possibilities in life other than that of a village schoolteacher in a humdrum marriage. We meanwhile register Signoret's growing despair as she knows her plan is failing and remain deeply moved when she commits suicide. Despite this tragic ending, the crucial point to this film is the fact that the central relationship becomes the one between the two women. There is an amazing tension between them that borders on narcissism and homoeroticism (something already hinted at in *Les diaboliques*).[43]

Continuing with this overview of Signoret's different types of feminities, in *Term of Trial* she plays the role of a worldly Parisian woman who has married an unambitious Englishman (played by Laurence Olivier), a pacifist during the war and now a schoolteacher. She is both pathetic and antipathetic as we witness her embittered, frustrated, lonely, and (apparently) domineering ways. But when her husband is accused of indecent assault, she rallies round and urges him to fight back—she believes he is too much of a mouse to have dared any such assault. Despite this set of interpersonal dynamics, which suggest she has the upper hand, the power play between the two constantly shifts and is quite complex. At times, she dominates; at others, he does. In the end, no one has the upper hand—and the camera works effectively to suggest this. Sometimes she towers above him; at other times, the roles are reversed. Within this bleak film, however, there are two extremely touching moments when they mutually seduce each other into lovemaking, one toward the middle of the film, when they are in despair at their failure to make each other happy, the other occurring at the end of the film, when she is filled with bemusement and admiration at his newly found boldness (as she says, he is less of a mouse than she thought). The resolution of their marriage is not, in the final analysis, one of compromise. They find an equality of terrain—based on the power to hold and respect one another—as the last shot makes very clear. In *The Deadly Affair* (Sidney Lumet, 1966), Signoret is made to age dramatically as the ravaged, unkempt widow of an assassinated MI5 agent. She herself is a concentration camp survivor who oozes pain and whose face is "a ghastly geography of experience."[44] She is, it transpires, a Soviet agent. But the characterization is such that we understand her treachery, and Signoret's performance is such that she elicits pity as much as contempt for her character. This is no mean achievement, given her bedraggled physical state and political views. There is a sense of horror as we witness her silent assassination by one of her own.

Finally, in the two Resistance films that she made during this period, *Le jour et l'heure* and *L'armée des ombres*, she embodies yet again very complex roles. In the first, she begins as a woman who has suffered enough from the consequences of the war (her husband is taken prisoner) and wants no engagement with it whatsoever, nor, it would appear, with life in general. Eventually she is tricked into participating in a Resistance exercise. She is initially furious, but subsequently she slowly takes on an increasingly active role and finally shows great courage under torture. This odyssey is paralleled by a love story in which she allows her dormant desire to be gradually awakened. She falls in love with the American pilot (played by Stuart Whitman) billeted into her care. In *L'armée des ombres*, she plays Mathilde, a leading Resistance fighter whose maternal love costs her her life—seemingly the two roles are incompatible. Mathilde is supremely intelligent, plans all the major escapes in this film's narrative, but transgresses the Resistance's code of practice by keeping her daughter's photograph on her. She is arrested by the Gestapo and later released. We assume (although nothing is confirmed) that, rather than betray her daughter, she has talked. The film closes with her being gunned down in the street by her Resistance colleagues.

In summary, in these roles Signoret shows us a range of aging femininities. But she also reminds us that, despite her changed, more mature and plumper body, the woman of passion does not disappear with middle age.[45] Intriguingly, some critics of the period refer to her beauty not in sensual or feminine terms but as a "masculine type of beauty"[46]—suggesting, not an androgyny, which is something with which we are more familiar in relation to more contemporary stars, but an ability to emanate a dual or perhaps even a blurred sexuality and a sex appeal that is not necessarily uniformly heterosexual, or tied to heterosexuality. In this regard, Signoret offers another possibility where desire is concerned that is not gender-bound, but is certainly sex-based. Clearly, then, Signoret's star body opens the door for a doubly desiring subjectivity on the part of the audience. But I would contend that her star body does more and suggests a third way of desiring that can comfortably accommodate all sexualities and sexual persuasions. Furthermore, it confirms that this desiring was always possible, was already happening, and that audiences were certainly aware of it.

Signoret has "it," this third sex appeal, as the popular television magazine *Télérama* made clear when, with extraordinary lucidity, it declared: "Madame Signoret is the third sex!"[47] Silent film stars Clara Bow and Louise Brooks suggested it before her. They possessed, as did Signoret, a feminine allure where beauty is not necessary but physical attraction is a must and acts as a magnetism that attracts both sexes. It is earthy and even vulgar. It is witty and disregarding of rules. It is based on the sexual potential that, though not enacted, is suggestively present and, as such, is closely tied to our own imagination. The power of this attraction lies, then, in its hint of excess and lack of self-consciousness and, finally, in the paradoxical visualization or embodiment (through the star body) of sex as a structuring absence—in some ways not dissimilar to the structuring absence of the unconscious mentioned earlier as a key to Signoret's performance style. Signoret's "presence," which we defined at the beginning of this chapter as a presence of counterpoints, now takes on a deeper resonance still, particularly, I would argue, in relation to the concept of clean erotics. By this I mean she offers pleasures in viewing the star body in a nonvoyeuristic way. The erotics are palpably there, albeit explicitly absent.

Part Three: 1970–1982

Signoret made fourteen films in the period 1970–1982 (1982 is the date of her last film, *L'Étoile du Nord*). She averaged, then, one a year, which is a considerable output and a rare achievement for an actor in her fifties. It is also a rare achievement because, for the last three of those years, she was often indisposed through illness. It is worth pausing a moment to examine the range and types of films she made during this period because of what it can tell us about the star body and national cinema. Seven of the fourteen films were coproductions, primarily with Italy, and were made during the first half of the 1970s. This fifty-fifty distribution of coproductions and home products mirrors exactly what was happening in the film industry at the time. Signoret's subsequent career pattern (during the second half of the 1970s) graphically illustrates the moment when this practice of coproductions decreased between the two countries because of Italy's own declining film industry. Thus, in the period 1970–1973, coproductions averaged around 50 percent; by 1976, they were down to 20 percent. Both industries suffered huge drops in audiences because of the advent of television, and if France's film industry survived where Italy's did not, it was thanks in large part to the generous system of state aid provided by the French government. However, where coproductions were concerned, a marriage of convenience that had lasted for nearly thirty years (1948–1975) between France and Italy—and which had helped each nation's film industry through difficult technological changes (color and Cinemascope, in particular)—was now at an end.

An important part of Signoret's output coincides, therefore, with this period of progressive severance from coproductions, during which France had to develop strategies for its own industry's survival. This it did in a number of ways, first, by maintaining a very high level of gangster/thriller films (known as *polars* in France) and comedies; second, by returning to the "tradition of quality" of the 1950s—namely, the literary adaptations and script-led films so derided by the *Cahiers du cinéma* group and French New Wave filmmakers. This tradition of quality also included what became known as "retro" cinema, nostalgic heritage films principally from the 1930s. Apart from this, there was a third type, labeled "civic" or political cinema, which examined the sociopolitical context of the 1970s with a critical eye, particularly questions of class and workers' conditions, political and economic scams.[48] Much of this civic/political cinema was labeled social-realist for obvious reasons, set as it was in the contemporary. Some of it was intentionally mainstream and was France's attempt to compete with the very popular series of American so-called political conspiracy films of the 1970s. Other films in this category were more hard-hitting with their exposure and did not intentionally target the mainstream. Some of these crossed over into the popular mainstream cinema by dint of audience attendance (for example, *L'aveu*, Constantin Costa-Gavras, 1970, garnered over two million spectators in France and was ranked ninth in the year's box office).

In terms of Signoret's output in this last period, what is so remarkable is that it falls into all these categories of cinema, with the one exception of comedy (see table below). She stands metonymically as a star body for the trajectory and the strategies of the French film industry during the 1970s. Thus, seven of her films were coproductions, seven were in the *polar*/thriller genre (including three Georges Simenon adaptations), and all but two (*Les granges brûlées* and *La chair de l'orchidée*) did very well at the box office. Seven fall into the category of civic cinema (including three of the *polars*), and five fall into the "retro" and "tradition of quality" categories (including one costume drama).

This table allows us to make other points with regard to Signoret's career. First, it by and large mirrors the first part of her career, which was also a mixture of "quality" and auteur cinema. Second, it echoes her earlier relation to auteur cinema in the second part of her career. We recall that, in the late 1950s

TYPOLOGY OF SIGNORET FILM OUTPUT, 1970–1982

Coproductions	Polars/thriller	Civic/political	Retro/quality
L'Aveu (Fr/It, 1970)	*Comptes à rebours*	*L'aveu*	*La veuve Couderc*
Comptes à rebours (Fr/It, 1971)	*Le chat*	*Le chat*	*L'adolescente*
Le chat (Fr/It, 1971)	*La veuve Couderc*	*Rude journée pour la reine* (1973)	*Chère inconnue* (1980)
La veuve Couderc (Fr/It, 1971)	*Les granges brûlées*	*La chair de l'orchidée*	*Guy de Maupassant* (1982)
Les granges brûlées (Fr/It, 1973)	*La chair de l'orchidée*	*Police Python 357*	*L'Étoile du Nord*
La chair de l'orchidée (Fr/It/Ger, 1975)	*Police Python 357*	*La vie devant soi*	
Police Python 357 (Fr/It/Ger, 1976)	*L'Étoile du Nord* (1982)	*Judith Therpauve* (1978)	
L'adolescente (Fr/Ger, 1979)		*La vie devant soi* (UK/USA, 1977)	

and early 1960s, the French New Wave wanted nothing to do with Signoret, (deeming her of the "old tradition," yet the British New Wave eagerly embraced her (for example, in *Room at the Top*). Similarly, in the 1970s, whereas the French New Wavists continued to shun her, she was used by the emerging class of French or France-based filmmakers who became associated with the civic and political cinema of that period, including Allio, Chéreau, Corneau, and Costa-Gavras. Several of Signoret's civic films (*Le chat, Police Python 357*, and *Judith Therpauve*) are in the vein of social-realist civic cinema. Others in that same category (*Rude journée pour la reine* and *La chair de l'orchidée*) are more radical and take a stand against the potential "comfort" of social realism by offering a more complex way of examining the class struggle and rapacious capitalism. They either juxtapose or even counterpoint fantasy and reality (as with *Rude journée*), or they go for a form of hybridization between the real and the surreal (as with *La chair de l'orchidée*), grounding a surrealistic narrative within an eclectic, almost gothic, set of real locations.

Equally intriguing is the broad set of 1970s political, social, and historical discourses that Signoret embodies in these various categories of films. Several films have a double-layered history—past and present—in which the contemporary is represented as unable to remain simply located within the reflected reality of the present context but necessarily finds itself looking back toward earlier histories. Similarly, films that are located in the past also project forward and have contemporary value. Let us take a few illustrative examples. The oppression of the "now," as seen in *Rude journée pour la reine*, speaks to a past of oppressions. In this film, Jeanne (Signoret), the cleaning woman and central protagonist, is doubly oppressed, by her work and her home situation. To escape this double drudgery, she flits in and out of romantic fantasies set in past times, where she becomes "queen" (or a person of the haute bourgeoisie). In real life, she is frumpy and constantly clothed in a housecoat; in the dreams, she is adorned with all the regalia befitting her elevated status. These dreams, it becomes clear, are mediated by the popular magazines she avidly consumes. Thus, these fantasies are nothing more than a strategy of the bourgeoisie to co-opt the working-class imagination ("the good old days"). So, in a third way, Jeanne stands oppressed, this time by the media that propagate a vision of a hermetic and unquestionable social order that has "always" existed. As such, this film acts metonymically for all the historic models of oppression that work to profit the existing social order. And it uses Jeanne, first, to display that oppression, then to function as the site/sight of capitalist oppression, only to show her finally reacting against it by defying stereotypes and refusing to do the respectable thing (which all her oppression has taught her to do). She defies her husband (played by Jacques Debary) and the law by helping her stepson (played by Olivier Perrier), a small-time criminal, to elope with his girlfriend (played by Arlette Chosson), a minor and the mother of his child.

In *Judith Therpauve*, Signoret again is astride history: the contemporary and the Occupation period. She is a former Resistance fighter and deportee to Auschwitz who is brought back out of retirement to help save a newspaper of which she is a shareholder, but which is being threatened with a hostile takeover bid by a press baron. She agrees to fight the cause even though she believes, rightly, that it is a lost one. She engages a young man (played by Philippe Léotard) as the new editor to help her wage this battle. However, her refusal to sack people to make the paper viable and the refusal of the trade union workers and leaders to agree to her terms, which are realistic in the context of her own resources, preferring to sell out to the press baron in the end, lead to the paper's folding. The intertextual reference within the contemporary scenario of the 1970s is the press baron Robert Hersant, who, during this period, became known as the "*papivore*" (paper eater) and who had just bought up one of the last regional independent newspapers, *Paris-Normandie*.

The newspaper in the film, *Libre République*, is also astride history—this time a conflictual one. During the Occupation, it was a collaborationist paper. After the war, it was taken over by former Resistance members, including Judith Therpauve, and came to stand for a new kind of republican integrity. For twenty years it acted as a voice that ran along the principle of the fourth estate (the voice that challenges those in power). But now the paper is threatened with a new takeover, this time based purely on the principle of capitalism, embodied by the greed of the press baron. This paper risks once more losing the cachet of independence through an erosion of freedom of expression. Therpauve for her part stands for a generation that took risks during the war and counted for something in the immediate postwar period, but which then was allowed, by younger generations, to slumber into indifference—a fate that is about to beset the newspaper.[49] She stands also for a generation of Resistance fighters who worked collectively in the political battle for liberation.

Numerous worlds are in collision in this film: old guard journalism against new technology; independent journalism versus grasping and powerful press barons; the despair of a past generation whose collective action reaps only indifference versus the despair of young people (as exemplified by the editor) for whom the political battle is a solitary, and therefore equally doomed, battle. The film also shows the ambiguities of the political moment, particularly in relation to the Left—namely, the sellout of the trade unions by the French Communist party (PCF). Not for the first time in this period had the PCF urged its members to lower their demands and accept the deal offered by the capitalist bosses. This happened in 1968, when the PCF told its members to pull out of the nationwide strike and return to work. It happened again when Hersant was in the process of pulling off the bid to take over *Paris-Normandie*. The film also reveals how trade unionists, through their lack of solidarity in relation to a collective good, can bring down a paper, just as much as press barons. As Chéreau said, *Judith Therpauve* was about "a painful exposure of certain struggles within the left."[50] This uncertain world, in which progress at any price is the order of the day—including, in this context, the erasure of the importance of history and memory—is never without its casualties. It is hardly surprising, therefore, that Judith Therpauve commits suicide at the end: she has lost everything to save this newspaper (including her home, which she remortgaged).

In a final example of this double layering of history, *La veuve Couderc*, we are looking the other way: from the past, the 1930s, and its relevance to the present, the 1970s. Set in rural France in 1934, this adaptation of a Simenon novel is located in the period when France was experiencing the worst effects of the Great Depression. It was also the period of the Stavisky affair and other corruption scandals, as well as the most active period of strikes following World War I. These examples of scandal and civil unrest are rumbling around in the background of the film. But, because *La veuve Couderc* is set in rural France (the Côte d'Or region), it is primarily the individual hypocrisies and economic hardships caused by the depression that are revealed in the film. Signoret, as the widow Couderc, occupies a number of intriguing positions: first, a proliferation of sexual roles through which, ultimately, the story is told; second, a series of economic positions that act also as motors to the narrative. In terms of sexual roles, she is the older woman who befriends the young man, Jean (played by Alain Delon), an escaped prisoner, whom she looks after and eventually seduces. As such, she is both mother and lover. Her proto-maternal role replaces the one she never got to occupy as Madame Couderc; now that she is a widow in her fifties, it is too late for her to bear children. Her quasi-filial relation with Jean brings her lover relationship into the arena of incest and taboo; however, the potential threat to morality is completely naturalized by the muted and under-stated way in which she expresses her desire for him (a look, a few words is all she uses). In the same vein, although it is the case that she has power over him (because she has given him shelter), her seduction is not a manipulative one but an open invitation to share her bed.[51]

There are two triangular sets of relationships that complicate and comple-ment this initial proliferation of sexual roles. First, Couderc has a rival in the young and nubile Félicie (played by Octavia Piccolo), who is part of the extended Couderc family and lives just across the way, on the other side of a canal. Félicie, unlike the widow Couderc, is fertile and already has one child (by another man) and, given her sexual appetite, is likely to bear quite a few more. She also seduces Jean. The widow has to learn to share her young lover with Félicie. But the widow is also being pursued by a much older man, her brother-in-law (played by Bobby Lapointe), who shares the house she has inherited from her husband, an inheritance that the entire family greedily contests. Thus, ques-tions of value come into the equation. The widow Couderc is of value to the grasping family only insofar as the brother to her dead husband might be able to ensnare her into marriage. Otherwise, they would prefer her dead, which in the end they bring about by denouncing Jean to the police (both are gunned down by the police at the farm). In this way, they retrieve all the patrimony. Furthermore, she, Couderc, can only hold on to Jean as long as she is prepared to compromise on how much of him she can have. In the end, the only way she can keep him to herself is to choose to die with him.

Thus, the widow Couderc negotiates her pleasure and her death just as uncompromisingly as she manages her farm. Determined to make a financial go of her inheritance, she attempts to modernize one of her earning assets, chick-ens, by purchasing, through mail order, an egg incubator. For a while this new enterprise works, although it is much ridiculed by the family, and in the shoot-out at the end it accidentally goes up in flames. Ultimately, the film tells the tale of an individual locked into an incessant battle against reactionary values.[52] The widow Couderc and Jean are victims of society's rigid incomprehension and reactionary attitude toward sexual freedom: Couderc, because she both wants to move forward with the times and not deny her sexual being; Jean, because he is young and beautiful and generous with his sexual being. They are also victims to a mood of anti-integration. The entire family persists in seeing them as out-siders. The themes of exclusion and marginalization, the fear and dislike of youth and its emblematic association with sexual freedom (read promiscuity), the dislike of technological change and mistrust of women handling it are, as film critic Maryse Degallaix, suggested, as much a phenomenon of the 1970s as the 1930s.[53] Interestingly, in this context, this film predates many of the 1970s films that deal with these issues and which in large part expose the establishment reaction to, even backlash toward, the events of May 1968. The claim is not that this film heralded the new civic cinema of the 1970s; far from it, especially because it can be read as a "retro" film. The point, rather, is that director Pierre Granier-Deferre, as with his other adaptation of Simenon, *Le chat* (which he updated into the 1970s),—infused it with some contemporary debates, including, arguably, feminism, and that Signoret's and Delon's strong profiles in the contemporary context (she as an engaged woman of the Left, he as a very bankable star) made it possible to read it as more than a parable of 1930s rural prejudice.

This impacting of stars on a film's eventual form needs a moment's consideration. Signoret repeatedly stated that she made no attempt to "improve" on the script (and there are abundant examples to support this). However, there is evidence, at least in this last period of her film career, that she had an effect both on the script and on the outcome of the narrative. There is also evidence that her star body was a part-vehicle to attempt new approaches to the genre. An exemplary film in relation to these three points is Alain Corneau's *Police Python 357*. Corneau worked with Signoret and Yves Montand on the characters to provide them with a history before the film starts. It was during this process, according to Corneau, that Signoret's tremendous skills as a dialoguist emerged, to the extent that her part as the bedridden mastermind became largely her own character treatment.[54] Although her presence on screen is not as great as that of her costars, Montand and François Périer, she ends up indirectly holding the pivotal role in the narrative as the string puller. In this thriller, Signoret plays Thérèse, the invalid wife of a senior police officer, Ganay (Périer). He is having an affair with an ex-prostitute (played by Stefania Sandrelli), a relationship that is condoned by his wife. Unbeknown to him, this prostitute is also involved with one of his detectives, Ferrot (Montand). When Ganay does find out, he kills her in a fit of jealous rage. Problematically, however, it is Ferrot who is the last person to have been seen leaving her apartment, not Ganay. Equally problematically, Ferrot is the police officer assigned to the case, but all clues lead to him. In the end, Ferrot resolves the enigma and kills his boss in a defensive shootout. There is no one left who can prove his innocence. Meantime, Thérèse—who had been pulling all the strings in a desperate attempt to save her husband—no longer wants to live and is helped by Ferrot to commit suicide.

In terms of genre, Corneau presented a thriller that is not based on the contemporary American tradition of extreme violence, as in the Arthur Penn and Sam Peckinpah films that were such trendsetters in Hollywood. Corneau stated that, although he admired American thrillers, he did not want to copy them. Instead, he felt that France had to find its own specificity and not imitate Hollywood slavishly.[55] Thus, the film stands as an attempt to find that new way, a way that is achieved through counterpoint if not, indeed, a dialectical approach. It is a violent film, but without a drop of blood and without a great deal of action—a thriller where the camera is almost immobile, much like Thérèse, the immobilized string puller. In fact, in this context, Signoret, as Thérèse, is the embodiment of this attempt to rethink the genre. Violence comes in the form of aggressive editing and mise-en-scène, especially the types of shots, and is counterpointed by the lighting, which is soft and "carnal," to quote Corneau.[56] The violence also finds its place in the suicidal nature of the three main protagonists, all of whom are fascinated by death. Finally, the violence comes through the revelation of the complexity of class relations and tensions. Whereas Thérèse embodies the rich provincial bourgeoisie and its rigid fixity (epitomized by her infirmity), and her husband, the inflexible hierarchy of institutions (in this instance, the police), neither of these characters, nor the worlds they represent, can be simplified into categories of good or bad. Thérèse pulls strings (because she can; she has the tacit respect that her class commands. But she engineers her own suicide, emblematically inviting, in her own demise, that of her class, or its power, at least). Furthermore, she compassionately condones her husband's liaison.

The political edge of this film comes down, then, to its style as much as to its content. But it also is indelibly linked to the star body. I want to take this point a little bit further because there are some interesting permutations to this star effect in other Signoret films of this period. For example, in *L'aveu*, undoubtedly an important political/civic film of the 1970s, Signoret's role as Lise London, the wife of Arthur London, a victim of the Stalinist-influenced trials in former Czechoslovakia, is, in relation to the original text written by London, considerably diminished. In the book, she occupies a great deal of the author's writing, and we come to understand her actions, particularly the reasons why she denounces her husband after he has "confessed" at the trial. It is also made clear that he pushed her very hard through his letters to her to renunciate him so she could be given a visa to leave and return to France with the children, where they would be safe. The film, however, considerably truncates her importance as well as the tremendous pressures she was under to make terrible decisions. In the end, we do not really obtain a favorable image of her. She seems more married to the communist line than to her husband (played by Yves Montand), and the subsequent reconciliation between the husband and wife at the end does not ring convincingly. Thus, within this rewriting of the text (approved by London, incidentally), Signoret/Lise is implicitly judged for lacking faith in her husband and taken to task for not having taken that faith beyond politics.[57] This considerable shift in meaning provides a somewhat misogynistic reading of Lise and foregrounds a very male-centered reading of the original—an outcome possibly influenced by the huge success of Costa-Gavras's earlier film, *Z* (1968), also starring Montand and very much a male-centered text, where a similar reduction of the female role occurs. As reviewer Michael Sragow made clear, Signoret's role "is as underwritten as Mrs. Lambrikis' in *Z*."[58]

In *Le chat* and *La vie devant soi*, Signoret's presence again considerably altered or impacted upon the narrative, although in a converse way to *L'aveu*. In *Le chat* her role bears no resemblance to the character in the original Simenon story.[59] The circumstances of the couple's marriage are completely different. In the novel, it is a second marriage, embarked upon in the couple's mature years and one of convenience. In the film, the couple marries young, and they are in love. Unlike the novel, where this second marriage has always been without passion, in the film it is a marriage of long standing that began in passion but has gradually fallen apart because time and circumstances have worked against it. Even the body type of the wife is totally different. In the novel, she is described as scrawny and puny—two epithets that cannot be attributed to Signoret. In the film, therefore, Signoret is larger than her original; indeed, her character is considerably fleshed out. Furthermore, the narrative is told as much from her point of view as that of her husband (played by Jean Gabin), an equality of subjectivities that does not occur in the far more misogynistic Simenon text. Finally, in the novel, her character is someone who needs a man, any man, to help her around the house. Not so with Signoret's character. She had a career as a successful trapeze artist, which a fall put an end to. Thus, her only physical infirmity is a limp. She is just as competent around the home as her husband.

In *La vie devant soi*, Signoret's presence as Madame Rosa, the aged prostitute, ends up, again, by giving her a greater role than that of the original text. The story, in both the novel (by Emile Ajar/Romain Gary) and the film, is narrated from the point of view of Momo (played by Samy Ben Youb), a young Arab boy. In the film, there is a role reversal in that Madame Rosa becomes the stronger presence, whereas in the novel, it was Momo who dominated. Critics argued that director Moshe Mizrahi was so taken with Signoret and somewhat in awe that he gave her prominence in her role as the old and ugly woman she portrays.[60] Whatever the case, she dominates the cast. Signoret worked extremely hard on the role, and in it she became some kind of totem to history, which is possibly why she came to occupy such a dominant position. In the film version, Madame Rosa's body and mind become the site of the history of the persecution of both the Jews and the Arabs. She incarnates the past persecution of Jews during the German occupation of France. Moreover, she embodies that time with a strong degree of iconic specificity in that, as she tells us, she was first rounded up and taken to the Vel' d'Hiv and subsequently deported to Auschwitz. She also incarnates the contemporary (1970s) Arab-Jewish problem (to which she often refers) and the attempts to broker peace between the two parties, even to the extent of pretending to Momo's father, who has come to reclaim him after years of being in prison, that his son has been raised as a Jew, not an Arab. In an age when racial tolerance as a discourse was not high on the political culture agenda, Madame Rosa leads through her example. As she says, whatever your origins, what really counts is the ability to love. The love between her, an aging Jew, and Momo, an adolescent Arab, stands as a testimony to the potential for harmony between the races. However, despite the fact that her body and mind are worn out, that her body is bloated, her heart subject to the effects of hypertension, and her mind suffering from senility, it would seem fair to suggest that her body as a totem to history is worn out by the impossible weight of this history. There is nowhere else for her to go than to hide—physically, by holing up in her secret refuge under the stairs and, mentally, by entering dementia—a withdrawal that ends in death.

SIGNORET: THE STAR BODY AND THE UGLY

In this concluding section, I want to pursue this aspect of Signoret's later career, namely, the mutation of her body into a swollen excess of its former self. Signoret's star embodiment was a continuum toward the "ugly," not just the aged (the deterioration of her looks began in 1961), which is not what we associate with female stardom. Stars as signs of their times—especially female stars—are expected to sustain their looks and bodies (for example, Catherine Deneuve and Charlotte Rampling). Therefore, how was it that Signoret continued to occupy a high profile as a star given that she aged, became "ugly" before her time? And, finally, how do we account for the fact that she is still, in her films of this period, represented as a desiring subject, either in nostalgic flashbacks, as in *Le chat*, or in fact, as in *La veuve Couderc* and *L'Étoile du Nord*?

It is highly instructive that Signoret was called a *monstre sacré* and compared to that other *monstre sacré* of French cinema, Jean Gabin.[61] This comparison with the masculine warrants a closer look. Also, it is worth querying what this form of shorthand, in categorizing her along with the masculine, is hiding. Let us take a closer look. I suggested earlier that Signoret's performance offers a blurring of sexualities that produces pleasure for both the male and the female spectator. I have also made the point (in Chapter One) that Signoret was an intelligent woman and perceived as such at a time when women, particularly the female star body, were supposed to be the site of sexual beauty—in other words, the body, not the mind. But we can take this reading further and suggest that her body as performance violates "natural" boundaries, in this context the ideological straitjacketing of female performance into the body as beauty and not as intellect. Signoret, in her middle-period performances, perpetuated this violation by transcending these boundaries in her proliferation of femininities and, by extension, sexualities. In her last period, she continued to violate boundaries just as she had done throughout her career, but she did it this time by counterposing her mutable body (in its bloatedness, outsized nose, swollen eyelids and cheeks, etc.) to the concept of "finished" (or fixed) beauty, as in Brigitte Bardot. It is instructive that this mutable body—unlike that of Bardot—did not disappear but continued to attract huge audiences to her later films (several ranking in the top ten in the 1970s).

In answer to the questions posed above, I want to suggest that, by comparing Signoret to the masculine, what is avoided is the idea of a feminine star body violating boundaries. That is, it avoids dealing with the notion of the female body as a mutable body, one that can become grotesque, "ugly." It is also an attempt to lessen Signoret's real force and function. By labeling her outside that sphere of the feminine (as masculine), the attempt is to reduce her power to challenge the "accepted" norms of beauty and femininity. If this is the case, we can get behind the referential smoke screen and can now start to understand what is really going on with Signoret's body as performance in terms of cultural politics. Let me start with a quote from Robert Stam's book *Subversive Pleasures* (1989, 157–158), in which he talks about Bakhtin's view of the grotesque body:

> For Bakhtin, the body is a festival of becoming. . . . Bakhtin is fascinated by the unfinished body, the elastic malleable body, the body that outgrows itself, that reaches beyond its own limits and conceives of new bodies. He praises the body in movement . . . the active body, the sweating, farting, lubricating, defecating body . . . all the body's secretions. . . . Bakhtin's vision exalts the "base" products of the body . . . in sum all that has been banned from respectable representation because official decorum remains chained to a Manichean notion of the body's fundamental uncleanliness.

In other words, ideological aesthetics demand that the body remain contained within "natural" and clean boundaries, whereas in truth, the body's central principle, to quote Stam (1989, 159), is "growth and change; by exceeding its limits, the body expresses its essence." This is Bakhtin's "mutable body," the one that passes from one form to another through its "gluttony, creative obscenity, indefatigable sexuality" (Stam 1989, 158). Bakhtin celebrated this mutable grotesque body. Indeed, as Stam (159) explains, by "calling attention to the paradoxical attractiveness of the grotesque body, Bakhtin rejects what might be called the 'fascism of beauty,' the construction of an ideal type or language of beauty in relation to which other types are seen as inferior 'dialectical' variations." Thus, the ugly can be just as valued as the beautiful. Equally, the ugly can be seen as just as desiring and desired as the beautiful.

Signoret's success in the 1970s, despite her aging, her thickening body, and her swollen face, suggests that we are dealing here with the paradoxical attractiveness of the grotesque body and not spectator prurience, precisely because Signoret rejected any masochistic relationship to her physical decline. She was quoted as saying, "I am fat and ugly and I am going to use it to my advantage" (Monserrat 1983a, 271). Fat and ugly though she was, then, she harnessed these traits and used them to her advantage. Excess in this different form becomes a source of creative energy. Thus, a first reason for Signoret's continued success and attractiveness, is that her body as performance ties into Bakhtin's notion of the rejection of the fascism of beauty. Implicitly Bakhtin's analysis of the grotesque body also "dehierarchizes the senses" and challenges the supremacy of sight (we like what we see) over the other, more base, senses of smell and taste, senses that are more readily associated with the body and sexual pleasure (Stam 1989, 159). As a system of signs, therefore, Signoret's performance stands for the whole body and acknowledges (as do we, the audience) its odors, its secretions, and its appetites. We can smell the effects of physical labor on her body in *La veuve Couderc* and *Rude journée pour la reine*, to say nothing of the alcohol on her breath in *Le chat*. So whereas before her gestures suggested "the more to come," now she remains "bodily present" in her entirety (inside and out).

A second reason for her attractiveness again comes to us through a Bakhtinian reading. Her body, by exceeding its limits, does indeed become grotesque, obscene. But it visibilizes its essence, puts on display its truth. In the context of Simone Signoret, that truth is both personal and political. In other words, she refused on both personal and political counts the ideological notion that the body (including the body politic) must remain contained within natural and clean boundaries. She rejected, therefore, ideological censorship of the citizen's body politic. Instead, she asserted its right to be voiced, heard, and—in its refusal to conform—to be eccentric in the true sense of the word, as outside the center. Signoret's bodily discourses can be read as a reaction against and rejection of ideological discourses, both sexual and political, of the time. And her aging body in her later films conveys a clearly oppositional image that was as forceful as it ever was. Indeed, her body evolved from her earlier performances, when her minimalism and lack of excess was already a challenge to the ideological hierarchy of containment and displacement (punishing women, denying them agency), to a later performance, when she challenged other hierarchies based on the concept of female beauty and the supremacy of sight over the other senses.

Viewed in this light (Bakhtinian, to be sure), Signoret's body and performance situate her body as democratic and unhierarchical. She suggests the normativity of diverse sexualities and challenges the fixity of gender, to the point of suggesting a gender-free body. She also challenges the primacy of sight and the narcissism and voyeurism implicit in that hierarchy. She stands as a metonymy for all our bodies—smells and all—and reminds us of their constant self-differentiation (we change all the time and are all different). Finally, she proposes a view of the body that is not based on masculine rationality but on the idea of an active commonality, that is, the notion that all bodies are motivated by desires, pulsions, and organ movements (from mouth to bowels and genitals). In this way, the body is both inner and outer matter and not identified by its sexual organs. Thus, her body as performance throws down the gauntlet to the monadic (we are our sex) and dyadic (we are our gender) notions of a fixed subjectivity as the sole marker of identity. She offers—and did so long before any such discourses were in place at least in cinema—a new kind of cultural politics that was beyond sexual politics.[62] She is, then, the body political in its widest sense: the body as a site of history and contesting histories, as a site of economics and economies of desire, and, finally, a mutating body that has as its beginning a proliferation of feminities but that remains, in the end, unfixed and plural.

Chapter Three

Signoret's Theater Work

IMONE SIGNORET is known primarily for her film work. However, on three occasions she took to the stage: twice in Paris (at the Théâtre Sarah Bernhardt, now known as the Théâtre de la Ville) and once in London at the Royal Court Theatre (she never appeared onstage for her potential debut performance at the Théâtre des Mathurins in 1942). Her first appearance was in 1954, as Elizabeth Proctor in the French adaptation of Arthur Miller's *The Crucible* (*Les sorcières de Salem*, script adaptation by Marcel Aymé). This production ran for a whole year. Her second, in 1962, was as Regina in her own adaptation of Lillian Hellman's *The Little Foxes* (*Les petits renards*). This ran for six months. Finally, she played Lady Macbeth opposite Alec Guinness in William Gaskill's production of *Macbeth*, which ran, in repertory, for six weeks in 1966.

In a career that spanned forty-three years, from 1942 to 1985, Signoret appeared in fifty-seven films. So, with only three stage performances to her name, theater represents only a very small percentage of her performing life. Of the three theatrical performances, only the first was a success. The other two, by Signoret's own admission, were qualified failures. Her brief and not too successful encounters with the theater left her with the realization that it was not her world. However, the point is that she did take these risks, for either political or personal reasons, and they represent moments when she was confronted with the limitations of her actorly skills.

When discussing theater work, we are bound to come up against the problem of how to write about performances that can no longer be seen, that no longer exist for all intents and purposes. Without the visual evidence, one has to rely on the directors' notes, photographic evidence, critics' reviews, and, of course, actors' accounts of their own performances. It is also clear that it would be helpful to consider the venues of the plays themselves in terms of their contexts, for they too will yield clues.

THEATER VENUES

The Théâtre Sarah Bernhardt is one of the two big theaters in Paris; the other is the Théâtre du Châtelet. Both are located on the Place du Châtelet, more or less across the square from each other. The Sarah Bernhardt has 1,500 seats, the Châtelet, 3,500. The Sarah Bernhardt was a theater with an international vocation and still is, under its present name of the Théâtre de la Ville (the theater carries high up on its facade, in huge lettering, its former, more famous name, Sarah Bernhardt). This theater was first built in 1860 during the Haussmannization of Paris. It was then known as the Théâtre Lyrique and was one of the many theaters that had been relocated into the city center as part of a major program to centralize theaters away from the infamous Boulevard du Temple (known also as the Boulevard du Crime) and to prevent aristocrats from mingling with riffraff and dissidents in this perceived den of iniquity. The boulevard of attractions (crime and all) gave way to the sanitized Place du Châtelet, conveniently located near the administrative nerve center of the city (embodied by such buildings as the Hôtel de Ville and the Palais de Justice, to name two). Interestingly, the Lyrique was burned down during the Paris Commune of 1871, a symbolic revenge by dissidents. It was rebuilt, and, in 1898, the internationally acclaimed actress Sarah Bernhardt (1844–1923) leased the theater and renamed it after herself. This name prevailed until the German occupation of Paris during World War II, when, because Bernhardt was a Jew, it was changed to the Théâtre de la Cité. Under Franco-Nazi anti-Semitic laws, buildings named after Jews had to be renamed. In 1944, the theater became the Sarah Bernhardt once again and remained as such until 1968, when it was completely rebuilt and named the Théâtre de la Ville.

Thus, when Signoret performed in this theater, it was still the Sarah Bernhardt. We need to be mindful of this theater's political resonances because they are not without their reverberations where Signoret's own personal and political history is concerned. The theater was a site of sociopolitical engineering. By locating it in the center of the city, Napoleon III (with Haussmann's city planning to help) was effectively controlling the citizenry of Paris. The theater was also a site of protestation against repression, when it was burned down during the Paris Commune. Finally, it was a "victim" of Nazi anti-Semitism. Given Signoret's own trajectory as a defender of human rights, the fact that her own body (through her Jewish heritage) had been a site of interdiction, it is possible to trace some lines, in the Deleuzian sense, between Signoret's circumstances and the theater's own history under its illustrious namesake.

The Sarah Bernhardt Theater's original stage size was huge: 25 meters wide and 35 meters deep. Match this size with the depth of the auditorium (1500 seats), and it becomes obvious that actors had to have voices that carried and gestures that could be seen. Clearly, a problem would occur for a performer such as Signoret whose experience with theater work in her very early years was fleeting. Although she had been coached at the renowned cours Sicard in the early 1940s, she was destined not to make her career in that arena because her voice was too weak. Another problem was her performance style, which resided in its vocal and gestural minimalism. Signoret's performance style relied primarily on small facial gestures—a look, a slight lip movement, a moue—to make the point. Her gestures were equally at a minimum—an occasional hand gesture for phatic value, hands on hips, a shrugging of the shoulders—but other than that there was little going on that could be visually measured. She was far removed from the more hyperbolic and carnivalesque visual language of theater. Thus, what she tried to express fell, within such a large arena as this theater, into a vacuum. In film, camera proximity worked to give her performance style the power it had. With the stage, no such proximity was possible, thus, the performance lost its power. In terms of voice, Signoret in her films was quiet; even when she was angry, she seethed more than she screeched. Furthermore, she did not often say a lot, but when she did speak, both what she said and how she said it mattered. On a huge stage, and at a distance from most of her audience, it must have been extremely hard for her voice to reach them with any great precision or depth. Thus, again, establishing contact with those people out there watching and evaluating her stage potential must have been a daunting exercise.

Signoret was conscious of her limitations, and so too was the director of *Sorcières* (her friend Raymond Rouleau). In order to compensate for her voice (or lack of voice), the set's ceiling was lowered by the set designer, Lila de Nobili, and acted as a resonating box—Nobili used real wood for her interiors, which facilitated this task, as wood resonates on stage (Signoret 1978, 130). In her autobiography, Signoret (130) spoke of her unease on stage while everyone else seemed perfectly at ease. This would be an unease she would never lose and why twelve years later she gave up completely on any thoughts of further theater work. This did not prevent her from going on to appear in plays adapted for film or television, however. She played in Sidney Lumet's film version of *The Seagull* in 1968 and in French television's 1970 broadcast of Brendan Behan's *The Hostage*.

As for the other venue where Signoret appeared, the Royal Court Theatre, given its size (a small stage, with an auditorium of 700 seats) and its reputation as a radical theater, it should have suited her perfectly. The Royal Court had staged John Osborne's *Look Back in Anger*. Samuel Beckett's and Arnold Wesker's plays were also part of this forum's repertory that made it so famous during the 1960s in particular. It had gained a reputation for radical stagings of the established canon of plays. Thus, when Gaskill decided to produce *Macbeth*, audience expectations ran high. Instead of being able to adapt to the stage and auditorium size, however, if anything the smallness of the theater magnified Signoret's shortcomings. Although there might have been no objections to her French accent with this very English playwright's text, she was unable to scan the lines with a cadence that carried conviction and clarity of meaning, as she herself acknowledged (Signoret 1978, 324–328).

THREE PLAYS, ONE ACTOR

Before turning in more detail to Signoret's performances, let us first consider the plays themselves. All three are non-French (two American and one English), so why did she elect to do these and not others? As will become clear, in each instance a different reason motivated her choice. The two American plays are, in terms of their authors, radical texts. Miller and Hellman were both liberals, and both were, during the 1950s, affected one way or another by the McCarthy era. In other words, they were touched by the intolerance of the times. *The Crucible* was a plea against intolerance—ostensibly, the intolerance of the seventeenth-century witch-hunts in Salem, Massachusetts. But it was also a thinly veiled indictment of McCarthyism and the condemnation of the Rosenbergs, who were sentenced to the electric chair in 1953 for supposedly spying for the Russians. John and Elizabeth Proctor in the play were preincarnations in the historical sense of Julius and Ethel Rosenberg. However, as an adapted work for French audiences, the play also had intrinsic national resonance, namely,

France's own intolerance, targeted especially against Jews, during the Occupation. Thus, Signoret wanted to do the play because of its political value. Both Signoret and Yves Montand, who played John Proctor, believed in the innocence of the Rosenbergs. Indeed, they had spoken at the huge rally held in June 1953 at the Vel' d'Hiv in Paris to protest against the execution of the Rosenbergs. But they also believed in the play as a general plea against intolerance, from which France itself was far from free. In the climate of the cold war, the political Left and, in particular, the French Communist party and those associated with it were subject to frequent attacks. France was a divided nation over its own struggles with decolonization, which was bringing the nation to the brink of civil war. In this climate of political instability, censorship was rife. In a broader context, we need to recall that just as in the West there was a fierce anticommunism (the worst of which manifested itself in McCarthyism), so too in the East there was a purge of ideologically suspect political personages and intellectuals. Thus, in the East there were the Moscow and Prague trials (see discussion in Chapter Seven). In the West, there was the U.S. House Un-American Activities Committee. People denounced each other. The director Elia Kazan, for example, did not hestitate in 1952 to write an open letter to the *New York Times* calling on people to denounce communists. In 1954, he made *On the Waterfront*, a potentially radical film which spoke out against corrupt trade union bosses. But Kazan distorted it to his own purposes with a special pleading on behalf of informers. Perhaps the real lack of clarity of this period—when every political body imaginable was trying to assert an ideological clarity—is in some ways metaphorically pointed to by the fact that Marcel Aymé became the adaptor of *The Crucible* to the French stage and not Sartre, who had been Miller's first choice. Aymé was deeply anti-American and, unlike Sartre, certainly not a man of the Left. He was a staunch Frenchman, but he was also brought before a *comité d'épuration* after the war for fraternizing with the enemy and collaboration (which took the form of writing film scripts during the Occupation). For this he was given a nine-month sanction. He was not a clear-cut character. But he was considered a great man of letters, so much so that a few years after being sanctioned, he was offered the Légion d'Honneur, which he refused. On this issue, Signoret merely recorded that, during the Occupation, Aymé had a number of friends who were a bit "encumbering" (Signoret 1978, 134). Whatever the ambiguities surrounding Aymé, they were not enough for her to pull out of the project.

As far as *Les petits renards* was concerned, here Signoret readily admitted that she made a mistake and fell into a trap of her own making. Having translated the play, she wanted to get it staged because she saw it as a groundbreaking piece that demystified the gallant South. Set in the post–Civil War period, it was for Signoret the reverse image of *Gone with the Wind*. Indeed, she saw it as closely aligned with the powerful Billie Holiday song "Strange Fruit" (Signoret 1978, 315). Not satisfied with just translating the play, Signoret also wanted to act in it and take on the role of Regina, the ruthless, ambitious woman who will stop at nothing to make money. Hellman's play, written in 1936, had already been made into a film starring Bette Davis as Regina (William Wyler, *The Little Foxes*, 1941). Davis's version was, then, the template for Signoret's own embodiment of the role: would she be able to play a monster with the same conviction, venom, and general nastiness that Davis had managed? Overall, critics thought not. Signoret seemed unable to inhabit the role; she seemed distanced from her character.[1] Critics found her too voluptuous for the part and lacking in the edginess the role required; others found her ungainly, too buxom and wooden.[2] Signoret herself recognized that she was too busy playing the author of the piece (and watching how the cast dealt with their delivery of "her lines") that she forgot to act the part (Signoret 1978, 315). A further complication, suggested by Signoret herself, might have been that her friend Pierre Mondy directed the play and did not call her to task enough.[3]

Signoret's last stage performance was *Macbeth*. Gaskill, as director of the Royal Court Theatre, had been more or less obliged to drop his earlier practices of only staging radical new plays in repertory. The Royal Court was facing a serious financial crisis; audiences were snubbing the radical productions. Gaskill decided that the only way to save the theater from ruin was to bring in some Shakespeare, albeit in an experimental way, and to attract audiences by casting international stars. He went over to Paris to woo Signoret, seeing her as someone who could help fill the empty seats. She was finally coaxed into it by Alec Guinness. At first, she wanted to say no. This role had already defeated many an English actor, so why should she take the risk, especially because she would be the first French woman to play Lady Macbeth in English? Eventually her friendship with Guinness held sway, and he was able to persuade her to do it. Given her popularity with English audiences, Signoret thought she could give it a try, even though she had no idea what the outcome would be.[4] She had never seen a performance of *Macbeth*, but she knew this version, produced by Gaskill, was going to be very modern in its interpretation and rendition and would therefore be controversial. She rightly assumed she had been invited to play the role because of her anticonformist reputation.[5]

Indeed, Gaskill's interpretation was strongly inflected by his current interest in Bertolt Brecht. The staging was austere. There was no decor, and the stage was fully lit. The witches were male and played by black actors. The stage—perhaps in itself too small for such an epic as *Macbeth*—was stripped bare, thus leaving the actors with a huge burden to shoulder in performance terms. The British press found fault with Gaskill's whole conception of the production, saying there was no atmosphere of terror.[6] In an interview before rehearsals started, Signoret stated that she would quit if she felt she was not up to the demands of the role, in particular, the demands of the Shakespearean language.[7] She studied six versions of the play (Signoret 1978, 324) and learned her role by heart.[8] But she could not scan correctly and made very little progress during the two months of rehearsals. Still, she stuck with it, almost perversely—and none of her colleagues told her it was time to pack up and go. When she did acknowledge she had made a terrible mistake, it was too late to pull out. Rather than cause the six-week scheduled performance to fold, she went through with it. It was a terrifying experience for her (Simone 1978, 327). Gaskill was also taking a risk with Guinness. The public did not like Guinness in Shakespearean mode.[9] Thus, the play's anticonformism and choice of lead actors, which would shock any Shakespearean purist, were bound to lead to a mixed press reception.

Although it might be tempting to claim that the broader contexts of the play's mise-en-scène weighed against a favorable reception, unfortunately, the British press was unanimous in its critical dismissal of Signoret as dreadful. *The Guardian* spoke of Signoret as the worst Lady Macbeth ever.[10] These terrible reviews did not deter people from coming to watch. Indeed, all tickets had been sold before the performance began its run of six weeks; audiences wanted to see

Signoret—the famed, sexy French actor. Undeterred by the critical reviews, they came, and the house was packed each evening. Furthermore, the price of black-market tickets inexplicably soared.[11] Like ghouls at a sacrifice, people were curious to see for themselves just how bad this production was.

Signoret's stage performance—one play *Les sorcières de Salem*

In terms of the roles embodied by Signoret in these three plays, the first and last were ones that had her cast against her usual type. Although, by 1952, she was an international star (thanks to *Casque d'or*), she had become associated with a narrow set of characterizations. Almost without exception she played a prostitute, a trollop, a bitch or a gold digger—someone who could use her sexuality to good avail. Only occasionally did she have more "noble" roles—as a Resistance fighter, or a brilliant pianist recovering from a nervous breakdown, or an unhappy and lonely housewife. In *Les sorcières de Salem*, she played a Puritan and in *Macbeth*, a tragic and flawed queen. Only with *Les petits renards* did she resume some part of her more typical screen persona, as the bitchy, gold-digging Regina.

When we consider Signoret's characterization of Elizabeth Proctor in *Les sorcières de Salem*, there is much that would lead us to consider that she is playing against screen type. She had to drop her sensual and assertive body type—be in denial of her incendiary eyes and impersonate precisely a person whose body is not used to provoke any response. Indeed, critics of the day repeatedly used the word *dignity* to describe Signoret's performance.[12] Others noted how silent she was.[13] Others still remarked how all her emotions appeared to be concentrated in her clenched fists.[14] These comments lead us to speculate that these were strategies Signoret used almost as if to contain her real self. With Elizabeth Proctor, we find a character who is truly puritanical and sexually frigid, not attributes we associate with Signoret. Furthermore, Elizabeth Proctor is so convinced in her righteousness that she holds the moral high ground right until the end of the play, when, to all intents and purposes, it is too late. As we discover, her change of heart cannot save her husband. However, in these closing moments of the play, when she lets her love shine through, the repressed Elizabeth Proctor gives way to a woman of passion (the Signoret we know)—a woman who believes in her husband and affirms his refusal to perjure himself. In her own stance against intolerance, Elizabeth Proctor becomes, then, someone whose courage readily aligns her with Signoret's own political persona: a woman with strong views who is not afraid to speak out against abuses of human rights. In this play, Montand is also cast against type. The crooning music hall singer drops his smooth charm to become the rugged pioneer-spirited John Proctor. In the public arena, though, he was equally associated with the same causes as his wife.

The play ran for a year and was a huge success. Undoubtedly, if we go by the reviews of the period, the Signoret/Montand ticket was *the* big attraction. For *L'Humanité*, their presence on stage made this production the theatrical event of the season.[15] But the question remains just how much the political persona of these two stars influenced, or even got in the way of reading, critically, the true value of the performers and their performances. The very mixed reviews their performances received can act as a partial answer, even if they cannot account for the actual audience response. Let us start first with a quick overview of the reviews in the three principal quality newspapers that cover the political spectrum. The reviewer Guy Leclerc, writing for *L'Humanité*, the PCF's official newspaper, is full of praise for the newborn stage actors Signoret and Montand. He also leaves the reader in no doubt as to the polemical nature of the play.[16] For the PCF, this play was hugely topical as an allegory about McCarthyism and the witch-hunt that brought the Rosenbergs to their execution. Not only was the play itself grist for the PCF's anticapitalist mill, so too was the presence on stage of Montand and Signoret—two star personas they had systematically portrayed as their traveling companions.

As far as the right-wing newspaper *Le Figaro* was concerned, the focus of critic Jean-Jacques Gautier's very positive review was more on the staging of the play by the director, Raymond Rouleau, and Lila de Nobili's sets and costumes than on any actors in particular. He does, however, mention Signoret's extraordinary dignity and comments on Yves Montand's sober performance.[17] However, the review lacks *L'Humanité*'s enthusiasm for the play's star actors. Finally, the theater critic Robert Kemp, writing in *Le Monde*, a centrist, nonpartisan newspaper, again notes Signoret's dignity in the role of Elizabeth Proctor, and singles out the brilliance of Rouleau's direction and staging, but overall the review is lukewarm with its faint praise.[18]

In general, reviews of the time where Signoret is concerned fell into two camps: either they praised her or they damned her. Those who liked her work thought she had an inner sensibility that showed great depth in her acting.[19] They perceived her as restrained and self-effacing within her role.[20] For some, she was able to convey the iciness of Elizabeth Proctor's character with utter conviction.[21] As for those who did not like her performance, a major criticism was that she was unable to make the shift between screen and stage.[22] Her voice was too thin, she was swallowed up by the stage.[23] Not only was her voice thin, one critic complained, but her face was lifeless and her eyes extinguished.[24] Yet another critic drew attention to her lack of expressivity and added that in her minimalism she overplayed her restraint to the point of being brittle.[25]

Significantly, the press was virtually unanimous in its appreciation of Raymond Rouleau's production. (The play won the *Grand Prix de la Mise-en-Scène* in 1955.) Rouleau's style of direction was based on ensemble work—he used his principle of teamwork to progressively build up the play's tension. Critics spoke of the play's vigorous and fast pace and its solid construction.[26] Rouleau was a perfectionist and knew exactly what he could achieve with his actors, although he never went for easy solutions.[27] He made the best of his actors' limitations, and, because of his focus on ensemble playing and his sense of pace, the less able were sustained by the group and not allowed to flounder. Signoret and Montand were friends of Rouleau and had made it clear they would quit if he found they were no good. Rouleau found no reason to recast.

If her role as Elizabeth Proctor got Signoret out of type, it did not change her mode of performance practice—even though this undoubtedly caused some problems with her performance. As we know, Signoret speaks of being inhabited by her characters; they become her. We note that this is the opposite of method acting, where the actor becomes the character. The character, Signoret says, enters her, then becomes exteriorized by her body.[28] This form of doubling (*dédoublement*) is one where she is taken over by the "other," as she refers to the characters she plays (Signoret 1978, 116–117). Once she agrees to a role, the character grows in her like a seed.[29] The incubation period is the preparation.[30] Then, on day one of the appearance, on stage or at the studio, she is the "other," and that "other" takes over, becoming her (Signoret 1979, 20–21). Signoret's performativity consists, then, of emptying herself out, of disembodying herself, to make room for the "other." Typically, as part of her preparation, Signoret also researched her role. This could take the form of reading (as, for example, for Lady Macbeth) or of going around the streets, or, indeed, into prisons and hospitals, if necessary, observing the character she was to embody.

For her role as Elizabeth Proctor, Signoret read all of Ethel Rosenberg's letters from prison (Signoret 1978, 132). The kiss at the end of Act 4, as John Proctor is taken off to be hanged, was based entirely on the Rosenbergs' last kiss (Signoret 1978, 133). Thus, Signoret was inhabited not by one persona but by two: the textual Elizabeth Proctor and the subtextual Ethel Rosenberg. Signoret's body, therefore, made space for the occupation of two other textual bodies—albeit both authentic historically marked bodies (Elizabeth Proctor of the Salem trials of the seventeenth century and Ethel Rosenberg of the McCarthy era). Signoret had then to square this cohabitation between three bodies with a suppressed emotional self. As she herself said, she had to remain icy cold until Act 4, when she had to completely reverse her character and let her repressed passion out. Signoret stated that she was able to achieve this transformation, thanks to Ethel Rosenberg's own letters of love and passion to her husband (Signoret 1978, 132). Thus, during the major part of her performance, Signoret was harnessed, reined in, frozen. The way she found to play this difficult atypical role was to opt for a subdued, self-effacing presence. As we know from our discussion of her film performance, there was nothing subdued or self-effacing about Signoret's minimalist style, which was all about fire and passion. So we can imagine that until Act 4 Signoret was a shadow of herself—hence, her own sense of unease. If her stage performance was anything like the film version (and there is a lot to suggest that there is was substantial difference), then she was indeed rather gray and self-absorbed, in an almost sullen manner.

What I am suggesting is that Signoret overprepared and overcompensated for the fact that she was not (and was aware that she was not) a stage actor. She went cold in an arena where projection and bodily presence matter enormously. Signoret readily admitted that she found the stage terrifying because "the audience is right there and judges you immediately, whereas in the cinema theatre, they see the film as an end product—an assembly of the best shots."[31] The mechanics of film technology gave her the means to assert her magnetic power in a way that she would never master on the stage—through, for example, the use of close-ups, doing several takes of the same scene, and so on. There were, of course, points of convergence where her minimalist style added to the overall stage performance in *Les sorcières* and gave an effect, particularly the way her weighty silences counterpointed the prevailing hysteria of the young women and the inquisitorial judges.[32]

Signoret's performance as Elizabeth Proctor was not a straightforward success. Her embodiment both worked and did not work. Her interpretation, then, raises questions in relation to the cinema–stage crossover. It is not just that in a stage performance the actor is of necessity different every single night and can in fact choose to do something different every night—as opposed to the cinematic performance, where the actor is always the same, captured on film in a set of fixed images, even though that same is made up of many different takes. Theater acting has a spontaneity to it that cinema cannot emulate. Furthermore, it is easy to speculate that Signoret might have lacked spontaneity because she was weighed down by too many intertexts (or interbodies) and too much knowledge. But the crossover also raises the question as to how much a star's film aura can allow him or her to get away with certain inadequacies—Signoret's lack of experience and voice projection being two major cases in point—at the same time as it can expose his or her limitations. The risk involved was worth it as far as Signoret was concerned, and would continue to be worth it, even though her next two stage performances only further highlighted her limitations as a stage actor.[33]

Chapter Four

Postwar Films—1946–1951

*I*N DISCUSSING Signoret's postwar films, it is worth considering her star persona against that of the Italian Anna Magnani, *the* icon of Italian Neorealism because this tells us something about national identity and the codes of femininity that were conflated onto the female body at that time. Several of Signoret's films fall into the category of *réalisme noir* (black realism), a type of film whose style became associated with that of Italian neorealism (the other influences being American film noir and France's own poetic realism). Italy, like France, was committed to renewing its image postwar, and among the star personas that the Italian film industry appropriated was Magnani. She was chosen not only for her ordinariness, but, even more pertinently, because she exuded intelligence, integrity, and authenticity in her roles; she came to embody the moral and ethical strength of the people. In France, no such national value was ascribed to any particular female French star in the same period, especially not Signoret—even though, as we have seen, she had all of the above attributes. Her roles were primarily perceived as representing France's economic underbelly. Indeed, most of the narratives in her films, for which she was a central vehicle, rather than being about nation building, were about duplicity, fear, and vengeance.

Codes of Femininity and National Identity

Signoret's output of films during this period includes eight major roles and two smaller ones, the other three being a cameo (*La boîte aux rêves*), a short sketch (*La ronde*), and a very brief walk-on part (*Sans laisser d'adresse*). Leaving these three roles aside, in the ten films that concern us, she plays a prostitute three times (*Les démons de l'aube*, *Macadam*, and *Dédée d'Anvers*), a gold digger twice (*Four Days' Leave* and *Manèges*), and twice a woman who has risen in class (*Impasse des deux anges* and *Le Traqué/Gunman in the Street*, Boris Lewin and Frank Tuttle, 1950). In only two films is she truly born of the rich bourgeoisie (*Fantômas* and *Ombre et Lumière*), and finally, she appears as a Resistance fighter—and in a British, not French, film (*Against the Wind*). Thus, half her films have her registered in the lowliest classes and professions. A fifth have her rising through the ranks, albeit to deal with her murky past (*Impasse des deux anges* and *Le Traqué*). Only a third have her as truly "respectable" (*Fantômas*, *Against the Wind*, and *Ombre et Lumière*). Significantly, all of these films are contemporary (or near contemporary, as two are about the Resistance). As this chapter will show, in each one it is possible to discern running discourses that refer to France's postwar unease or lack of optimism in its ability to rebuild the nation's psyche.

Interestingly, in Signoret's films, this focus on the present does not come at the price of a denial of the past, even though, initially, the characters may attempt to do so. Rather, the films point to the inevitability of the past returning to haunt. Thus, several films use Signoret as the vehicle for this struggle between the desire to transcend or deny the past and the need to confront it in order to be able to move forward. In *Impasse des deux anges*, *Le Traqué*, and *Ombre et Lumière*, she plays women who are trying to forge a new and bright future. However, the past catches up with them and threatens to destroy their potential happiness, and it becomes clear to each character that the only way to build that future is by confronting the past. The protagonist might lose out, seriously, as in *Le Traqué*, when she is shot dead by the police while attempting to help her former lover escape. Or she might get lucky and see the demons of her past off, as in *Ombre et Lumière*, when she admits to her fiancé that she had a nervous breakdown (and even thought she was mad). Finally, the outcome might be far more ambiguous, as with *Impasse*. In this film, a former lover resurfaces into the life of Marianne (played by Signoret) after a seven-year absence. For a while, she is seemingly tempted to drop her new life and leave with this man, Jean (played by Paul Meurisse)—the first passion of her life—and forgo a rather dull marriage with the marquis (played by Marcel Herrand), to whom she is betrothed. When she discovers that Jean was and still is a top-class safecracker and jewel thief and that he has arrived uninvited to her prenuptial reception intent on stealing her valuable necklace (an heirloom belonging to the marquis's family), she is still undeterred in her decision to go with him. During their nocturnal walk—in which they return to their old haunts in the Impasse des Deux Anges (in the sixth arrondissement of Paris)—they catch up on the past. She now finds out that he spent the last seven years in jail. She, meantime, has built herself a career as a successful stage actor. Despite Jean's accusations that she has betrayed her class, she retorts that she has nothing to reproach herself for. A first impasse is reached, then, one that is based on class. But this is not what causes their separation. It is only once she witnesses his cruelty and violence that she decides to pull away and return to the promise of a future with the marquis. As she tells the marquis, at the end of the film, when the two of them drive off to be married, "I had a past. I no longer have one. Now I am free." One senses from her distant gaze that this is a compromise—or unlikely to be a marriage based on passion. Indeed, it is noteworthy that there are many more close-ups of Signoret in her exchanges and scenes with her former lover, Jean, than there are in scenes between her and the Marquis (the ratio is 4:1).

In three of these ten films, *Macadam*, *Impasse*, and *Le Traqué*, the confrontation with the past comes in the form of a "mystery man," an outlaw returning from places unknown to his former territory or mistress. The crucial point is that it is a man "out of law" who provokes this confrontation. The destabilizing factor is the criminal past and its inescapability. It is possible to read into this preoccupation with the criminal past a concern of the nation with its own recent history, for, at the time, France showed every desire not to confront the past other than to mythologize it (as in the mythification of the Resistance). These films, then, seem to suggest—through this repeated trope—that there is some work to be done: that, where France is concerned, its own criminality during the Occupation cannot be hushed over. These films, as well as the very dark *Dédée* and *Manèges*, are readily aligned with the black realist tendency of post-war French cinema, because of their themes of treachery and vengeance, to say nothing of their very dark mise-en-scène and the predominantly negative representation of women as the source of the male's malaise. As such, they have been read as expressions of the postwar disillusionment with the political and economic situation of the time.[1] They are this, but they also stand as metaphors for the unspeakable, censored reality of the Occupation. Crucially, they use the female body as a modality through which, however problematically and paradoxically it might be represented, this censored reality can find an expression.

Moving away from this category of *réalísme noir* (black realism), but still within the realm of the confrontation with the past, *Ombre et Lumière*, a psychological melodrama, is of a very different nature and takes place in the psyche. Having collapsed at a concert and been diagnosed as suffering from a form of narcissism induced by mental fatigue, Isabelle Leritz (Signoret's character) is hospitalized for two years. When she comes home, she seeks a quiet life. Her sneaky sister, Caroline (played by Maria Casarès)—who wants nothing better than for Isabelle to have a relapse, especially because she has unwittingly stolen Isabelle's boyfriend, Jacques (played by Jacques Berthier)—hints at the idea that the madness might be hereditary. As Caroline reminds Isabelle, their father went to war, went mad, was put in an asylum, and never returned; indeed, he died in the same asylum where Isabelle was hospitalized. Here we have the case of one female preying on the mental fragility of another—a form of subtle torture—for Caroline has never forgiven her sister for being her parents' love child, born in passion and adored by her mother (whereas she was a "mistake"). This idea, that men who went to war went mad and women who overwork also go mad, suggests that there is something lacking in both—a nervous fragility, since neither had the inner strength to sustain, let alone overcome, trauma (one suspects that Caroline's obsession with work is located in her own trauma and that she too is a little mad). We discover, thanks to Caroline, that where Isabelle is concerned, it is her self-regarding nature that led her to use her love affairs both to bring her work to new, dizzying heights and to gain extra publicity. Thus, her narcissistic breakdown is directly related to her egocentrism and desire to excel in the public sphere. However, now that she has met the love of her life, she realizes she is no longer driven in this way. As we saw in our earlier discussion of this film in Chapter One, the sister also manipulates the situation so that Isabelle will have to tell Jacques the truth and reveal her past to him. But Isabelle also needs to confront it within herself and be sure she will not collapse again.

Throughout the film, there is an excessive play with mirrors—all, of course, connected to Isabelle's earlier breakdown. At first, she runs from mirrors that hold her reflection. A little later, when in the office of her doctor (played by Pierre Dux), she has a flashback to the moment of her breakdown. We see her seated at her piano, but the camera focuses on the multiple reflections of her on the inside of the piano lid. Later still, when she is in the countryside at her lover's home, she has all the mirrors taken down, so afraid is she of the madness induced by narcissism. Only once she has told Jacques the truth about her past and decided to confront her fears herself does she feel strong enough to have the mirrors reinstalled.

The way in which she ultimately comes to face her own innermost fears, however, is by resuming her career as a concert pianist and playing, emphatically through to the end, the dreaded Tchaikovsky Piano Concerto no. 2. Curiously, she has to get back to the top as a professional before she can relinquish her fears—in other words, she has to demonstrate that she can give up that which previously forged her identity in order to prove that she is sane. She thus breaks the "mirror" (her narcissism). In this way, she dispels any fears she or her fiancé might have. By breaking the "mirror," she also rids herself of her wicked sister's insistent mirroring of her madness. Isabelle can now stand up to her sister, which she does by telling her that, henceforth, she will only have business dealings with her and nothing more. She delivers this trenchant dismissal with a wonderful gesture of contempt: dropping her cigarette into her sister's ice bucket. After the concert and buoyed by the proof that she is cured, she can now embrace marriage and domesticity, in other words, make her proper entry into the private sphere (where she "belongs"). As if to confirm this message, the director, Henri Calef, is on record as wanting to show in this film, in particular, through Signoret's character, that love is necessary for a psychologically balanced life.[2] As with *Impasse*, therefore, the female can only be recouped into her "proper" function of nation building (of marrying, procreating, and keeping the home clean) once she has confronted the past—something that France itself was seemingly incapable of doing.

This realization of what will make for a balanced life where women are concerned is something that the dreadful Dora (played by Signoret) in *Manèges* never achieves. She too has gone mad, mad for money; so mad, her lust for material wealth becomes a hysteria that only total immobilization in the form of a near fatal accident, which leaves her paralyzed from the neck down, can put a stop to. Her lack of regard for her husband, Robert (played by Bernard Blier), a former prisoner of war, leads her to bankrupt him not only financially but also morally and sexually. Such is her greed, she fleeces him of all his money, so he is obliged to take on black market labor. Such is her lust for young flesh and rich bodies, she leaves him bereft of his conjugal rights. The treacherous female has eaten every single bit of him away. The voracious female, indeed—as we see in a set of increasingly tighter close-up shots of Dora's open, laughing mouth, teeth and all (a Freudian nightmare). Beyond the deep-seated misogyny of this film, it is not very difficult to read, into this parable of fear and loathing, the anxieties of emasculation felt by postwar France (and men) in the face of the modern woman emerging from her independent role of importance during the war to that of enfranchised voice after the Liberation.[3] It is surely no coincidence that, in two films already (*Impasse* and *Ombre et Lumière*), Signoret's character has given up a lucrative career. The point in *Manèges* is also, however, to demonize women for the sexual role they supposedly played during the Occupation. Dora, once immobilized by the accident, willingly confronts her past. She denounces herself or uses her mother (played by Jane Marken) to denounce her past. She sees relating her past as a means of hurting the ineffectual male, of showing that he is less than her, of using her past as a relationship of power to humiliate him—in the same way that, during the Occupation, France was humiliated by the treachery and deviousness of many (read many women) who elected to collaborate and thus sustained a life based on self-interest and not on the common good of the nation.

The theme of duplicity runs very strongly through all of these films. In *Ombre et Lumière*, Isabelle has two names: Leritz, her professional name, and Moreux, her adored mother's name. As the title makes clear, although it refers in the first instance to the difference between the two sisters, there are also two sides to Isabelle's character.[4] She is light and dark. As Leritz, she has known the dark side of madness; as Moreux (the name she currently uses to disguise her fame), she is light and full of hope. However, she conceals the truth of her fame and madness from her lover for fear of losing him. Thus, her Moreux side has a duplicity of its own—and, as we noted earlier, she does not tell her lover the truth until she is in the country and her hand is forced by both her sister and her agent, who threaten to reveal everything. In *Impasse des deux anges*, there are two angels: again, light and dark, good and bad. But it is not entirely clear who is which. Indeed, it is more a case of all major characters being a mix of both. Marianne and her future husband both have to learn to compromise. She has to give up the theater, he has to give up being so traditional in his view about women and love (namely, that you must never show it since it is a sign of weakness). Signoret's character has a duplicitous nature in terms of names. Her real name is Anne-Marie, but when she took to the stage, she became Marianne— she literally turned herself around. As her future husband, the marquis, jokingly asserts, she will have to change her name back (reverse the order) because otherwise he will feel as if he is sleeping with the republic. This renaming is something she categorically refuses to do. If she has rejected her earlier name, it is because it aligns her with a past she would rather forget: that of an orphan, an abandoned lover, living in material unease and belonging to a class that her recent wealth has allowed her to leave. In the end, though, she is obliged to face that past—as Anne-Marie, Jean's lover—before she can truly claim to be Marianne (emblematically the name of republican France).

Nobody in these postwar movies has a clean record, not even the apparently more sympathetic characters. Francesco (played by Marcel Pagliero) and Monsieur René (played by Bernard Blier) in *Dédée d'Anvers* are engaged in some dubious gun-running affair. Indeed, the men in this film either denounce, act treacherously, or are careless with their talk, and it is the women who keep the secrets. The men cost people's lives. Monsieur René inadvertently lets slip to Marco (played by Marcel Dalio) that Dédée (played by Signoret) is going to leave with Francesco. This sets in motion Marco's vile act of murder. Throughout the film, men behave in ways more readily associated with female characterizations in film noir, a reversal that is surely significant and that points both to a masculinity in crisis and a fragmented identity where men are lacking in clarity. Marco, for all his awfulness, is constantly ridiculed and humiliated. Monsieur René's sexuality is ambiguous, and, as we have just mentioned, Francesco—the only truly "masculine" man (to whom Monsieur René is very attracted)—is involved in dubious business activities. Perhaps it is because masculinity was in crisis postwar that the ending of the film had to depart so strongly away from the original text (by Ashelbé) and it is Dédée who metes out justice (albeit using Monsieur René to do the deed), since none of the men know what to do. In the original text, it is Dédée's friend Germaine (played by Jane Marken) who, under duress from Marco, blurts out the secret. Marco then shoots Dédée in the back, and Monsieur René, as an act of justice, strangles

Marco to death. But an equally intriguing reason for this gender shift is surely that, in the film adaptation, the narrative point of view has become Dédée's. It is she who, having found agency, is now empowered with the authority to carry out the decisive avenging act—weak (feminized) men being punished for betrayal. This film acts, then, as part of a pair with *Manèges*, where the hysterical this time is located in the male (Marco), not, as with *Manèges*, in the female (Dora).

Even the heroic men in *Les démons de l'aube*, the French Resistance movie, are not spared this lack of clarity. Although this film heroizes a recent past, it shows our heroes as flawed. An entire Resistance cell gets captured and wiped out by the Germans because of the negligence of the entrusted messenger, Lieutenant Legrand (played by Georges Marchal), who later in the film leads the commando force that lands at Toulon. As the film begins, we see him returning to France from Germany. As a prisoner of war, he is being exchanged as part of the notorious Service de Travail Obligatoire (STO) program, whereby one prisoner is returned for every three workers sent to Germany. On his train journey home, Legrand crosses a train carrying men in the other direction, some prisoners, some exchange workers. One of them, a Resistance fighter named Serge Duhamel (played by André Valmy), gives him a vital note to deliver. Legrand fails to deliver the message because he and his wife (played by Jacqueline Pierreux) get into an argument over her infidelities. The wife has had a live-in lover during his absence. To put an end to the argument, she decides to seduce Legrand. This takes some doing, and during her efforts she discovers the note, reads it, and tears it up. A little later, she proceeds to denounce her husband to the *milice* (militia), and, we assume, to give them the contents of the message. When they arrive to arrest him, he makes his escape. But the damage is done.

The sexual infidelities of a treacherous wife were what all husbands feared during their emprisonment. Here, Legrand's wife not only sleeps around, she sleeps with the enemy. So she conforms to a constructed stereotype and a deep-seated fear. Sex creates problems elsewhere in this film—which, of course, because it is about the Resistance, should be about heroic men and not about the dangers and trespasses of sex (that is, women). Even good women are problematic in this all-too-male narrative. Lili (played by Signoret), the adored barmaid and prostitute at the Café au Petit Verdun, ends up wreaking havoc in one young man's life, albeit unwittingly. The young commando, Simon (played by Dominique Nohain), is the butt of all his fellow commandos, who see him as a weakling and a kid. He is the telephone engineer, but the men call him "the telephone mistress." Lili offers him sex, free of charge, to help him enter into manhood. But the offer backfires. The night before he is due to go on a very dangerous mission, which will, to all evidence, cost him his life, he comes to Lili's room (we assume they have sex). At first, it appears as if he has fallen asleep and missed his curfew, so now he is too late for his mission. Instead, it transpires he is not asleep, but has killed himself. In the end, his beloved Lieutenant Legrand was unable to protect Simon by preventing him from going on the fatal mission, so he chose his own death. The point is, though, that he has died in Lili's bed, not outside his commanding officer's tent. Unable to confront his lieutenant with both his terror at the mission he has to carry out and his sense of betrayal (after all, the lieutenant had always protected him before), he has taken himself off to the female sphere to enact, not an assertion of his masculinity (by having sex with Lili), but what will appear to his fellow commandos as an act of cowardice. Containment and displacement are fully engaged here. The "feminized" Simon takes his "weakness" to where it "belongs" (woman's place). Even Lili, when she touches his skin, remarks how soft it is, "like a girl's." The message is clear: women do not belong in this very male world (including Simon). As Simon prophetically says to Lili after she has kissed him: "In my dream, I dreamt of death, and she looked like you."

By way of comparison, in *Against the Wind*, Signoret has a far more active role in the Resistance. She is a leader, a commanding officer in the Belgian Resistance, and has a great deal of official power over men. But there is also duplicity and treachery in this film. One of the fighters is a traitor who is weeded out by intelligence for Signoret to kill. Unsurprisingly, given the very masculine nature of the representation of the Resistance in French cinema, French reviews of this film were pretty dismissive.[5]

The only film in this period where everything is starkly black and white is *Fantômas*. Here, Fantômas (played by Marcel Herrand), the eponymous villain and perpetrator of evil, is to be sought out and destroyed. Fantômas—a far more sinister creation than earlier, or indeed later, versions of this character—is hell-bent on asserting his tyrannical power over Paris. Equipped with all the latest gadgets of surveillance technology and torture, including rotunda-shaped cells that crush their prisoners as if in a press, he also runs a laboratory that is developing a secret weapon, a death ray (an instrument for mass extinction using lethal gases). He intends to use it on the citizens of Paris if the authorities do not give him the money he demands. At one point in the film, he flies over Paris in a helicopter, making a leaflet drop that warns the citizens of his intent to systematically execute one million of them (half of Paris) using his lethal weapon if he is not obeyed. Fantômas has a daughter, Hélène (played by Signoret). She is in love with and about to marry Fandor (played by André Le Gall), a journalist who, along with the police, has pursued Fantômas with a view to putting him firmly behind bars. Fantômas makes every effort to thwart this marriage, including attempting to kidnap his own daughter. He later captures police Inspector Juve (played by Alexandre Rignault) and Fandor and throws them into his crushing cell, which he threatens to use on them. Later still he captures Hélène, but not before she has got hold of the formula for the death ray and secreted it away. Eventually, thanks in large part to Hélène's initiative, courage, and ingenuity, they all make their escape, then proceed to pursue and kill Fantômas.

It is not too difficult to interpret this overly determined evil Fantômas as a parody of Hitler, particularly given the sophistication of his tools of death, torture, and mass destruction and his system of control and propaganda.[6] As one of his aides says of his secret death-ray machine, which can kill at a distance, and the crushing machine, "It isn't clean," thus closely associating this uncleanliness with the practices of Nazi Germany and the "final solution" of cleansing the nation of Jews. Indeed, the film opens with a map of Paris and a huge letter *F* superimposed over it—as if the shadow of fascism were looming menacingly over the city. Furthermore, the idea of extortion of money (value) for human beings (the one million citizens he threatens to exterminate) parallels the way French bodies were treated during the Occupation: as items of exchange under the STO. The difference, of course, in this instance is that the tyrannical patriarch gets brought down, on the one hand, by a combination of representatives of law and order and the fourth estate and, on the other, by his own daughter.

Against the Wind (1947). Signoret as resistor in action.

All resist and overcome his authority. The daughter is far from filial. Indeed, she helps to free Fandor and Juve by breaking up the technology in her father's laboratory. She participates, then, quite markedly in destroying the patriarch who wants totalitarian control.[7] Clearly, unlike some of the young scientists who are into Fantômas' "scientific" experiments for the money, these two young people (Fandor and Hélène) have no time for the trappings of high modernity: namely, a technology that kills on a massive scale. Instructively, the zealous scientists and technicians also meet their death, one of them at the hands of Hélène, who is more than handy with a pistol.

Female power in this film is consistently asserted. Apart from the two examples already cited, on several occasions Hélène is represented through mise-en-scène and narrative development as commandingly active. Thus, when she and Fandor go into hiding after her father's first attempt to kidnap her, she is frequently framed in a three-shot, where she towers over Fandor and Juve, desperate to get some action going. At one point, in her frustration at what she perceives as the men's passivity, she says: "If I were a man, I wouldn't stay here, with all the guns you have; I'd do something." She paces the floor impatiently, expressing her frustration by picking up a chair and firmly setting it down again. She refuses to be infantilized by Juve. When he tries to "protect" her by insisting she stay put, she retorts, "Listen, Juve, I'm not twelve years old; I don't need protecting." And, indeed, she does not stay put. When Juve and Fandor do not return from their reconnoitering exercise, it is clear to her that they have been taken prisoner, so she decides she must take action. Arthur, her minder (played by Yves Deniad), keeps trying to prevent her, to no avail. She discovers where her father's emporium of death is (a laboratory ironically named Laboratoires Gentil), tracks down Fandor and Juve, and briefly gains possession of the secret formula to her father's deadly weapon. Even once she is caught by her father, she refuses to divulge the whereabouts of the formula despite his brutal ways. And, although she almost causes Juve's entrapment plan for Fantômas to fail, thanks to her overzealous attack on her father's technology (she smashes the control panels), nonetheless, at the crucial moment, she cuts the lights and thus prevents Fandor from mistakenly killing Juve (who is disguised as Fantômas).

Sex, Class, and Modernization

Beyond this uneasy relationship with the past that runs through the films, there are three other preoccupations that deserve comment not just because they resurface with enough regularity to merit it, but also because all are attached to Signoret's persona: these are, sex, class, and modernization. Sex in film noir movies, when embodied by the woman, is seen as predatory, threatening, the source of chaos, even death—with the men sitting passively by while all this destruction is going on, as it were. A quote from the Press Book (dated 1952) accompanying a 1952 British release of *Dédée* makes this point rather well. Speaking of Signoret, it states that from her very first films, "she was marked for the part of *femme fatale*, easy of virtue and headstrong, weaving tragedy, destroying and being destroyed." As Lili, Gisèle, Dédée, and Dora, she enacts all the above. But she also brings something else to her role as femme fatale. That something is speaking the truth—an ability to see what is really going on and to articulate it. Thus, for example, Lili in *Démons de l'aube* puts the lieutenant right in no uncertain terms as to why Simon, his *chouchou* (darling) committed suicide. She did not lure Simon to his death, as might a femme fatale. He did not die for "a bit of skirt," as the lieutenant puts it, but because he, Simon, believed in his lieutenant and believed he could fix everything. The mission he had been given was too much for him, so he killed himself because he was afraid to die and therefore afraid to fail. The lieutenant now realizes this suicide was a way of preventing the mission from going wrong. He also comes to realize that such a sacrifice cannot be asked of a rank soldier and that he must do it himself: in other words, to lead through example. Thus, Lili's ability to articulate the truth teaches him to be responsible. Gisèle in *Macadam* refuses to put her happiness before the safety of the man she loves, François (played by Jacques Dacqmine). She recognizes that because of her past involvement with Victor, the murdering gangster (played by Paul Meurisse), she is no longer free (or entitled) to have happiness. She states categorically to François: "I am responsible. I love you too much to be selfish." Having unwittingly brought him into a life-threatening situation, she now acts to save him. In *Dédée d'Anvers*, Dédée leads the way to avenge her lover's murder by instructing Monsieur René how to kill Marco. Even the evil Dora in *Manèges* breaks her silence and reveals the truth to her duped husband, awful though it is. This has the effect of freeing him from the delusion he was under. Now that he knows how much she loathed him and systematically stripped him of everything he owned, he feels free of any further responsibility toward his wife. Her truth releases him.

In postwar France, masculinity may well be in crisis in these movies, but, as the above examples show, the men seem unable to take action for themselves or see the truth. Ironically, it would appear, they need the quintessential embodiment of betrayal—the femme fatale, the very person who is traditionally represented as the least trustworthy—either to act for them or to spell out clearly what they must do or need to know. In a sense, there is this extraordinary "rehabilitation," however intentional or not, of a specific kind of proletarian woman—the prostitute—and it is in this context that class enters into consideration when discussing Signoret's roles in these films. As we know from Chapter One, politically, Signoret came from a left-wing position and had always been authentically engaged within the political arena. This does not mean that she could not play a *garce* (bitch), as Dora demonstrates. What it does mean is that her authenticity allowed her, first, to give more depth to the role of the prostitute than limiting it to her practising sexuality. Second, as a "bitch," she still holds on to some kind of integrity with herself. In the former case, it is instructive that Gisèle and Dédée, both prostitutes, once they have fallen in love, are always thinking what their next move should be or how to solve a problem. Thus, this specific proletarian class is not confined to a single set of signifiers (as treacherous and untrustworthy), nor to a simple economy of exchange. Furthermore, as if to make the point about working-class diversity, in *Macadam*, Gisèle's proletarianism is contrasted with that of the mother and daughter who run the seedy Hôtel Bijou, an illegal *maison de passe* (brothel), where Gisèle and the other prostitutes live and work. Both the mother, Madame Rosa (played by Françoise Rosay), and the daughter, Simone (played by Andrée Clément), are willing to break the unwritten codes that exist among the working and criminal underclasses and denounce people who get in their way. With the mother, it is the gangster Victor, whose money she wants to steal, that leads her to denounce, a cupidity that she will pay for with her life. As for her daughter, jealousy drives her to denounce Gisèle, who has "stolen" her boyfriend, François.

For some, life is cheap in this underground, illicit world. But for both Gisèle and Dédée, there is a way to make life have value. This belief is emblematically signified by them when, once they have found love and agenced their desire, they make a shift in their clothing. Thus, they dress more demurely, signaling a new awareness of their selves. Dédée, for instance, when she goes to meet her lover, Francesco, wears a dress with a high collar, as opposed to her former dresses, with their plunging necklines. Gisèle moves away from the sparkly and showy sequined outfits (designed by Jacques Heim) that make her, visually, a younger mirror image of Madame Rosa, whose jackets are a monument of sequined excess (also designed by Jacques Heim). Rather, Gisèle now wears practical, ordinary street clothes. There is, then, a desire not to make the body a display, a spectacle for visual consumption. The body becomes contained, unadorned, and understated. As such, it can clearly do more; it is no longer pure glittery surface but has inner and outer substance. Here, the representation of class through Signoret's body and her codes of femininity (particularly her dress codes) are motivated toward undermining or deconstructing the stereotypes associated with her class and profession, forcing the spectator to see these prostitutes as individuals with feelings who can touch us (especially Dédée). It is possible that even the repellent Dora moves us in her paralyzed state because she, in matters of greed, is her mother's best pupil and, in matters sexual, has been first primed and then pimped by her mother. If anything, these considerations of class issues allow us to read these three films—*Macadam, Dédée,* and *Manèges*—in a less misogynistic light. This does not mean that we gloss over the negative construction of femininity explicit in these films. But it does seem possible to argue that class awareness predominated over sexual consciousness—Yves Allégret, a committed man of the Left, was, after all, the director of *Dédée* and *Manèges*. However, it is worth making the point that Simone de Beauvoir's book *The Second Sex* was published in 1949, and so the issues were there on the Left's debating floor. Clearly, as far as cinema was concerned, even if from the Left, consciousness was yet to be raised. Thus, the class struggle was the major debate of the intellectual Left; feminism had to wait another twenty-five years.

There is an interesting and different play with class in *Impasse des deux anges.* Here Signoret has moved up the economic ladder in a big way. Formerly, a salesperson in a store, by the time we meet her she has fulfilled her ambition to become a major stage actor. In the opening sequence of the film, we first get to see Signoret/Marianne in medium close-up in the form of a magazine photograph, possibly a fanzine. The man holding the magazine and looking at the photograph is the one masterminding the theft of the marquis's necklace (which Jean is to carry out), and he refers to Marianne as being "a star in the firmament." But there are two rather peculiar things about this photograph. First, the actual photograph is a still of Signoret that was used to promote an earlier film of hers, *Macadam.* Thus, it is an odd intertextual reference because, within the diegesis of *Impasse,* it is supposed to represent a portrait of Marianne and not Gisèle (Signoret's character in *Macadam*). More significantly, in this photo she is scantily dressed in black lingerie—suggesting a character with a certain ease of virtue—and we do not know if the image refers to the actor Marianne playing a role or if this is a picture of Marianne as herself. We next see her in the second sequence in a full shot coming onto stage during a dress rehearsal. This time she is cross-dressed in the costume of an eighteenth-century marquis, suggesting a different order of sexual play, one that crosses gender, but also making a statement about her relationship to her betrothed, namely, that it is one of equality (whatever the marquis might think) because both are coded as the same. There is also an element of parody and masquerade at work here that suggests that class is about both appearance and the ability to disguise or dissimulate the real person, because one only has to don a costume to be a marquis. This idea of sexual equality and class as a masquerade continues in the next series of shots. The actors are taking a break, and Marianne/the marquis is talking with her understudy. She has arrived on stage with a cigarette inelegantly stuffed in her mouth and puffs away at it in a quite vulgar manner, only to stomp it out on stage when the moment has come for a photo of the cast. All of these gestures are ones more readily associated with masculine comportment, particularly because in the previous sequence, we have just seen Jean execute precisely the same gestures with his cigarette. So now we are all the more perplexed as to how this woman will fit into the world she is about to enter through marriage, namely, the aristocracy. She is sexually ambiguous, lacking in basic (high society) etiquette, a bit vulgar, and appears to have a colorful past, if her lingerie attire from the photo is anything to go by. Yet marry she does—and arguably the marriage is able to occur, because both parties have given up a way of the past. This marriage brings together *la vieille France*, the traditionalist and, indeed, antirepublican France of the aristocracy, and the new, slightly brazen, modern republican France. Certainly, after the war and the occupation of France, there was a need to heal the political factions that this difficult period had opened up. Furthermore, if France was to bring itself into line with the rest of twentieth-century Europe, so that it could compete economically on even ground, it would have to embrace modernization on a grand scale. Thus, to modernize, France had to work away from its past and let go of archaic and corrupt ways. But it also had to transcend class and accept the republican ideal of equality that got so badly trampled on during the Occupation. In short, postwar France must take on Marianne and not attempt to infantilize the new democracy by changing her name back to the sweet, innocuous Anne-Marie. When Marianne refuses to allow the marquis to dictate to her how she will be called, she is asserting herself and, in her namesake, the new republic and with it the newly found enfranchisement of women.

If few films in the postwar years were advocating the above principles in relation to sex and class, the third preoccupation running at the time, that of modernization, was more commonly in evidence and continued to be so throughout the cinema of the 1950s. Unsurprisingly, modernization was met in France with ambivalence. The price to pay for bringing France securely into the twentieth century was to make its market available to the United States in exchange for massive aid in the form of the Marshall Plan. The United States similarly plowed aid into other Western countries that fought the war. Although that aid system is now long gone, the colonization of Western European market economies by the United States remains unabated. Any number of French films of the late 1940s through the 1950s reflect the ambivalence felt by France in relation to this new market economy, which it believed threatened its culture. The form this took in films was the crude establishment of a series of binary divides between American and French goods, from food, cigarettes, and alcoholic beverages to cars. French stars were used as vehicles for a cultural chauvinism that was put on display at seemingly every opportunity. Thus, for example, Jean Gabin, in *Touchez pas au grisbi* (Jacques Becker, 1954), will only drink French wine and eat in French restaurants. He refuses American cocktails in the Pigalle nightclubs where they are on offer. He eats paté and French bread for a midnight snack. In *Impasse des deux anges*, Jean/Paul Meurisse refuses Lucky Strikes and insists on Gauloises. In *Ombre et Lumière*, Isabelle/Signoret declines the cocktails her sister, Caroline, so easily takes to, preferring an aperitif. "I don't drink cocktails," she asserts. Ironically, it is this difference in taste that leads to her meeting and falling in love with Caroline's erstwhile lover, Jacques. She leaves Caroline in her fancy American bar and takes off to eat and drink French style in a local brasserie. There she bumps into Jacques. "I like my quartier," she declares as she takes a seat in one of her favorite French restaurants with its French *chansons réalistes* playing away in the background. For her assertive support of French products, she is handsomely rewarded: she and Jacques fall in love and marry.

In the 1947 film *Fantômas*, evidence that the hybridization of French culture is already under way is signified by the presence of American objects, such as a pinball machine and a Wurlitzer playing American jazz, housed in the archetypally French local café Mimosas. In response to these objects, Hélène/Signoret can only counterattack—as she does in the face of the sophisticated state-of-the-art technology owned by her father—with her intelligence and by valiantly smoking Gitanes or Gauloises, driving around in French cars and wearing French fashions. In that same film, the contrast between modernity and the crumbling facade of old France is clearly illustrated by Fantômas' secret high-tech headquarters, kept hidden inside the decrepit-appearing (*Laboratoires Gentil*). There is, however, a clear nostalgia for that un-Americanized France—hence, perhaps, the name Gentil (nice or gentle). One of the ways this is demonstrated is by a series of comic gags, most particularly those that take place in the forecourt of the factory. These comic scenes between protagonists recall the prewar days and are particularly reminiscent of Jean Renoir's characters in *Le crime de Monsieur Lange* (1935).

French cinema at this time was fighting quota systems with the Americans. The industry formed lobbying groups (such as the Comités de la Défense du Cinéma Français) and led numerous protests against the Blum-Byrnes agreements. These agreements effectively gave the United States carte blanche to dominate French screens (for example, in 1946–1947, 70 percent of the films shown in France were American). Thus, the dislike expressed by the French commandos of the Coca-Cola poster in *Les démons de l'ombre* comes as no surprise in this context, any more than the product placement that also goes on within this film. Posters in the Café au petit Verdun advertising Orangine stand out in their wholesomeness against the vulgarity of the pinup girl on the Coca-Cola advertisement that adorns the commandos' cafeteria door. The soldiers describe it as "offensive" (the pinup is in a swimsuit holding a bottle of Coke) and the colors as "garish." The Orangine poster in the café has less nudity on display, although we do see a pair of reasonably exposed legs. But, of course, these are French legs and therefore entirely inoffensive, as are Lili's/Signoret's when they are shown as she climbs down the cellar steps to kiss Simon. Additionally, the naming of the commandos' jeep, an American invention, as Madeleine-Bastille, with all its French revolutionary connotations, is deliberate, particularly given that this arterial Parisian boulevard is one of two that has traditionally been used for civil protest and worker demonstrations (including the 1948 marches against the Blum-Byrnes agreements).

To conclude this section, it would seem pertinent to argue that, during this postwar period, there was a crisis in representation where women were concerned—an essentializing of women as bad and little else. As Burch and Sellier (1996, 224–237) explain so compellingly in their book, there appears to have been a continuous recycling of the same stale images of women as treacherous and ruthless, as victimizers of men, hardly ever as victims themselves. Instead of embracing the newfound emancipation of women postwar, French cinema seemed determined to represent women as a permanent threat to masculinity. But—and this is an important but—even within this pathological display, a careful and close reading of Signoret's performances makes it clear that her persona functioned as an intertext for all the divergent and conflicting discourses that had running currency in the French nation during that five-year period after the end of the war. With the exception of *Manèges*, Signoret singularly failed to comply with the dominant discourse that demonized women. In fact, the nation's "truths" of the time seeped out—with and through Signoret's performances—and continued to do so throughout the 1950s. Her performances refused to submit or conform to the attempts to place the blame for France's postwar unease on women. As such, through her performative resistance, and despite the general trend of misogyny in contemporary cinema, she exposed the lack of moral and ethical strength of her nation.[8] She gave evidence to its internal struggle as it sought out a sense of identity. In short, she became the nation's "appropriate" body even though it elected not to appropriate her—and, as we know, a bit later it would choose Brigitte Bardot, who would soon become its major export item.

THE EROTICS OF POWER:
TOWARD SELF-REPRESENTATION

This section will now go on to analyze how Signoret's body and intellectual mentality were the tools to this performative resistance. Although, as we shall see, expressing this resistance was, initially, not without its own internal struggle. In Chapter Two, I spoke of Signoret's "presence" and suggested that part of this came down to a clean eroticism. I want now to take a closer look at this question of eroticism with a view to opening up a discussion of Signoret's performances in this first set of films. The intention is to try and discern how, given her inexperience at this early stage of her career, Signoret achieved this performative resistance. I also want to establish what is meant by what I term her "erotics of power." As we shall see in chapters to come, this power became a major hallmark of her subsequent performances. However, let us first consider its presence in her first films. We begin by remarking that we are faced with a paradox because this power is not yet there as a constant. What immediately strikes us is that up until her 1950s films *Manèges*, *Le Traqué*, and *Ombre et Lumière*, with the exception of *Dédée d'Anvers*, there is something rather stilted about parts of Signoret's performance. There is an unevenness to it: part is natural, part is forced. Thus, in this latter context, she often looks and moves around more as an adolescent than as a woman in her mid-twenties. Her voice is light and girlish, which her lisp serves merely to reinforce—even to the extent that in her first significant role in *La boîte aux rêves* she is made to appear rather simpleminded. In this same film, she mumbles her lines, and there is a forced elegance in her comportment. In *Les démons de l'aube*, a certain awkwardness still prevails. In her first encounter with Simon, when the soldiers have brought him, blindfolded, to her to be kissed, she gives all sorts of knowing winks and nods to the men—in short, she overplays the moment of the preinitiation rites (even though the actual kiss itself is beautifully handled by her). This gaucheness and lack of naturalness are further marked in her films of this first period by the way in which her elbows seem pointed at times and her arms stiff and straight, making her appear wooden, as if she does not quite know what to do with herself. This unease is also expressed through her hands. If she has no object to hold on to (cigarette packet, darning, etc.), she tends to rub her right hand up her stiffened left arm and vice versa, a gratuitous and seemingly nervous gesture since it does not add to the performance, except to reveal an unease.

Thus, the question becomes, how does this awkwardness square up with my claim that Signoret's performance style challenges the received representation of femininity? I want to suggest that it is in these early performances that we can trace the blueprint to Signoret's power as a star, because, although all of the above is true, in these same films, the moment that her role is sexualized, everything changes. She stops being stilted, and her performance becomes rounded and engaging. Thus, for example, in *Against the Wind*, at the beginning of the film she is quite frozen (her limbs, especially her arms, do not move easily). However, the moment she falls in love with Johnnie (played by Gordon Jackson), she performs well and convincingly—she matures from girlishness to a knowing, sexy woman (where, incidentally, her lisp works to reinforce her sexiness)—and it is instructive that, henceforth, she exerts far greater agency once she has asserted her erotic self. She kisses Johnnie fulsomely on the mouth. She also courageously executes Max (played by Jack Warner), the traitor, by making him face her as she pulls the trigger. Again, in *Fantômas* she does not come alive in her performance until she takes matters into her own hands. It is as if Signoret herself does not know why she is in this film, until, that is, she throws down her darning and insists that her minder help her locate Fantômas's hiding place so she can help her lover escape. In *Macadam*, once she has met François and managed to seduce him, she becomes soft and loses the hard-edged, almost caricatural, stereotyped performance style she had adopted for her role as a prostitute-cum-con artist. In brief, then, the variations in her performance seem to be dictated by whether a role allowed her to have sexual agency or not. As mere object or as desexualized/de-eroticized woman, she does not perform well. In these performances, she is seemingly obliged to repress her eroticism. For this reason, she lacks conviction, and an awkwardness emerges. However, the moment she takes full charge of her body, her eroticism is able to seep to the surface, and her performance becomes electric and compelling to watch.

The dichotomy of performance in some of Signoret's pre-1950 films (*Démons*, *Macadam*, and *Impasse*) has another source as well, one that comes down to a struggle between, on the one hand, the French film industry's construction of the femme fatale and its attempt to reiterate through that construction a fixed image of the treacherous, demonized woman and, on the other, Signoret's ability to play the role of a woman who is not convinced of her depravity—a belief she confirms totally in *Dédée* and, later, *Manèges*. Signoret, in these roles, refuses to accept her punishment or any form of discipline as morally correct—which she would have done had she accepted the attempts to fix her either as a femme fatale or as depraved and treacherous. She refuses the mentality of the oppressed, nowhere more significantly than in *Dédée* and *Manèges*. In the latter film, it is instructive that both her version of the truth and her mother's, told in flashback, correct Robert's earlier version, also related in flashback. In his version, he sees Dora as the victim of his penury and inability to provide for her. As he will learn from the two women, he was taken for every franc he had. His reading of events, then, is not the truth. That privilege lies with the women. In this regard (misogyny aside), this film with its construct of flashbacks runs counter to the common practice in American film noir, where it is the man's version of events that counts, and the man who corrects or renegotiates the woman's flashback (see, for, example, *Mildred Pierce*, Michael Curtiz, 1945).

In these early roles, Signoret resists the essentializing of woman, often using body language (the minimal gesture to suggest there is more) and the brief, well-chosen word to assert that there is an inner as well as an outer being and that she cannot be compartmentalized as "other" and "bad." In short, her performances are a battle of the will—she embodies characters who fight to establish a socially recognized self (for example, strikingly, in *Les démons de l'aube*, where she asserts her identity as a woman against the dismissive and brutal Lieutenant Legrand, who describes her as a *poule*/whore). She does not, then, act in deference to the dominant force, be it the patriarch or other institutionally sanctioned embodiments of power. Rather, to be even more effective in her defiance, she ensures that her challenges to those who would oppress her have an audience, a witness. The effect of ensemble playing functions to sanction this form of challenging behavior, it supplies her with a diegetic audience. Thus, in *Dédée*, she exposes the tyrannical behavior of her pimp, Marco, at mealtimes when all the inhabitants of the Big Moon are gathered at the table. In *Démons*, she proudly displays her art of seduction in front of the assembled men at the Café au petit Verdun. They can only watch in suspended silence and admiration as she kisses the young Simon. In *Impasse*, she stays the hand of the marquis, who wants to "tear her away from her sordid milieu" (the theater) and "mold her like wax"; she tells him "to leave my past out of it." And she makes it clear in the ensemble scenes (and in front of him) that she has every intention of remaining a woman in her own right (a position much admired, incidentally, by the marquis's aging aunt, if not by the bishop present at her prenuptial reception).

Signoret's performances assert a freedom based initially on the erotic order, not the rational one. She shows how mind and body do not need to be split, as they are within the culture of rational Western discourses. Indeed, as we have argued, where Signoret's characters are concerned, if body and mind are split, she becomes brittle and ill at ease with her body. Part of her erotics of power lies, then, in her performative body exposing the pathology of Western civilization's obsessive focus on the control of mind over body, a control that is manifest in many of the actors whom she plays opposite. Marcel Herrand (*Fantômas* and *Impasse*) and Paul Meurisse (*Macadam* and *Impasse*) are two actors whose icy cerebrality contrasts with her deep earthiness. Civilized repression of the libidinal self is what produces, on the one hand, the cold savagery of Victor and Jean (Meurisse's roles) and, on the other, the cruel inhumanity of Fantômas and the marquis's assumption of rational superiority (Herrand's roles). It is surely significant that the Meurisse characters die for their cruel rationality either at the hands of a woman or as a result of being rejected by a woman. In *Macadam*, he is shot dead by Madame Rosa's avenging daughter. In *Impasse*, he is gunned down by gangsters. In the latter film, Jean has chosen death, and lets himself be killed, because Marianne no longer loves him. His cruel rationality has cost him her love and now his life. As for the Herrand characters, as Fantômas he is driven to his death by his daughter (in a car chase) and, conversely, is brought to all his senses by Marianne in *Impasse*.

Surprisingly, with the exception of *Manèges*, this erotics of power is at its most understated in Signoret's costume. This does not mean to say that it is not powerful; quite the opposite, in fact, for it is once she has given up the trappings that identify her as femme fatale that her power adorns her whole being. Thus, in the closing sequence of *Dédée d'Anvers*, she is far more powerful as the Dédée who sets out purposefully and neatly attired in her beret and black-belted raincoat to join her lover, Francesco, than she ever was dressed up in her fur coat turning tricks. She is no longer costumed in excess as seductress incarnate. These clothes leave space for her desire to be palpable—there is no forcing or masquerade. Indeed, it is as if Signoret's own minimalism has spread out all over her character's body and into her clothing. This power takes on extraordinary dimensions a little later in the final sequence when, still in the same attire, she shifts from lover to avenger by bringing Marco to justice.

Manèges constitutes the one exception to this link between the erotics of power and costume. If anything, in this context, the film is about the fear of such power. Dora is the clothed embodiment of the fetishized femme fatale, that is, until she is ultimately stripped of any masquerade through her hospitalization and is totally immobilized, with her neck in a brace and her one visible arm in a splint, with the rest of her body apparently held together by bandages, much like a mummy. Now, only her painted fingernails remain as a reminder of her former phallic glory. Gone are the breeches and leather gloves she wore for riding (a truly parodic mise-en-scène of her fetishistic status). Gone too are the fur coats and silky satin negligees. Viewed in this light, there is nothing left of the phallic femme fatale to torture the impotent husband, not even her voice or her

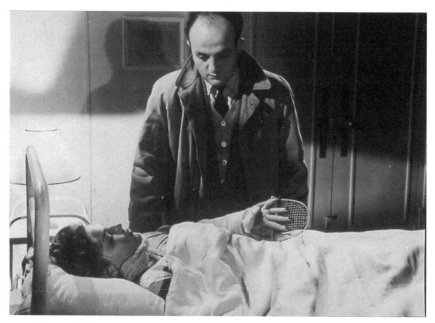

Manèges/The Wanton (1950). Dora immobilized; only her painted fingernails remain of her former phallic glory.

sadistic laughter. The fear of castration is finally safely contained. The woman is silenced and immobilized. However, the severity of the punishment shows the extremes to which patriarchy must go. Even so, Dora remains unrepentant, using her mother to reassert her narrative, her identity, and thereby her own refusal to acknowledge any depravity. Thus, although she is now without physical or sexual power, she still has her autobiography—a tool based on language—as an erotics of power. It is her means, however desperate, of counterbalancing the fetishization and ultimate castration that attempt to deny her her power. Significantly, that power has greater limitations than with other Signoret roles of this period, based as it is on a negative representation of her independence and sexual agency and on a desire to destroy another human being. Let us return to these other roles.

We rarely see Signoret in fabrics that imitate the skin (satins and silks, in particular), but we do occasionally have her in furs. Mostly she remains fully clothed, which in itself is quite remarkable, given how many times she plays either a prostitute or a treacherous woman on the make. Thus, her power does not lie in the display of nudity. Nor, ultimately, does this power reside in that other conventional cinematic practice, fetishism—using clothing and adornment to contain the female form as safe (as phallic). I noted earlier how, in both *Macadam* and *Dédée*, once the characters have found their true love, their clothing shifts. In other words, they move away from the standard cinematic procedures of stereotype or fetishism and gain power in that found freedom, as is exemplified by their change of clothing.

A closer look at Gisèle's clothing in *Macadam* will help to make the point. The first shot of Gisèle is a high-angle one as she comes into the restaurant and rushes up the stairs to her "sugar daddy," Léon (played by Félix Oudart). We see her gloves and feathered hat, her décolleté dress and sequined jacket, all from atop. She looks more like an exotic bird of prey or paradise—it is not yet clear which until we see her try to pull the scam on Léon. Gisèle puts on a show: she claims she has just fallen victim to an armed robbery in which her necklace (an expensive present from Léon) has been stolen. She flutters around like a rapacious animal and is clearly intended to represent, through the excess of femininity, which her clothing connotes, what men regard as "evil incarnate" (Doane 1982, 82). Later, when she meets up with Victor, her former lover and partner in crime, she has switched hats, this time wearing one adorned with artificial flowers. As for the rest of her attire, she is still in sequins. The greedy beast of prey has given way to a different type of masquerade and artifice, arguably less predatory and more inviting. However, later, when Victor is in prison (thanks to Madame Rosa's denunciation), she has made a radical shift. Now she wears a soberly cut white dress with a puritan-style collar. She looks the image of demure womanhood. There is no attempt to draw attention to the self, as with the former outfits. And indeed, during her conversation with Victor, it is clear that her main preoccupation is how to protect François from Victor (whom Victor believes to be an undercover policeman). We, as the spectator, are in the know and are aware that Gisèle has fallen in love with François and given up on her previous ways. Indeed, her relationship with him has grown apace from her earlier seduction, when we saw her gleefully sitting on a chair in her black lingerie about to remove her stockings as she warmly welcomed him into her room and invited him into her bed. When we now see them together, she is unostentatious in her dress code. Thus, at a local dance she wears a simple flower-patterned dress, very much the attire of the other young women present at the event. She melts into the social environment. In terms of looks, of course, she remains the most beautiful, and the camera focuses enough on her that she necessarily stands out. In her last appearance, as she is about to leave with François, she is wearing a bland raincoat and a beret —again, the common dress attire of the time. In short, the sartorial trajectory has been toward normalcy.

A similar sartorial evolution occurs for Dédée. Whereas both women's earlier dress code was charged with only one meaning—their sexual availability (as prostitutes)—progressively they come to embody more complex sets of meanings (and depth of emotions) as their dress code simplifies. As the masquerade of femininity drops off, so an erotics of power can emerge. With Dédée, there is a gradual process of demasquerading—marked by her clothing and the framing of shots—from the moment she first meets Francesco (the eye contact at the port) to that of deciding to risk everything, defy Marco, and embark on a relationship with her lover. In this process, we get to sense all her feelings and their authenticity. Thus, in the first scene with Francesco, we sense her toughness, even cruelty, but also her desire for him. Later, we feel her desire turning to passion. And finally, we sense her numbness when Francesco is murdered.

In this film there are three major sequences where her desire for him is palpably expressed. Interestingly, the first two are precisely ten minutes in length, the third only two minutes long. In the first, she is fully dressed in her female masquerade as a sexually available prostitute—fur coat, black dress with a deep V-neck, at the point of which is pinned a diamante brooch (this brooch draws attention in its glittering to her cleavage). She is returning to the Big Moon after

Dédée d'Anvers/Dédée (1948). Dédée fully dressed in her female masquerade as a prostitute.

turning her latest trick with a rich businessman. By the time of the other two sequences (respectively, halfway through the film and toward the end), she wears a simple, long-sleeved light-colored dress with a high collar adorned with a simple brooch. She is quasi-virginal, although underneath, her lingerie is black, reminding us that she is, in fact, a fully sexual woman.

Let us consider these sequences. In the first, she is unceremoniously dumped near the port and left to cope with being dropped into the middle of a brawl between sailors. She runs for cover to the nearest doorway. A few seconds later, one of the sailors throws a knife at his attackers. It is a poor throw and narrowly misses her, landing instead on the door behind her. The door opens to reveal Francesco (perhaps also hiding from the brawl). The two remain framed in the doorway watching the fight—a vicious conflict between rival gangs, where some men are handcuffed by others to the railings and beaten senseless. All of this is watched with ever-increasing glee by Dédée and indifference by Francesco. It is a shocking moment in the film, paralleled only by Marco's brutal torturing of Dédée, when he burns her with his cigarette. It is shocking also because her reaction is so unexpected and uncharacteristic. Up until now, Dédée had spent most of her time trying to avoid being brutalized by Marco, in a sense occupying more of a victim space than any other. Now she shifts to that of semi-sadistic voyeur because she derives such pleasure (as she herself tells Francesco) from watching men fight. "They never hurt each other enough," she declares, as we see them being beaten to a pulp. Francesco then inquires: "Don't you like men?" To which she replies: "No, or rather I like them too much, which is the same thing." We gather from this exchange that she sees men as capable of extreme hurt, which is, of course, why Francesco is so appealing, because he appears to

Dédée d'Anvers/Dédée (1948). Dédée's masquerade of femininity drops off.

be an exception to this rule. But this exchange also reveals a tough, even cruel, side to Dédée, which makes the audience uncertain how to read her. The point is also that with all this violence circulating, this chance encounter is hardly auspicious. Finally, in terms of mise-en-scène, the damp, foggy, and dark setting does not augur well for the birth and subsequent burgeoning of a happy relationship between the two.

Other differences are revealed. Francesco emerges from this sequence as the more romantic of the two, Dédée as the more erotically desiring. He walks her along the canal. She clearly wants to stop him in his tracks and kiss. Nothing happens. She declares she must get back to her job. He pays her to stay with him. She believes it is for a professional exchange (those are her terms), and she sits down to make herself available, evidently disappointed that Francesco appears not to desire her for who she is, but as a piece of trade. It is clear from her expression that she believes she has misread their earlier eye contact, so she shifts to a business-type mode, demands a cigarette. However, she wistfully regards him as he unwraps a packet, as if to say "Why can he not see how much I am in love with him?" Again, nothing happens, even though she says "Let's get on with it." Francesco then explains to her that he just wants her with him to hear a woman's voice. At that point, she again shifts her comportment and becomes again a desiring subject, as is evidenced by the way she takes a second cigarette from his packet and puts it in her mouth. Dédée invests this moment with huge eroticism—there is no mistaking what she wants. Not until the next encounter do we and Dédée get to understand why Francesco did not want to make love then. He wanted it to be special, clean, and in a bed—not on some pile of disused sacks. Francesco is the one who remains enigmatic, therefore, not Dédée. She is observant and witty in the face of Francesco's undecipherability. She unambiguously stakes her claim as a desiring body yet can also shift and adjust to, as she puts it, "expressions of brotherly and sisterly love"—which is how she reads Francesco's position at one stage. Equally, she is unafraid of reiterating her own desire when she senses there is desire lurking within Francesco's rather broody exterior. In short, she occupies the more active role in this seduction (a role more typically associated at the time with the male).

During this entire first sequence, the two are mostly framed in a medium two-shot (fourteen in all). Other than that, they are shot in close-up but separately (Dédée's thirteen shots to Francesco's nine). These separate close-ups give evidence that the time for the consumation of love has not yet arrived. Yet the density of close-ups on the individual characters (twenty-two in all) signals their status as desiring and desired bodies. There are, then, no close-ups of the couple. These will only occur in the next sequence, when they meet up and finally make love (eight close-ups). This second sequence is in three parts. First, Francesco comes to the Big Moon, and the two of them dance together. In terms of two-shots, five medium shots and one close-up make up this section. In the single two-shot close-up, Dédée insists on Francesco holding her closer and tells him how nice he smells. Again, this is an interesting reversal of roles, with the woman expressing her needs and desires in the way that is more typically associated with the male. Second, they move on to a nearby hotel (three full shots). Dédée leaves in just her dress. The fur coat—the signifier of her "otherness," her masquerade of femininity, her sexual availability—is left behind. We fade into the next morning and come across the two lovers in bed. Most of this section is in close-up. There are five very tight two-shot close-ups. These are interspersed with five single close-ups on Dédée and two on Francesco. In the close-ups on Dédée, we see her kissing his hand, touching his lips with her fingertips— palpably expressing her love. Her lips are moist, as if she has consumed this love like a fruit. But we also see in her face the pain that her desire causes her. Francesco almost says the words "I love you," something we know he has never felt for any woman before. She swoons back in a very tight close-up, over- whelmed with passion and understanding of the importance of his unspoken words. In the final section of the sequence, the lovers have left the hotel and are making their way back to the Big Moon. Francesco offers her his jacket to keep her warm and his scarf (which she will keep as a token of his love). The two- shots that frame them mark a movement away from their earlier intimacy. There are three full shots, three medium shots, and only two close-ups. Furthermore, there are two medium shots of Dédée on her own and one of Francesco. During this section, Dédée faces the reality of her life outside the bubble of their love. Her fear of Marco comes flooding back, the reality of her "work" also, and the seeming inescapability of it all. Only then does Francesco tell her that he will take her away from all of this horror. She rushes into his arms and asks him to kiss her. Fade out on a close-up of their kiss. So again, as in the two former sections of this sequence, Dédée moves physically to agence desire (holding and touching her man). In so doing she asserts a reciprocity of erotic power.

But it is in the last sequence of the two lovers together that we are intensely privy to a fully and erotically charged female gaze. It is an extraordinary moment and one that marks Dédée's full entry into a desiring self that is free of her enslavement to the other (that is, Marco). The sequence begins with Dédée rushing downstairs and out of the Big Moon. She is running from Marco and his latest horrible request (that she fleece Francesco). The camera directly occu- pies her position, and all we see is her hand holding the banister rails as she charges downstairs. Next, we are in Francesco's cabin; the camera is still placed in Dédée's position. She is to the left of the screen in the foreground, Francesco is in full view in a close-up. Her back is to us, but all we see are her hands in close-up (as before). Her person is reflected in a medium shot in a mirror on the cabin wall behind and just to the left of Francesco, forming a triangle (Dédée on two points of the triangle, Francesco on the third). Dédée's hands reach out to Francesco and caress his face. It is as if we are she, reaching out for the desired, eroticized Francesco. Only her reflection reminds us that this is not so, that it is she who is holding and desiring Francesco. This mise-en-scène is almost immedi- ately mirrored when Francesco moves, left to right, across the cabin to a port- hole. As the spectator looks at the screen, Francesco is now to the left of the screen and Dédée is offscreen to the right. This time we do not see her hands, only her face reflected in this porthole, which, again, is just behind Francesco and to the right. Once more the reflection lies between the two lovers.

In the two minutes of this sequence, we have been presented with two trian- gulations that mirror each other. These triangulations are made up of Francesco as a single and Dédée as a double presence (her unsubstantial reflection and her real self). The effect of the mirroring is first to intensify the desire. We are sutured into Dédée's position thanks to the camera's positioning. But we are also pushed out of that suturing by her reflection, which functions to reassert her ownership of the gaze. The way the spectator is pulled in and pushed out of a desiring subjectivity constitutes one aspect of the intensity and power of the eroticized gaze in this sequence, and this operates at an extra-diegetic level. But, because we also get to witness her desiring gaze in the reflections as well as her physical gestures of desire, diegetically speaking, there is a mise-en-scène of a doubly desiring subjectivity—Dédée's. However, and here is the dialectical rub, in an entirely symbolic way, these reflections also signal danger (Eros and Thanatos are copresent in this scene, thanks to these reflections). Indeed, they foreshadow death. Francesco is caught between these two Dédées: the real and the unsubstantial. He is aware of the real Dédée before his eyes but unaware of the reflection that lies in the shadows behind him. We know that Dédée comes from a violent past, that she is desperate to leave, and that she knows the danger involved in that leaving. Thus, her reflection, her shadow behind Francesco, acknowledges the ghosts of her past, including her recent past with Marco. The desiring reflection is also, then, the specter of death. However, Francesco remains unaware of this, seeing only the new Dédée before him.

Such are her erotics of power that she causes both Marco and Francesco to reveal their true colors—a self-exposure that leads paradoxically and ironically to both their deaths. Francesco emerges, finally, as a man capable of trusting and loving a woman; Marco, as cowardly and treacherous (in short, the embodiment of the stereotype of the femme fatale). In terms of her own being, Dédée may well have lost the love of her life, but she has gained her sense of worth—she is a woman in her own right—which is why it is she who organizes the final denouement of the plot and supervises Marco's summary execution.

Dédée marks the moment when Signoret's star persona is truly brought to the fore. Her role in this film represents a culmination of a style. As if to sanction this moment of arrival, it is significant that a radical shift in her physical representation on screen occurs. Until this film, where framing Signoret (in a one-shot) was concerned, there was a balance between medium shots and full shots on the one hand, and close-ups on the other. With *Dédée*, Signoret receives star treatment, with 60 percent of her solo shots being in close-up—a percentage that prevails or increases for three of the other films of this period that she made after *Dédée*: *Impasse* (70 percent), *Manèges* (60 percent), and *Ombre et Lumière* (65 percent).[9] The point is, with this density of close-ups, eroticism becomes palpable; its power to magnetize the spectator reflects its power to affect the diegetic viewer. What is so significant about this viewed eroticism, however, is that, consistently, Signoret's characters are not defined solely in relation to men but also to other women. The diegetic audience is mixed. Women, just as much as men, act as counterpoints to Signoret's own role. Thus, among the older women characters, there are bad mothers (the proto-mothers Madame Rosa in *Macadam*, Lady Beltham in *Fantômas*, and Dora's real mother in *Manèges*) and good mothers (the proto-mother Germaine in *Dédée* and the absent but significant mothers in *Fantômas* and *Ombre et Lumière*). In the same vein, there are good and bad sisters or proto-sisters. These characters act as a foil to Signoret's own beauty (because they are, for the most part, less graced with spectacular good looks). But they also function to affirm the authenticity and depth of her performance and help sharpen the focus on the range and palpability of emotions felt by Signoret's characters (from hate and contempt to passion, loneliness, and despair).

There are two further, tightly interrelated aspects that need briefly to be addressed in relation to Signoret's power, and these are to do with space and mobility. Space is taken here in its largest meaning of physical space and social relations as well as mobility in terms of freedom of movement. Space is both ordered and chaotic, whether urban geography or social relations. Interestingly, Signoret's characters not only embody this order and chaos, but, in that they enjoy a relative mobility, they also act as their go-betweens. To take *Dédée d'Anvers* as an example, whereas all her fellow prostitutes remain physically limited within the confines of the Big Moon (the farthest they get is to look out of the window), Dédée can make her way to the port, to the docks, and to Francesco's cabin. The limits of her world are, however, Antwerp (hence the meaningfulness of the film's title: Dédée *of* Antwerp) despite the fact that she says to Francesco, "I am free to go where I like"—indeed, his death puts an end to those dreams, and we assume she will resume her earlier circulation within the city. But certainly she is not the bearer of chaos (unlike the femme fatale), even though she is part of it. In fact, in this film, completely counter to stereotype, the biggest embodiment and generator of chaos is Marco. His clothes are a chaotic mismatch, his hair often in disarray, and his behavior frequently hysterical. Significantly, there is no emblematic figure of order, although several strive to achieve this impossible goal based on man's rationality. Monsieur René comes closest in his obsessive neatness and his ability to manage the social relations within his nightclub. But he too is a source of chaos once he tells Marco of Dédée's plans to leave him. Francesco equally appears to be a source of order, but his illicit gun running delays the escape plans put together with Dédée and gives Marco time to find him and kill him. Within the compound of the Big Moon, Germaine is, emotionally, the one with the most wisdom and insight into other human beings and as such provides some much needed stability for Dédée. But, unlike the men who aspire to rationality and order, she realizes the impossibility, if not the futility, of such a goal. Meantime, Dédée circulates in and among all these people and places. In this way, she acts as a conduit between the two extremes and comes to embody, in a broader way than her proto-mother, Germaine, the necessity of their coexistence.

It is not just a question of accepting that order and chaos are the principles of space, both social and geographical. Many of Signoret's characters are able to do more with this knowledge and thus become empowered by it. Only one character, Dora, is destroyed by it. Her frenetic displacements between the two do not lead to a balanced outcome but to bedridden immobilism and to a complete destruction of her sexual identity. Sometimes that empowerment comes with the facilitators of class and capital—again, two things that Dora never obtains (she never achieves class, and she is profligate with all the capital). In *Against the Wind*, *Fantômas*, *Impasse*, and *Ombre et Lumière*, Signoret's characters have class and capital. They enter in and out of the precariousness of the chaotic spaces and find moments of order and pleasure. They take that precariousness in stride, use it to enhance and enrich the moments of emotional and physical stability (Isabelle's trajectory is a good example of this). But class and capital do not have to be the signifiers of empowerment, as the outcome of *Macadam* makes clear. Gisèle has managed to hold herself together through the push and pull of the two entities and obtains a satisfactory outcome. No assumptions about its durability are made—that too is part of this empowerment. Thus, Signoret's characters, emboldened as they are with this knowledge, exude an intelligence about life (and being in it) in ways that the superficial, stereotyped femme fatale is never allowed to enjoy. Body and intellect join together in Signoret's star persona to place before our eyes a powerfully erotic woman whose strength in performance can only grow to take on further dimensions.

Chapter Five

Trajectory to International Stardom—1952–1959

HIS CHAPTER focuses on the period 1952–1959, during which Signoret's status and reputation as an international star were firmly established. It is noteworthy that, although she played fewer roles in the 1950s than in the previous six-year period (for reasons already explained in earlier chapters), the cumulative effect was to bring her the very prize she no longer particularly sought: international fame. The six films from this period—*Casque d'Or, Thérèse Raquin, Les diaboliques, La mort en ce jardin, Les sorcières de Salem*, and *Room at the Top*—constitute a key to our analysis of Signoret's star persona and body-text and fall into three sections. In the first section, I shall do a brief analysis of the way in which the star persona is framed. In the second, I shall examine three of her films with regard to the interface between the star body and literary adaptations. The final section will consider questions of costume and color and the star body as a readable text.

SHOOTING THE STAR

The period 1952–1959 marked Signoret's full entry into international stardom, with her performance in four of the six films gaining prestigious prizes: the British Academy Award for Best Foreign Actress in *Casque d'Or, Thérèse Raquin*, and *Les sorcières de Salem* and three awards for *Room at the Top* (the British Academy Award, Best Actress Cannes, and the Oscar). These six films represent a pinnacle in her career, during which she averaged an audience, in France, of two million per film. It is worth considering this figure if only because it more or less matches the average for her earlier films. We need to be aware that in the 1950s, film attendance figures in France were not yet on the decline. In 1950, the official figure was 370 million, rising to 395 million in 1955 and reaching a peak of 411 million in 1957. The point is, therefore, that whereas Signoret managed to hold on to her audience numerically speaking, in real terms, the two million figure actually represents a drop in the potential audience rather than an increase. This comes as a surprise, given her international star status at the time. Doubtless the attraction of American movies, which had reflooded the market after the war, taking 50 percent market share, drew away some of the audience. But so too did the attraction of other, more sensationally sexy and febrile stars breaking onto the scene during this period, such as Brigitte Bardot. It is also worth making the point that this figure is one she would never equal again, even in her later, equally successful career. However, by this time the major reason for the decline in attendance for Signoret's films can be attributed to the overall drop in audiences (to 180 million in the 1970s). Indeed, in the period 1970–1985, she averaged around one million, half her original audience.

Earlier chapters discussed the sociopolitical reasons behind Signoret's lack of domination within the star arena of the 1950s in France, but we can also see that market forces and the phenomenon of new star bodies were equally significant factors. Nonetheless, she was a star, and a careful examination of how she was shot as a star will reveal intriguing data, which in turn can help us seize what was different about her representation from other female stars of that era, such as Brigitte Bardot, Danielle Darrieux, and Martine Carol. The following tables show the distribution of shots between her roles and those of the male lead (or leads, where appropriate) or other central female characters. I have had to leave out *Les sorcières de Salem* because there is no video available (and I have managed to view it only once, at the Cinémathèque Française).

Let us begin with an analysis of the solo shots of Signoret and the percentages of close-ups over these five films in relation to the other lead personalities. Crucially, these percentages are worked out based on the number of close-ups (CUs) and medium close-ups (MCUs) in relation to the total number of solo shots of Signoret or the lead characters, and not on the total number of shots in the film (which gives a less clear picture as to the treatment of star personas).

The high percentage of close-ups in the British film *Room at the Top* points in the first instance to a cultural difference in filming. The French film industry is known for its more economical use of close-ups. French critics, particularly in the 1930s through the 1950s, often commented negatively if a film, to their mind, had too many close-ups—as indeed was the case, according to some of the French reviews, with *Room at the Top*.[1] As Ginette Vincendeau (2000, 9) points out, French cinema of the classical era (1930–1960) tended to prefer medium and long shots to close-ups. The more distanced shots served either to reveal the stars' own actorly style (gestures, etc.) or to show them in relation to other actors through ensemble play. Close-ups were used for emphasis and a momentary illusion of intimacy with the star, rather than for the fetishistic value they retain within classical Hollywood cinema.[2] What I have chosen to look at here is the percentages of close-ups based on the total number of solo shots of Signoret and compare these with those of the other lead characters because they allow for a very interesting story to unfold.

With 73 percent of Signoret's solo shots in close-up in *Room at the Top*, we would be correct to consider that, in shooting terms, she received the kind of female star treatment that is generally practiced in mainstream classical (Hollywood) narrative cinema. However, when we consider her costar Laurence Harvey, he is very strongly flagged up with a much greater number of close-ups (83 percent) than Signoret. Furthermore, in terms of the percentage of close-ups of Heather Sears (79 percent), she too is more often in close-up than Signoret. This is especially remarkable considering the significance of her role where the narrative is concerned, which is very much secondary to Signoret's. But to return to the two top-billed stars: because Harvey is present in virtually every shot of the

SOLO SHOTS OF SIGNORET

	Casque d'Or	Thérèse Raquin	Les diaboliques	La mort en ce jardin	Room at the Top
Close-up	18	4	3	1	35
Medium close-up	25	50	15	7	18
Medium shot	15	38	41	19	19
Long shot	14	12	13	3	1

SOLO SHOTS OF MALE OR OTHER CENTRAL LEAD(S)

	Casque d'Or	Thérèse Raquin	Les diaboliques	La mort en ce jardin	Room at the Top
Close-up	Serge Reggiani: 18	Raf Vallone: 6 Roland Lesaffre: 3	Vera Clouzot: 9 Paul Meurisse: 4	Georges Marchal: 1 Michêle Girardon: 3	Laurence Harvey: 79 Heather Sears: 7
Medium close-up	15	Raf Vallone: 17 Roland Lesaffre: 20	Vera Clouzot: 51 Paul Meurisse: 16	Georges Marchal: 1 Michêle Girardon: 6	Laurence Harvey: 79 Heather Sears: 4
Medium shot	42	Raf Vallone: 24 Roland Lesaffre: 22	Vera Clouzot: 35 Paul Meurisse: 24	Georges Marchal: 22 Michêle Girardon: 5	Laurence Harvey: 20 Heather Sears: 0
Long shot	22	Raf Vallone: 7 Roland Lesaffre: 9	Vera Clouzot: 26 Paul Meurisse: 0	Georges Marchal: 21 Michêle Girardon: 1	Laurence Harvey: 13 Heather Sears: 3

PERCENTAGE OF CLOSE-UPS AND MEDIUM CLOSE-UPS

	Casque d'Or	Thérèse Raquin	Les diaboliques	La mort en ce jardin	Room at the Top
Percentage of CUs and MCUs, Signoret	60%	53%	24%	27%	73%
Percentage of CUs and MCUs, other leads	Reggiani: 33%	Vallone: 43% Lesaffre: 43%	Clouzot: 50% Meurisse: 45%	Marchal: 4% Girardon: 60%	Harvey: 83% Sears: 79%

film, we are not surprised at the large number of solo shots that he has. What is striking, though, is the ratio of close-ups to medium and long shots of him (just under 5:1) compared with Signoret (just over 2.5:1). In other words, Harvey, ratio-wise, is held more often in close-up than the central female protagonist, Signoret. Granted, the point of view within this film is Joe Lampton's, the role embodied by Harvey. Nonetheless, the predominance of close-ups does suggest that the male star is more of an attraction than the female star or, again, that Harvey, whose breakthrough role this was, is in some way being fetishized, even feminized, by the camera, or finally—because this was a British vehicle—that his star persona was necessarily being forefronted. Thus, we could claim that there is a nationalistic motivation to his greater exposure. Yet we could also express surprise given that Signoret was brought in as the foreign presence needed by director Jack Clayton to facilitate greater sexual explicitness.

Let us continue with this analysis and take two other films, for there are more surprises. Signoret is the lead star, with top billing, in *Les diaboliques* and *La mort en ce jardin*, yet we can hardly fail to notice the very low percentage of close-ups of her in either of these films. With regard to *Les diaboliques*, when we compare her percentage of close-ups (24 percent) with Vera Clouzot's (50 percent) and take into account that Clouzot has 121 solo shots compared with Signoret's 72, then we could be excused for thinking that Clouzot is the star of this film, not Signoret. However, even though she is less than half as present in terms of single shots as the other main female protagonist, Signoret, as an actorly presence, dominates the film (in much the same way as she does in *Room at the Top*). As with *Room at the Top*, these statistics present a similar set of contradictions: we see less of her, even though she is the dominating force of the film. Moreover, where Signoret's star persona is concerned, there is an unexpected inversion in *Les diaboliques* in terms of the ratio of close-ups to medium and long shots (1:3). This is hardly star treatment, and the inversion becomes even more dramatic when Signoret is compared with Clouzot, who has as many solo close-ups as she does medium and long shots. More dramatic still, the male lead (played by Paul Meurisse) is more often in the close-up frame (45 percent) than Signoret; with regard to the ratio of close-ups to medium and long shots, he averages 2.5:3, which brings him close to Clouzot's ratio. Arguably, in this film, as with *Room at the Top*, Signoret occupies the least feminized of the positions in relation to the camera.

What about *La mort en ce jardin*? Again, Signoret had top billing, but as we can see, her close-up percentages are very low, especially when compared with the other main female lead, played by Michèle Girardon (Maria in the film), who, proportionately, has more than twice as many close-ups. However, something of a paradox emerges when we consider Georges Marchal, who plays Chark, the action hero who saves the day at least a couple of times in this film (once by helping the miners beat the army into retreat, by blowing up their ammunition depot, and another when he manages to lead Maria to safety through the rain forest). Throughout the film, he appears in only two solo close-ups, and both of them are of his hands, not his face. The first is an MCU of his hands as he snuffs out the candle before going to bed with Djin (played by Signoret). The second is a very tight CU on his hands as he lights the matches to blow up the ammunition depot. Otherwise he is continuously in medium or long shot. In fact, we see more of him in ensemble shots or two-shots than we do in solo shots. Most of this film is in medium and long shots, so in fact the singling out of the two female leads for close-ups, albeit in a small way, represents an exception, not the rule, in this film. As such, the percentage of close-ups where Signoret is concerned is hardly commensurate with the codes and conventions of classical narrative cinema. But Luis Buñuel is not a mainstream director. Indeed, as an art filmmaker much associated with surrealism and with the Left, his choice of shots have clear ideological resonances. Thus, medium and long shots predominate, particularly for Chark, who is the only one to show any kind of group or class solidarity in this brutal film, where human beings are exposed for their venal nature. Within an ideological reading, the character of Chark stands out as the single embodiment of the class struggle. Djin, as we shall see, is completely the opposite, seeking to advance her status by all means, fair or foul.

But back to the issue of discrepancies, for they continue—this time with *Thérèse Raquin*. In this instance, although 53 percent of Signoret's solo shots are in close-up and she has twice as many solo shots as either Raf Vallone or Roland Lesaffre (104 vs. 54), regarding actual time, more importance is given to Lesaffre than to either of the main protagonists. Lesaffre, who plays the blackmailing sailor, is only present in the film for a maximum of 25 minutes out of a 117-minute-long film (in percentage terms, 21 percent of the film time), yet he ends up with as many solo shots as Vallone, the top-billed male lead. In terms of close-ups, the two men both have the same number (twenty-three); similarly, they share the same number of medium and long shots (thirty-one). It is not difficult to place a queer reading on this discrepancy where Lesaffre is concerned, as the following contextualization allows us to make clear. Marcel Carné, who was openly gay within the studio confines, had befriended Lesaffre, who was also gay, after meeting him in 1949, and was very keen to provide him with a role in this film. So he wrote one in for him, which is pure invention on his part and which does not exist in the original text by Emile Zola. Interestingly, at the time of the film's release, critics remarked favorably on Lesaffre's performance, thereby vindicating Carné's decision to cast him.[3] This allowed Carné to offer him a key role in his next film, *L'air de Paris* (1954). In the latter film, the homoeroticism surrounding Lesaffre is made even more explicit through the way in which his athletic body is put on display (Dyer 2000, 128). But, as Dyer (2000, 130) notes, although in *Thérèse Raquin* there is "less body-baring," there is "one telling sequence, much more gay iconographic: a striped sailor top is torn to reveal a nipple and a bicep flexed to hold a hand mirror, imagery that could come straight from . . . 1950s gay pornography." A great deal of attention and focus is paid to Lesaffre's movements by the camera from the moment we first meet him in *Thérèse Raquin*. His body sways and undulates. He moves sensually, as compared with the brutally assertive manner of Laurent (played by Vallone). Indeed, Laurent's masculinity acts as a perfect foil to Lesaffre's queer identity. Furthermore, Lesaffre is the agent of fate, the angel figure who spells disaster for Thérèse and Laurent. As Dyer (2000, 134) points out, "There is a long tradition of representing gay desire in the figure of the [male] angel in . . . high gay culture."[4]

Until Lesaffre put in an appearance at the shooting, Signoret was delighted to be working with Carné (Signoret 1978, 121). But once Lesaffre was on board, relations cooled considerably, and Signoret made it clear that she did not particularly care for Carné's obvious sexual preferences (Monserrat 1983a, 85). She also disapproved of Carné's major rewriting of the Zola original.[5] The introduction of this non-Zola character does skew the film, and Signoret intimated as much when she expressed her fear that Lesaffre's role killed off the psychological tension that should have driven the two main characters (Turk 1989, 381). She clearly perceived that her role and Vallone's were being diminished by the excessive focus on Lesaffre. To a degree she was right, even though I would not go so far as Edward Baron Turk (1989, 382) who stated that "in the film's second half . . . erotic interest shifts to the sailor." It is not so much that it shifts, as Lesaffre's insertion into the narrative takes it away from the two lovers. Once the blackmail is on the table, the dramatic tension between the lovers shifts from eroticism to a despairing sense of doom, thus completely changing Zola's intentions. If Lesaffre's performance threatens, as Turk claimed, to eclipse Signoret's and Vallone's, then I would argue that it is less Lesaffre's actorly skills that makes this threat possible than the sheer volume of shots to which he is privy in such a short period of time. The spectator is more or less obliged to speculate on this actor's body at the expense of the two star personas. Signoret argued that Carné had turned the film into a thriller (Turk 1989, 381), and she is right. However, what she failed to note is that he achieved a reversal of the traditional trope of the thriller and offered us an *homme fatal* in the form of Lesaffre's sailor, thus effectively bringing this film into the realm of the queer and, incidentally, removing any possibility that Signoret might occupy the role of femme fatale.

These queering shifts are intriguing particularly because this is not the only film of this period where this occurs. Let us briefly return to *Les diaboliques*. The original text on which this film is based had a lesbian narrative. Given the homophobic climate of the times and the fact that director Henri-Georges Clouzot wanted to cast his wife, Vera Clouzot, as Christina (and she was determined to have a central role in this film), it is more than likely that this motivated the decision to straighten the story out.[6] However, as we can determine from the distribution of shots in this film, Signoret occupies the least feminine of all the spaces. Indeed, Paul Meurisse as Michel, the lover and no longer (as in the original) the victim—a crucial shift, which heterosexualizes the narrative—occupies almost as strongly a female position as Christina, the intended victim in this rewritten tale. We see Signoret being extremely active in medium and long shots, moving the murder plot along and essentially occupying the role that traditionally should have been that of Paul Meurisse's character. Conversely, his character is feminized, and it is Michel's disappearance, his enigma, that gets investigated. Thus, rather than participating in anything that could be qualified as action-packed masculinity in practice, he takes on the role more traditionally associated with the femme fatale in film noir: namely, the body as an object of fascination and scrutiny. So once again a male occupies or usurps the place that should have been that of the female lead. Michel's passivity and feminization—which begins by his being the "victim" who is murdered, then continues as he remains the invisible subject—is strongly counterbalanced by the no-nonsense practicalities of Signoret's character, Nicole. She occupies, not necessarily by default either, given her short-cropped hair and her rather unsexualized clothing, a masculinized space. Her dress barely changes throughout the film, and the cut is consistently the same. She wears a daytime functional tunic that can be belted to give a certain severe elegance or left unbelted, as it is later on in the film, for comfort.[7] The only elements that hint at an iconicity of femme fatale are her painted fingernails and her high heels, which she quickly shelves in favor of carpet-slippers as soon as she can, as if disinclined to inhabit such a prescriptive space.

Signoret's evacuating of her role as femme fatale causes a disruption within the narrative, and it is as if the strength of her characterization permits the original text to bleed back in. As with *Thérèse Raquin*, we are permitted a queer reading. But this time it comes about in a completely opposite way, through repression. As an effect of heterosexualizing the relationship, *Les diaboliques* confronts us with sexualities that fail to run true to type or refuse almost to conform with the film noir generic narrative's expectation of them. In a "normal" film noir, the femme fatale leads the man to his doom, but we do at least sense his passion for her. As the next section of this chapter goes on to explain, there is a mismatch in this film between sex and gender and ultimately desire that appears to have been completely erased at the heterosexual level, in any event. Thus, we are presented with incoherencies that have the converse effect of the desired outcome, and, as such, it is heterosexuality that in the final analysis is destabilized.

Yet another pattern emerges with *Casque d'Or*. Overall, Serge Reggiani, who plays Manda, the male lead, has more solo shots—97—than Signoret, who plays Marie, the lead female, with 72, a ratio of 4:3. Signoret has more close-ups than Reggiani (43 to 33), but, compared with her, he has more medium shots (42 to 15) and long shots (22 to 14). However, Signoret is in twice as many ensemble shots (46) as Resgiani (23), and that is surprising. Given that this film is, in part, about nostalgia for a certain working-class solidarity that has now died away, we could have expected to see more of Reggiani/Manda in ensemble shots, particularly because he is the protagonist. Instead, we see him principally in two-shots—98 overall, of which 45 are with Marie and 13 with his old friend Raymond (played by Raymond Bussières). Manda stands for certain values, as is made clear throughout the film, and these are integrity and friendship. But his lack of presence within ensemble shots as opposed to Marie tends to suggest that he is an outsider and she very much part of the community. Certainly he does not belong to this milieu in the way that Marie does. Nor is he part of their treacherous and inconstant ways, as Marie is in the first half of the film and Leca (played by Claude Dauphin) is throughout. In fact, there is no class solidarity—at least not like the mythic class solidarity at the Paris Commune at 1871 to which this film points with its constant reference to the song "Le temps des cerises." Instead, for Manda, the question of class solidarity becomes reduced to or replaced by one of friendship with fellow ex-convict Raymond and passion for the rather selfish Marie. The class solidarity song of the closing sequences of the film, "Le temps des cerises," remains an ironic nostalgic throwback to earlier times of the Paris Commune.[8] Paradoxically, in this context, Dauphin, as the manipulative Leca, appears in an identical number of ensemble shots as Reggiani. Yet Leca can hardly be said to represent class solidarity, since he schemes all the time to get the things he wants, among them Marie. Moreover, Dauphin has more solo shots than Signoret (78). Thus, where we might have originally thought that the two men were the foils of Signoret, we are obliged to conclude that Signoret and Dauphin would appear, numerically at least, to be the foils of Reggiani. Certainly, at the very least, we can argue the case that visually this is not so much a female-centered text, as Signoret's strong performance might lead us to believe, but one that puts masculinity in center frame and, in particular, boosts male friendship as the greatest value of all. Signoret was clearly aware of this dynamic when she remarked that it was indeed a virile film—even though, as she added, it was full of tenderness for women.[9] I would add that it is an interesting unfixed image of masculinity, given both Reggiani's performance style (he moves and speaks very little) and costume (of soft fabrics).

There are several conclusions we can draw from this analysis. In terms of shots and shooting the star persona, as far as the five films under consideration are concerned, in each one there occurs a triangular formulation, with three main characters occupying different points on the triangle. In every one of these triangulations, Signoret's character is not where one might expect the female star persona to find herself, namely, at the apex of the triangle, but instead on the base. In *Casque d'Or* and *Room at the Top*, the star persona at the apex is the lead male character; in *Thérèse Raquin*, proportionately speaking, it is the secondary male character, and in *Les diaboliques* and *La mort en ce jardin*, it is the secondary female character. Thus, at the peak of her stardom and good looks, Signoret occupied the least typical position for a female star. Indeed, she occupied the place more traditionally associated with the male star. Take, for example, Jean Gabin, the male star to whom she is so frequently compared. He averaged 25 to 36 percent in terms of close-ups to his total number of shots, a figure not dissimilar to Signoret's own.[10] She occupies, then, like most male leads, a place of action, not passivity. Equally, she does not occupy the position of the fetishized body. The body in focus is not hers, but the one that finds itself at the apex, or even, as with Paul Meurisse in *Les diaboliques*, very close to the apex. Hers is not the body to be investigated, but Reggiani's Manda, Lesaffre's sailor, Vera Clouzot's Christina, Meurisse's Michel, and Harvey's Joe Lampton. Even in *La mort en ce jardin* this holds true, for the enigma is Maria—how did she lose her voice, we wonder, since, at the end of all the trauma and thanks to Chark's perseverance, she gets it back? Ultimately, Signoret's character is far less passive than her male counterparts. Manda has things happen to him, Laurent always wants to act but is constantly blocked (by women, feeble men, and later Lesaffre), Michel has to wait for things to happen, and Joe, who may well engineer his way to the top, does so at the expense of letting things happen to him. Ultimately, all lack agency.

As for Signoret, compared with her earlier period, there is a slight drop in the percentage of close-ups (of 8 percent). Whereas, on average, she is in the close-up frame for 55 percent of her shots in the period 1947–1951, during her true star period (1952–1959) she is only there on average for 47 percent. She does, however, meet the standard criteria used in shooting French female stars because her average is not that dissimilar from her contemporaries (averaging from 33 to 51 percent). What is different, as we have attempted to show, is just how unpassive and unfetishized she is by the camera. This does make her a star, unlike her contemporaries, and suggests that there was more to her performance that the camera was intent on observing and keeping *en scène*, such as her intelligence, her purpose and drive, which marks her out as a woman with agency; her energy, which cannot be confined to the intimate and constraining frame of the close-up; and her physical and mental wit as well as her sensuality, which need more of a frame in which to express themselves bodily than a close-up can permit. Signoret's actor's craft—where the tiniest gesture is of such significance—commands a bigger picture. Minimalism, like miniaturism, is all about detail, yet here with Signoret it necessitates the larger frame. Thus, just to cite one example, consider the medium shot of her in *Thérèse Raquin* as she dictates the letter to the blackmailer. While her face shows composure, her thumb agitat-

edly rubs the tablecloth, and it is that little detail that allows us to read her true
fury and irritation at this man who so unfairly holds her fate and her lover's in
his hands.

LITERARY ADAPTATIONS AND THE STAR BODY

Of the six films made during this period, only one was an adaptation of a literary classic: *Thérèse Raquin* by Emile Zola. *Les diaboliques* was based on the
novel *Celle qui n'était plus/She Who Was No More* by Pierre Boileau and
Thomas Narcejac. *Casque d'Or* was loosely based on the life story of a popular
icon of the criminal classes in Paris at the turn of the last century, Amélie Hélie.
Hélie wrote her own memoirs, which were published in the popular magazine
Fin de siècle, entitled *Mes jours et mes nuits/My Days and Nights*, by Casque
d'Or, the Queen of the Apaches. But it is not clear if Jacques Becker accessed
them for his film. *Les sorcières de Salem* was adapted from the Arthur Miller
play *The Crucible*. *La mort en ce jardin* and *Room at the Top* have as their
sources best-selling novels (by José André Lacour and John Braine, respectively).
Arguably, only *Thérèse Raquin* falls into that dreaded category of "quality cinema" that the *Cahiers du cinéma* applied to so many French films produced during the 1950s. Thus, we can see that this association of Signoret with a cinema
that is *passéiste* yet again really does not apply. However, I have already discussed this issue in Chapter Two, so this is not the debate I want to have here.
What is intriguing at this juncture are the shifts from original text to adaptation
and how those shifts get played out by the star vehicle. In this section, I shall
investigate three of the six films: those where the most radical shifts occur,
namely, *Casque d'Or*, *Thérèse Raquin*, and *Les diaboliques*. Of the three other
films, *La mort en ce jardin* remains true to the original, *Les sorcières de Salem*
has a slight shift in political emphasis, and the changes to the original text in
Room at the Top were discussed in Chapter Two in relation to questions of censorship.

The film versions of *Casque d'Or* and *Thérèse Raquin* take interesting liberties in so far as they make their protagonists much softer versions than their
earlier referents. The original Casque d'Or was Amélie Hélie, renamed Marie in
the film version. Unlike Marie, who meets and falls in love with Manda (a love
affair that sets in motion the narrative), Amélie was in real life already Manda's
mistress and was two-timing him with Leca. So there is nothing in the original
that permits us to see Leca as the ruthless predatory male he becomes in the film
who will stop at nothing to get Marie/Casque d'Or for himself. Both Manda
and Leca were leaders of rival gangs (termed *apaches* in the film) and, although
it is true that in the original the two of them got into a fight over Amélie, wounding each other, there were no deaths involved. Amélie was a great beauty and
used to men fighting over her. Even women attacked her, seeing her as an
unbeatable rival once she set her sights on their man. Manda was no more the
true love of her life than any of the other men and, when he was denounced and
sent to prison for life, she moved on to other lovers. Not, however, without
some retribution. A few years later, one of Manda's gang members attempted
to stab her to death, but she survived the attack, despite receiving some severe
knife wounds.[11] Thus, we can see that, where Marie in the film is concerned,
there is a considerable shift in characterization. Although she may play tough
and hard to get in the first part of the film, thus bringing about Manda's fateful

pursuit of her, she softens considerably once she takes stock of the enormous sacrifice he has made to win her love (his freedom). She is not the heartless *garce* or femme fatale so traditionally associated with this type of film genre, nor, indeed, of the original.[12]

It is worth commenting on the fatal fight in which Manda kills Marie's pimp, Roland (played by William Sabatier), and her harsh reaction to it. It can be read as her continued ruthlessness (making her consistent with the real Casque d'Or, who is referred to in the film's press release of the time as "a cruel heroine"), or it can be read as Marie asserting her refusal to be a piece of merchandise fought over by men, thereby bringing the character closer to Signoret's own star persona (as a woman of agency). We must recall that it is the two men who provoke the fight, not her. Thus, it is Manda's desire and Roland's refusal to let her go that causes the head-on clash between them, rather than Marie per se. Indeed, by the time of the fight in the backyard of the Ange-Gabriel café, Marie had every reason to believe that Manda was engaged to another, so she had already given up on him and had agreed, arguably out of frustration, to become Leca's mistress. And even though Marie sends Leca out of the café to keep an eye on the two rivals, she never intended that Leca interfere in the way he did by providing the fatal weapon (his knife) to be used in the fight. The density of masculine aggression surrounding her person—with all three men trying to gain possession of her (to say nothing of her drive to survive and not be implicated in Roland's murder)—can explain her icy abandonment of Manda after the fight. She is not an object ("merchandise," as the gangsters regularly refer to women in this film, including Marie), nor is she for sale to the highest bidder.

In the film, Marie, unlike her original, also enjoys good relationships with her fellow prostitutes. We see her staying with her friend Julie (played by Dominique Davray), for example and sharing her bed. At the beginning of the film, her women friends cheer her on to dance with Roland. These same women, just as much as the men, enjoy watching her as a spectacle and as a spectacular beauty (they beseech her to perform a dance: "Go on, Marie"). They also comment on the unsuitability of Roland as her current lover, thus setting the scene (as a diegetic audience) for us to "understand" why she would find Manda so appealing.

Manda is completely transformed in the film. Unlike his original, he is an ex-convict who is trying to go straight. He is good and constant, reacts only when provoked, and speaks very little, believing that actions count more than words. He is faithful not only to Marie but to his friend Raymond, whom he refuses to let take the blame for Roland's murder. In the film, Marie and Manda are lovestruck, and we believe in their love; we feel its intensity through the looks and smiles they exchange. We sense their satisfaction with each other when we see them on the morning following their one and only night of lovemaking. So understated is their passion that it feels authentic.

The transformation of meaning in terms of Marie and Manda not only softens them but brings about an equality between the two of them. A greater fluidity between the sexes occurs, destabilizing their gender construction as fixed entities. What is suggested, instead, is sexuality as flow both within and between bodies rather than something rigid and contained and measurable only against the phallus. Thus, Manda wears soft fabrics (velvet trousers), and he is more often in solo shots than Marie. Softness and desire even enter his deadly fight with Roland when, at the end of the fight sequence, the two men lie on the ground, their bodies entwined, as Roland gradually expires, his hand softly strokes Manda's face, as if he were a lover caressing the face of his beloved. Similarly, Marie can be strong and assertive (in claiming her right to love Manda and to help him escape); she can also be fully surrendered as a desiring body. In other words, both Manda's and Marie's bodies can occupy or flow between many states, such as desiring, aggressive, and surrendered.

Becker was considered a social filmmaker, a label he accepted; he also saw himself as something of an entomologist.[13] This suggests that he delves deeply into both social contexts and the minutiae of people's lives. With *Casque d'Or*, he wanted to make a film about pure love, to show the gestures of love rather than the act itself.[14] He also saw his film as coming somewhere between Jean Renoir and Eugène Sue—the joy of love from Renoir and the plotting and intrigue from Sue.[15] Indeed, there is an intense sensuality to the film that is matched by Signoret's own "challenging sensuality," to quote Becker,[16] and Reggiani's quiet, restrained intensity. But the context of this film and its making add further dimensions to its meaning. The chance to make this film had been around since before the war.[17] Had it been made then, it would have coincided either with the time of the Popular Front or with its demise post-1939. In the former case, the narrative would have focused on male working-class solidarity; in the latter, it would have been a deeply pessimistic film and focused on working-class masculinity in crisis (much in the vein of Carné's poetic realist films of that time). Becker's film does neither. Instead, it is an elegiac treatise on sexual equality, a theme common to all his films. It is also an appeal against the inhumanity of the death penalty, which makes it a very modern film. It is therefore interesting that he should have chosen to locate his film in an apparently nostalgic evocation of the Belle Epoque rather than in the contemporary and used this particular background to foreground his radical ideas about equal rights (for men and women) and social progress (abolition of the death penalty).[18]

It is also possible to read, in Becker's softening of his characters, a nostalgia for and commitment to an ideal image of the working classes, both male and female. Thus, his choice of a costume drama as a background for radical statements becomes clearer when we consider that by 1951, when the film was being made, the political climate was dramatically shifting. The emblematic party of the working class (the PCF) was no longer in political office. Besides, the Right was clearly on its way back into power for the first time since the end of the war. Furthermore, among other draconian measures to contain civil peace, censorship was tightening its grip. In this light, the film takes on metaphorical, even mythical, value. In speaking from the past, Becker was in fact making a statement about the present. Becker was a man of the Left, and from his viewpoint there was much to be dismayed about. Since 1947, France had been governed by a coalition of the Left and centrist parties (called the Third Force). But gradually the effects of the cold war and the Marshall Plan created a climate of increasing instability for this coalition, which effectively meant that it, and therefore the Left, could no longer govern. Arguably, the end was in the beginning. The Americans made it clear that aid would be conditional on the PCF having no voice of authority, and so in 1947, the Communist cabinet ministers were relieved of their governmental functions. Even though it was the most popular party with the electorate (with nearly five million votes), the PCF was not in a position to take power on its own. It still garnered only 26 percent of the nation's electoral vote. Nor could it any longer be part of a coalition with the Left, partly because of the American embargo, but also because the Soviet Union forbade any alliances with the Left. So the PCF withheld its support of the Left coalition, and by 1951 the coalition began to show its cracks and fall apart (the more centrist parties refused to support certain socialist proposals and vice versa). This left the way clear for the Right to take over power, which, by 1952, it did. Former collaborators were now officially allowed back into office, most famously Antoine Pinay, a member of Pétain's Vichy government during the Occupation, who in 1952 was appointed prime minister. Read in this light, the shooting of Leca, a collaborator with the police and an informer, now takes on stronger political connotations, as does the film as a whole. Thus, although working-class solidarity is revealed in the film's narrative to be under threat and close to erasure, nonetheless, there are those few individuals who can still carry the torch, or at least the memory. Raymond is dead, Manda is dead, but presently Marie/Casque d'Or lives on. The closing image of the film is precisely of her memory, with, intoned over the image of her dancing in a tight embrace with Manda, the emblematic song of that class and its communard solidarity of 1871, "Le Temps des cerises" (one of Jean-Baptiste Clément's revolutionary songs published in 1868).[19]

A similar softening of the central characters Thérèse and Laurent occurs in Carné's film version of *Thérèse Raquin*, which he updated to the 1950s. Thérèse is represented as the victim of her circumstances, stuck in a marriage out of gratitude to Camille's mother (played by Sylvie) who took her in as an orphan. She is not the scheming, avaricious Thérèse of the novel, nor is Laurent. Indeed, as he pleads with Thérèse to leave Camille (played by Jacques Duby) and run away without further delay, he embodies almost the existentialist desire for freedom, to live each day as authentically and fully as possible, to not be bound by convention or a false sense of duty, and, even less, by an attachment to a certain bourgeois well-being that is riddled with *mauvaise foi*. The ill-fated couple never schemed to murder Camille. Thérèse makes every attempt to do the decent thing by him and find a humane way to leave him, starting by telling the truth—as she says to Laurent, "I haven't yet learned how to lie." For this reason, she even consents to go to Paris with Camille to see if they can save their marriage. It is only because of Laurent's impetuousness that Camille ends up dead. Unable to bear the idea of her going to Paris with Camille, Laurent jumps on the train and attempts to take her away with him. In the ensuing struggle, Camille falls to his death from the train. Ultimately, his death in the film is an accident, not a premeditated crime, as in the novel.

Michel Perez (1986, 22) makes an interesting point about the shifts in this film. He believes Carné portrays the passion between Laurent and Thérèse with an energy that has a "moral nobleness" to it that cannot help but be violent if the lovers aspire to be free. Thérèse desires freedom, but not, as it turns out, at any price, nor indeed at the cost of poverty. We are made conscious throughout the film of a certain caution in Thérèse when it comes to matters of economic security. Thus, although there is the expression of mutual desire within the film version of Zola's novel (unlike the original where it is one-sided), she is also more afraid of it than Laurent. This is partly because it is so unfamiliar to her and partly because, if she were to run away with him, she would lose financial security (one of the prime reasons she agreed to marry Camille in the first place). She also makes the point to Laurent that "gratefulness and pity keep [her] chained" to Camille. Her ambivalence means she cannot, in her passion, aspire to freedom through violence (unlike Laurent, who acts impulsively and often erupts irrationally). She is, therefore, incapable of such acts as premeditated

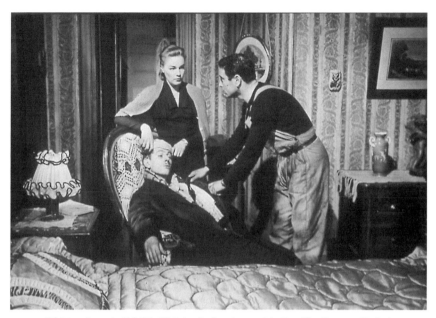

Thérèse Raquin (1953). Thérèse before love with Camille (Jacques Duby)
and Laurent (Raf Vallone).

murder, unlike her counterpart in Zola's novel, whose lust for Laurent leads her
to agree to murder Camille. Carné's Thérèse remains throughout ambivalent,
enigmatic even, as if this newly discovered passion is almost beyond her. When
we first meet her, she is quite frumpily dressed in a dreary coat, sensible hat, and
sturdy shoes, all of which more befit a middle-aged woman of the 1950s than a
young woman. We sense her lack of zest for life. At home, she wears somber
clothes, almost as if in mourning for her lost self. When she is in the apartment
above the shop, most often she is to be found wearing a pinafore and carpet-
slippers. Her hair is rigorously kept in place in a half-chignon, heavily clasped
with a thick tortoiseshell clip. There is not a stray hair in sight. Only once she
has enjoyed sexual passion with Laurent does her hair come down, her clothing
give way to a sensual white blouse revealing just a tiny bit of cleavage. This is
maintained for just the briefest of times. This "undoneness" lasts from the first
sexual encounter, which occurs just under a quarter of the way into the film
(twenty-five minutes in), until Thérèse's departure with Camille to Paris, which
takes place two-fifths of the way through the film (forty-two minutes in, some
seventeen minutes later). After that time and for the rest of the film she is back
to her former attire. As she says to Laurent, "I only know how to do sad things:
sewing, looking after people, counting money." As for him, she adds, all he
wants is "everything, like happy people do."

In a poignant way, the mise-en-scène makes this point for us about Thérèse:
how can she aspire to this violence in passion that Perez (1986) speaks of when
her whole life is, and has always been, as ordered as the drapery shop she runs
with her mother-in-law? The immaculate but bleak and austere tidiness of the
shop is matched by the overwhelmingly gloomy atmosphere of the apartment

Thérèse Raquin (1953). Thérèse after love: "undone" on bed with Laurent.

above, created by the ponderous provincial nineteenth-century furniture. If it is airless below, it is even more ferociously stuffy above, where there is too much furniture and where the soft furnishings, from the thick velvet curtains and the embossed tapestry wallpaper to the heavy lace net curtains and oil-cloth table-cloth, literally pinion Thérèse into her place of submission. All passion is surely going to be starved or suffocated in this environment.

In Zola's novel, the shop, which is a haberdashery and small-wares business, is described as filthy and unkempt. This dirt and slovenliness is directly associated with Thérèse, whose name adorns the sign outside. Everything is neglected; objects in the window are faded by the sun. The quality of the goods is "lamentable" (Zola 1867/1953, 16). We are a far cry from the film version of Thérèse's establishment, with its neatness and order and tidy bolts of quality cloth, which she constantly smooths and refolds. Zola's Thérèse is presented to us as physically unattractive. Indeed, Laurent when he first encounters her finds her ugly and only begins the affair with her so he can get sexual gratification for free. Zola's Thérèse is described to us as completely unappetizing. Her face, for example, is white, dry, thin-nosed, and thin-lipped, her body skinny and wiry— hardly adjectives to qualify her reincarnation in the form of Simone Signoret. Ugliness and dirt typify Zola's Thérèse, whereas order, cleanliness, and dormant sensual beauty qualify Carné's version. We must recall that Zola was part of a group of authors known as the naturalists and that he was fascinated by what he termed a "scientific interest" in physiology. Each chapter of his *Thérèse Raquin* is a case study in abnormal physiology. Zola wanted to investigate, in a scientific way, the temperament of people who are dominated by their blood and nerves—people who are without free will but who are driven by their fateful corporeality (whether the result of generations of alcoholics or inbreeding or "bad blood" through miscegenation, as is the case with Zola's Thérèse). Zola's Thérèse and Laurent are without a soul, human brutes; no more, no less. Their physiology is what drives them; there is no pretense at intelligence.

Carné's characters are far different. Thus, we witness Thérèse's intelligence shining through as she desperately tries to save the situation. Moreover, we feel sympathy for her, trapped as she is in a marriage that deadens her soul. We also understand Laurent's frustration as he tries to persuade her that they can lead a better life together. We even sympathize with the two of them when they accidentally kill Camille. Carné's Laurent loves only Thérèse. He is not driven by economic self-interest to the point of concocting a plan to murder Camille, as he is in the novel. Rather, he is a hard-working truck driver. He is a foreigner, Italian—a stranger, therefore, and not, as in Zola's novel, an old school friend of Camille's. Carné's Laurent is emblematic of the authentic, hard-working immigrant working class (last seen in Renoir's 1933 film *Toni*), not the philandering, lazy, would-be artist of Zola's text. Finally, in this context of shifts in characterization, we sympathize with Thérèse because of the awfulness of her mother-in-law. Here, the mother-in-law is frighteningly possessive of her sickly son, and even before Camille dies, she has very little regard for her niece— Thérèse's only use in her eyes is that she will act as a guarantee of continued care for her son once she dies. In the novel, conversely, Camille's mother is a sweet if rather naive woman who loves her niece and wants only the happiness of her son through marriage to this young woman. When Camille is murdered, so duped is she to the nature of the crime and its perpetrators (she believes it is a boating accident) that she warmly encourages Thérèse and Laurent to marry, and even goes to the point of bestowing her entire fortune on her niece as a dowry.

In other words, as opposed to the novel, where all is internally and physiologically predetermined, a plethora of external reasons are provided within the film's narrative to explain why Thérèse is open to the pull of sexual desire and to show how frustration precipitates the fatal accident. We are very far removed from Zola's eugenics here. For example, there is no mention in the film of Thérèse's miscegenated blood, to which Zola refers as "that African blood burning through her veins" (Zola 1953, 59). We are also far removed from his notion of fatalistic corporeality (the idea that people are doomed through "bad blood" to commit terrible crimes). Instead, Carné produces a third person, the blackmailing sailor, as the instrument of fate. He externalizes the inner fatal drive that Zola speaks of and gives human form to it. In so doing, Carné deprives the narrative of its original motivation. Equally, in making his two central characters sympathetic, he changes Zola's intentionally moral tale—about the gruesome but inevitable psychological tension between two people governed by bad blood and genetic greed—into a melodrama with a thriller twist. Frustration and repressed desire drive these characters, not inner flaws. Thus, Carné's characters are unlucky not to find happiness, whereas Zola's merit the terrible end they meet (they commit a double suicide). Carné's adaptation reverses the dynamics of the original text and makes Camille and his mother the embodiments of nastiness and mean-spiritedness. It is this scheming duo who behave dishonorably in their plot to keep Thérèse prisoner once they are told by the more than honorable Laurent about his love for Thérèse. André Bazin (1953, 23) was right to see this version as a betrayal of Zola's text. This betrayal is perpetuated by the casting of the central characters. Signoret's luminous intelligence was never going to allow her to embody the raw bestiality of Zola's Thérèse. Vallone's exotic otherness and Italian Communist party credentials place him a long way away from the crude and avaricious Laurent of the novel—it is as if, peculiarly, the exotic of the original Thérèse (due to her miscegenated blood) has been transposed onto Vallone's Laurent. Indeed, Vallone's foreignness arguably makes him more "exotic" as a source of spectator pleasure than Signoret. I say "arguably" because the two are wonderfully matched in their first kissing scene, where he first kisses her and then she, so obviously hungry for more, returns the kiss with intense fulsomeness.

The cleanliness and order of Thérèse's environment, matched as it is by her own neatness, reflect the stifling nature of provincial France in the 1950s. Although set in Lyon, this town is an abstract anonymous one that could be anywhere in the northern half of France. Signoret's actorly body evokes the effects of this monotonous, claustrophobic, and petty world in a number of ways. First, through the measured, efficient, and crisp manner with which she executes certain gestures (such as first smoothing and then folding the bolts of cloth away and setting the table at mealtimes), she shows how ingrained this conforming behavior is and how routinized her life has become. Second, the spaces through which she has to move almost consistently have her contained or trapped. Thus, for example, she is shot either in medium or long shot as she ascends the spiral wrought-iron staircase that leads up to the apartment. In the medium shot, she is seemingly caged within the spiral; in the long shot, she is trapped within her own loneliness (evoked by the emptiness of the mise-en-scène). When in her room upstairs, she can only look out onto the street below through the small square panes in the windows that keep her prisoner. Later, toward the very end of the film, when all is lost, she peers through slats of the venetian blinds. The slats are lit in such a way that they form bars across her face, again emprisoning her. Finally, she barely speaks during the film. Her virtual silence is broken just once when she tells her now mute and paralyzed mother-in-law how dreadfully abused she has been by her and her son. This monologue lasts three and a half minutes. This is her longest delivery throughout the entire film, and it is remarkable for a number of reasons. In the first instance, we could reasonably expect such a momentous moment of volubility on her part to be reserved for Laurent (for example, in a declaration of love). In the second instance, it represents Thérèse's single violent outburst. Her violence, then, is reserved not for her passion, but for a lengthy declamation on the abuse she has felt of her rights as a woman—as she declares vehemently to her mother-in-law, "I am young, I am alive." Indeed, she is not meant to be buried under all this submission.

Carné's updating the film to the contemporary scene of the 1950s means we can read Thérèse's statement within the context of the times. Even though women were by this time able to vote and were therefore officially enfranchised, they were still far from free—and once married they were, as Thérèse so rightly points out, their husband's chattel. She depends on Camille for financial security. Her job provides her with no income; all of that goes into the family pot. It is also worth making the point that, in terms of the law governing marital status, the wife was not free to find work elsewhere unless her husband gave his permission for her to do so (this law was not rescinded until 1965).[20] So Thérèse, who is tyrannically ruled by both her mother-in-law and her husband, is unlikely to find a route to freedom through work elsewhere (as Camille insists at one point, "you are my wife and you have to do as I say; the law is on my side"). She not only has to run the shop for no remuneration, but also the household upstairs. Again, as Thérèse exclaims, this constitutes an exploitation of her labor. Small wonder she is depressed, feels downtrodden—a state to which her carpet-slippers so admirably attest—of course she is trapped into this marriage; how can she possibly make her escape with a man who has no means to support her? Their difference in class is just one more oppressive nail in the coffin of their love affair. Significantly, then, when she does come to speak, to break her silence and assert her voice (her *voix*, meaning her voice but also her right to vote, her enfranchisement), she speaks of what matters to her, and she speaks it to one who cannot answer her back but who is obliged to listen—her mother-in-law, who very much upholds patriarchal law. If we return to Perez's comment about violence and passion and the desire to be free, where Thérèse is concerned we can now read her passion as a desire first and foremost for her own freedom including the assertion of her own rights, without which, as she readily acknowledges, she is not free to pursue love.

It is instructive how much the press releases of the time remain blissfully unaware of the force and true direction of Thérèse's anger and violence at her entrapment, something that Signoret's own performance brings so strongly to the fore. They speak of the story being about "a powerful man and an unfulfilled woman." In part this is true. But she will only fleetingly feel fulfilled sexually. All else is a struggle until she makes her final stand (albeit at a verbal level only) against the masochistic positioning to which patriarchy has consigned her and so many other women of that period. This is something that the American distributors also singularly, but unsurprisingly, failed to notice if their title release for this film, *Adulteress*, is anything to go by—or indeed the press release advertising it as "the absorbing drama of sin" and the promotional photograph used: the only shot in the entire film where Thérèse's clothing is in disarray.

With regard to the last film text under consideration in this section, *Les diaboliques*, Clouzot also radically changed the narrative and plot line. Clouzot heterosexualized the original lesbian text written by Boileau and Narcejac, where it is the two women who are lovers seeking to eliminate the husband so they can run away together. However, as we shall see, the lesbian text seeps through. In Clouzot's version, it is the mistress and her male lover who plot to do away with the wife. The wife, Christina, is married to the ruthless and sadistic headmaster, Michel, with whom she runs a private boys' boarding school just outside Paris. Nicole (Signoret), a science schoolteacher (as opposed to a doctor in the original), is cast as the headmaster's lover (and not as the wife's lover, as in the novel). In the original story, the two women plot to kill the husband, who suffers from a weak heart. Clouzot reverses the tale, and it is the husband and Nicole who plot against the wife, who is now the one with a weak heart. In order for the plan to succeed, the mistress has to befriend the wife. This she does by ganging up with her against the husband, who behaves quite brutally toward the two of them, even to the point of giving Nicole a black eye. His sadism includes publicly humiliating his wife, forcing her to eat disgusting food, and raping her. The two women enter into a complicitous relationship against Michel, a complicity that, to the viewer, is utterly convincing, since we do not know, until the very end of the film, that Michel and Nicole were plotting to cause Christina's eventual heart attack. In other words, we are led to believe that what we are seeing is the truth, the duplicity being revealed only at the end.

Les diaboliques/The Fiends. (1955) A queer triangle: Christina (Vera Clouzot) and Nicole (Signoret) together, Michel (Paul Meurisse) in the window.

During this period of seeing what we believe to be the truth, we witness the close friendship between the two women. Indeed, as one schoolteacher remarks, although they should be rivals, in fact they are close allies. This closeness is clearly signaled by the number of two-shots of the women together (eighty-two in all) as opposed to those of Michel and Nicole, who are almost never in a two-shot (there are only six) or those of Michel with his wife (fifteen). This female relationship, then, has greater visual importance than any of the others. Even the three-shots are few and far between, which is unusual, given that that there is a triangular relationship between these three main characters (there are only eleven three-shots). Thus, the actual framing of the characters lulls us into this belief that the relationship between Nicole and Christina is a close, primary, even intimate one. At one point, the two women are framed in a bedroom window in their nightclothes. In the background, a double bed is untidily unmade as if slept in—indeed, later, when they have enticed Michel to Niort and murdered him, there is a shot of them in bed together. In the earlier shot, Nicole is wearing dark pajamas and Christina white ones. Nicole stands, as if protectively, behind Christina. They stand framed like any couple might. However, this light/dark motif that runs throughout warns us that not all is unambiguous. Nicole wears dark, severe utilitarian-styled dresses with straight skirts firmly belted at the waist, whereas Christina wears light-colored patterns with full skirts (which hint at her Latin American origins).[21] The only reversal in coloring is with the hair: Nicole's hair is blond and cropped short, whereas Christina's is long and dark. However, this reversal does nothing to undo the image of Christina's exotic foreignness and femininity, as opposed to Nicole's more severe,

Les diaboliques/The Fiends (1955). Queerer still: Christina and Nicole in bed together.

"masculinized" appearance. Thus, Christina comes across as the exotic fragile female and Nicole as a strong-willed, modern woman. Unlike Christina, who has given over her economic rights to Michel through marriage, Nicole is economically independent. She not only has a paid job, she is also a property owner. She is purposeful and no-nonsense—even hard-nosed and tough. Nicole smokes her cigarette in a "masculine" manner, pulling the butt from her mouth with her thumb and forefingers and stamping it out with considerable force. She is quite "masculinized," therefore, in relation to Christina. Furthermore, she teaches science and geometry, "hard" male-identified subjects, as opposed to Christina's, "soft," language subjects. As the science teacher, it is she who obtains the sleeping potion and knows the right amount to put into the whiskey, which only then will Christina be allowed to pour and serve to Michel. The roles are clearly defined here, and as far as we know, it is Nicole who devised the crime.

Not all is "masculine" in Nicole, however. Her black high heels and deep red fingernails are, of course, markers within the thriller codes and conventions of her femme fatale status. Iconically speaking, then, she represents here the traditional femme fatale of film noir, with her clothing marking her as the safely contained phallic woman. But, this apparent investment in noir iconography stops dead in its tracks at this juncture with regard to Nicole's clothing. Other things intrude to stop it short. The carpet-slippers she wears while carrying out the murder and at the end of the film, when she is finally apprehended for her crime, do enormous damage to her status as a sexy femme fatale. How can this homebody in any way be associated with the glamour of the phallic woman of the film noir genre? Her gestures lose their extraordinariness, their excess, for when she is at her most ritualistically phallic (killing Michel), her dress code stresses her ordinariness. Her dress is unbelted in this scene so that it hangs, totally unrevealing of any contours, like a shapeless housecoat. That is one way in which the iconographic coding is in conflict, but there are others. Her dark sunglasses and the casually worn cardigan over the shoulders suggest a sporty persona, one not associated with the langorous femme fatale. Even that iconography is destabilized by the fact that Nicole knits (presumably for herself—a new white cardigan perhaps), although her needles do flash with considerable vigor, pointing to her prickly nature. Curiously, as if to give weight to this conflictual or fragmented characterization, it is noteworthy that she is not the object of Michel's investigatory gaze. She is not, therefore, the enigma that has to be unraveled—which, as a femme fatale, she most assuredly would be. Indeed, this probing of the enigma itself gets fragmented. In the first instance, there is a reversal of this film noir trope, and it is Michel who, once he has been "murdered," becomes the enigmatically vanished body that is the constant object of the two females' searching gaze. In the second instance, it is the rather grubby, unkempt, and sleazy-looking retired policeman-turned-private eye, Inspector Fichet (played by Charles Vanel), who probes and investigates Christina, not Nicole, to get at the truth and resolve the mystery. Finally, in this series of role reversals, where the two men are concerned, to Michel's rather feminized role (as the enigmatic evanescent body) corresponds to Fichet's own lack of sexualized masculinity: he is not the sexy private eye of noir tradition, even though his persistence finally pays dividends.

To return to Signoret's role as Nicole: when she walks, with her grand strides, she comes over as sexually powerful, predatory even. But here again there is something incomplete, as if she is lacking a target. There is no hint of passion between her and Michel (in a sense, there cannot be, or else the twist in the

Les diaboliques/The Fiends (1955). Nicole holds Christina.

narrative would be given away). Thus, this power seemingly has to find another outlet, and this it does in the form of her relationship with Christina. Nicole/ Signoret takes charge of and has control over the other woman, much as she does in the original novel. As such, she occupies a masculine space, which, in this instance, transforms their relationship into a simulacrum of the heterosexual couple. This is confirmed in a number of ways. First, on several occasions Nicole holds Christina from behind in a proprietal way that is similar to the way Michel grabs hold of his wife, pinning her arms to her side. Second, she has arguments with Christina that are more like a couple's tiffs than straightforward disagreements between friends or colleagues. For example, in one sequence the two women are sitting side by side marking the boys' homework, trying to "behave normally." But Christina keeps fretting about the crime. Nicole's silent seething at her partner's feeble weakness eventually reaches the breaking point, and she begins to make all sorts of brutal gestures, including violently throwing a pencil eraser at her.

In his review of this film, Derek Prowse spoke of Signoret as "big and dominating" and Vera Clouzot as "small and harassed."[22] Within these sets of contrasts, Nicole looms as the dark shadow to Christina's virginal transluscence. Theirs is not quite a butch-femme relationship, however, even though it appears to come close. As we shall see, it meets with several twists that challenge this stereotype. Nicole orders Christina about magisterially but also comforts her when she is abused by Michel. But, as with all the other embodiments mentioned above, the dramatic tension stops there, and things start to contradict themselves and fragment as the film tries to reassert its heterosexual bias. In a sense, the fact of heterosexualizing the narrative gets in the way of the plot having conviction, denaturalizes it, and forces it to a series of grinding halts. Several

Les diaboliques/The Fiends (1955). Michel grabs his wife.

critics of the time made the point that the plot was empty, absurd.[23] That is too harsh, although they do have a point that something does not quite gel (for the reasons I have suggested). The film is full of suspense and minute observations that make it compelling to watch, particularly the moments when the complicity of the two women is forefronted. We get a grip on a narrative line that seems to be taking us somewhere—and that somewhere is into their relationship—but as soon as we move away, things become dislocated, contradictory even. Thus, the lesbian intertext is always present, clashing with the reinscription of the hetero-sexual one. Interestingly, even within the now straight version of the story, we are not totally without sympathy for these two women. For example, the mur-der scene where they drug and eventually drown Michel in the bathtub is a mas-terful piece of horror. Yet we believe we understand their motivation, given how much they have suffered at the sadistic hand of this man, of whom they are now (apparently) disposing themselves.

Just as this film fluctuates uneasily between text and intertext, so too the nar-rative fluctuates between two contradictory types of relationships. First, there is the intense same-sex relationship between Nicole and Christina. Second, there is the doubly dosed sadomasochistic one between Michel and his wife, on the one hand, and Michel and Nicole, on the other. In the novel, there is no real match to this. We hardly meet up with the lesbian couple. Only at the end, once the twist in the plot is revealed, do we realise what their true relationship was, so nothing is developed there. Nor do we get much sense of the husband and wife relationship. The only point of comparison between the novel and the film, then, is the rather nasty dynamic between the book's doctor (Lucienne) and her supposed lover (the husband), which is the relationship that dominates the nov-el's narrative. Meantime, Clouzot filled the film with an extraordinary set of relational mirrorings and complexities that make his narrative far denser and in excess of the original. I would argue that there are two reasons for this. First, the film adaptation has a political intertext that is not present in the novel (first printed in 1952). I have already pointed out in Chapter Two that there are indi-rect references to the Algerian war and the use of "clean" torture (the film was released in 1955, a year after the Algerian crisis was in the public domain). This film can also be read as redolent with the immeasurable guilt that is the legacy of the Occupation.[24] Guilt is everywhere, pervasive and paradoxically ungrasp-able, much like Michel's disappearing body. This guilt takes the projected form of cruelty through a criss-crossing of sadomasochistic relationships that shift and mirror each other, leaving us unclear as to who, if anyone, is the victim; in fact, all the adults are monstrous. Suspicion is rife, and no one, not even Chris-tina, is a true innocent.

This reading of the film, within the context of the contemporary, certainly holds true and provides some of the clues to this textual density. But the other reason for its greater density comes down to the complexity of Nicole and Christina's relationship. It can, as I have already explained, be seen as a simula-crum of the heterosexual relationship (a first inverted mirroring of sorts). How-ever, it can equally be seen for what it is—albeit the filmic text tries to hide it away—namely, a lesbian relationship. It can also be seen as a mother-daughter relationship. Nicole takes care of Christina; she speaks to her at times as a mother would to a daughter. She patiently and meticulously explains why the murder must be done and why it must be done in a particular way. She is protec-tive of Christina's sexual immaturity. She soothes her when Michel is cruel to her, and so on. Already, we are looking at three types of ambiguity here, unfixing the social order of things. Nothing remains in place. Thus, it should not surprise us that there is also a power shift within this same-sex relationship. Christina, who at first seems so submissive to Nicole's dominant ways, takes the upper hand once Inspector Fichet gets involved in the story. Christina is still full of fear at her "crime" and will finally die, terrorized by the mysterious haunting of Michel's "ghost." However, until that moment of her death it is, paradoxically, Christina who takes charge, even dismissing Nicole from her sight, as Fichet becomes increasingly nosy with his questions. In fact, it is she who fields them with intelligence and Nicole who becomes more and more anxious. Of course, at the end of the film we come to understand why Nicole reacts so badly to the detective's intrusive questions (because he might blow apart the scheme to cause Christina's death). But until then, it looks as if there is a role reversal and Christina has taken command of the situation. Thus, in this same-sex relationship, power relations shift, sexual positionings and sexuality itself shift.

There is fragmentation and excess, both of which are played through the body and both of which function to challenge constructed orders, social restrictions, established laws, and hierarchies as they relate to sexuality. Yes, Christina does die in the end, and, yes, the two conspirators do get found out (unlike in the novel, incidentally, where we are left to believe that, having gotten away with the crime, Lucienne will now get rid of her rather sickly lover, Mireille). So order of a sort is reestablished in the concluding moments of the film (by a very scruffy patriarch, the detective), but not before a great deal of social disruption has taken place in which gender norms and political censorship are challenged. Sexual and political boundaries within this film have been stretched, transgressed even, beyond the historical and ideological order in which it was produced—the mid-1950s—a time of severe censorship and profound homophobia. Despite the film's unease as to its nature (as straight or queer), this was Signoret's highest-ever scoring film in France, with an audience of 3.7 million. People go to see thrillers to be frightened. They also go because it is a chance to see a representation of the unrepresentable. The attraction lies in the challenge to the architectonics of social order—the carnivalesque disruption of knowable boundaries. And it is surely this that makes this film still hold such fascination for audiences today.

COSTUME COLOR AND THE STAR TEXT

In this section, I am taking *costume* to refer broadly to both costume drama and contemporary film. Signoret made only a handful of costume dramas—six in her entire career, three of which were in the 1950s: a cameo appearance in *La ronde* and star roles in *Casque d'Or* and *Les sorcières de Salem*. Yet, the 1950s, costume dramas, along with comedies and thrillers, were at their peak in popular mainstream French cinema (Vincendeau 2000, 12). I have already discussed costume in general terms in this chapter, most especially in relation to *Thérèse Raquin* and *Les diaboliques*. In this section, I want, first, to focus on the interplay between Signoret's body and her costume, and to this effect will take one costume drama, *Casque d'Or*, as a case study, although I shall precede it with a short discussion of *Les sorcières de Salem*. After that, I shall turn my attention to Signoret's apparel in *Room at the Top*. The chapter will conclude with a third case study, in this instance Signoret's first color film, *La mort en ce jardin*.

In that they offer fashion on a truly spectacular dimension, costume dramas typically target the female audience. Furthermore, costume drama generally sidelines history using it as a backdrop for the romantic involvement of the protagonists (Bruzzi 1997, 35). As we have already seen, where *Casque d'Or* is concerned, both history and melodrama are at its core. This broadens its appeal to male and female audiences alike. Indeed, on the one hand, it tells a double history: that of a working-class collective and that of a woman's individual life at the turn of the nineteenth century. On the other hand, it relates the doomed love affair between Marie and Manda. The historical and the political come to the fore once more in Signoret's other major film in this genre, *Les sorcières de Salem*, which, as a politicized costume drama, is as far away from historical romances as one could imagine. The type of costume dramas Signoret was making, therefore, were quite distinct from the average fare of the time. It is worth remarking that Signoret's close friend Gérard Philipe was one of the leading male stars of the 1950s associated with the mainstream romantic comedy version of the popular costume drama, for example, his eponymous role in *Fanfan la tulipe* (Christian-Jaque, 1951). Philipe, therefore, figured as a matinee idol, being consumed by female spectators, whereas Signoret was not. As we shall see, her play with costume will equally go against the tide of the times.

In *Les sorcières de Salem*, costume serves to shield Elizabeth Proctor/Signoret's body not just from others but from herself. Her body is completely buttoned in and up. The coarse wool texture of her clothes, the plain stitching, and the wooden buttons all keep her perfectly hidden, but they also make us sense

Les sorcières de Salem/The Witches of Salem (1957). Two opposing sets of bodies: the buttoned up Elizabeth Proctor (Signoret) and the undone Abigail (Mylène Demongeot) and John Proctor (Yves Montand).

the hair shirt she might be wearing underneath. The proof of her virtue and puritanism is writ large on the fabrics that enclose her. No one can approach such a body, as John Proctor knows only too well when he says, "Sometimes a woman condemns a man because she likes virtue too much." Her body is as much in crisis through sexual repression as is her husband's and Abigail Williams's through sexual frustration. This is clearly symbolized by the way the two opposing sets of bodies wear their clothes. Whereas nothing of Elizabeth's body can be seen, apart from her face, John's shirt is undone to the waist, exposing a beautiful torso, and Abigail (played by Mylène Demongeot) wears front-laced blouses that temptingly expose her shoulders and rounded bosom, to which her tight-fitting aprons serve as a match by revealing her waist and suggesting her hips. Elizabeth's clothes keep her straight-backed and unbending. Her movements are slow and deliberate, and she often appears to be frozen stiff, so encased is she in her moral rectitude. Her rigidity becomes an exercise in power over John, her daughter, Fancy (played by Chantal Gozzi), as well as Abigail. Thus, her clothes become a way of disciplining not just her body but also those of others—they are emblematic of the true path that should be followed. As if to reinforce the rigidity of her disciplined body, she is enormously silent, lacking in a desire to communicate with humankind, preferring her God as an interlocutor. Similarly, her face is shot fully lit—there are no shadows of ambiguity for her. Her soul, like her face, remains two-dimensional, therefore, unable to tolerate the black side that everyone carries. Thus, she remains hard as moral nails, until near the end of the film, when at last her body changes shape and her clothing reveals a woman of flesh and love beneath. Signoret conveys this transformation with great economy. Her face is transformed from the severe, pinched features of before into a round, soft aura, much like her rounded pregnant body (she is carrying John's child). Indeed, her pregnancy points to her fertility and to the maternal body, to hope. Her voice now breathes emotion: the harshness, heard up until now, gives way to a weeping, choking voice as she speaks her love to John, beseeching him to look at her with the desire he felt for Abigail. Her body surrenders to love, knowing that despite all her efforts, including refusing to denounce him, there is nothing she can do to save him from death— nothing, that is, except to give him the strength, through her change, to face death without fear.

Let us now look at *Casque d'Or*. In terms of the costumes themselves, we are struck by three dominant types: Marie's, Manda's, and those of the gang members, in particular, Leca's. I have already spoken of the softness of Manda's attire and want now to focus primarily on Marie's but without losing sight of Leca and his gang, since their clothing acts as a foil to both Marie's and Manda's costumes. Over the duration of the film, we see Marie in four different examples of outward clothing (three of which are day outfits and one evening) and three different ones of inward attire (underwear and/or nightclothes).

Only once are Marie's clothes commented upon by the diegetic audience in the form of Julie's discussion with Marie of her evening attire the fatal night they go to the Ange-Gabriel (the night Manda kills Roland). In this scene, Marie appears at first to be dressed in black, in a tightly bodiced dress, with a small amount of white frilly lace effects across the bosom and at the bottom of the sleeves. She enters with considerable flounce, aided by the feather boa she wears around her neck and under which, we soon discover, lies a black onyx choker necklace. The dangling pieces of the necklace look like long, sharp teeth. The fetishistic value of the plumed female body is a common enough stereotype of the devouring femme fatale, as is the notion of the plumed female as dangerous and predatory, which the necklace serves to enhance. However, Marie's dress is completely at odds with everything else she has worn up to this point. Before, she had no need to signal anything about herself through clothing by excess. Her clothes were quite ordinary, and it was more the seductive effect of her eyes and smile that gave her power over others, including Manda. So why this dress? Why this excess? The first point that needs to be made is that this radical shift in costume attire occurs at the turning point in the drama, when Manda kills Roland. Indeed, a first reading would lead us to interpret Marie's attire as a typical femme fatale's masquerade. Her dress marks the entry of the black widow, ready to "witness" the death of her present lover and be the "cause" of Manda's own eventual demise—death by guillotine.

A second reading of her costume, however, can be made when we measure her costume against that of the high-society women who arrive at the Ange-Gabriel in their startlingly white attire. White furs, feathers, and satins for the aristocratic women abound. This begins to complicate the first reading. So, too, does our perception of Marie's own dress, which we observe upon closer scrutiny is a composite affair of black striped tafetta over white satin. As far as her outer shell is concerned, Marie is in black, in contrast to the other, rich women's white. But underneath she wears the white satin that corresponds to their outer shell. She also wears frilly lace bits, which, like the feathers on the aristocrats' heads, point to spectacular adornment. As Stella Bruzzi (1997, xvii) points out, after the great masculine renunciation of the nineteenth century, whereby men gave up "the desire for exhibitionism in their own attire" and transferred the

Casque d'Or/Golden Helmet/Golden Marie (1952). Marie/Casque d'Or's evening dress. Seated next to her is Julie (Dominique Davray); behind her is Leca (Claude Dauphin).

frills and furbelows to women, the "exhibitionist but passive woman" became "the embodiment of the man's desire—in short, his fetish." Only in part does Marie's dress code suggest that this might be the case for her, for the blackness of her outer shell points to the aristocratic men who surround their companions. They are dressed in the de rigueur black evening dress—top hat, tails, and starched white shirt. The rest of the men and women dancing in the bar or lounging about are in day dress, including Leca's gang in their showy costumes (striped shirts, checked jackets, light trousers, and fancy waistcoats). In other words, the other men, in particular, Leca's gang in the bar, have, in one way or another, not colluded with the grand renunciation, suggesting they occupy a more dis/playful, feminized space. Marie's outer dress color, however, aligns her more readily with male aristocrats—that is, a more masculine space. And Leca's gang's attire (in its femininity) serves only to enhance this impression. In the opening sequences Marie occupies such a space: when she rows Roland to the shore and when she invites Manda to dance with her at the *guinguette* (dance hall). At those moments we have been aware of her defiance of the norms. This begins to suggest that this dress—given its masculine connotations—is more about defiance than it is about sexual display or female predatoriness, as suggested in our first reading (of clothes befitting a femme fatale or vamp).

This leads us to a third reading. Marie's body has engulfed the dress; clothes and flesh have become one. The dress is neither a shield nor a projection of male desire. The dress tells us exactly where Marie's truth lies—and it is multiple. Thus, the excess here is about excess of meaning. First, Marie has worn this dress as a sign of mourning—for losing Manda. In the previous sequence, she had declared her love to him, by kissing him passionately, only to be told by his fiancée that he was already engaged. Second, and this is the significance of the frills, she is in mourning because she is selling herself to Leca (she has agreed to become his mistress, in a sense the embodiment of his desire as suggested by the frills on her dress, now that Manda is lost to her). This dress, then, represents the black moment of disempowerment but also a moment of parodic protest. Parodic, because her dress holds an opposite meaning to the first reading we offered the dress, then, becomes *not* the masquerade of the femme fatale, but both a power statement (it reminds us of the defiant woman of action) and a statement of disempowerment (it displays Marie's state of mourning, thus ironising her sell-out to Leca). Parodic, but also tragic in this moment, because it signals her own "death" as the free-spirited Marie we have known up until now (by giving herself to Leca). It is at this point that Marie becomes ambiguous and difficult to interpret simply as a manipulative and destructive woman. Just as the satin beneath her taffeta overdress, other meanings seep through.

To further elucidate this point, let us now consider the outer clothing she wears both sides of this central moment in the film. What first strikes is the balance and continuity within the dress code. We have already noted that Marie does not wear a great number of costumes, this is intriguing, because a function of the costume drama genre is the spectacle of clothing. Second, we also note that among the costumes she wears there is a considerable amount of recycling and repetition. The outfit she wears at the beginning of the film reappears in her first meeting with Leca. When she goes to find Manda at his place of work and declare her love for him, she wears a different outfit—a short-waisted flared jacket in light gray over a frilly blouse with a brooch pinned at the cleavage point. Her skirt is in a darker gray. In the second part of the film, except for one new outfit (which she wears to meet Manda on the riverbank), she mixes and matches what she has already worn in the first part. The significance is, of course, the continuity in her dress code (of which more below), a sense that costume is not on display in and of itself. We sense a life that is real and ongoing because clothing reappears and is combined differently, depending on the whim of its wearer.

At the beginning of the first and second parts of the film, Marie appears in a new costume. (Incidentally, these two openings represent in themselves a form of repetition: Marie rows to the *guinguette* and later rows to the bank to find Manda.) In part one, she wears a low-cut blouse worn on the shoulders with frilly collar and sleeves. The material (possibly satin, since it has a luster) is of white polka dots on a lightish background. It is fully buttoned at the back but has three small buttons at the front. The bodice-style cut means the blouse hugs the upper part of the body and is fully revealing of the shape of the breasts. The full-length skirt Marie wears is strongly pleated but flows easily (as if made of crepe). Along the bottom there are two black broderie lines running in parallel. The outfit is completed by the black leather belt she wears in the middle, which, in terms of shape, looks like a miniature corset. The cut of the blouse makes the cleavage almost perceptible; furthermore, it only just stays on the shoulders, slipping off from time to time to reveal a gloriously tempting Marie. The buttons (back and front) also hint at the delicious (and complicated) parcel to be unwrapped. Finally, the outer corset-like belt hints at what might be underneath in the form of further corseting.

In the second part, Marie appears in very similarly cut clothes, but this time the blouse is of striped cotton and the skirt is of dark satin with black broderie lines along the bottom. The belt is again corset-like. Her clothes mirror, in look

Casque d'Or/Golden Helmet/Golden Marie (1952). Marie meets Leca.

Casque d'Or/Golden Helmet/Golden Marie (1952). Marie meets with Manda
(Serge Reggiani).

but not entirely in fabric those of Manda (his dark velvet trousers and stripe
cotton shirt). They also mirror the clothes she wore both in the opening
sequence and when she went to visit Leca. These clothes, then, are layered with
the same meanings as the earlier ones. But there are further imbrications. The
stripes on the collar of Marie's blouse fall in the same diagonal direction as the
stripes on Leca's shirt (seen in part one). The design of this blouse recalls her
earlier polka-dot blouse, and that former blouse was itself a lighter mirroring of
Leca's polka-dot waistcoat. Thus, much as Marie's clothes (in part two) appear
to align her with Manda, they fail to be totally free from connotations with Leca
and his own desire for her, even though we know she does not reciprocate his
feelings. She may get cornered by him; however, she does not give of herself to
him (in part one, she agrees to become his mistress but is saved by Roland's
murder; in part two, she becomes his mistress only in order to save Manda). So
it is undoubtedly significant that, when she goes to meet Manda at the river's
edge, this is the only time we actually get to hear the rustle of her petticoats. As
she moves toward Manda, we hear the frisson of eroticism expressing her sexual
desire as she readies herself to awaken her sleeping lover.

As far as Marie is concerned, the fabrics, the rustle of petticoats, the buttons,
the hugging nature of the blouses, and the containing quality of the belts tell us
a great deal about her and her sexuality. She is both yielding and unyielding
(soft and hard fabrics), contained and uncontained (the buttons, corset belts,
and bodiced blouses, on the one hand, and the exposed shoulders, cleavage, and
petticoat rustle, on the other). But—and this is what is so fascinating—in the
two bedroom scenes (again, a mirroring of sorts) where we get to see Marie in
underclothing or nightwear, we perceive that there is no difference between the

Casque d'Or/Golden Helmet/Golden Marie (1952). Marie in her underwear (no corset).

outer and the inner subject. In other words, what is put on display outwardly with her clothes is merely repeated in her undergarments. In the first bedroom scene, when she has stayed overnight at Julie's, we see her in her white cotton underclothing. At this point in the film, Marie is in a completely female space (even when the men come to fetch her, they are not allowed into the room). Thus, the question becomes, as with the rustling of petticoats mentioned above, which only we, the audience, get to hear, who is this display for? Not her lover, since he is this time absent (later on, as we saw, he was asleep). So who? Moments of high eroticism are missed out on by the very ones they should concern—and there is surely a reason for this.

Let us investigate this underclothing further. The chemise has a bodice top and flared bottom, which is identical in cut to the blouses Marie wears. The cut also matches the flared jacket she wears later on. The underskirt is similar in design to her skirts, including the two strips running in parallel along the bottom. There is, however, no corset. Bruzzi (1997, 41) explains the fetishitic value of the corset. First, its tight lacing is motivated by the Victorian desire to assert difference. However, there is a "fundamental paradox" that, although the corset supposedly functions to assert "morality and modesty," in fact it also "arouse[s] desire" (42). In other words, the deep décolletage emphasizes the "impression of something very precious emerging from a complicated wrapping" (42). In principle then, the corset, like the petticoats, show/reveal what they hide and so have enormous erotic value for the perceiver and hearer (the male). They are on "the cusp between display and denial" (38). But we know that for Marie there is no corset and that no one hears her petticoats rustle.

As to Marie and her lack of a corset, in effect that desired object (as far as the male is concerned), that fetishistic object, is not just missing. She has put it

Casque d'Or/Golden Helmet/Golden Marie (1952). Marie puts the corset elsewhere—outside and reduced as a belt for all to see.

elsewhere. It is worn outside in the reduced form of her belt, and not on the inside. Thus, there is no transforming of the body going on because there is no corset—the body is not constrained into another shape, asserting the notion of difference. Where Marie is concerned, the body within and without is the same: the roundness and fullness of her body as well as its firmness (filling the dress and underclothes) is a constant, whether it is clothed or not. There is a reason for this lack of corset, therefore. Let us investigate still further. As Alexandra Warwick and Dani Cavallaro (1998, 86) explain, "Though the body in a corset is the same in physical terms as the body without, it is *not* the same body." They then add this intriguing piece of information:

> In the nineteenth century a woman wore a corset for more general reasons of fashion, or social status, and . . . the meaning produced was one of conformity to a masculine power structure that dictated passivity for the . . . woman, rather than one of explicit eroticism.

Marie's dress code becomes complex viewed in this light. The belt becomes an ironic commentary on masculine desire (she first exteriorizes it, then diminishes it). It also signals her refusal to conform and to act passively. Even when, later on, in her desperate attempt to save Manda, she "gives into" Leca, we are made aware that there is nothing consensual about her actions. Indeed, we feel it more as a form of rape than as a succumbing to another man's will. In other words, he will not get the thrill of undoing her corset.

But back to this earlier scene with Julie and continuing with Warwick and Cavallaro. Underclothes mediate between the body and the outer clothes. It is the space between the flesh and "the encultured image of the body that others will perceive" (Warwick and Cavallaro 1998, 61). It is the slash (/) that connotes the splitting of the subject (between inner and outer), pointing to the fact that we are not unified ideal beings (79). Underclothes also act as a boundary—a layer in between the flesh and the outer countenance. As such, in that they are seen before full nudity, they make the body less threatening and destabilizing. However, what strikes us with Marie's attire in her friend's bedroom is its sameness (outer and inner), its hint at continuity. In its repetition of the outer countenance, it actually reassures. In its liminality to the body, it ensures the authentic body and its authenticity beneath. In other words, there is a collapsing of the difference between body and clothing: the more you expose the body, the more it reveals itself to be the same. The purpose of this first bedroom scene now becomes clearer: it prefigures the later single night of lovemaking with Manda and announces that, as with this attire, so too the nightie she wears that night with Manda signifies the same thing. There is no disguising. There are no boundaries. The erotics out there is the erotics in here—an authenticity of erotics (referring back to what I have already termed a "clean erotics") that is not concerned with such issues as the split subject but is very clearly about a fully desiring body. In essence, Marie/Signoret epitomizes fashion designer Vivienne Westwood's idea that "the underlying rationale for clothing is the discovery of nakedness" (Bruzzi 1997, 33).

Thus, Marie's clothes and her body make sense together—the costumes do not override the body, nor do they override the narrative. The rustle of the petticoats is *her* expression of desire. The lack of the corset means she has no need for erotic accoutrements. She is the erotic body. As Bruzzi (1997, 36) says, costume dramas, because they conventionally prioritize the eroticism of the costumes, tend to obscure the "moral, social or political message." In Marie's case, we have seen how this does not occur. Indeed, she ironizes the function of dress and, through her parodic play with it, proposes a political edge to the function of costume itself. Thus, insofar as *Casque d'Or* is a costume drama, the film does a great deal to posit a new way forward for the genre. And it is arguably its modernity that was not perceived by French critics of the time, or not liked, that made the film fail in France when it was released and that now makes it a classic. Signoret (1978, 117–118) precisely pinpoints the importance of the film's costumes as an aspect of its revitalizing the costume drama genre when she states:

> [Antoine] Mayo's costumes, which were so authentic, did not appeal [to the critics]. They were used to adapted reconstructions, namely, the 1950s style of the wasp waist and hourglass corsets, which today render virtually unwatchable the majority of the Belle Epoque 1900 films made at that time.

Indeed, Becker's film had none of the tradition of quality cinema about it. There was intentionally very little dialogue—Becker deliberately went against the trend of the times for script-led films.[25] Monetary constraints meant he had to keep things simple—sets, decor, and costumes, among other things. Thus, the film remains purposefully unostentatious or unspectacular as a costume drama. Dialogue, mise-en-scène, costume, but also editing, all work to offer a renewal of the genre. The film remains deeply authentic because it is grounded in history, however miniature, and in the real lives of a section of society we choose mostly to ignore. The clash of editing styles, sensuous yet brutal (the very last scene of the guillotine[26] best epitomizes this clash of styles within a sequence) says so much about Paris's underbelly in that period, when life had to be grasped, fought for, as well as enjoyed. In French cinema we would have to await the 1970s and the work of directors like René Allio, Jean-Louis Comolli, Bertrand Tavernier, and André Téchiné before costume drama once again dealt with popular history and gave a politicized reading of it.

Apparel of the ordinary is also what typifies Signoret's dress code as Alice Aisgill in *Room at the Top*. Indeed, in her plain cardigans and straight knee-length skirts she expresses both her class and her age. Her dress sense is honest in its middle-class classic style (reminiscent of Hardy Amies' ready-to-wear clothes of the 1950s) and truthful in that it does not seek to mask her age as a woman in her late thirties. And Alice *is* honest—as is made clear when Joe, in the same breath, expresses a wish that she were not so truthful, but then declares that he loves her for it. Alice is also all woman (so says one of her theater woman friends). We see this in the close-ups of her face and in her expression of desire for Joe. Joe recognizes just how much she is a fully sexual woman in their play with cigarettes—he lights them, then places them in her mouth; she holds on hungrily and fulsomely to them until he withdraws them to kiss her (this occurs three times in the film).

Alice's total womanhood contrasts with Susan Brown's teenage lack of sexual knowledge. To the older woman's depth of feeling based on lived experience contrasts the younger woman's superficially adult airs and naiveté about love

Room at the Top (1959). Alice's total womanhood (Alice/Signoret in bed with Joe Lampton/Laurence Harvey.

and sex. This is made eminently clear in the contrastive nature of the clothes they wear. Susan (played by Heather Sears) in her ballerina-type skirts and schoolgirlish buttoned up blouses is not much of a match for the cool sophistication of Alice's classic attire. Nor, of course, do we see Susan in underclothing or nightwear (in her one sex scene with Joe, she remains fully clothed and extremely wooden). But we do see Alice in various states of undress with Joe. There are four love scenes, three of which have some aspect of nudity. In the first, when she seduces Joe on Sparrow Hill, all we see is the foreplay with the cigarette mentioned above. In the second, it is her black slip and naked shoulders we see as she lies in bed with Joe and then lies upon him. In the third, we are led to understand that she is completely naked since Joe comments on her body and how much he would love to have a picture of her like that—we only see the naked shoulders as she gets dressed behind a screen. Finally, on their brief sojourn in Dorset, we know they are naked underneath their raincoats as they walk along the rain-drenched beach. In that same sequence, once in bed, Alice's nightie—though conventional in style—is low-cut and adorned with bows that are tempting to undo.

In the second and third love scenes, as soon as Alice gets up from their love-making, she quickly covers her body precisely because, as she says, it is no longer a young woman's body. Yet, as she also says in the third love scene during her first argument with Joe (he cannot bear that she once posed nude for an artist), "I own my own body and I am not ashamed of it. And I am not ashamed of anything I have [ever] done." Strong, assertive words. What drives Alice to cover up, then, is her own sense of comfort with her body, taking it for what and how it is. Interestingly, there are ways in which her lingerie reveals this. In the second scene, when she gets up, she puts on a black silk dressing gown that matches her black slip underneath and tenderly molds to her body. This conjuncture of soft fabrics and semi-nudity points to the erotic value of her body as a pleasured body (we sense her enjoyment of sex with Joe). At the same time, in covering her body (but not its contours), she modestly asserts her ownership of that body, takes it back to herself.

In the third scene, however, something completely different occurs. At first, Alice is standing naked behind the screen, and Joe exclaims how beautiful she is and how much he likes to see her with nothing on. She then proceeds to tell him something about her past, when she was proud to show her nudity as an artist's model. In this moment she is truly happy—glowing with the pleasure of sex and sharing her life with the man she loves. Joe cannot understand why she would pose nude, and they begin to argue. To his anger she responds with a cutting comment about his lack of sophistication. Signoret delivers this barb, her face full of irony with a knowing, caustic wink. A class gap opens up, wounding him. He, in vicious return, asks her—almost spitting—what she did forty years ago during World War I. An age gap looms large, wounding her. As this scene of destruction unfolds, Alice puts on a curiously shapeless white, pinstriped, cotton housecoat. We know she is naked underneath, but the clothing works to remove any sense of the erotic thrill that we experienced with the silk gown. Alice and Joe give as good as they get—equal in insults—but the love affair is broken, at least for the moment. Nowhere is this more sharply signified than through Alice's shift from sexy lingerie to banal housecoat.

Age is an issue for Alice throughout the film because she keeps coming back to it after they have made love. She is found several times in the film to be looking at her face and examining the age lines and the less taut nature of the skin

Room at the Top (1959). Alice tells Joe she is not ashamed of who she is.

around her chin. The first time Joe meets her she is removing stage makeup (a mask/disguise for age) in front of a mirror. This is their first encounter—behind the scenes at the local amateur repertory theater. It is instructive that Joe is not looking at her, but at Susan, and that Alice is looking at Joe's reflection in the mirror. The relay of looks does not bode well, even if the removal of the mask points to Alice's moral integrity about her age. She is realistic about her age and

Room at the Top (1959). Alice faced with multiple images of herself.

her body; Joe is far more in denial. And, although she wants to believe that he will give everything up to be with her, she is honest enough to realize that the age difference between them (ten years) does matter. It is surely significant that, after Joe has left her for good and before she drives off to her fatal accident, she looks in the mirror in the pub, checking for herself just one last time to see who indeed she is, only to be faced with multiple images of herself (front and back, down an interminable series of reflections). In that simple but complex shot, she begs the question How do I come back from this kind of devastation?

In the end, Alice is the older woman who helps Joe grow in confidence. As she says to him, "I was a good teacher." So good, in fact, it took several attempts for him to leave her. The fullness of her embraces reveals a woman whose body is unashamedly in tune with her lover's. One wonders how Joe could ever relinquish her rich voluptuousness for the gangly and prudish awkwardness of Susan's immature body. There is no prudishness where Alice is concerned—as is exemplified by their first love scene, which begins in the car. She remarks, with bemusement written all over her face, that English cars are rather prudish when it comes to matters of sex. The gear stick is in the way, so she invites him out of the car into the more inviting wide, open spaces of the Yorkshire hillsides. As she puts it, Sparrow Hill is "somewhere cold and clean where there are no dirty people." There is nothing sordid to her mind, then, about their having sex. In their second love scene, her hands tenderly hold his head as he lays against her breast, the openness of her fingers speaking to the warmth of her sexuality—to say nothing of her serene silence after lovemaking (as opposed to Susan's irritating chatter and questions after Joe seduces her). Alice, unlike Susan, knows "it was alright." Each time we sense it gets richer, deeper, more— always more fulfilling, as the Dorset sequence makes clear. Alice is right when, as she boards the train home, she voices her fear to Joe that nothing will ever be the same again.

Alice, however strong her resolve in this love affair, is someone who will break—contrary to what, at an early stage in the film, she, unprophetically, asserts to Joe (she is playing his lover in a play rehearsal, and says, "I'm not fragile, I won't break"). Ironically, Joe has joined the repertory company hoping to get closer to Susan, not Alice. And this is the crux of the problem: Alice will love him to the point of full vulnerability, even when it is clear that he has set his sights on Susan (the "girl" at "the Top"). The first time Joe leaves her, Alice grieves in silence supported only by her friend Elspeth (played by Hermione Baddeley). When he comes back and declares that he loves her and not Susan, Alice values every moment as if she knows it will be the last. She does finally believe in his commitment (after the Dorset sojourn), even though she is terrified of the fragility of their love out there in the real world. Justifiably so, since her husband and Susan's father eventually trample all over it. Both men issue Joe an ultimatum ("Leave Alice alone"/"Marry Susan, or else"). Joe is faced with a dilemma: either behave heroically and defy everyone by running off with Alice, or act as a coward and marry Susan. Joe had told Alice the truth about himself in that same love scene when they had argued: when he was a prisoner of war, the last thing he wanted to do was try to escape—why be a hero like the upper-class "toffs" who were conducting the war as if it were run according to some kind of gentleman's code of honor? Ever a pragmatist, Joe bows out to the cowardly alternative. Alice is right when she says that as soon as he is among the people "at the Top" he becomes timid and conforms to their wishes. In all their meetings she had asked him to be true to himself always, as he was when with her. As she says: "You had it in you to be so much bigger than them." However, it is something he cannot achieve, and it is she who will suffer for his ultimate lack of authenticity. It is something she could not teach him and that he failed to learn for himself. This time, Alice's devastation is total and very public. She goes to the pub where he had once unreservedly declared his love for her and gets extremely drunk in front of a rather subdued diegetic audience, only to leave, dignified and distraught, to drive to her death.

It is a deeply moving role that Signoret embodies. There is no trite melodrama in her nuanced shifts in feelings from joy to despair—as, for example, in her last scene with Joe, when her face decomposes in a few minutes from happiness, through shock, restrained pain, and utter devastation as he rejects her (repeatedly saying he is going to marry Susan). There is nothing mannered in her gestures, which are utterly convincing as she seeks out the core of the man she loves and strives to share her being with him—her marvelous wave at him from the back as she walks away from him down the street remains etched in Joe's mind as the moment he knew he wanted her (its strength can be measured by the fact that this is the image that repeatedly returns to haunt him after her death). Signoret makes us believe that her Alice knows herself intimately even as she struggles with the contradictions between her self-knowledge and the mores and hypocrisies of late-1950s Britain, in which women are still perceived as men's property. As Alice's husband (played by Allan Cuthbertson) makes very clear, he will never let her go, not because he loves her, but because she belongs to him. Rather than return to the bleak emptiness of her married life and conform (hence, perhaps, the multiple reflections of her in the pub's mirror), she chooses nothing (death). Sometimes nothing is better than something.

The popular and the surreal merge in Raymond Queneau and Luis Buñuel's adaptation of José André Lacour's novel *La mort en ce jardin*, which is our last case study. Buñuel's film was shot in Mexico (where he was in exile), and it was Signoret's first color film. Significantly, it was shot in Eastmancolor, a new and less expensive system of color cinematography that had come onto the market in the early 1950s. It had two major advantages over Technicolor (the other system available at the time). First, Eastmancolor is a tripack single-strip color film and, based as it is on the three primary color registers for film (red, green, and blue), it has a greater sensitivity to light and allows for faster speeds. As such, it is an accurate color recorder with different speeds for night/interiors and daylight shooting. It also films distant objects more distinctly. Eastmancolor's tripack system uses filters to add or subtract color and, because of this, is particularly sensitive to the rendition of the three primary colors, red, yellow, and blue. Given its rather simplified nature (single strip, three base registers), it can have a tendency to rather gaudy color effects in film, especially in its early years of use (the 1950s). So if green is stressed, thus turning it into a dark green, it can become oppressive and nauseating. It can be used, in coloring the landscape, as an extension of the characters' psyche or inner disturbance. Red is the most aggressive of the three colors, and blue can become intensely cold. As we shall see, all three of these colors will mark Signoret's body—singly and to a specific effect—at one point or another in the film's narrative.

In Buñuel's film, most of these properties of Eastmancolor come into play. Thus, throughout, the depth provided by the fast tripack system makes the surroundings tactilely omnipresent. The background rocks and river at the gold mine are just as much a reminder of human frailty as is the deeply verdant greenery of the giant rain forest that threatens to engulf the five main protagonists lost in the "garden" (at one point, the branches "eat" Maria's hair). In terms of color and to give meaning to his mise-en-scène, Buñuel plays with the flexibility of Eastmancolor by either adding or subtracting color (through using different filters). In the first half of the film, the exterior colors are bleached out to the point of pale yellow hues, reflecting the heat of the beating sunlight. Interestingly, at this stage, we only see Signoret in interiors—and here, as opposed to the exteriors, the color has tonality and depth. The overall impression is one of great realism. In the second half of the film, however, when Signoret and the four other fugitives flee into the rain forest (the "garden" of the film's title), the color—predominantly an oppressive green—takes on a deep, at times, thick and unguent quality, which, coupled with the choice of shots (in particular, the close-ups of the flora and fauna), brings it far closer to a visceral, surrealist painterliness.[27]

Because of the dramatic effect of Eastmancolor on Signoret's image, in the analysis that follows the primary focus will be on her and her bodily relationship to color. In her character role of Djin she has basically three embodiments. The first embodiment is of Djin the prostitute who successfully runs her business, a very overt bar-cum-brothel in Cachazu, a small mining town on the Amazon. In terms of clothing, she is first seen wearing a bright red silk dressing gown that has slipped off her right shoulder, leaving it temptingly exposed. She is sitting watching over Chark as he lies asleep in her bed. The red of her robe acts as a strong foil to the blondness of her skin and hair. Her blondness becomes a point of contrast against the darkness of all the skins that surround her in her bar and elsewhere, including Maria's darkness, and points to a European body that is strongly out of context and (if we pay attention to the red robe) one that is being signaled as potentially hazardous to know (at least corporeally). To compound this idea, in this scene, Djin's mouth is heavily made up, with her lips painted a deep, garish red. The effect is to draw attention to the whiteness of her teeth and in particular to expose her top teeth as if she has an overbite. They effectively speak to her greed and venality—words Djin uses to describe herself to Chark when he wakes up and she negotiates her fee with him. As she does this, she accompanies her words with a broad, cynical smile, fully displaying her fiercesome molars. Overall, the juxtaposition of color and texture works in this scene to suggest an eroticism that is dangerous and unsafe (the Freudian/surrealist image of the vagina dentata springs to mind). Indeed, Chark's trust in her seduction of him will be misplaced. She steals his gun, denounces him to the police, and takes a share of his money as a bribe. Henceforth, throughout the first half of the film, Djin will always be closely associated with this first of the primary colors—red. Thus, when, in a subsequent sequence, she is fully clothed, her body is segmented into three by this color as our eyes travel from her thick red lips to her thick red belt to her sling-back red high heels (all of the same red, incidentally). Our eyes, impelled by the color red, move down the erotic female form. In order, the red leads us to gaze upon the lips, then the waist and bust (lying in between waist and lips), finally the hips and legs. Intriguingly, the fingernails are not painted red, but the hands are drawn attention to by the heavy fake-pearl bracelet she wears.

In her second embodiment, Djin is a fugitive on the run. She arrives at the getaway boat dressed in a white shirt, slacks, and high-laced boots and sporting a green scarf. At this stage, she is made up as before. But none of this outer cleanliness lasts. Indeed, the nightly downpours of rain in the forest make sure of this, as they mercilessly strip her hard outer shell away. Over the numerous days that the group roams aimlessly around the forest, Djin is progressively divested of her trappings of femininity—in effect, the dangerous body described above disappears. The first accoutrement to go is the painted face. By the second day, all traces of red have gone, and her teeth recede. By day three, her shirt is soiled by the nightly downpours, and her face is starting to look very grubby, her hair knotted. By day four, her shirt is torn on her left shoulder and at the back, revealing unclean, greenish flesh—highlighted by the deep green of the forest (and the tripack color register). Only one button secures her shirt at the front. Thus, not only are her cleavage, shoulder, and back exposed but also her belly. However, this availability of the flesh is not in any way alluring. Her face by now is truly filthy, her lips blistered by the sweltering heat, her hair a mess and held back by her green scarf. Her overall squalidness contrasts with Maria's general lack of dirtiness. Maria is slightly grubby and her shirt somewhat the worse for wear, but she does not look filthy. Nor for that matter do Chark or the priest Lisardi (played by Michel Piccoli—in fact, his white trousers remain remarkably white, although not pristine, throughout this ordeal). Castin, the last member of the group, already wounded and sullied from the pitched battle with the army earlier on, looks no different from when their escape began. Thus, the one for whom there has been a monumental change in terms of outer appearance is Djin. She is, sartorially speaking, totally without artifice, her entire body encrusted with dirt. And as her appearance gradually disintegrates, so a nicer, more considerate person emerges. The dangerous body disappears, the treacherous female is temporarily undone—it is as if the rain has forced the inner body, the former, venal Djin, out into the open. Metaphorically speaking, all the evil and scheming green pus has seeped through to the outer skin, where it lays for all to see. Thus, we believe her when, at the end of their ordeal, she

La mort en ce jardin/Evil Eden/Gina (1956). Djin, her face totally filthy leans over Castin (Charles Vanel).

apologizes to Chark for her previous treachery and tells him she loves him. This time we are convinced by the integrity of her seduction as she leads him off to "bathe" in the lake—to wash herself clean of the cleansing process, as it were.

Sadly, we are as fooled as he is. Once the trappings of fine clothes and jewelry become available, the former Djin begins to reemerge. Miraculously, the fugitives are rescued thanks to Chark's dogged refusal to give up hope. His intrepid exploration of the forest brings him to a lake shore and more miraculously still to a plane that has crashed, leaving no survivors but plenty of loot—fine food, fine clothing, and very expensive jewels. Maria and Chark quickly dress themselves anew. Maria dons a white dress. It is not dissimilar in color and cut (high neck and ballerina skirt) to the one she wore in the first part of the film, but it is more refined. She comes across some jewels, which she, not unreasonably, wants to keep for herself. But the priest swiftly puts her right and proceeds to bury them under a tree where she cannot find them. In the meantime, Djin, who by now has bathed and made love with Chark, is making herself ready. Using one of the dead person's raincoats as a dressing gown, she already has her hair in curlers and is about to make up her face (thanks to another dead person's makeup case). As she quietly reconstructs herself, she observes the priest burying the jewels and subsequently goes to retrieve them. In the next stage of her return to "beauty," her hair is immaculately done, her nails manicured, her face red-lipped once more and her body encased in a deep blue brocade evening gown that is strapless and sleeveless. The haute couture gown hugs the body like a sheath, and its deep blue color resonates with coldness. The masquerade is nearly complete: Djin looks like "a real lady," as Chark puts it. She offers the jewels to Chark (to make up for her former betrayal and theft), and he proceeds to attach the necklace and bracelet to her body. She is truly adorned—from top to toe—in the stolen trappings of another class. Chark remarks: "You are now

La mort en ce jardin/Evil Eden/Gina (1956). Djin restored to her former glory with an added touch of class (with Georges Marchal as Chark).

attired for a new life." Nothing could be further from the truth, as the clothes themselves make clear. She cannot masquerade as what she is not, she has not relinquished her former self, and she pays the ultimate price for not changing from within. There is a suffocating elegance to the gown that gives no space for movement. Djin is completely trapped both by its tubular cut and its stiff, unyielding material. There is literally no way out—and a few seconds later, when she stands fully illuminated by the fire, she is shot dead by Castin (played by Charles Vanel). She falls stiffly backward, all of a piece, as it were. Nothing bends or buckles as she topples over like a statue from its plinth. The phallic, tainted, icy female in all her iconicity is forcibly removed, pushed over to make way for the innocent, virginal and warm-hearted Maria, with whom Chark makes his eventual escape.

Eastmancolor in this film does not flatter Djin/Signoret. The primary color registers, which can so easily be forefronted by this tripack color technology, distort her face by overemphasizing the teeth (through the use of red), reduce the star image to a deeply unattractive green-colored skin, and strap her into a blue dress that makes her body stand out so startlingly she is an unmovable fixed object and therefore an easy target for the male to wipe out as a threat to his masculinity. Two types of women die in that moment: the conforming, constrained, and fetishized exponent of 1950s haute bourgeoisie and the equally fetishized scheming femme fatale of no determined class origin so common to the American film noir of that period. The filthy green woman who emerged between these two types does not meet with salvation in Buñuel's Garden of Evil (incidentally, the British title is *Evil Eden*). Djin will lay petrified on the ground and, like the snake earlier on in the film that was killed by Chark, she will be eaten by the carnivorous ants that show no mercy where available flesh is concerned.

Chapter Six

Working the International Scene—1960–1968

By 1960, Signoret had been consecrated an international star. Having won the Oscar for Best Actress for *Room at the Top*, her career, for all intents and purposes, should have taken off in meteoric fashion. Within the French context, she was finally elevated by the popular film magazine *Cinémonde* to the status of star and won this fanzine's popular and prestigious Victorine prize for Best Actress in 1965. Yet in the eight years immediately following her Oscar she made an eclectic range of films—twelve in all—that were far from typical of an international star's trajectory. Of these twelve films, four were cameo parts. And although eight out of those twelve gave her top billing, she had a central role in only six. Of the other two top billings, the first was an ensemble film (*Ship of Fools*), the other a spy thriller (*The Deadly Affair*), in which she had a key part to play but only a brief time on screen in which to do it. Compared with her greater presence on the international scene, where she made six films, all with top billing, she had only two star roles in French films (*Les mauvais coups* and *Le jour et l'heure*); the rest were cameos, as shown in the table on page 130.

Signoret was thirty-seven when she made *Room at the Top*. By the time she received her Oscar, she was 39—no longer in the first throes of youth, therefore. The French New Wave was taking off and, in the early 1960s, according to the prevailing myths, was seeking out new and unknown talent, especially young actors. Somehow the only female actor to make the crossover from the 1950s to the French New Wave was Jeanne Moreau, only seven years Signoret's junior. Signoret's aging body did not exclude her from the international scene, however, and of the films she starred in, *Adua* was entered for the Venice Film Festival and *Ship of Fools* had several nominations for an Oscar (Signoret and Oskar Werner, among them). Nor did it exclude her from playing the role of *l'amoureuse*. As critic Henri Vinneuil so astutely pointed out at the time: "The more she advances in her career, the better she plays the *amoureuse*, and shows the perfection of a profession known through and through."[1] Olivier Delville remarked that, with her increasing loss of looks, a strange femininity emanated from her in the films of this period. She was no longer beautiful in the conventional sense;

SIGNORET'S FILM ROLES, 1960–1968

Central Roles	Top Billing Roles	Cameos
Adua e le compagne (1960) (Italy)		
Les mauvais coups (1961)		*Les amours célèbres* (1961)
Term of Trial (1962) (UK)		*Dragées au poivre* (1963) (France/Italy)
Le jour et l'heure (1963) (France/Italy)	*Ship of Fools* (1964) (USA)	*Compartiment tueurs* (1965) *Paris brûle-t-il?* (1966)
	The Deadly Affair (1966) (UK)	
Games (1967) (USA)		
The Seagull (1968) (UK)		

rather, she had become fascinating.[2] Her body had taken on a thickness—already hinted at in *Room at the Top*—that allowed her to bring a different depth to the roles she embodied: lover, schemer, murderer. Although Signoret was never typecast, these roles continued in a similar vein as her earlier ones, and were threaded through with the same passion and violence as before—what changed was her reference, as a character, to an aging body (briefly alluded to by her in *Room at the Top*). In a number of the films she portrayed a disgruntled, bitter, disillusioned wife who desperately attempts to shake the marriage back into passion; in others, she was the aging mistress who tries to cling to her lover. In all instances, she peered at her body in mirrors or made reference to her aging. In many of her roles there is a terrible sense in which she is doomed, destined to die from drugs or alcohol, to be murdered, or to be relegated to a dreadful loneliness. Of the twelve films, she comes out as something of a winner in only four of them: *Adua, Le jour et l'heure, Games,* and *Term of Trial.* As for the rest (not including *Paris brûle-t-il?,* in which she appears very briefly), they can be classified as shown here:

Dies of Drugs/Alcohol	Murdered/Killed	Loneliness
Les mauvais coups	*Les amours célèbres*	*Dragées au poivre*
Ship of Fools	*Compartiment tueurs*	*The Seagull*
	Deadly Affair	

CAMEO ROLES TO DIE FOR

In *Paris-brûle-t-il?,* Signoret makes the briefest of appearances. Along with Yves Montand, she had promised director René Clément that she would be in this monumental film about the liberation of Paris. But she has a very minor role, serving drinks to soldiers returning home. This film would be the last in a line that adopted the Gaullist take on the importance of the French Resistance during World War II. Four years later, as de Gaulle lost his censorial grip over France, Jean-Pierre Melville's film about the Resistance, *L'armée des ombres,* along with Marcel Ophuls massive *Le chagrin et la pitié/The Sorrow and the Pity* (1970), finally put an end to the heroization of the French during the Occupation. Clément's film, in its attempt to rehabilitate France, bends history over backward and glosses over all the tensions between the various Resistance factions (the Gaullists and the Communists, to name but two). Given its play with historical truth, one wonders why Signoret and Montand agreed to be in the film. Certainly, Signoret had already made with Clément in 1963—again, much in the Gaullist tradition of *La France résistante—Le jour et l'heure* which would indicate that she had some sympathy with the Gaullist view that France had been a resisting nation. It is significant that a few years later, Signoret (1978, 344) readily admitted that it was not until the Events of May '68 that she finally became totally disabused by the Gaullist myth: "I had come to an end with the sentimentality which secretly had always been with me since 1940." Signoret was on record as stating that the reason she made Resistance films was in an attempt to regain a lost past and a past in which she was not active.[3] Thus, she made a number of such films during her career, but the only two that point to the moral ambiguities surrounding that period are *Against the Wind* (1948) about the Belgian resistance movement (so, in effect, not touching upon France), and *L'armée des ombres,* which, as much as it showed the courage of resistors, also exposed the less heroic side of the Resistance. In the same vein—some twenty years later—Signoret would do the narrative voiceover for *Des terroristes à la retraite* (Mosco, 1983),[4] a film that seriously challenged the French Communist party's take on the Jewish émigrés' involvement in their campaign of terrorism in Paris during the Occupation.

As for the other three cameo roles, the baseline of the film narrative remains constant as that of the older woman clinging to her younger lover and failing. In *Dragées au poivre/Sweet and Sour,* she is reduced to the humiliating role of having to beg on the telephone that her disinterested lover visit her (a role in some ways not dissimilar to her radio performance of Jean Cocteau's *La voix humaine,* 1964).[5] Things take a far more sinister turn in the other two cameo performances from this period. In *Les amours célèbres/Famous Love Affairs,* she attempts to keep her lover by her side by physically maiming him, and in *Compartiment tueurs,* she is the murder victim of her feckless lover, who abuses her clinging ways and finally sets up a very complicated plot to kill her for her money. It is these two latter films that I want now to investigate in relation to Signoret's performance because, beyond the victim/victimizer themes, they raise interesting issues about sexuality.

Les amours célèbres, directed by Michel Boisrond, is made up of four sketches, each about twenty-five to twenty-nine minutes long, supposedly based on the lives of historical people. In fact, the sketches are inspired by *Les amours célèbres* by Paul Gordeaux, which had been adapted as a comic strip of the same name that appeared in the early 1960s in *France-Soir,* a popular daily newspaper. The film sketches portray the love lives of different historical characters ranging from the Middle Ages through the time of Louis XIV to the First Empire and, finally, the late nineteenth century. The sketches are not ordered chronologically; thus, the film begins with Dany Robin and Jean-Paul Belmondo starring in a bedroom farce set in the time of the Sun King. Signoret appears in the second sketch, entitled "Jenny de Lacour," which is a dark melodrama situated toward the end of the nineteenth century. The third sketch zooms back in time to the Middle Ages and stars Alain Delon and Brigitte Bardot. The fourth sketch fast-forwards to the First Empire and stars Edwige Feuillère and Annie Girardot.[6]

Signoret's sketch of the older, scheming, love-panicked woman is located between those of Dany Robin (then aged thirty-five) and Brigitte Bardot (age twenty-eight). Signoret was forty-one. In other words, she is squeezed in between two women whose reputations rested as much on their beauty as on the roles of ingenues that they typically played. Signoret's role is heavy to their light burlesque or comic embodiments as the object of male lust. Robin is a frivolous courtesan, Madame de Monaco, who is currently the mistress of the dashing Count Lauzan (played by Jean-Paul Belmondo). When her beauty catches the eye of the predatory King Louis XIV (played by Philippe Noiret), the count successfully endeavors to prevent the seduction by the king of his seemingly willing mistress. Bardot, the daughter of an apothecary, astounds the Duc de Bavière (played by Alain Delon) with her beauty. He hastily marries her to keep her to himself, thus ending all other men's suffering because she is no longer available. We get to see Dany Robin seminude as she rollicks around in bed with Belmondo. As for Bardot, in the opening sequence of the film sketch, we get our first sighting of her as she rises naked from the river in which she is bathing, observed both by the audience and by the duke, who immediately falls for her.

Of Signoret, there is nothing to see. She is strapped into the formal dress code of late-nineteenth-century decorum: tight-bodiced dresses made in heavy silk (designed at the time by Charles Worth and authentically reproduced by Lila de Nobili for the film). The dress code bespeaks repressed desire, passion even, as does the dark decor of her apartment.[7] Jenny (Signoret) very soon gives up the deep crimson ball gown, worn in the opening sequence, for black. Hints at exotica in the form of fans and Oriental screens are few and far between in the overstuffed interiors, where what dominates is a somber brown ocher. All the trappings of respectability are present, including several aspidistras. Even the billiard table—doubtless the scene of earlier frivolities in the days of the empire—is covered with a brown cloth and used as an ordinary table. The time of the story, the narrator's voice tells us, is the 1880s, under the presidency of Jules Grévy, a rigorously austere man who governed at a time when "love was darker, more cruel and was not permitted in marriage nor allowed outside." Jenny de Lacour is a demimondaine whose beauty formerly broke men's hearts. A prince once blew his brains out for love of her. In earlier times, she was the emperor's mistress. But now, under Grévy, moral probity is the order of the day. She is therefore an anachronism —a relic from the days when courtesan life was part of the moral landscape. In the repressive climate of the late nineteenth century, she is something that has to be hidden away, as the chief inspector makes clear to the investigating Inspector Massot (played by François Maistre): knowledge of her sexual practices must be consigned to the unmentionable.

Decor and dress code tell us a great deal about Jenny's predicament. She is no longer the self-assured beauty of before, and, along with her environment, she represents a struggle—one that is all but lost—between the past and the present. Mirrors that once reflected her former beauty abound but are lost in the draperies and faded heavy furnishings. Even her interactions with her lover bespeak her uncertainty as she fluctuates between using the formal *vous* and the familiar *tu* without any apparent justification. The truth is also that Jenny knows she is an aging beauty and will soon be consigned to oblivion. This is made poignantly clear in the opening sequence when, upon returning home from dancing with her lover, the Comte de La Roche (played by Pierre Vaneck), she immediately goes to the mirror and looks at her face, then pulls on her sagging chin to tighten it. She knows he will soon abandon her. Not only has he nearly wiped out her fortune through his gambling debts, he is just about to make an advantageous marriage. So she plots to keep her lover by blinding him (by getting an accomplice to throw vitriol into his eyes). In this way, so her failing logic would have it, he can no longer witness her decline, and in his infirmity he will be bound to her through dependence. Her plan works, and he eventually proposes marriage.

However, Inspector Massot keeps probing, and had Jenny not played the coquette with him, nor treated him as an inferior socially and sexually, she might have got away with it. She shows off in front of him. First, she gives him a disquisition on sexual practice and status when he feels unable to name the nature of her relationship with the count. "Why can't you say lover?" she asks. Being a lover, she assures him, is "beautiful," but being a fiancé is "foolish;" a husband, "lugubrious." As she says all this, her body is draped in langorous elegance over a sofa, and she gives the inspector the knowing looks of a woman with vast experience in matters of love. Her second, more fatal display of arrogance, however, is to show him her collection of perfume and, most particularly, to show off the newest gadget—the atomizer. Unwittingly, she has given him two vital links: first, to the perpetrator of the criminal act and, second, to the method. The tables are now turned, and the inspector begins to add things up. The supplier of her perfume, Gaudry (played by Antoine Bourseiller), uses vitriol to fix his new synthetic perfumes. And how better to target the count's eyes than with an atomizer? All that remains to be understood is the motive. The inspector sets a trap into which Jenny falls, and the crime is solved. Appalled at being found out, she makes her escape, only to be run over by a horse and carriage—a victim to the increased and speedier (thanks to gaslight) night traffic in Paris.

This is true melodrama at its worst where women are concerned. Jenny de Lacour is punished for crossing several lines. Her transgressions are related to her sexuality, her age, and her class. She transgresses in her active sexuality that contradicts the moral mood of the times. Through her terror of loss through aging, she transgressively destroys the very love she so desperately clings to. And despite her ability to dress the part, her lack of breeding manages to seep through, particularly when it pleases her to shock and behave with vulgarity in front of those she deems her inferiors. Jenny's bold assertions of her sexual power leave her blind to the intellect and astuteness of the inspector. Her impatience at the slowness of things, the investigation, the carriage taking her back home one day (stuck in the same traffic that a few hours later will strike her down), all point to an unconscious truth that, despite what she believes, she is not in control of the situation. In the carriage, her eyes dart from one side to the other, desperately trying to move things forward, to no avail. When she says, in response to the inspector's suggestion, that it might be the count's fiancée who has committed the crime, "One does not use vitriol in high society," she as good as gives herself away. She is nothing but an "adventuress" (as she admits herself in this same conversation) and, therefore, presumably, a woman capable of a base crime. She is not of this upper class, and the inspector knows it. She has used her charms over Gaudry to get him to do her bidding, just as she tries over the inspector. As the *de* in her name so ironically hints at, she is de Lacour—but from the court or the courtyard? It is a cruel love story, and she pays a heavy price for her unseemly desires.

In *Compartiment tueurs,* Costa-Gavras's highly acclaimed first film, Signoret's character again dies a victim of her own lack of astuteness—or so it would appear. She plays the role of an aging actor, Eliane Darrès, who only manages to get small roles in films, radio, theater, and television. Like Jenny de Lacour, it is her lack of self-reflexivity that brings about her downfall. She is a self-important starlet ("I have given ten years of my life to the theater," she declaims at one point). If only she had not been so caught up in her own incessant self-promotion, Inspector Grazzi (played by Yves Montand) might have believed her version of events, and thus her life would have been spared. She actually saw the truth of what happened on the train, but Grazzi does not believe her. The sleeping car murders are in fact a red herring to cover up a more sinister plot of financial intrigue and murder. The film is so named because, after a first murder in the sleeping car, a further three out of the six passengers meet with their death at the hands of an unknown murderer. Until the very end we do not know that it is in fact Eliane's lover, Eric (played by Jean-Louis Trintignant), who has plotted with his male lover, Jean-Loup (played by Claude Mann), to do away with her so he can get his hands on her fortune and they can make their getaway. The idea is to befuddle the police because there is no motive behind any of the murders (except, of course, Eliane's). This befuddling is further assisted by the fact that Jean-Loup is a police officer working with Grazzi on the murders. Because he can provide insider information to his lover, the murderer is always one step ahead of the police.[8]

It is worth pointing out some of the intriguing intertextual links between the film text and the stars themselves. First, there is the clash of culture and class between Grazzi and Eliane Darrès that pastiches Signoret and Montand's own dynamics (Signoret was a well-educated Parisienne and Montand an emergent from the Italian immigré working classes brought up in Marseille). Eliane's hoity-toity educated Parisian manner contrasts marvelously with Grazzi's down-to-earth Marseillais accent. Second, Bambi (played by Catherine Allégret), is one of the travelers in the sleeping car who gets bound up into the plot, and bound up also with a young man with whom she begins an affair. Allégret, Signoret's daughter, was only seventeen at the time, and her character misbehaves in defiance of a putative mother, all the while saying, "If my mother only knew what I was up to" and "What would my mother say if she saw me doing this?"—which, of course, in a sense, with her real mother Signoret present on the set as Eliane, she does know and see. Third, Eliane is terrified of the aging process—something we know that Signoret, far from fearing, did not shy away from. She liked, she declared, the fact that when watching the rushes of *Room at the Top* she saw that she was without artifice, virtually without makeup (incidentally, the way that Montand liked her to be). In short, she was herself, playing her age, and she realized that henceforth she could play roles that resembled her.[9] Finally, in *Compartiment tueurs* Eliane has just been jilted by Eric, but up until that recent event she had given up all her engagements at his insistence and given up on all her artifices (makeup, wigs, hairpieces, etc.). Signoret, never one to like artifices and preferring plain, comfy clothes and virtually no makeup, had been prepared at one point to give up her career for Montand, but he had more or less forced her back into it (Signoret 1978, 120–21). Eliane, in a flashback on her life with Eric, says at one point: "I know that I irritate him and that he thinks I am crazy and that I am a woman who clings on to his youth just as old age pursues me." Eric for his part describes her as a pathetic character who made a lot of dust rather than any sparkle. Yet he rejuvenated her and took her to all the hot spots in Paris in the Saint Germain-des-Prés quarter, where Signoret spent so much of her younger life.

When Eliane was with Eric, she was, as her brother puts it, "his mistress, his mother, his sister." However, she reverts to type once he has abandoned her. And, when Grazzi comes to visit her in her overstuffed apartment, she is heavily made up once more and wearing a very loosely tied peignoir that reveals her black brassiere and her long legs—a hybrid between a femme fatale and an aging coquette. This fragmented set of femininities provides us with a female body and subjectivity that is in excess of meaning: mistress, mother, sister, femme fatale, aging coquette. She cannot be all these things without being in contradiction. Eric complained that she had become "invasive," yet he also said that she was more dust than substance. Again, she could hardly be both. The problem lies with the fact of aging. It is the fate of all women who grow old that society does not know how to place them and would rather they not "be" (unless they play the role of grandmother). Because to "be"—as in being middle-aged—is still to be sexual, even though the contemporary focus on youth attempts to deny that function in women of a certain age. Eliane was living, she says, a passion that was total and terrifying, both to her and to Eric, but for very different reasons. It was terrifying because Eliane knows that in less than a minute it can all be destroyed, and it was terrifying to Eric because such passion in an older woman is unseemly to patriarchy. Thus Eliane's dilemma—excess of meaning—reflects the pain of loss of social and sexual power: she is dust. Grazzi is just as dismissive of her witness account, preferring to accept the only male witness's testimony over hers, as Eric is of her sexual being. In narrative terms, the older woman is punished (murdered) for loving a younger man. She is also punished, it seems, for not realizing that he was even more of a masquerade than she was, in that he was a homosexual. Eliane was not, however, in the final analysis, a dupe to the sadomasochistic nature of her attachment to Eric. As she says to him: "You played with me with the luxury of unnecessary cruelty"— much like a cat with a mouse, one suspects.

Love's Naked Truth: *Les mauvais coups* and *Le jour et l'heure:* Two Exceptions to Signoret's *traversée du désert*

In the post-Oscar period of the early 1960s, Signoret had only two starring roles in French films: *Les mauvais coups* and *Le jour et l'heure*. Earlier chapters have suggested why Signoret's career suffered during this fallow period: political reasons were foremost, but the New Wave effect and her age also played into this. These two films merit being dealt with here as separate studies from her international roles because they mark a temporary ending to her career as a top-billed star in her own country. As we know, she would reemerge in the late 1960s and successfully continue her career until her death in 1985. She was one of the first postwar female stars to make such an important comeback and to confound those in the French film industry and elsewhere who believed that there is no place (in major roles, at least) for women over a certain age, especially not for those who have lost their looks.

In both these films Signoret plays a middle-aged woman consonant with her own age (late thirties to early forties). Desire is at the core of the two texts: in the first, she is desperate to hold onto her man by any means; in the second, she is awakened to desire by a chance encounter with a foreigner. Both films are linked by the authorial hand of Roger Vailland. He wrote the script for *Les mauvais coups,* which is based on his novel of the same name; and in collaboration with René Clément, he wrote the screenplay for *Le jour et l'heure.* In *Les mauvais coups,* all characters suffer from an implacable selfishness, but Signoret makes hers the most palpable in her portrayal of a morally bankrupt woman who knows that she has lost the freshness and beauty of her youth. Vailland, who was full of praise for Signoret's performance, said that she was so good she frightened him.[10] In *Le jour et l'heure,* Signoret's character is certainly not morally bankrupt, but she has chosen to stand outside of history and have nothing to do with the war or the German occupation of France. Thus, she remains closed off from life until a set of circumstances forces her into action, and she becomes an active participant in the Resistance and sexually open after years of denial.

Les mauvais coups was director François Leterrier's first film. He had worked as an assistant with Yves Allégret (Signoret's former husband), and he was the escaped man in Robert Bresson's *Un Condamné à mort s'est échappé/ A Man Escaped* (1956). Much is made, in critical reviews of Leterrier's film of the Bressonian influence.[11] Certainly, the slow pacing and the way the characters' psychology gradually unfolds have something of a Bressonian feel, as does the choice of Reginald Kernan, a nonactor, for the central male role of Milan.[12] The starkness of the exterior shots (filmed in October in Saint-Fargeau and along the Loing River, near Auxerre in the Yonne) makes us think briefly of Bresson. However, Leterrier's shots are lush in their starkness, and at times there is a strong contrast of light and dark. At other times a terrible dampness emanates from the misty morning shots and the general wetness of the landscape. Shot in Dyaloscope, these rural images, because they are spread so wide, obtain a heaviness and darkness that make them painful and violent in their beauty. In short, Leterrier's shots lack the flattened, bleached out effect that Bresson strove for and are richer and more redolent with explicit meaning than Bresson's austere style would ever permit.

In this film, Signoret plays Roberte, the disabused and disaffected wife of a former racing driver, Milan (Kernan). Roberte and Milan have rented a property on a chateau estate for a year, during which time Milan intends to write his autobiography. Roberte, a former Paris socialite, renowned for her brilliance, beauty, and excesses (particularly in gambling), gave up her exciting (to her) life to be with Milan on his racing circuits. But now theirs has become a love-hate relationship, very much in the vein of *Who's Afraid of Virginia Woolf*, directed by Mike Nichols, which was released five years later, in 1966. Roberte drinks heavily to compensate for their lost passion and eventually commits suicide when Milan takes off on his own to start up a racing career once more. But it is what occurs within this petrified relationship, what Roberte does, that is of interest to us here. Milan and Roberte have a sexless marriage. In its place they exchange cruelties, banalities, and sometimes words of love. Milan goes to prostitutes from time to time. Once he had an affair with a close friend of Roberte's, a younger woman named Juliette. For a brief while a triangular relationship was sustained until Roberte kicked Juliette out.

So when the new schoolteacher, Hélène (played by Alexandra Stewart), arrives in the village, Roberte decides to take charge of a situation that she is convinced will lead to Milan's seduction of the young woman. There are three key moments in this process. First, Roberte befriends Hélène. Next, she fills her in on the emptiness of her marriage with Milan. Finally, she attempts to make Hélène over into her own former self, ostensibly in the hopes that it will rekindle Milan's passion for her instead. Milan in the meantime perceives all the traps Roberte is setting and decides to leave before succumbing to Hélène's charms.

In Roberte's play with Hélène there is far more at stake than the above synopsis would indicate. Indeed, a contemporary reviewer recognized that the two women's preoccupation was not really with Milan but with each other. Interestingly, for this critic, it was the only part of the film that gave it any drama and made it come alive.[13] It is worth recalling that this film was made five years before Ingmar Bergman's *Persona* (1966), to which it bears some resemblance, particularly with regard to the relationship between the two women. There is one shot in particular of Roberte and Hélène framed as a reflection in a mirror in which Roberte is making Hélène over as herself that recalls Bergman's more famous shot of Liv Ullmann and Bibi Andersson in a similar pose. Both shots are about fusion of identity and the narcissistic mirror moment, and in this latter respect signal not only the problem of misrecognition but also the death of the subject.

There is an amazing tension between Roberte and Hélène that reaches certain peaks within the narrative, and there are three pivotal scenes or moments that are as much about sexual play as they are about identity and power. These three scenes accrue in intensity. In the first, Roberte, Hélène, and Milan are returning by car from an evening at the casino. Roberte falls asleep on Hélène's shoulder. Once back home, Roberte asks Hélène to fix her a drink. Before, it had always been Milan who carefully measured out the tots of alcohol; now it is Hélène who executes precisely the same gestures (that is, she becomes Milan). Roberte, lying on the sofa, grabs Hélène's wrist and pulls her down to sit next to her. Hélène wipes away Roberte's tears. Roberte falls asleep, and as Hélène makes to leave, she kisses Roberte on the forehead. Milan, impassive, watches. Hélène says to him, "I love her."

The second scene takes place in Roberte's bedroom (again, with Milan as a silent witness). Hélène, who has just come in with Milan from the pouring rain, stands by the window gazing out. Her pose reminds Roberte of the day, ten years earlier, when Milan had declared his love for her and how happy she had been. As she narrates the story, she first draws Hélène closer to her, then pulls her down onto the bed, holding her face tenderly between her two hands. Roberte reenacts the scene of this declaration of love with Hélène as her former self and herself as Milan.

The third scene between the two women occurs without Milan's presence until the very end, when he bursts in on them and, horrified, runs away. This scene is a complex play of mirror images and ultimately seduction—a seduction (through the mirror almost) whereby Roberte seduces Hélène into becoming her former self. It takes place both in the salon and in Roberte's bedroom and is dominated by a series of mirror images (seven in all).

During this set of mirroring images, Roberte dresses Hélène, applies makeup, and does her hair. At each stage she makes comments about Hélène's body— "You have beautiful breasts, you must show them"; "Your hair is so silky"— caresses her hair and shoulders, and, when she has completed the transfor-

Les mauvais coups/Naked Autumn (1961). The narcissistic moment of misrecognition:
Roberte (Signoret) makes Hélène (Alexandra Stewart)
over into her former self.

mation, kisses her on the forehead (returning Hélène's kiss of before). The masquerade is now complete. Roberte draws Hélène in (and into) her own image, all the better to throw her at Milan. Hélène will become Roberte's former self in this travesty. Because Milan has already made it clear that he will not seduce Hélène, the game, in Roberte's mind, becomes one of replaying ten-year-old scenarios, including the one hinted at in the earlier scene. It is for that reason that she takes over Hélène's body completely. The erotic interest where Roberte is concerned is to "become again" the desired body she once was and to use Hélène's body to effectuate that desiring. For Hélène, who by now has become sucked into Roberte and Milan's story, the desire is to become Roberte and thus appeal acceptably (as a rejuvenated Roberte) to Milan. Thus, the two women are desiring a body (Roberte's) that essentially no longer exists but that hangs between them in the mirror, as it were, as a tremendous attraction. They are, in other words, attracted to each other for what they are not (Roberte of ten years ago)—hence the notion of misrecognition and narcissism that runs so strongly through their relationship. The lesbian intertext is quite palpably there and is, in essence, what gives this scene its tension and erotic suspense. Indeed, it is the queering of the film provided by the interaction between the two women that gives it its interest (Milan's presence within the film singularly fails to interest).

As if to underscore the "danger" of this attraction, this whole scene is intercut with shots of Milan outside in the wintry landscape shooting at ravens. He eventually kills one and brings it home, bursts in on the above scene, throws the carrion bird down at Roberte's feet, and storms out. Clearly, Milan fails to remain as the third presence within the mirror—he asserts no patriarchal veto over the misrecognition of desire between the two women. He throws down an emblem of treachery and denunciation and leaves.[14] The strength of and between the two women disempowers Milan; he can only retort by this angry gesture suggesting their perfidy.

It is a bleak and savage film. In this broken marriage, Roberte chooses fight rather than flight (Milan's preferred option). However, rather than just play the role as a vicious and self-destructive woman, Signoret shows us how Roberte is both manipulative and lost, hard and vulnerable, cruel and yet heartbreaking because of her pain. Her voice breaks; at times it carries such sadness, just as at other times, in its harshness, it tears the surrounding silence of the countryside.[15]

In *Le jour et l'heure,* Signoret plays Thérèse Dutheil, who has married into the haute-bourgeoisie. Her husband, presently a prisoner of war, is a textile industrialist. She has two children by him and lives in a luxurious apartment building in the Trocadéro area of Paris—a building that also houses her deeply unpleasant sister-in-law, Agathe (played by Geneviève Page). Agathe happily collaborates with the Nazis while Thérèse remains detached and apolitical. As her voiceover to the trailer of the film makes clear, she has said no to everything and wants to remain there—until, that is, one day when a set of circumstances draws her into having to act and help American pilot Allen Morley (played by Stuart Whitman) make his escape through France to Spain. Having survived the war by ignoring it ("It doesn't concern me," she says in an early interrogation by the French *milice*), she gradually dispenses with her hard shell and bourgeois respectability, thanks to the transforming effect of her love for this man.

Although this Resistance film is fast-paced and thrilling, undoubtedly it is Thérèse's awakening that is at the core of the narrative. Given Signoret's reputation as a *femme engagée* (politically engaged woman), certain critics of the time had trouble accepting Signoret's casting as a woman who lacked political commitment—as *une endormie* (a sleepwalker) who suddenly wakes up to the absurdity of her existence.[16] However, although Thérèse declares that war does not interest her, she gives early signs of defiance. When, at the beginning of the film, she is interrogated by the French *milice* and is slapped for her seeming insolence she does not react other than to stare at the officer, pick up her belongings, and, once outside the building, wash her face clean from his touch. Although Signoret may appear to be cast against her true persona (at least in the first part), in fact, in her role as Thérèse, she embodies the story of many women whose lives were profoundly affected by the war and who found a strange kind of freedom and sexual liberation during that period.

Married in 1933, we pick up on Thérèse's story in May 1944. We do not know of the circumstances that drove her into this marriage, which forced her to leave her much loved native village (an idyllic space in her consciousness). By the time we meet up with her, her only interest is to ensure her children's safety and their survival through the war. Having spent the weekend with her relatives in the country, she is intent on getting back to Paris with her suitcases packed with food for the children. An old school friend, Antoine (played by Michel Piccoli), gives her a lift. Unbeknown to her, he is a member of the Resistance, and hidden in the back of his truck are three fighter pilots shot down by the Germans (two British and Allen, the American). When the truck breaks down and the men jump out to help, she reacts angrily at Antoine's dissimulation. But one thing leads to another, and she finds herself having to give shelter to the American pilot.

Her chance meeting with Allen is the moment when, as director René Clément said, "the war comes and finds her and awakens her."[17] Until meeting Allen, she has lived her married existence bound by rules (there are, she later tells him, "too many rule makers in my life"). Once she brings him into her home (to hide him until he can make his escape), she starts to assert herself against these rules. She begins to challenge her awful sister-in-law, Agathe, both in words and in action. Allen also helps her to loosen herself from the entanglements that stunt her life. The real turning point for her occurs in a remarkable scene in which the two of them, in complete silence, tacitly acknowledge their feelings for each other. During an air raid, which interrupts their candlelight dinner, Allen asks her to go down into the cellar with her children. She refuses, asserting thereby her desire to remain with him. At this point he almost kisses her, but a nearby bomb explodes, shattering the moment. Everything is pitch dark for a while until he calls out for her, and we see her backlit from the fired buildings outside. She is standing on one side of an enormous tapestry loom, he on the other. The strings of the loom are lit so that they simultaneously look like Cupid's harp/ heart strings and a spider's web. The double metaphorical value of the loom as an object of love that could unite them or a symbol of all that which separates them (rules, her husband) is powerfully felt as the shot is held for several agonizing seconds before fading.

In the previous sequence to this one, Thérèse had asked Allen, her voice full of tears, "What do you do when you can't go on anymore?" His response: "I apply the rule: Never entomb yourself." In this conversation it transpires that both Allen and Thérèse hate rules. But Allen tells her that he felt he had to fight this war even if it meant having to obey rules. He could not ignore what was going on and entomb himself. He shows the way by example—and it is one that Thérèse begins to embrace. She cuts through the conventions that bound her. After the bomb raid sequence, the tone of her voice changes, aided perhaps by Allen's drunken declaration of love the following day. In twenty-four hours the tear-driven voice has gone, and she starts to act decisively, first in asserting her right to privacy by taking her apartment key off Agathe, and second, by announcing to Allen that she will take him to the station—a decision that accidentally leads to her boarding the train to Toulouse with him.

Emboldened by these decisive gestures, Thérèse grows in stature, and crucially it is she who safely delivers Allen to the *maquis* in the French Pyrenees. Without her naive courage and defiance this would have been impossible. She is not set up heroically, however. Indeed, before their escape from Paris there are several occasions when her ignorance of the Resistance's ways results in her making mistakes that put people's safety in jeopardy (for example, she talks too loudly when she passes a message on to a cell member in the church, and she telephones a safe haven unaware the phone might be tapped). But that naivete also gives her tremendous strength because it allows her to behave with candor. Thus, when she and Allen are arrested in Toulouse and taken for questioning, it is her comportment that is remarkable for its unhesitating rawness and that contributes eventually to the authorities' decision to set the couple free. When one of the torturers grabs at her breasts, she resoundingly slaps him, and he is forced to let go.[18] While being questioned by Chief Inspector Marboz (played by Pierre Dux), the head of the French *milice*, it becomes clear that they have mistaken her for one of the Resistance leaders, a certain Sophie. Thérèse reacts spontaneously by laughing, not just at their mistake but also at the ludicrous nature of their mistake (she knows she could never *be* Sophie). Marboz promises her her life and Allen's if she will tell him where the head of the *maquis* (code named Titus) is hiding out. The point is, of course, that even if she wanted to she could not betray "Titus"—and this adds to her, by now, hysterical laughter. She realizes she will be executed for what she does not know. This realization does not lead her to despair, however. Rather, she attempts to turn the situation to her advantage and suggests to Marboz that because the war is nearly at an end, he could help his case if he were to release her and the American. He appears to take no notice of this suggestion and orders their transportation to the Gestapo headquarters. Once in the police van and sensing that all is lost, Thérèse declares her love to Allen, and, finally, they kiss. A few minutes later, they are dropped off some kilometers outside Toulouse and left to fend for themselves. Marboz has heeded her words.

The metaphorical web of the loom by now is in shreds and has made way for the exchange of love. What is remarkable is that its decomposition occurs in virtual silence. Apart from two occasions when the silence is broken, neither Allen nor Thérèse has spoken of their love—all has been revealed through the gaze, through a series of endless looks, not all of which have necessarily been exchanged.[19] Thus, the first time Thérèse sees Allen, it is in the rearview mirror of Antoine's truck, as he helps to push it into action once more. This shot is matched a little later by one in the truck when Allen, sitting in the back of the truck, peers through the cab's rear window and looks down at her as she sleeps. Much later, while on the train to Toulouse, Thérèse looks down at Allen with a similar loving glance as they sit in the crowded corridor. He is unaware of her gaze, just as he is unaware of the expression of terror on her face once he is arrested on the train a few moments later and dragged through the sea of passengers by the Gestapo officer. Her face expresses it all. Completely distraught in her belief that all is now lost, her face progressively decomposes. The look of love has turned into the anguished expression of grief. There is such humility in these various unrelayed sets of looks, a poignancy also, that when, on the rare occasions they do get to gaze on each other and embrace, the love we feel between them is one of tender vulnerabilty before it is one of violent passion. Thus, at the end of the film, as Thérèse's expression makes clear, their separation is almost unbearable. In this shot, Thérèse/Signoret makes the sense of loss tangible through an intense play with silence and the barest of facial movements. It is a scene familiar to many women of that generation for whom the war was an extraordinary, often destabilizing, period in their lives.

Signoret's performance captures perfectly the madness yet peculiar elation of this time lived, almost ineluctably, on a knife edge. She felt it was one of her best films, after *Dédée d'Anvers* and *Casque d'Or*.[20] In certain respects the heroines' trajectories are not dissimilar. All three characters find a new sense of fulfillment through an intense experience of love that liberates rather than entraps them, and in each case they experience the devastating truth about the impermanence of things—a knowledge from which they learn rather than succumb to. As such, *Le jour et l'heure* is more than a Resistance film; it is a film with strong feminist resonances, speaking as it does to an authentic moment in women's history.

AN INTERNATIONAL CAREER 1960–1968—THREE SETS
OF STARRING ROLES

British Social Realism in *Term of Trial*

We can date Signoret's international career from 1960 with her performance in Antonio Pietrangeli's *Adua e le compagne*. However, since I have been unable to see it, in this section I shall focus exclusively on Peter Glenville's *Term of Trial,* an intense, claustrophobic social realist drama tightly shot by Ossie Morris and starring Signoret opposite Laurence Olivier. Signoret made this film three years after *Room at the Top,* with which it has some affinities, not least of which is the same Woolf production company (now renamed Romulus Films). Similarly, the film is not without its own controversy in regard to sexual issues. Although it is not a *Lolita*-type film (Stanley Kubrick's *Lolita,* also shot by Ossie Morris, came out in 1961), a core thread to the film is a fifteen-year-old schoolgirl's infatuation with middle-aged schoolmaster Graham Weir (played by Olivier) that turns nasty when he very gently rebuffs her advances. Humiliated by his rejection of her, she accuses him of indecent assault, and the case goes to court.

Sarah Miles plays the "knowing, sensual innocent"[21] Shirley Taylor, and her performance as the awkward but determined teenager is utterly convincing. However, she is no match for the schoolmaster's wife, Anna (played by Signoret). The frailty of her pubescence stands out against Anna's mature body. Her voice pleads rather than seduces. But, for a while, she is a force to be reckoned with. In order to obtain access to the schoolmaster, she persuades him to give her extra English lessons, and eventually a peculiar triangular relationship is established between the three main characters. This is graphically illustrated at one point in the film when all three are seated around the table having tea in the Weirs' home. For Graham, Shirley embodies the child he and Anna could never have. As far as Shirley is concerned, she is the appropriate rival to Anna for Graham's affections. Only Anna sees things as they are, and it is instructive that the three-shot of them at the table is taken from her point of view. To her mind, Shirley represents not so much a threat to her marriage as a young woman in the throes of her first sexual infatuation, which could get out of hand. Later in that same sequence Anna warns Graham of the situation and tells him to be careful in case Shirley gets hurt. Anna clearly sees it as Graham's responsibility to monitor the sensitive dynamics, but he laughs it off.

Graham's inability to heed his wife's words and his rather naive refusal to understand Shirley's quite explicit advances until it is too late do not necessarily mark Graham out as simply a weak and spineless man, as some critics of the time argued.[22] His story is more complex. He is a man who is so wounded by his lack of a child of his own that he can only see the few bright schoolchildren he teaches, including Shirley, as just that, children. He is also a man who has been hurt professionally because of his pacifism during the war. It cost him any high-powered teaching post he might have anticipated in light of his qualifications. He accepts, unquestioningly, his impoverished state, but in his wife's eyes he lacks ambition. In Graham we see a man who suffers both from blind spots and a tired resignation to his lot in life. He carries this resignation around with him to the pubs he frequents, where he drinks too much, and into his home, where he wearily submits to his wife's disparaging comments. He plays the passive to her aggressive. Thus, in effect, the film's real drama is between the husband and wife and their struggling relationship that fluctuates between passion, anger, tenderness, and open resentment. The other drama, Shirley's misguided attraction and Graham's fumbling ineptitude—for he is undoubtedly flattered by her attention—acts as a powerful foil and forces a number of outcomes, which ultimately serve to save the marriage. If Graham does not succumb to Shirley's seductive charms, it is not because he is not tempted, but more that he is fully aware how much he loves his wife—something he declares persistently to both Anna and Shirley. What causes a radical shift in Graham, however, is the trial and subsequent acquittal. In a long and impassioned speech from the dock, he stands firm by all he believes in and denounces British hypocrisy for deliberately misreading what he describes as an innocent love. He tells the truth: there was an attraction, it was not acted upon, and, had Shirley not been pushed to accuse him of wrongdoing by her parents, then what was so special between them would not have been destroyed by filthy-minded prurience. His display of integrity brings Shirley to withdraw her false accusations. Reinstated at school, he becomes more assertive still. He finally stands up to his bullying headmaster by refusing to resign. Then, at the very end of the film, he engages in a spirited game of verbal poker with his wife whereby he prevents her from leaving him.

This film is something of a hybrid between British social realism and British New Wave. It depicts quite faithfully the various struggles at that time between generations and questions of class. In the early 1960s, teenagers were becoming rebellious and sexualized, quite prepared to challenge their parents' stricter codes of behavior. There is an angry young man in the form of Mitchell (played by Terence Stamp), an impudent teenager who cannot wait to leave school. But there is also the angry middle-aged woman, Anna Weir, who is desperate to leave the miserable confines of the anonymous uncultured northern town Graham has brought her to and find a life that more resembles her memory of a former Parisian life. Shirley is trying to better herself in order to leave her working-class roots so grievously (to her) embodied by her parent's lack of culture and capital. Another pupil, Thompson (played by Ray Holder), who is cruelly bullied at home, also aspires to better things in life through education. But the focus is not, in the end, the youth class. Thompson evaporates after forty minutes. Mitchell disappears just over halfway through. Only Shirley remains to pursue her pathetic fabrications, later to be dragged back into the bosom of her family. The driving force of the film in terms of enigma is whether the Weirs' marriage will survive. Thus, the film is ultimately a portrait of a marriage. We sense the very real physicality of Anna and Graham's relationship in all its complexity. They torment each other. He puts her down in front of others in small but insidious ways, for example, by revealing to their snobby dinner guests (whom he insisted on inviting) that she was a barmaid during the war, or ridiculing her in front of Shirley for calling his study "the library." She, in turn, takes every opportunity when they are at home together alone to remind him of his lack of ambition. But they also love each other, and just as they are at times brutally honest with each other, they equally have a strong sexual relationship. On several occasions we see them passionately drawn to each other. Anna is always alluringly dressed, with her low-cut dresses and décolleté lingerie. Graham is conventionally dressed but conveys a schoolboyish charm, exemplified by the way he tucks his thumbs (rather than his hands) into his trouser pockets. It is this charm that seduced Anna in the first place, as she frequently reminds him (even in her rows with him). Furthermore, they defend each other. Anna literally stands by Graham's side when the police officer comes to their house with Shirley's allegations of indecent assault. Graham defends his wife against Shirley's criticisms that she is cruel and bitter. Anna believes in her husband's innocence and is not only present throughout the trial but also visibly engaged. It is significant that, during Shirley's testimony and cross-examination, it is Anna, not Graham, who is in the frame. We see her from Shirley's point of view from the witness box. Thus, we see Anna's reactions both to Shirley's accusations and to the undermining of them by the defense lawyer. Through this mise-en-scène, which excludes Graham, it is as if the two "rivals" are battling it out.

As if to emphasize the strength of this nonetheless difficult marriage, the camera mostly holds Anna and Graham in two-shots in the domestic interior scenes, a strength that is underscored by Anna's various dress codes (see the table below). Thus, we are privy to the full impact on both of them of what they say and do when they fight and when they are loving. Signoret and Olivier are well matched, his self-deprecating irony only occasionally giving way to real anger in the face of her more energized fury and despair as she fluctuates between love and near contempt for him.[23] We first meet Anna in the bathroom. The camera catches her in medium close-up in the mirror as she is brushing her teeth. She is furious that Graham has humiliated her in front of their dinner guests. This develops into general anger about his job. Intermittently, she stops her brushing action to turn to Graham and snarl at him. She further punctuates her fury by spitting out words and water into the basin at the same time. Graham leans passively against the door, defending himself, only just, by repeating lines he must have delivered time and again in the face of this kind of onslaught. But then things shift. Still arguing, Anna removes her dressing gown, ready to take a bath; she is in medium close-up, so we see her exposed shoulders and slip straps, one of which has fallen off her shoulder. Her facial expression, however, has lost its hard edge and now is full of amused irony that is warm and sexualized. The steam from the hot water rises, as does Graham's desire for her. Very soon they are locked in a tender and mutually desiring embrace. The anger has subsided, the pain and sorrow dissolved.

We see this pattern repeated several times during the film, all within the domestic sphere. There are four key sequences, two that occur in the first forty minutes of the film and two that occur in the second half, one after Graham's arrest and the other after the court case. These two sets of sequences are separated by one other interior sequence, in which Shirley comes to the Weirs' house. The following outline of these scenes demonstrates the use of changing point of view (POV) and camera work—close-ups (CUs), medium close-ups (MCUs), and medium shots (MSs)—to reveal the relationship between the protagonists.

As we can see in the first three of these four sequences, the passive-aggressive dynamic follows the same pattern. Although this dynamic is potentially very destructive, ultimately it ends up being a tool to bring them closer. Thus, Anna gets more and more incensed as Graham attempts to defend himself. Yet when he gives up, this only increases her anger. Things threaten to snap, but then something gets said or done that breaks the tension, and peace, even love, is restored. Signoret and Olivier play it as if they had lived it all their adult lives. In their squabbles, her voice is raised as she seethes inside. His voice, by contrast, is soft, conciliatory, mellifluously even, as—ever the pacifist—he seeks to smooth things over. But he too can erupt with passion, coming out of his timid shell, which is presumably why she stays. But it is a close call, one feels. On two occasions she makes the point that she wants more fire. During her angry scene in the kitchen (sequence 2), she says, "Show some spunk . . . go on and hit me if

Term of Trial (1962). Portrait of a marriage: desire in the bathroom
(Anna/Signoret and Graham/Laurence Olivier).

you like . . . go and get another woman . . . cut loose . . . do something human
for a change. . . . I can't go on like this . . . in a vacuum. . . . There's nothing
even to fight." And right at the end of the film, in the second bedroom sequence
(sequence 4), she declares: "As far as I am concerned, I'd much rather be badly
treated by a man with some spirit than have to put up with your endless mush."
The curious thing is that he more or less fulfills her demands. He "almost" has
an affair (with Shirley). He does slap his wife—in the first bedroom sequence
(sequence 3). And he does "treat her badly" in that, in the closing sequence, he

1. Bathroom (11 m. 53 s. into film):	2. Kitchen (20 m. 32 s. into film):	(34 m. 25
Anna in CU reflected in mirror; launches several "attacks" on Graham shot in MCU on both; scene ends with embrace in two-shot CU. Dissolve. Anna in deshabillée. (length: 2 m. 27 s.)	Anna, cross at having to wait for Graham, gets crosser as she puts out his food. Her outpourings are punctuated by domestic gestures, all of which are loaded with annoyance. This culminates in her lighting a cigarette with vigor. Meanwhile, Graham sheepishly holds his hands between his legs. Scene is shot in a series of shot-countershots in MS, with Anna standing and Graham sitting (high angle on him from Anna's POV, low angle on her from Graham's POV). Brief respite as they talk of the child they never had. Graham stands next to her; she is nearly in tears. She then explodes again and calls him a coward: series of shot-countershots in CU. They separate. She sits in living room, he ascends stairs. Shot from his POV high angle on Anna as she apologizes. Dissolve. Anna is wearing a low-cut dress under a cardigan, showing her cleavage. (length: 5 m. 10 s.)	s. into film) Shirley comes to the Weirs' house.

lies to her by saying that he was guilty, the court had got it wrong, and he had assaulted Shirley. At this point, Anna gets to slap him back in her outrage (either at his lie or his infidelity). Signoret said she found it almost impossible to do this scene: "I have never hit a man in my life," she declared in an interview.[24] Indeed, slapping Olivier with conviction must have been difficult, and you can see her hesitation, but it actually enhances the performance. As Anna, she is in two minds whether to believe him or not. By slapping him she is doing one of two things. Either she is accepting what he has said as true, or she is agreeing to collude with his lie. To not slap him would be to acknowledge that he is weak ("a mouse") and that she must carry out her threat to leave him.

The two bedroom sequences can be seen as mirroring each other (arguments leading to a slap, then reconciliation and close embrace). But the difference with the second bedroom sequence is that there are moments when the couple is separated in CUs. There is space for them to measure each other up. You can see Anna/Signoret doing this with her eyes and Graham/Olivier more with his mouth and hands. She is asking herself should she believe him, he is desperately hoping she will. Up until that moment she thought she knew him inside out. She appeared to be the domineering one of the couple—as the kitchen sequence, in part, tends to confirm (with the angled shots). Now the power base has shifted. He has the power to play a card that might keep her, she has the power to leave. The point is that Graham has broken free from his former weak passivity and has discovered strategies within him that, though not aggressive, are certainly not submissive. Thus, the constant holding of the couple in two-shots that we witnessed in the previous bedroom scene, although it could indicate that they are solid as a couple despite their arguing, could imply that there

3. Bedroom (74 m. into film):
The entire sequence is in two-shot MS. Camera 1 is on his side of bed, camera 2 on hers. Anna and Graham are in bed; they are discussing the case. Camera 1 POV. She is quite reasonable to start with but gets crosser. Camera 2 POV from her side of bed as Graham starts to get agitated. He pleads with her that they "stop lashing at each other." Back to camera 1 POV, his side of bed. She reaches over him to get a cigarette, which she shares with him. She then asks him what will happen if he loses his job. They start arguing again. She again taunts him for being a coward: "I bet it's pure funk that stopped you. You didn't have the guts to go through with it." He is so riled he shouts at her and slaps her. Camera 2 POV, her side. They argue more calmly until he begs her: "We must stop tormenting each other." Camera 1 POV, his side; he is lying on her thigh. She reaches out to him and tells him she has got him the number of a lawyer. Camera tracks into MCU on both. Fade out. Anna wears décolletée nightie.
(length: 6 m.)

4. Bedroom (98 m. into film):
Graham has come home to discover that Anna is going to leave him. She has found the gun he intended to use if he lost the case. This time she is no longer cross. She is waiting for him in the bedroom to announce her decision. She is calm and reasonable. Sequence opens with high-angle full shot of the two: Graham is standing by the bed; she is sitting on it. (It is not his POV.) She accuses him of being a coward. He sits down on the other side of bed. Cut to two-shot MCU from Graham's side. She starts to taunt him, saying she wishes he had done it. He tells her that in fact Shirley's original accusation was true. Cut to a series of single-shot CUs as Anna accuses him of lying and he denies it, ending on a CU of Anna. She moves round to his side of the bed, still in CU, camera tracking—her eyes flicker, registering her surprise and anger. She slaps him. Cut to MCU of Graham as slap lands. Camera tracks with Anna to mirror. MCU on her in mirror with Graham in background. Cut to a series of separate CUs as they discuss (not fight about) the situation, ending in MS of Anna smiling ironically. She moves toward Graham, saying she will have to keep an eye on him. He pulls her down onto him. Camera tracks into a CU of the two of them. Dissolve.
Anna is wearing a low-cut costume showing her cleavage.
(length: 5 m.)

is a strong symbiosis that keeps them together. Viewed in this light, the new dynamics of the closing sequence, where there is separation as well as togetherness, suggest that there is a possibility that Anna and Graham have renewed themselves and found a better way to relate. So there is both optimism at the end (Anna: "You're less of a mouse than I thought") and a degree of uncertainty (Graham: "Am I, dear?") as to how this will be sustained. Old patterns die hard.

The Mother of Lost Causes: *Ship of Fools* (1964) and *The Deadly Affair* (1966)

Among the films Signoret made on the international scene during this period is her first American film, *Ship of Fools,* which arguably came some thirty years late (if we recall that she had signed with Hollywood in 1949[25]). The film was

Term of Trial (1962). Relations of power: Anna (Signoret) appears as
the dominating one of the couple.

made by the independent producer-director Stanley Kramer, a filmmaker who
swam against the tide and whose films dealt with the flaws in the fabric of American life. In his autobiography, Kramer (1997, 2) speaks of himself as being "the
most picketed American producer in American film history." Because he wanted
to "run his own show" (4), he established his own production company in the
late 1940s. A little later, in 1953, after a two-year stint as an independent with
Columbia Studios, during which time he felt too constrained, he set himself up
as producer-director.

Kramer had a reputation as a filmmaker with strong moral principles (on
questions of racism, see *The Defiant Ones*, 1958; on Nazism and fascism, see
Judgment at Nuremberg, 1961, which won an Oscar for Best Actor for Maximilian Schell). During the 1950s he supported as best he could victims of the
McCarthy witch-hunt, not because he was anti-American and pro-Communist
but because he was a fervent liberal. *Ship of Fools* speaks out against all types
of intolerance. Based on the novel by Katherine Anne Porter and set in 1933—
the year Adolf Hitler was made chancellor of Germany—the film relates the separate but interwoven adventures of a diverse group of voyagers aboard a
German passenger freighter bound from Veracruz, Mexico, to Bremerhaven,
Germany. En route, it stops at Cuba to pick up a Spanish noblewoman (Signoret), who is being deported to Tenerife for acts of sedition. She had supported
the Mexican workers' strike in Cuba against their redundancy and subsequent

virtual kidnapping to work on sugar plantations in Tenerife (Kramer 1997, 203). She had also embraced the Cuban revolutionaries' cause. Given Signoret's characterization, as well as her and Kramer's political stances, we could have expected a meeting of minds. Doubtless, during the shooting of the film, there was because Signoret gives an exceptionally moving performance as the morphine-addicted countess who espouses lost causes. However, shortly after the release of the film in France, in 1965, Signoret publicly lambasted Kramer for his sins of omission. Here is what she said:

> You know how much I love America, but the Americans have a blind spot in their brains when it comes to the crimes of the Nazis. They immediately think of the Jews, only the Jews, as if the Nazis hadn't first and foremost emprisoned communists; a man like you [Stanley Kramer] does not have the right to make a film on Nazism and omit the communists, because in that omission there is a lot of malice and a lot of hypocrisy.[26]

There is some striking bad faith in this statement because the film is based on a novel that refers, historically, to the early 1930s. The novel itself is set in 1931; Kramer moved it forward to 1933 precisely because that was the year Hitler came to power and he believed it was important to talk about this impending threat to democracy (Kramer 1997, 204). But this was a period before the Communists were actively persecuted, even though the National Socialist views on Jews and Bolshevism were well known. Furthermore, Kramer's film is not "just about" the Jews; it is far more broad in its attack on intolerance. Bigotry and racism are as much at the forefront of his critical eye as is anti-Semitism. Finally, Signoret may have been unaware of Kramer's courageous stance during the McCarthy era, but she certainly knew him to be a man with strong liberal views, and this was a motivating reason to work with him. It is hard to understand where this attack comes from, particularly since she had abandoned her close association with communism by the late 1950s.[27]

We need to recall that this was a period in the United States of considerable internal and external political strain. Barry Goldwater, a staunch right-wing Republican, was running against Lyndon Johnson for president. Soviet-American relations were at a very low point, and, within the United States, blacks still suffered massively from racial abuse and discrimination. In this climate, Kramer stood out as a man who was prepared to make films about issues that would not go away (Kramer 1997, 2). In her autobiography, Signoret (1978, 297–300) spoke warmly of this film's production and her time spent with the whole team of actors. She reminisced about a couple of outings made with Kramer, both of which point to the contemporary issues at hand and, one feels, to Kramer's engagement with the world. The first trip was to a track meet, at Los Angeles Colosseum, between U.S. and Soviet athletes, the first of its kind in America. Inside the stadium, crowds cheered their heroes, mostly blacks, yet, as Signoret remarks, how many would have invited these same black people into their homes for tea (299). Outside, the bigoted, anti-Communist and racist John Birch Society handed out leaflets claiming the Soviet athletes were undoubtedly spies (300). This was an experience, then, that spoke metaphorically of this period of suspicion and hate. The second excursion was to a drug rehabilitation center. The visit was not purely to give Signoret firsthand experience of the effects of drug addiction but also, more humanely, to show her how critical a problem this affliction was for young people.

In *Ship of Fools*, Signoret gets second billing after Vivien Leigh, whose last film this was. Leigh plays the role of a "gay divorcée" who—as one of the ship's fools—periodically and unsuccessfully makes these cruises on the hunt for a new husband. Oskar Werner plays the ship's doctor, Lee Marvin a bigoted and racist has-been baseball player, and José Ferrer a pro-Nazi German. The dwarf actor Michael Dunn is the gently ironic but tolerant and observant narrator of the film. Finally, among the major roles, Heinz Ruehmann is the kindhearted but deluded Jew who is returning home to Germany. In response to Hitler's accession to power and his anti-Semitic position, Ruehmann simply declares: "We are over a million Jews in Germany; what is he going to do, kill us all?"

Kramer shot the film in black and white because he felt the "theme was just too foreboding for color" (Kramer 1997, 205). He had wanted to cast his good friend and partner on many films, Spencer Tracy, in the role of the doctor but Tracy was too ill to work (he did, however, come on the set to watch the proceedings, along with Katharine Hepburn). Instead, Kramer cast Oskar Werner, who was "fantastic in his role . . . [because] he was able to convey power as well as sympathy, pathos and love" (206). According to Kramer, nobody liked Werner, and he was difficult to work with even though, in front of the camera, he was "a true genius" (206). Kramer added that casting Werner opposite Signoret was also a stroke of genius. From the moment of their first scene together—when he eventually relents (or rather, is seduced) and gives her morphine—"their relationship is the emotional and dramatic center of the picture" (207).

Although Leigh's name is the first billed, she very much plays the foil to Signoret's Spanish countess. Her hard, embittered Mary Treadwell, a woman disillusioned by life and love, contrasts with Signoret's warm sensuality, a woman who accepts the ironies of life but is ever open to new opportunities and experiences. Physically, the two women could not be more distinct. Leigh's body is thin, starved of nutrition (or love), her face lined by life and unhappiness. Signoret, with her lived-in body and face, is slightly plump and warmly attractive. Leigh is always fully clothed in top fashion designs (by Jean-Louis). There are no top designers for the countess. Other than the clothes she boarded with, she has only one other dress (an evening gown). We do, however, get to see her in her night attire in her cabin and lying in bed. And it is easy to see why the doctor is so simply seduced by her, since she is luscious in her state of semi-undress, her body and face inviting him in. As the countess, Signoret is unafraid to be who she is, intelligent, perceptive, but also vulnerable and needy (Kramer 1997, 208). Her humor is funny and ironic, not acerbic and cutting like Leigh's character. The countess tried to help the poor, she was the "voice of the politically disenfranchised" (208), actions for which she is to be emprisoned. Mary Treadwell, one suspects, has only ever helped herself: "She is a drunk in the picture, filled with venom and dreaming about earlier days when she was beautiful, popular and happy—forgetting that she was never actually happy" (208). Indeed, she spreads her venom and unhappiness over all whom she encounters. In the film, she offers several disquisitions on love, all of them full of bitterness as she waits for fear and loneliness to do their work, whereas the countess lives her feelings in the moment. Presently, they are those of love for the doctor. She is unafraid to try, willing to be vulnerable and suffer loss again, as she knows she will.

Although Vivien Leigh received top billing, it is really Signoret and Werner who are the core of the film, as Kramer (1997) noted. He also acknowledged that Leigh's role had less depth than Signoret's (208). Leigh was already ill by this time and would die two years later, in 1967, of tuberculosis. But she had also become ravaged by the breakup of her marriage to Laurence Olivier. Given her mental and physical frailty, both Kramer and Leigh knew she could no longer obtain starring roles, but he wanted to cast her despite the fact that "every producer in England and America knew how difficult it was to get a performance out of her" (208–209). She was, as he says, "a tortured soul" and must have recognized herself in the role (208). Her precarity as an actor meant her role was necessarily more secondary. Indeed, in terms of length, Signoret is on screen for 18 percent of the film to Leigh's 12 percent. Signoret is held more in close-ups and medium close-ups; Leigh more in medium shots, to avoid close scrutiny of her damaged looks (which she cruelly ironizes at the close of the film when, in very tight close-up reflected in the mirror, she lards her face up with makeup). More significantly, in terms of average appearance time, Signoret is on screen ten times, at an average rate of two and a half minutes, compared with Leigh's eleven appearances, averaging one and a half minutes. In short, Signoret has more time to make things happen. Arguably, Leigh has less time to falter. Having said this, she produces a remarkable scene toward the end of the film when, completely drunk and on her way back to her cabin, she breaks into a Charleston. It is a heartbreaking moment when star persona and role merge as one. Leigh's story now takes over that of Mary Treadwell, as she is flooded by memories of her past when she was beautiful and not the overpainted wreck she has become.[28]

Leigh functions as a foil also in terms of acting technique. As a Southern belle from Virginia, she plays her role in a slightly excessive/phatic way that is reminiscent of (or, indeed, pays homage to) her two great Oscar-winning performances as Scarlett O'Hara and Blanche Dubois.[29] To her overplaying comes Signoret's and Werner's underplaying. The countess and the doctor's life weariness is tempered by a softness that allows them to be touched deeply by each other's vulnerability. Neither the doctor nor the countess are well; he has a weak heart, she is a morphine addict (for which she makes no excuses). It is their love affair that structures this otherwise proliferating narrative. Their relationship begins and ends with the countess's arrival and departure from the boat. Between these two moments there are four matching scenes:

Scene 1 (length: four minutes and forty-five seconds): This first meeting and exchange with the doctor (as with the other three scenes) is shot entirely in medium close-up (shot-countershot). Signoret is clad in a satin robe, which she has to remove for the doctor to examine her. She teases him: "Are you sure you are the ship's doctor?" She looks very sexy in her black slip as she humorously complies with the doctor's commands to breathe in and out. It takes time to win him around because he refuses to give her sleeping medication to begin with. But they talk all the time, gently, teasingly. The doctor becomes less stiff as time progresses. However, once the countess's facial expression shifts from humorous irony to clear despair he decides to help her with a morphine injection. The point of this sequence is not just to demonstrate that as a doctor he is humane (he also stays with her until she falls asleep), but to establish the credibility of

Countess arrives on board the ship; she is cheered on by a huge crowd of Mexican farmworkers.	*Scene 1 (her cabin):* The doctor comes; they talk, She is in a state of undress; she "seduces" him, and he nurtures her (gives her morphine).	*Scene 3 (her cabin):* The effects of drug withdrawal force her to leave the dinner dance. She goes to her cabin; he follows and nurtures her (gives her morphine). She is in a state of undress. They talk; they kiss.
	Scene 2 (on deck): She watches over him as he sleeps (nurture). They talk; she "seduces" him.	*Scene 4 (his cabin):* The effects of his weak heart force him to bed. She nurtures him (tucks him into bed), reads to him; they talk.
		Countess leaves ship, having embraced the doctor goodbye in her cabin. She leaves in silence and alone; there is no audience watching over her or cheering.

their love affair. The exchange is flirtatious, yet discreet, the erotic warmth quite tangible.

Scene 2 (length: three minutes and fifty-five seconds): In the previous scene, the doctor nurtures the countess. But she also gives him something that he has not received in a long time: tenderness and warmth from a woman. This second scene reverses the nurturing, albeit at a more symbolic level. The doctor has been asleep on deck for some time, and the countess has been watching over him for the best part of half an hour (she informs him). She has tucked a rug around him, which she now adjusts with care. She smiles tenderly over him as he awakens. In their conversation that follows she enumerates adjectives that best describe him, ending on the assertion that he is "charming." He is clearly touched and pleased, and it is obvious that he is being slowly seduced by the genuine attention she pays him.

Scene 3 (length: six minutes): The countess has returned to her cabin. She has just danced briefly with the doctor but has had to leave because of an attack of the shakes. Visibly moved by her predicament, the doctor goes to her cabin and once again helps her by giving her some morphine. He asks her why she is doing this to herself. She explains how once a man took over her life. He also controlled the lives of five thousand workers whom he kept in abject poverty. When she witnessed that poverty, she set out to fight it with all her might. Implicitly we infer that her drug addiction is a by-product of that traumatic time. The doctor is moved by her willingness to be committed to change (rare to his knowledge). They inquire into each other's lives—completely expose themselves in their vulnerability. She sums up their relationship: although they are two strangers on a ship, they are talking like friends, even lovers; he should, she says, have been the innocent love of her childhood. Their exchanges are tender and sweet and this time end with a kiss. The scene fades out, but it is obvious they make love.

Scene 4 (length: four minutes): Once again the roles of nurturing are reversed. The countess comes to the doctor's cabin to look after him. She insists he go to bed and that she read to him until he dozes off. Her choice of reading, though, is hardly the stuff of somnolence, but it is significant on a number of levels. She reads from D. H. Lawrence's *Lady Chatterley's Lover*—not just any scene, but the scene where the two lovers (Chatterley and her gardener) meet up and kiss and she exclaims: "Why, Jonathan, you are violating me!" It turns out the countess is reading from memory—the actual book she has in her hands is a volume of the good doctor's medical journal. The excerpt selected from Lawrence's novel refers indirectly to the countess and the doctor's own lovemaking earlier. But there are other significant intertextual links. Lawrence's book, written in 1921, had been banned for obscenity. However, he had had it privately printed in Florence in 1928. Thus, copies were obtainable, if with difficulty. Looking further at its checkered history, censorship of the novel meant that it was not published in its integral version in Great Britain until 1961 after winning a famous court case in 1960 that challenged the obscenity laws. The context of the film is 1933. Soon Hitler would be burning books such as this one, deemed obscene. The countess has memorized the book as a strategy of resistance (reminiscent of Ray Bradbury's novel *Fahrenheit 451*).[30] How did she obtain a copy in the first place? Her quoting from memory points to her commitment to resist oppression of all sorts, as witnessed in the previous scene. In 1964, the context of the film's release, the novel's publication was still a hot topic and certainly helped spearhead the move toward the abolition of censorship in Britain (which did not occur until the mid-1970s). Thus, Kramer's inclusion of this "reading" from memory is far from innocent and, in terms of the contemporary context, refers on numerous levels to the question of intolerance and censorship in Britain but also assuredly the United States. Signoret's own association, once more, as a star body linked with this issue of censorship (sexual censorship, in this instance) recalls her earlier association with it in *Room at the Top* (discussed in Chapter Two).

In sum, the countess arrives with a flourish and leaves with dignity. In her own cabin class she is the only one with courage. Even the doctor lacks the final ability to act courageously and leave with her. He stays on board and collapses from a heart attack, crying out that he should have left with her. She may well have espoused lost causes all her adult life, but we are left feeling that she, at least, remains remarkable—untainted as she is by any evidence of bad faith.

In *The Deadly Affair*, adapted from John Le Carré's *Call for the Dead*, matters are far less clear.[31] Ambiguity and treachery abound in this cold war spy thriller set in 1960s London, whose drab and wintry cityscape is marvelously rendered by producer/director Sidney Lumet's and camera operator Freddie Young's intelligent mastery of Technicolor. Lumet wanted to shoot the film in black and white. However, because he had to use Technicolor, he elected to kill off as much color as he could. This was achieved, first, by preexposing the film (to a dead-white card in a black room) and, second, by Young closing "his shutter down to sixty degrees opening which gave him roughly thirty percent exposure."[32] The effect was to remove the top and bottom color registers and produce the grainy, gray, cold feel of the film as we know it. It is not a glamorous spy thriller à la James Bond, so popular in the 1960s. The lead characters—James Mason as MI5's Charles Dobbs, Simone Signoret as the Soviet spy Elsa

Fennan, and Harry Andrews as Dobbs's helpful retired detective Inspector Mendel—are all middle-aged. The London we see for the most part is made up of the dreary Surrey suburbs ("Wallaston," where Elsa lives), Battersea warehouse garages, and the boathouses on the Thames' World's End in the (at that time) unglamorous part of Chelsea. The streets are damp and gray, and everywhere feels very cold—people remain well wrapped up even indoors (for example, Elsa wears thick gray woolen socks over her stockinged feet when at home). As Penelope Huston put it so eloquently: "This is real Le Carré country, the meeting of middle-aged survivors on the barbed-wire of their ideological frontiers."[33] As the story unfolds, one gets the feeling that it is the barbed wire of their personal pain that is really center stage here, for Dobbs is as much in pain and haunted by the treachery of his promiscuous wife as Elsa is by her past (during the war she was a Jewish victim of Nazi concentration camps).

In the film Dobbs is sent to investigate the apparent suicide of Samuel Fennan, an MI5 senior official. He comes to realize that the suicide was in fact a murder. Slowly, with Mendel's help, Dobbs gets to unravel the mystery and works out that Fennan, who had high security clearance, must have discovered that his wife was passing copies of documents he took home to the Soviets. Rather than denounce her, he starts by bringing innocuous documents home, then sends an anonymous letter denouncing himself to MI5. As Dobbs continues his investigation, everything leads back to Elsa. He deduces, therefore, that it must be her spymaster (code-named Sontag) who ordered Fennan's murder and that Elsa knows full well that there was no suicide. He works out how the spy ring and Elsa arranged their exchange rendezvous—via a postcard sent to Elsa asking her to arrange a theater date. Dobbs decides to set a trap to catch the spymaster and send such a postcard to Elsa. Unsuspectingly, Elsa arranges to meet the spymaster at a matinee performance of *Edward II*. To Dobbs's horror, the spymaster turns out to be none other than his trusted friend Dieter Frey (played by Maximilian Schell), a comrade from wartime espionage days when they were both on the same side. Frey, who had come to London under the guise of a business trip to find out why the source of information had dried up, uses his friendship with Dobbs to advance his own investigation. He succeeds in killing off Fennan and other small-time players in the spy ring, but he is not smart enough to have seen Dobbs's hand in the theater trap. Only once he arrives and sits next to Elsa does some kind of light dawn for the two of them. Once they both realize they have walked into a trap (through rapid intercutting of close-ups between the two), it is a matter of seconds before Elsa understands that Frey must kill her. The gentleness with which he puts his arm around her suggests she accepts her death as inevitable. He makes his escape, only to find his own death at the hands of Dobbs in the freezing gray waters of the Thames.

Neither the Soviet KGB nor the British Intelligence Service come out well in this story.[34] Dobbs is deluded about his wife (played by Harriet Andersson) and equally allows his weakness around women to cloud his judgment of Elsa. He is moved by her pain, seeing his own mirrored in it. He considers that she is more a victim of the KGB that saw in the "punished life" of this Jewish prisoner an easy prey for Communist dreams. However, Elsa for her part believes in nothing, has no dreams, or so she would have Dobbs believe. She makes it clear that, whichever side you are on, the secret intelligence services are as bad as each other, with their deadly and ruthless games. We never fully discover why she turned traitor not just to Britain but ultimately to her husband, who had rescued her after the war and whom she claims, in an outburst to Dobbs, was her life. Why, if this was the case, was she prepared to have Dobbs believe that it was her husband who was the double agent? At one point she explains that he spied in the name of social justice and gave the money gained to charity. Is she perhaps talking about herself? Did she believe she was helping the cause of peace? Was her treachery, as Dobbs surmises, motivated by the desire for a better world?[35]

Such is the force of Signoret's performance that we never resolve the ambiguity surrounding her. We sense her as victim, but we also sense her as hard and determined. Indeed, she remains shockingly calm throughout most of her ordeals (the interviews and her murder). She appears four times in the film, as outlined below.

In the first two sequences, Elsa is subjected to Dobbs's intense questioning. But the dynamics are such that what occurs is a double exposure. Mason's performance as the earnest, truth-seeking Dobbs, with his desperate attempts not just to elicit information from Elsa but to justify his own comportment with her deceased husband, is perfectly matched by Signoret's interpretation of Elsa as an honest cynic. She is a woman wounded by experience, much like Dobbs, as it transpires. Somehow she manages to deduce this when she asks Dobbs about his wife. It becomes clear to her that they are both emotional cripples. She is unable to feel because she was so brutalized during the war, and Dobbs is unable to let himself feel. Thus, these two encounters—incidentally, the only times when Signoret speaks—are far more like sparring matches than they are interrogations. Elsa in her interlocutions with Dobbs gets to question his practice (as an agent for MI5) far more successfully than he does hers. And this is her power—she turns the mirror back on Dobbs. She refuses his image of her as a victim and a woman who has been deluded into believing that communism offers the solution to the ills of society. She exposes the pathos of Dobbs's own insecure beliefs around patriotism and treachery ("You're a fool, Mr. Dobbs, you don't even know the rules of your own game."). She eyes him glacially as she tells him off about the sordid pettiness of his job. Spying is a game, she says, with human beings as pawns on a chessboard.

What gives these two encounters even greater power is Signoret's tremendous sense of timing. In the first sequence, once Elsa has let Dobbs into her house,

Scene 1	Scene 2	Scene 3	Scene 4
(15 m. into film):	*(70 m. into film):*	*(82 m. into film):*	*(86 m. into film):*
Dobbs interviews Elsa in her home in Surrey.	Dobbs again comes to Elsa's house to interrogate her.	Mendel follows Elsa to London; she has swallowed the bait and gone to buy tickets for the theater.	Elsa, sitting alone in the theater, awaits her spymaster. When Dieter Frey turns up, she realizes that something is wrong. Frey kills her.
(length: 9 min. 30 s.)	(length: 5 m. 17 s.)		
		(length 3 m.)	
			(length: 9 m.)
Film length: 104 m.	Signoret on screen: 26 m. 47 s. (25% of time)		

she leaves him standing in her front room as she goes through to the kitchen to fetch the kettle and comes back into the living room area at the rear. Dobbs stands in the foreground, his back to us, while Elsa is in the background facing toward him (in a long shot). She slowly and methodically makes a cup of instant coffee.[36] This chillingly silent shot of her coffee making lasts one minute and forty-five seconds. She says nothing. It is an eerie, uneasy moment, but it is also a moment in which it is clear that power is not in the obvious place. She keeps Dobbs waiting as if it were he who is about to undergo the interrogation—as if she is stalking him in her own home, not vice versa. She moves forward slowly to center frame (the camera cuts, goes behind her into a medium close-up of her feet in thick socks). She puts on the fire to cut the increasing chill (medium shot on her from Dobbs's point of view) and, turning the spoon slowly in her cup (medium close-up on her), she finally indicates her readiness to engage with Dobbs by asking: "You're the man who interviewed my husband about loyalty?" The tone of her voice throughout this interview is dull, heavy, and laced with suffering, which, as she says, she has learned to bear with discretion. When she speaks, her voice is out of breath, expressing with it the pain of loss and her lassitude at all the suffering she has endured. She even tells Dobbs of the heaviness of her body, which she drags around and that will not sleep. Her delivery is painstakingly slow, as if she is drained from the effects of shock. She makes questioning her unbearable for Dobbs, the weight of her pain and shock being too close to his own with regard to his wife. There is no quick cross fire of interrogation going on here. Rather, it is a heavy, soggy mass of suffering that gets thrust from one to the other. The exchange ends with Dobbs leaving, exhausted, framed in a low-angle shot from Elsa's point of view (she is held in medium close-up in profile). Once he is gone, Elsa, equally exhausted, drops her head.

In the second interview, Dobbs comes in with far more energy and anger. The story has moved on considerably, and he is convinced that Elsa is involved in the treason. He interrupts her packing (she is moving) and shouts at her to get some reaction, accusing her of being a spy. But only when he screams "What kind of daydreams did you dream, Mrs. Fennan, that had so little of the world in them?" does she finally respond. This is the first of two speeches she makes, both of which have the effect of depleting Dobbs of his energy, casting him back into impotence. He leaves visibly shaken. It is not just the content of the two speeches, it is the incredible slowness of their delivery that has the impact. The first response is only fifty-three words long, but it takes two minutes to deliver. The camera slowly pans to her face in medium close-up (twelve seconds); she gently snorts and begins to speak, at first in a virtual whisper, then moving into a voice full of tears:

> Look at me [whisper, she looks at her body to her right]. Look at me [louder whisper, she looks at her body to her left]. What dreams did *they* leave me [softly]? I dreamt of children [tearfully], I had none. I dreamt of . . . err . . . of a beautiful body, they marked it. [Long pause] That's when Samuel found me. He pitied me, he loved me, and he took me away. *He* had dreams. I had none. But he . . . [her voice tails off]

Dobbs hesitates, then resumes his aggressive questioning. Attempting to push her further, he grabs her shoulder. She shrugs him off, as the camera cuts to a close-up. This time she is angry. Her speech is seventy words long and takes one minute and forty-five seconds; it works to forestall him once again:

> Get your hands off me! Now go and kill Sontag. Keep the game alive. But don't think I am on your side. I am on no . . . nobody's side. I am a battlefield [at this point, she removes her rubber gloves] for your toy soldiers. You can march on me [throws gloves aside]. You can bomb me. You can burn me. You can make me barren. . . . But never pity me, Mr. Dobbs [wags her finger], never pity me. Never tell me you understand *my* feelings. . . . Now go away and kill!

We only get to witness Dobbs's reaction once he is outside her house. She has truly dismissed him, and he is in shock. It is not just her words, but her gesture of removing the gloves that makes her dismissal so emphatic: she peels them off like a surgeon, having completed an operation. So emphatic is the gesture that we do not even see them being pulled off; we merely hear the sound of rubber—the sound of her contempt.

Signoret's performance brings tremendous tension to the film even though she is present for only a quarter of the film time and speaks very little. The point is she makes the tone of her voice and her face fill so much space with meaning that we sense she is central to the enigma. This again breaks with the contemporary tradition of spy films, which were male-dominated (the Bond series, for example) and where treacherous women had small roles and, more significantly, were invariably beautiful. Even though her swollen features are not yet within the realm of the ugly, Signoret's face is showing the ravaging effects of drink. Only her lips (which still glisten with sensuality) and her eyes (so expressive in this instance of pain and shock) remain of her former beauty. These are the two features that she puts to such astonishing effect in her final scene, when the terrible spy game ends for her. She is murdered in the theater just as Edward II is murdered on stage by "a beautiful friend" (to quote Edward).[37] We hear Edward's screams as the hot poker is inserted into his arse by the friend he trusted and yet who betrayed him, just as we witness Elsa's silence as she succumbs to Dieter Frey's pressure on her neck. Shock, anxiety, terror, sadness, acceptance—she says them all through her eyes and mouth.

The Return of the *diabolique* and the Monstrous Ego: *Games* (1967) and *The Seagull* (1968)

These last two films under consideration are interestingly matched in that, in both, Signoret plays a female monster. In *Games,* she is a ruthless con artist who wreaks havoc in a young couple's marriage and succeeds in institutionalizing one, murdering the other, and getting away with the bounty. In *The Seagull,* she plays Arkadina, the egotistical mother who is more interested in her fame and her love affairs than in her tragic son's efforts to impress her. Although they are strong roles, and certainly Signoret has played the *diabolique* before, nonetheless there are unnerving moments in both films in which her consummate actorly skills temporarily desert her and she overacts. The result is not disastrous but bizarre and unexpected. In *Games,* this overacting occurs only in the first sequence in which we meet her and for some reason she hams up her role (masquerading as a traveling salesperson). Arguably, it could be that she struggled at first to find her way into the character. Signoret had just come from her

The Deadly Affair (1966). The end of the spy game: at the theater Elsa (Signoret) and Dieter (Maximilian Schell) realize they have fallen into the trap.

failure as Lady Macbeth and, in an interview, said she was still haunted by her character. Such was the effect, she claimed, that she found it difficult to switch roles.[38] Paradoxically, director Curtis Harrington was delighted with her performance.[39] But this overacting is not limited to the one film; she does it again in *The Seagull*, directed by Sidney Lumet, with whom she had already worked. As I shall argue, it could be the staginess of Lumet's direction that forces her to overact.[40]

Lumet had chosen to shoot Anton Chekhov's masterpiece as a filmed play and wanted the film to be the same length as the play. With a running time of 140 minutes, it feels very long, particularly because, in order to keep the theatrical feel, Lumet used long takes and elected to shoot primarily in long shots, ensemble shots, and full shots over medium and close-up shots. The effect is to slow everything down and make the film seem slower and longer than the play.[41] According to Signoret (1978, 333–335), the cast spent two months together, and the film, which was made in a cooperative style, was shot in twenty-eight days.[42] Even so, this does not save it from a certain woodenness. And there is an odd fluctuation between intimacy and distance. As a French critic noted, Lumet's attempt to adhere to the alienation effect, which was in vogue in the 1960s, meant he used too many general shots, slowed things down, and kept viewers away from the characters' emotions.[43] The staginess, according to other critics, made the actors all "too much": James Mason as Trigorin is "too English," Vanessa Redgrave as Nina "too passionara."[44] Unfortunately, the effect of this staginess for Signoret is to make her lack of stage-acting ability (see

Chapter Three) impinge on her performance. She cannot sustain an evenness of style over the long takes. Indeed, she becomes far more gestural, her hands and arms waving all over the place. One critic found she "overacts to the point of caricature."[45] Her minimalism, for which she is so renowned, evaporates, and we rarely get to see her facial gestures that she normally uses to convey so much meaning. Only in a couple of intimate scenes—one with her son, Kostya (played by David Warner), when she tends to his wound (after his first suicide attempt), and the other with Trigorin, her lover, when she tries to win him back from his latest infatuation—which are shot in medium shot and close-up, does she recover her more typical style of performance. In these two scenes, which are back to back, she gets to express some tenderness as well as irritation toward her son, followed by tenderness and fury toward her lover. She even weeps some tears with her son, kisses his forehead and cheeks, and begs forgiveness for being such a "sinful mother." She never finishes changing his bandage, however. Her lover arrives, and two seconds later she is enacting the same behavior and emotions with him as she beseeches him not to leave her. She is a consummate manipulator who must have her way. Signoret conveys Arkadina's selfish hypocrisy well in these intimate scenes. She shows how Arkadina just rolls over anyone else's desires and needs—eyes, mouth, hands, and voice all work with urgency to push the son or the lover into the corner she wants him in. Arkadina is, after all, a famous stage actor, so her performance has to win the day. As Signoret rightly stated, Arkadina remains throughout "an actress for whom life resembles a theatrical performance which fluctuates between comedy and tragedy."[46]

The Seagull takes place on Arkadina's lakeside estate. As it opens, Kostya is about to stage a play he has just written. The performance is abandoned quickly, however, because Arkadina is very rude about the play and repeatedly interrupts the performance. She reacts against its modernity, refusing to keep an open mind; but she also reacts against the nubile Nina on stage, whose beauty and youth reflect unfavorably on her own aging. Indeed, Chekhov's play is as much a discourse on writing, the theater, and acting as it is on love. There are numerous love triangulations, just as there are several aesthetic antagonisms. Trigorin is an established writer in the realist tradition who, when it suits him, likes to play the role of the artist riddled by creative self-doubts. This lack of confidence successfully seduces Nina, a local landowner's daughter with aspirations to become a stage actor. Kostya is a young aspiring Symbolist playwright (a modernist, therefore) who is in love with Nina. Arkadina is a renowned stage actor in the old tradition who both hates her son because he reminds her that she is aging and remains unimpressed by his own work. Thus, in aesthetic terms, the traditional fights it out with the modern, first, in the writings of Trigorin and Kostya and, second, in the actorly embodiments of these two trends, Arkadina and Nina. In terms of love relationships, Arkadina tries to keep Trigorin by her side, but he chases after Nina. Kostya loves Nina who loves Trigorin. Masha (played by Kathleen Widdoes), the estate manager's daughter, loves Kostya who loves Nina (and so it goes, with several other secondary characters also caught in triangular fixations). Two years pass. Trigorin eventually tires of Nina, who fails to make it as a stage actor, suffers terrible loss at Trigorin's abandonment, and finally goes mad in the process. Trigorin returns to Arkadina. Kostya, by now a published writer, is still full of genuine self-doubt. Having attempted unsuccessfully to commit suicide after the debacle of his first play, it takes

Nina's reappearance, destroyed by her affair with Trigorin, to send him over the edge. This time he successfully shoots himself.

In Act 1, when Arkadina turns up for the performance of Kostya's play, she makes a grand entrance wearing a bright yellow dress that outshines the drab black worn by Masha and the virginal white worn by Nina. Her face, however, is made up as if it were she who was the actor about to go on stage. A close-up of her reveals her as almost a drag queen, grotesque in her excess, so thickly caked on is the makeup. Equally her costume strains at her body as it attempts to disguise her girth and create the illusion that she has a waist. As she sits impatiently during the performance, she cracks nuts in her hand and talks over Nina's words, essentially attempting to take over the stage. She is ugly in nature and looks. Cruelly, the camera shoots Signoret on her left side, which reveals her puffy face, thus accentuating her grotesqueness. Later in the film, in her more tender scenes with Kostya and Trigorin, she is shot from the right, and, viewed from that side, her face remains still quite beautiful. Thus, when Arkadina states proudly in Act 2—as she demolishes everyone in a croquet game—"I've kept my looks because I've never let myself become dowdy, I have never let myself go as some people do," it is transparently evident that she has not looked in a mirror for a long time. Indeed, this declaration, coming as it does from Signoret's lips, is not without its irony. As we know, during the 1960s, Signoret was pleased to embrace roles that allowed her to look her age. Thus, her own star persona mitigates against Arkadina's desire to look thirty-two when she is in fact well into her forties.

Arkadina's monstrous mother and *meneur du jeu,* however, are nothing compared to the awful Lisa Schindler of *Games.* If she enjoyed playing "the abusive Arkadina who refuses to age," then she equally enjoyed embracing the ruthless role of Lisa—as she said, "I get tired of playing the nice roles" and "Too bad if when I play an evil femme fatale some of my real *me* seeps through."[47] Fortunately for Curtis Harrington, some of Signoret's style and polish does come through after a rather uneven start. Harrington was an independent filmmaker and one of the pioneers of the American Underground. He was a friend of Kenneth Anger's, and he also worked with Roger Corman.[48] So a mixture of horror with the avant-garde is not uncommon in his films. *Games,* however, was Harrington's first attempt at a mainstream thriller with a major studio (Universal). It certainly is not a great film; it feels stiff—a sensation not helped by Katharine Ross's very awkward performance as the beleaguered and terrorized wife, Jennifer. Nonetheless, it did manage to win the Ann Radcliffe Prize, awarded each year by the Count Dracula Society.[49] References to Harrington's association with the American Underground abound in this film: from the contemporary art (modern and pop) that is strewn around the New York town house of the wealthy young couple, Paul (played by James Caan) and Jennifer, to the flirtations with the occult that all three characters indulge in, to the pacing and framing of the shots, and, finally, to the use of Technicolor, which, though it has painterly depth (like an avant-garde film), is strong, even garish at times (like many of the paintings in the house). You could imagine Andy Warhol living in such an environment. Even the film's outcome, where Lisa (Signoret) makes away with the loot, having murdered her accomplice, provides an anarchic resolution that has little to do with mainstream narrative.

Harrington ends up with something of a hybrid film. The narrative is based on a fairly stock plot: husband and accomplice scheme to get the wife's fortune by driving her insane, to the point that she actually murders someone. They do this by playing a series of nasty tricks on her. In one of the games, Paul persuades Jennifer to play a trick on Norman (played by Don Stroud), the grocery delivery boy. She is to give Norman the come-on, and Paul will come in pretending to avenge his honor. He waves a pistol at Norman and appears to shoot him dead. Both Jennifer and Paul had believed the gun contained blanks. Now Norman lies dead at Jennifer's feet. And so begins her trajectory toward madness. We do not know until late in the film that Paul is in cahoots with Lisa, nor do we know that he has not in fact killed Norman. His increased indifference to Jennifer as she becomes more and more of a zombie does, however, signal his complicity. It is all rather obvious. In the end, Harrington, who developed the story with George Edwards, is not really interested in a plausible plot line; rather, he is interested in effect (that of suspense and horror) and style, based on an aesthetics of the avant-garde. However, as one critic of the day said, Harrington is not Jean-Luc Godard, and thus there is not a great deal to say about the film once one has examined the performances and evaluated the film's look.[50] For example, Godard is always getting the audience to notice what he is doing with his camera. Similarly, color is always used for a reason. Godard is into a politics of aesthetics, not just an aesthetics of reference. In Harrington's film, the use of color is painterly but entirely suited to the narrative and mood of the film. There are no challenges there. In the same way we are rarely aware of the camera's presence. Characters are often held in single shots to register their emotions; there are some two-shots on the couple, a few three-shots, all of them occurring at obvious times. Similarly, the camera tracks around from time to time, but nothing remarkable occurs.

To illustrate this point, let us take the pivotal sequence that sets the ball rolling in terms of the three characters' commitment to game play. This sequence occurs half an hour into the film. In what has preceded we know that Lisa has managed to inveigle her way into the home, where she is now a guest. Jennifer is very taken with her and is beginning to treat her as a confidante. It is clear that Lisa has a past, as the trunk that arrives containing her worldly possessions makes clear. Much like Pandora's box, it contains all sorts of allusions to her secret past, including a pack of tarot cards, a feather boa, which she gives to Jennifer, and a pair of pistols, which she will eventually give to the couple. Within the present context of the narrative, we suspect that Lisa is a European woman of substance (and some class) who has fallen on hard times, which is why she is now a cosmetics traveling salesperson. Let us now focus on this sequence in which a challenge to enter into proper game play is thrown down by Lisa. Jennifer and Paul's house is crowded with all sorts of games (for example, a pinball machine where "Death" is the highest score). As Paul proudly puts it, they are symbols of American culture. Lisa sneers at them: "You Americans have it easy, being content with such simple amusements." She taunts Paul; she prefers real, more dangerous games to these "penny arcade amusements," as she puts it. Interwoven with these series of taunts, she produces a box containing two pistols, which she gives to Paul and Jennifer as a present, and starts to tell the story that is attached to them. Paul and Jennifer are seated, Lisa is standing and moves around the room. Each time she taunts Paul, she comes toward the couple, and they are held in a three-shot. Each time she picks up on her story about the pistols (how they were used in a duel between two of her lovers and, subsequently, for a suicide), she moves away, and the camera follows her in a tracking shot. This shot is interspersed with cutaways to a two-shot of the couple who sit mesmerized by her tale. This sequence of three-shot to a tracking single shot intercut with two-shots occurs three times, making things very predictable. And the mise-en-scène adds to the pedestrian nature of these shots: when Lisa recalls how her lover committed suicide, she is standing in front of a pop-art painting that looks very much like a target itself. Mercifully, Lisa brings all this to an end by firing one of the pistols, albeit off-screen.

Much of the rest of the film is similarly shot—always pointing to the obvious. This sequence, as indeed the entire film, plays on Paul and Jennifer's apparent failure to heed the dictum "Beware of strangers bearing gifts." Throughout, Lisa is seen as having the upper hand in all the games that are played. That she is the *meneur du jeu* is foreshadowed from the opening credits. Signoret's name is the first to appear, and several green egg-shaped graphics get set out in a line like cards. Then James Caan's name appears with the tarot card "The Sun," followed by Katharine Ross's "The Moon." The credit sequence ends on the thirteenth tarot card: "Death." A little later, when Lisa is unpacking her trunk, she drops her tarot cards, and Jennifer picks up the one marked "Juno." "This is not a gay card," Lisa informs her. However, as we can see, it is the card that—as the opening credits told us—symbolizes Jennifer and Paul because Juno is the moon goddess, Jupiter's sister. She, like Jupiter, is the goddess of celestial light (sun and moon). She is also the liberator and protector of the Roman wife. As far as we can determine, when Lisa says "This is not a gay card," she is offering yet another of her tactical lies. She knows that neither Jennifer nor Paul possesses the sort of cultural knowledge to challenge her interpretation, attracted as they are to a neo-Gothic late-1960s decadence and attached as they are to modern technological gadgetry. Later, after Norman's "death," Lisa will deal the tarot cards and read them for Jennifer. But it is she, not Jennifer, who picks out two to turn over: the first, she declares, points to a house struck by catastrophe; the second means Death. With hindsight it is obvious that she has stacked the cards. Lisa's skills in playing the occult know no limits, it would appear. During a Black Sabbath game that they play, the trio are interrupted by Jennifer's lawyer—he needs some documents signed. However, he cannot tell who is who behind their deathly masks, and it transpires that, unknown to him, Lisa signs the documents, not Jennifer. Later on still, dressed like a black widow, Lisa lures Jennifer out of bed to follow her and her crystal ball around the house in order to discover what is haunting her. Lisa successfully conjures up the image of the "dead" Norman for Jennifer, who not unnaturally, screams and collapses. Small wonder that the next time Norman reappears, very much alive, Jennifer grabs the gun and shoots him dead.

Lisa plays psychological games with Paul and Jennifer's reliance on mechanical toys that are external to their being. We sense her pulling the strings, even before we realize what deadly game she is up to. In and among these rather hammed up scenes of "terror," the measured Signoret does, however, occasionally emerge. Thus, for example, in the scene where she is about to read the tarot cards, she lights her cigarette in her usual casual manner, pours herself some coffee, and plops in three sugar cubes using her fingers instead of the tongs that are there. In the final sequence, in which she murders Paul, her accomplice, she is as chilling as she ever was in *Les diaboliques* or *Manèges*.

By way of conclusion to this chapter, I would like to compare Signoret's first and last appearance in this film—the contrast in acting styles is striking. In the forced playing of the first, it is as if either Harrington or Signoret was trying to reproduce the manic over-the-top performance associated with Bette Davis. As one French critic of the day pointedly remarked: "Ever since the American studios no longer avail themselves of Bette Davis and Joan Crawford (crucified by their last appearance in Robert Aldrich's *Whatever Happened to Baby Jane* [1962]) the Americans have latched onto Simone Signoret."[51] Lisa/Signoret arrives at Paul and Jennifer's house. Having successfully conned her way into their home by lying about a joint acquaintance, she proceeds to try and sell Jennifer some beauty products. Jennifer, not yet quite a zombie, realizes Lisa has duped her over her claim to know a mutual friend. Up until this point, Signoret's performance is adequate. Lisa's smiling face seduces Jennifer into believing her. She walks around the living room with an authoritative air. She even takes hold of an antique triptych mirror and places it on the coffee table, all the better to sell her wares. But, once exposed as a con, she begins to unhinge. Lisa stands up, as if expecting to be thrown out. Instead, she grabs hold of her head, wobbles on her legs, and half faints, collapsing on the sofa. This is so clearly a masquerade, and one could imagine a petulant Bette Davis carrying the pretense off considerably better. However, Jennifer, kindness itself, does not throw Lisa out but allows her to proceed with her sales spiel. First, Lisa starts to pull out all the different products and rattle off their virtues, faster and faster. Second, she positions the mirror so that it catches Jennifer's reflection in the middle mirror—she, Lisa, is in the two mirrors on either side of Jennifer. Jennifer's image, therefore, is trapped between the two of Lisa as she maniacally prattles on about what a woman needs to maintain her beauty. Jennifer, taking pity on her, offers to buy some. At this point, Lisa jumps up once more, runs across the room with her order pad, and sets about—hysterically—trying to fill the order, this time ranting on about having to ensure she meets her quota. She brushes Jennifer aside, who, sensing things are getting out of hand, only wants to help. Lisa stops what she is doing and rushes across the room once more to grab up some products, saying she wishes that she could give them away. Overcome with emotion she faints, dropping the products as she does so, and falls behind an armchair. Because Lisa later comments on this scene as a successful game where she conned Jennifer, the acting should not be sloughed off as bad melodrama— which in a way it is. Indeed, Signoret's performance here is reminiscent of Bette Davis at her most manipulative, but the difference is, of course, that with Davis, we do not expect to believe her; she lets us, the spectator, know all about her scheming nastiness long before the poor dupes in the film do. With Signoret, we have come to expect measured and authentic performances. Thus, this overacting is quite grotesque, if not downright queer. The film was shot, American studio style, in eighteen days. In this sequence one has to say that Harrington's lack of experience at working with tight deadlines shows itself. Signoret's timing is off. Her first collapse is gauche in the extreme. Similarly, there is no motivating reason for her to rush across the room to fill in an order. Finally, her faint and fall appear so poorly orchestrated it is as if no pretake rehearsals took place. She stutters on her feet and then makes herself fall rather than genuinely acting out the fainting.

Things do get better, however, and by the last sequence Signoret is back in top form. Up until this moment, we are not aware that Lisa has been working with Paul to destabilize Jennifer. Indeed, Paul had sent her packing after the crystal ball incident, and it is after this moment that the terror for Jennifer really begins. The telephone rings and no one speaks; the lights go out; ghosts whistle; the "penny arcade" games start up; Norman—whom she believes is dead—returns. In a fit of total terror Jennifer shoots at Norman, this time effectively killing him. Paul comes home just at that moment and calls the police. Jennifer, by now truly mad, is taken off to the asylum. Paul has the power of attorney signed over to him. He sells everything. It is at this point that, to our surprise, Lisa returns. She has abandoned her shabby shawls and dull blue cape and is glamorously dressed in a white mink coat and hat. She comes up into Paul's (very white) bedroom via the house elevator bearing two glasses of champagne on a tray. They toast their success. We discover that they met a year ago at a ski resort in Vermont, when they cooked up this plot to get Jennifer's money. Paul gives Lisa her cut (10 percent) and smugly continues to drink his champagne. He talks with swagger at the success of "his" scheme. Lisa replies nonchalantly: "Amateurs should not play games with professionals. Professionals have a way of dealing with things very simply." To which Paul retorts: "You couldn't call my scheme simple, could you?" and she very quietly responds by saying: "Precisely the point," as Paul starts to succumb to the effects of the potion she has put in his drink. She runs her finger round and round the rim of the glass, only slightly increasing the high-pitch sound as Paul falls onto the bed and dies (from an overdose of sleeping pills). Lisa expeditively tidies up, leaving no trace of her presence, and departs, taking all the money, presciently not forgetting to put her champagne glass in the attaché case. In this sequence, Signoret is a commanding presence. She fits the bill perfectly as the icy murderer whose resolve cannot be shaken and who has no need to do much other than let her prey fall into her snare. She is truly diabolical as she speaks softly, moistening her lower lip with her tongue as if she has just consumed a tasty morsel. Every gesture is economical but redolent with ruthlessness; as Paul dies, there is not even a flicker of emotion registered on her face.

Chapter Seven

The *monstre sacré* Returns to the French Screen—1969–1982

URING THIS last part of her career, Signoret made sixteen films. From 1969 to 1976 she appeared in ten films. She then took a break of two years to work on the television series, *Madame le Juge*, in which she starred. She returned to cinema to make another six films during the period 1977–1982. Her final piece of work was for television, a two part telefilm entitled *Music Hall* (1986). I have already remarked on how this output is quite phenomenal for an aging star, particularly one such as Signoret whose body over this period morphed and remorphed itself. Indeed, Chapter Two went into some detail on the political resonances of her body mutations and the function of the ugly body as a political response to the fascism of beauty, so I do not propose to go over that territory again. However, I do believe it might be helpful, just to remind ourselves, to provide a graph of her bodily changes during this period, for it reveals a body in constant mutation/mutilation: one that swells through overindulgence in drink, then shrinks after having been to a detox center. In the following graph, I have traced Signoret's body's trajectory on a scale from *A* to *F*, where *A* indicates when she is at her most svelte and *F* when she is at her most swollen.

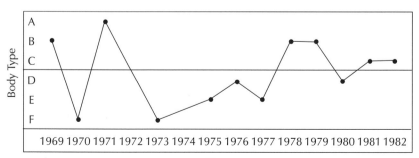

What is significant is the rapidity of these swings, particularly from 1969 to 1973—a pattern that gets repeated from 1976 to 1979—extremes that can easily be read on her face. After her Hollywood makeover in *Games* (1967), in which she looks glamorous, Signoret's face now resumes, in *L'armée des ombres* (1969), a puffy aura first observed in *The Deadly Affair* (1966). By the time of *L'aveu* (April 1970), her cheeks are pockmarked with the effects of alcohol; we can see the scarring under the heavy makeup when she is held in close-up, especially in right profile. We recall that in *The Seagull* (only two years earlier) her right profile was still quite beautiful, that has now gone, and her whole face is puffy. Yet only a year after *L'aveu*, in *La veuve Couderc* (October 1971), her skin is clear again, her face restored to that of a good-looking middle-aged woman. This metamorphosis is all the more extraordinary because her other major film of this period, *Le chat* (May 1971), was released in that same year. There her face and body continue to look swollen. Thus, there is only something like a six-month break between the shooting of *Le chat* (Fall 1970) and *La veuve Couderc* (May 1971) for this transformation to take place. But then, just over a year later, when she is shooting *Les granges brûlées* (Fall 1972, which came out in May 1973), her body has transmuted back to its puffy status. Curiously, these morphic movements do not work against Signoret's characterization—if anything, they work for her. And it is worth noting that a least once, during the period 1976–1979, this morphing was a deliberate decision for the purpose of embodying Madame Rosa in *La vie devant soi*.

SIGNORET'S FILM WORK, 1969–1982:[1] PERIOD AND TYPE

1969–1971	*1972–1976*	*1977–1982*
Comeback (Part One)	*Middle Passage*	*Closure*
Civic Cinema:	**Civic cinema:**	**Civic cinema:**
L'armée des ombres (1969) [1.4 million][1]	*Rude journée pour la reine* (1973) [72,214]	*La vie devant soi* (1977) [2 million]
L'aveu (1970) [2.1 million]		*Judith Therpauve* (1978) [190,313]
Cameo, civic:		
L'Américain (1969)[2]		
Comeback (Part two)		
Thriller:	**Thriller:**	**Retro/heritage/costume drama:**
Le chat (1971) [1 million]	*Les granges brûlées* (1973)[2]	*Chère inconnue* (1980) [511,601]
La veuve Couderc (1971) [2.1 million]	**Thriller/civic cinema:**	*L'Étoile du Nord* (1982) [1.6 million]
Cameo, thriller:	*La chair de l'orchidée* (1975) [552,107]	**Cameo:**
Comptes à rebours (1971) [1.1 million]	*Police Python 357* (1976) [1.5 million]	*L'adolescente* (1979) [437,875]
		Guy de Maupassant (1982) [109,892]

Source: Simsi, Simon. *Ciné-passions: 7ème art et industrie de 1945 à 2000.* Paris: Edition Dixit, 2001.
1. Figures in brackets are rounded attendance figures for France.
2. No attendance figures available.

For the sake of clarity, I have divided Signoret's filmic output into three periods. In Chapter Two, I had categorized these films in terms of typologies and genre (and, as we saw, there was some overlap), but this time I wish to consider them more systematically in chronological groupings and according to typological clusters. The table (page 166) shows these films grouped by period and type. These divisions are used in the rest of the chapter to discuss the films. Rounded attendance figures for France, are given in brackets. To give an idea of scale, the top-grossing films in France of the 1970s on average drew five million viewers, although *L'aveu*, with two million, came in ninth in its year.

COMEBACK—1969–1971

Part One: Taking on Another's Skin—*L'armée des ombres* and *L'aveu*

Signoret's role as Mathilde in Jean-Pierre Melville's Resistance film *L'armée des ombres* is, like the other main characters, a composite of several figures. Indeed, Joseph Kessel (1963, 7) the author of the novel of the same title on which the film is based, mentioned that his characters no longer referred to a single original but to a composite. Kessel published his novel during the Occupation in 1943, and for that reason he had to keep the identities of the fighters hidden. He talks of his bitterness in having to erase the identity of these heroic men and women for the sake of security, but explains how he managed nonetheless to spark something of them back into his consciousness if only by a single trait of theirs, whether a smile, a certain look, or just the sound of their voice (8). Both Kessel and Melville had been in the Resistance, and with *L'armée des ombres*, Melville manages to make a very intimate film about it. It feels lived from within. As we know, although Signoret had not lived it from within, she had lived close by it. To find her character, she recalled how, in her preparation for her role as Mathilde, she could only get to "know about it" through the experience of others (Signoret 1978, 364–365). Her first model was her makeup artist, Maud Begon, who had been in the Resistance and had been incarcerated in concentration camps. Her second model was someone who was also a reference point for both Kessel and Melville, Lucie Aubrac. In fact, Signoret knew her briefly during the Occupation, but only as her history teacher, Madame Samuel (see Chapter One). Later, in 1947, she discovered that her teacher and Lucie Aubrac were one and the same (37). Signoret spoke of her sense of shame in embodying a role that she did not play in real life when others close to her did, a feeling she again expressed, ten years later, when she played Madame Rosa in *La vie devant soi* (Signoret 1979, 11). We can see how the role of Mathilde represented a different challenge, even a deviation, from Signoret's normal practices of performance. She had always talked of how a character entered her skin.[1] This time, however, the process, by her own admission, was two way. Not only was she entered by the character Mathilde, she also was entering the skin of two real women: she is both occupied and occupying.

    The word *ombres* (shadows) in the title of the film refers to the hidden status of the Resistance army. It also points to the idea of invisibility, stealth. The fighters are shadows also because they are anonymous, their real identities hidden from others within the network—and, of course, from the Gestapo and the French *milice*, who try to track them down. All resistors attempt to survive in a world of counterfeit of their own creation (their papers are false, for example), a world where there are no rules. So how is it possible to talk about the Resistance since it is, above all, about invisibility? Hervé Aubron (1997), in a very illuminating article on Melville's film, points out how these shadows have no future; they are just that: shadows of the present whose sole purpose is to disoccupy (get the German occupiers out of France). They have no name, no substance, are evanescent; they embody the invisible. It becomes very difficult, therefore, to conceive of how a film "about the Resistance" can be made when erasure is at its core. Melville seems to have understood this when he said his film was less about the Resistance per se than it was about a certain idea of it.[2] Viewed this way, Melville's representation of the Resistance, as Aubron (1997, 148) makes clear, is more of a mental space, the essence of which is networking and transmitting. It is also a mental space that is based on ritual; hence the focus on gesture, particularly where Mathilde is concerned and Gerbier, the Resistance leader (based in part on Jean Moulin and played by Lino Ventura). Mathilde/Signoret's gestures suggest the scrupulousness of her preparations. We see the camera following her hands as she painstakingly plots escape routes; she takes her time to try out the different disguises she might need, and so on. Gerbier, for his part, is meticulous in all he does, for example, fastidiously folding his garments before he carefully closes his case (slowing the process down, one suspects, so that he can think).

This mental space is also conjured up within the film through the intense degree of silence that pervades it, as, too, a sense of enduring patience. But there is also nervous energy that comes in spurts, moments that disrupt the mental space and call for action, however rash. These are moments when extraordinary feats are accomplished, such as Gerbier's two escapes from captivity. However, there are also moments when the mental space is in danger of breaking down. So, for example, Mathilde carries her daughter's photograph on her (against express orders), a folly that will cost her her life. Gerbier, during his second incarceration, when all the prisoners in his cell are made to run the gauntlet in front of machine guns, mentally breaks down and cannot prevent himself from running like a scared rabbit even though he had told himself he would not. Jean-François (played by Jean-Pierre Cassel) denounces himself, knowing he will die under torture, but does so in an attempt to help Félix (played by Paul Crauchet), who is near death in prison. As Melville said, the film is "a tragedy with seven characters."[3]

With a few exceptions, until this film, the French Resistance had been represented as a man's world. And in some respects, when Melville talked about this film being about male friendship ("virile friendship," as he put it),[4] we could wonder if he was aware of the impact Signoret's performance as Mathilde had on the film. Certainly, Lino Ventura as Gerbier dominates; the point of view throughout is his. There are two male friendships at the core of the film: Gerbier's with the Resistance chief Luc Jardie (played by Paul Meurisse), also based in part on Jean Moulin, and Jean-François's with Félix. But then there is also Mathilde who, much as she is without friends, is equally a core element in the narrative/army of shadows, a fact Gerbier recognizes by taking her on as adjutant. All the men around her admire her for her skills. As Gerbier puts it: "I knew how remarkable she was, but she astounds me nonetheless. She is cut out both to lead and serve. She is willing, methodical and patient." Although it may be about virile friendship, this is far from being a "man's film." Indeed, in terms of the interplay between the masculine and the feminine, it is riddled with contradictions, most of which revolve around Mathilde or comparisons between her and Gerbier. Let us take a closer look.

Signoret figures in the film for only twenty-six minutes (19 percent of the total film time), and she is far from talkative during her appearances. In fact, she is more talked about than observed talking. In this regard her characterization remains true to the motivation of the novel. In the novel it is the male narrator (and at times Gerbier) who controls the narrative and provides the details of Mathilde's activities. These are very briefly recounted (if compared with the narrator's depiction of other male resistors' actions). Similarly, her direct speech is only reported eight times throughout the novel, the most detailed of which is in our first encounter with her, when she asks to join the Resistance (Kessel 1963, 113–114). It is at this point that interesting divergences from the novel occur, because the Mathilde we get to meet on screen is not the mother of seven of the novel whose husband is a bailiff and a regular reader of the right-wing/fascist *L'Action Française*. She is described as thin, drawn, with yellowing skin, and generally suffering from malnutrition (Kessel 1963, 112). It is this condition, which also affects her children, that drives her to join the Resistance and fight the *boches*, as she puts it. Signoret's Mathilde is a far more muted affair. She is a middle-aged educated woman who speaks German, which she uses to good avail in one of her escape plots. She has only one daughter, and she is far from thin. Other than that, nothing is known about her. The novel's Mathilde is aggressive and at times impulsive. She is tough, capable of ruthless decisions, and comes off as cold and calculating—all of which helps the Resistance cause. Signoret's Mathilde exudes warmth, noticeably when she takes Gerbier's hand after the terrible ordeal of his second escape. We believe in the instinctiveness of her compassion for him in his despair at his perceived weakness, and we see him momentarily register her warmth. In the novel, this same gesture is described as follows: "Mathilde made a movement of which she seemed incapable. She took one of Gerbier's hands and held it for a while. Gerbier hardly seemed to notice" (Kessel 1963, 232).

If the Mathilde of the film is less fleshed out, nonetheless, her role takes on considerably greater importance than her factotum in the novel. She is given far more space than in the novel, to begin with. We might get fewer details on her background and history—and in that she is a shadow—but we certainly see her in action a great deal more than we do her counterpart in the novel. Repeatedly in the novel we get to hear of Mathilde's activities in a few lines, whereas often her male colleagues' exploits get full coverage. The most striking example of this difference between the two Mathildes occurs in relation to one particular exploit. This scheme, devised by Mathilde, is given a full ten minutes on screen. This is the sequence where she plans and attempts to carry out Félix's escape from prison. In the end, although she successfully makes it into the prison, disguised as a German Red Cross nurse, and persuades the guards that Félix must be released to a hospital, his actual transportation cannot take place because he is too badly tortured to be moved. In the novel, this operation (which involves successfully getting a resistor out of the hospital) is summed up starkly in a three-sentence paragraph.

Mathilde may not be as "virile" as the men—she does not take her cyanide tablet when arrested by the Gestapo and questioned—but then this is not for lack of courage. The Gestapo have also arrested her daughter and are using her to blackmail Mathilde: her daughter will be sent to a brothel in Poland for the

German troops if Mathilde either commits suicide or refuses to give names. Later on, she is gunned down even though there is no proof that she has "spoken," just the fear that she will. This explains the complex set of expressions on Mathilde's face (surprise, terror, understanding)[5] when the car carrying her judges, jury, and executioners—Jardie, Gerbier, Le Masque (played by Claude Mann) and her faithful friend, Le Bison (played by Christian Barbier), who will have to shoot her—drives up and she is killed. She dies for excess of maternal love before, necessarily, treachery.

Additionally, Mathilde may be less "virile" than the men, but it is she whom we see constantly on the move: going from one place to another, plotting operations, making bombs. Conversely, Gerbier is mostly static, kept in a concentration camp, prison, or safe hiding. Mathilde is constantly on the move, too, in her ability to transform herself: from housewife to widow (brazenly walking into a German-run hospital and stealing a nurse's uniform); from prostitute to meddlesome do-gooder. She can change persona. Gerbier seemingly cannot, and the rigidity of his dress code is a clear indicator of this. For the most part we see him clad in a spotless blue serge suit and white shirt—his fetishistic dress code standing (in his mind, one surmises) for a set of rules that no longer exist in this lawless time. He is also clean shaven, but meticulously so. Thus, once he is arrested for a second time and held in captivity, unable to shave or keep himself clean, he looks diminished in his disheveled state—small wonder that forcing him to run the gauntlet is the final humiliating straw for this man of steely resolve.

Undeniably, Mathilde is controlled by the male discursivity of the text (as exemplified by Gerbier's voiceover in the film), but she is not reduced to a stereotype. In the film she has a stronger role than in the novel and one that is primarily represented at the visual level through action, as opposed to Gerbier and Jardie, who are mostly represented through their speech and through non-action. She is also represented as cerebral and therefore on an equal footing with the two men. She often declares, "I'll have to think this through" and "I'll find a way" when discussing her various operations with Gerbier. She is also smart: she warned Gerbier to lay low, but he ignored or was too slow to take her advice and was taken prisoner for a second time. She may not be their intellectual equal, but this is surely for lack of time: she is *doing* while they are *being*. Jardie writes philosophical texts, and Gerbier reads them (particularly during his three-month stint in safe hiding).[6] The point here is that Mathilde does not occupy a feminized position anymore than the two men necessarily occupy a masculinized one. In a lawless society there is no reason why gender boundaries should not also be flaunted, and Mathilde stands as an impressive and "remarkable" (as the two men say) exemplar of this. There are two ways, then, to read her ending. A first reading yields the following. As a woman and as a mother (on two counts of femininity, therefore), she can no longer be allowed to stay in this "virile world" of the Resistance. She has become a liability, and an end must be put to her masquerade in the masculine; that is, she is to be returned to the feminine (where she belongs). A second reading suggests something more complex and is more consistent with the contradictions around masculinity and femininity, as exemplified by the less than masculinized roles of Gerbier and Jardie mentioned above. First, she is not being made an example of, as was the case with the earlier assassination of a young man in the Resistance who had denounced Gerbier. The comparison with the young man is significant because, unlike him, she is not reduced (feminized). Even their deaths separate them. She is noisily shot down in broad daylight, he is strangled (so as not to make noise) in a darkened room. She is killed because the men sense there is no alternative. Indeed, in letting the men know what has happened, she has perhaps indicated that she would wish it (this is what Jardie argues). Thus, the shooting is an act of mercy and her death an act of courage. It is significant that in these closing moments, the subjectivity is as much hers as theirs—arguably for the first time in the film. Just before they kill her, the camera holds each man separately in a medium close-up as if being viewed, scrutinized by her. She knows, then, who are her judges and assassins, and she understands why they are such (even though there is no certainty that she has in fact talked and given names).

Given that audiences were already on the decline in France (having dropped by one-third in a period of five years),[7] *L'armée des ombres* was a reasonable success at the box office (1.5 million tickets sold, the top-grossing French film of that year; *Le cerveau* garnered 5.5 million). It was, however, strongly criticized by the two heavyweight film journals of the time, *Cahiers du cinéma* and *Postif*, which, after May 1968, had adopted a radical neo-Marxist position. They accused the film of being Gaullist, latching on to de Gaulle's brief presence in the film (albeit as a shadow) when he decorates Jardie for bravery. They also dismissed it as shallow and useless.[8] However, by the time of the making and release of this film, de Gaulle had resigned as president, so he was a very soft target for the militant Left. Undoubtedly, he was unpopular. By the late 1960s, he had become so authoritarian that his regime felt like a dictatorship by consent to many, and very few were sorry to see him go. Historically, though, he did have a significant role to play in the Resistance, and, factually, he did decorate resistors from his secret residence in London—hence his presence in the film and in the novel. But the values espoused in the film are not Gaullist; that is, the film does not reflect the notion of a glorious past. Indeed, as objectively as possible it shows the crises of conscience that individuals felt and the dehumanizing effect that this war from the shadows had upon them.

Far more controversial—in political terms—was *L'aveu*, which Signoret and Montand made with Costa-Gavras. This film, based on the personal account of the Czech Communist Artur London's imprisonment during the Prague purges of the early 1950s, caused considerable ripples among the Left and the Communists. The background is as follows: Over twenty-two months (1951–1952), Artur Gérard London, a dedicated Communist since his early youth, was arrested by the Czech authorities and subjected to brutal torture until he confessed to crimes he had never committed. London's credentials as a "good" Communist were such that, in 1949, he was appointed vice-minister for foreign affairs. He had fought in the Spanish civil war with the International Brigade, then worked for the Resistance in France as the head of the MOI, a secret Resistance cell of the immigrant workforce.[9] He was subsequently deported to Mauthausen, a concentration camp known as Night and Fog, and was one of its few survivors. In 1952, along with thirteen other prisoners, London was brought to court in a show trial, broadcast live to the nation, known as the Slansky trial (so-called because Rudolf Slansky, one of the fourteen accused, was the general secretary of the Czech Communist party, and as such the most senior member of the government until his arrest). Of the fourteen on trial, eleven were Jews. All had formerly fought in Spain as members of the International Brigade, all were subjected to similar treatment as London, and all confessed to being Trotskyites and having conspired against the state, to have worked with American and British agents to destabilize and, more significantly, bring about a regime reversal in favor of Western imperialism. Of the fourteen, eleven were sentenced to death and hanged; three, including London, were given life emprisonment.[10]

The point is, however, that London, as well as his coaccused, was seen, until 1951, when he was arrested, as a "good" Communist. Certainly, his belief was in the party (it could do no wrong), which is eventually why he succumbs to his torturers, known euphemistically as "referents," and confesses, believing that it is for the good of the party. This fervent commitment to the party also helps to explain why after the Rajk trial in 1949, when Lazlo Rajk was brought to trial in Hungary for conspiring with the West, London condoned his condemnation and signed the resolution condemning him to death.[11]

By 1951, three things combined to make London an undesirable and therefore someone to be liquidated. The first was Joseph Stalin's increasing sense that a third world war was on the horizon. The cold war was already a reality. In the United States, McCarthyism was biting deep into the paranoid fantasy of "Reds under the beds." New presidential elections were under way, and General Dwight Eisenhower, a staunch anti-Communist, was emerging as the leading candidate for the presidency. The second was Czechoslovakia's own internal problems. Slansky's economic policies had turned to disastrous effect, and in order to deflect attention from his failures, he decided to launch a purge, one that eventually backfired since, allied as he was to the other thirteen, he too was arrested under the orders of Czech president Klement Gottwald, a Stalinist poodle. The third connects to the involvement of all fourteen in the International Brigade (and for a certain number to their involvement with the French Resistance). In Stalin's view, at least, their communism was not forged under him, but was established during their period in the West. As such, it could be read as empathizing more closely with Trotsky's version of communism, than, say, either V. I. Lenin's or Stalin's. As London comes to understand during his terrible months of torture, Stalin was engaged in a systematic "removal" from power of the "cosmopolitan" (and predominantly Jewish) Communists who had formerly volunteered for the International Brigade. The first attacks started in reaction to the "Yugoslav affair," Marshal Tito's decision to create his own brand of socialism. The Rajk trial was a further nail in their coffin; the final one came with Gottwald's condemnation of the fourteen former members of his central committee (London 1968, 130).

This detailed context is necessary to understand why Montand and Signoret agreed to be in Costa-Gavras's film, and also why Jorge Semprun was persuaded to write the script.[12] Although Signoret never openly criticized the Eastern European Communist bloc, she had already taken her distance from the Communist party (in essence over the 1956 Soviet repression of Hungary). Montand, however, had not. It took his reading of London's book to finally accept that the socialism as practiced by the Soviet Union and its satellites was a travesty. He felt deeply compromised because at the time of the Prague trials he had accepted the confessions as the truth. Now the scales fell from his eyes.[13] Thus, this film for both Montand and Signoret was about their coming to terms with their convictions as former champions of communism—a recognition of their romantic beliefs in a pure revolution.[14] Making this film was Montand's rupture with communism, but not his (nor Signoret's, for that matter) rejection of the idea of a humanitarian socialism.[15] Undoubtedly, because of his own sense of guilt,

Montand played this role with total dedication, even going so far as to follow London's regime during the weeks of making the film. He lost over twelve kilos during the six weeks of shooting, often staying up all night so he would look like a man deprived of food and sleep.

Signoret for her part was quite troubled by the idea of being involved in this film. She did not want her or Montand's participation to be used by the enemies of socialism as grist for their condemnation of socialism.[16] She was equally troubled by the role of Lise, London's French wife, who repudiated her husband after his public confession and wrote a letter to President Gottwald, which, in turn, was broadcast over state radio. In this letter she stated:

> I believed that my husband had been a victim of the treachery of others seeking to hide their criminal activity against the party behind his case. Sadly, after hearing his own admission of guilt, my hopes have evaporated. He is a traitor to his party and his country. My suffering is huge and human. But as a communist I must be happy that the conspiracy against the state was uncovered and join all those who demand a just punishment for the traitors.[17]

For Signoret, it was inconceivable that a wife would denounce her husband. Eventually, it was her friend Chris Marker who helped persuade her to take up the role. He made her watch a documentary he had made on Lise London in which she explained why she wrote the letter (for a true Communist, loyalty to the party was above all other considerations). However, Signoret did so with reticence; she found it difficult to embody a character toward whom she felt such antipathy.[18] Indeed, how could Signoret allow her person to be invaded by someone who, on an ethical level, she detested?[19] It is worth recalling what Signoret once said about accepting roles: "I would be incapable of lending myself to an enterprise that went against my deepest convictions. I can perfectly well play the role of a Gestapo denunciator in an anti-fascist film. But I could not be a remarkable mother, or wonderful lover in a fascist film. I cannot and I never have" (Signoret 1978, 329). Because Costa-Gavras's film denounces the abuses of Stalinism, not socialism per se, she was able to see the project as an honorable one. But what undoubtedly finally brought her around was her sense of solidarity with Montand. Given their reputation as the star couple committed to political struggles, her absence would have been interpreted as a sign that she had "dropped" Montand.[20] *L'aveu* was a watershed film for her. It reinvigorated her politicized persona, and she became even more of a fervent defender of human rights after that film.[21]

As I have already pointed out in Chapter Two, Signoret's role is small within the context of the film. Given this, it is unclear whether the audience—unused to the idea of the sovereignty of commitment to the Communist party—would understand her character's renunciation of her husband. Crucially, as opposed to the original text, we do not realize that it is a renunciation that London expects, wedded as he is also to the supremacy of the party. Nor do we learn, as we do from the text, that he desperately hopes his wife will distance herself from him so that she can safely get back to her native France with their children and her aged parents. In her few appearances in the film Signoret's character remains strong and defiant in response to her husband's arrest and her own progressive marginalization from the party. She fights the system that attempts to disempower her and struggles to obtain information about her husband, that is, until she too believes in his guilt.

Signoret is only on screen for sixteen minutes (10 percent of the film time). She appears eight times—two of which are in the form of her husband's subjective flashbacks when in captivity. These flashbacks serve, not as tender moments of intimacy between the couple, but to establish her close affinity with the party. Thus, she declares in the first, "the party is always right," and, in the second, "Stalin has taught us that the most precious capital is man; when he is drowning we must help pull him out of the water." She makes both these pronouncements at dinner, potentially a time for a close sense of family. But that is not what comes through. What transpires is London's image of his wife (whom in the book he loves irrevocably) as an exemplary comrade. It is noteworthy that a bit later on he makes a similar declaration ("We always believed the party could not make mistakes"). Shortly after her husband's arrest, the secret police agents come to her house to search it. She fiercely stands up to them, demanding they first obtain a warrant. She uses her credentials as a good Communist (listing her trajectory: daughter of a Spanish Communist, two years' training in Moscow, International Brigade, French Resistance, emprisoned in Ravensbrück concentration camp), as well as those of her husband, to point out the foolishness of their quest—to little avail, it has to be said, since they search and remove papers and photographs. Her strong Communist militancy works at both the personal and the political level, therefore. She remains tough and resolute throughout, first, in her standing up for her husband and fighting his cause from outside and, second, in her fervent certainty, once he has confessed, that she must repudiate him as a bad Communist.

Signoret manages, just, to humanize this steely character. Our first sense of this is her care for her children and parents, of whom she is very protective during this distressful time. She fearlessly defends her home against the intruders by physically trying to prevent them going upstairs to disturb her family, and once their search is finished, she accuses them of being no better than the Nazis. After several aborted attempts to obtain details on her husband from top officials, we see fear start to creep into her eyes; here, Signoret successfully makes use of her ability to say volumes with just her eyes. She stands strong against the snide insinuations that her husband is in a difficult situation, declaring: "For me to believe he is guilty he must tell me himself"—something that certainly Signoret would stand by (even if in the film she is obliged to act differently). Signoret's aptitude at ironic delivery comes through when she is removed from her job as a radio journalist and told to find work in a factory. She retorts: "So that's the punishment; what that says for the proletarian-only party!" rightly pointing out that to see factory work as demeaning is an insult to the very class the socialist revolution is supposed to be putting above all other considerations. Finally, her ability to move with conviction from a stylish, well-dressed, and fully made-up French woman into the proletarian dress code of drab clothing and no makeup gives us more than a hint at how Signoret tried to play this character with honesty—because, of course, the real Lise London would have behaved in this way (as a good Communist who submits to the will of the party). She enters the poverty class and modestly sets about her given tasks. In this same regard, she accepts her removal from their comfortable home into a shared apartment with dignity, and just gets on with it.[22] But there is an added touch to this "transformation," which she undergoes as a result of her loss of status and which comes over clearly in her journeys home on the tram. Signoret wears a scarf that, in its plainness, points to the plainness of her unmade-up face, and also to the marked aging her personage has undergone as a result of the traumatic events.

All those involved in the film felt it was important to make it in the name of socialism. It was not, to their mind, an anti-Communist film, as several critics attempted to label it.[23] The film does expose the perverse and mad logic of a tyrannical system,[24] but clearly makes the point that it is men who misinterpret an ideology and mold it to their desires, not the ideology itself that is at fault. It was a humbling experience for Signoret as well as Montand. She said: "Ten years ago I thought I knew everything, now not. . . . I now ask myself questions with considerable violence."[25] Clearly she also saw it as a political/civic film in that she expressed the hope that it would "provoke some people into action."[26] The hot ticket of Montand and Signoret certainly attracted audiences, even if they did not at first know what they were letting themselves in for—the audience figures reached 2.2 million (the top-grossing French film of that year, *Le gendarme en ballade*, had 4.8 million).

Two Interludic Cameos: *L'Américain* and *Comptes à rebours*

A brief mention of these two films must be made, first, because *L'Américain* introduces a new type of persona where Signoret is concerned and, second, because *Comptes à rebours* provides some useful insight on characterization. Both were films for which Signoret agreed to do the part because the respective filmmakers, Marcel Bozzuffi and Roger Pigaut, were friends of hers. She helped by giving her name and by not taking a fee, opting for a percentage of the royalties, if there were any (which there were with Pigaut's: *Comptes à rebours* gained an audience of 1.1 million).

Bozzuffi's film relates the story of a young man, Bruno (played by Jean-Louis Trintignant) who comes home from America, where he had lived for twelve years, with a view to settling down. Home is the provincial town of Rouen. Over a few days he visits and meets up with his old friends but finds he does not fit in. A few have made a success of their lives, most have not, others have stayed the same. In any event, the great dreams and hopes they had when they were young have dissipated. We are privy to a number of flashbacks to twelve years earlier. At that time (1956–1957), the Algerian war was in full swing. Three of Bruno's friends were called up, but only two returned—to bury their friend. It is after the funeral that Bruno leaves for the United States. In effect, Bruno's absence covers the whole period of de Gaulle's presidency. By the time he returns—spring of 1969—de Gaulle has gone. His impact, of course, has not. *L'Américain* is a fairly truthful reflection of France of the 1960s: gray, monotonous, and one where the little man, particularly the specialist artisan, feels completely overpowered by Gaullist economic policies of modernization, which incorporated a massive building program, from expressways to high-rise buildings. It was also an era that had not come to terms with its loss of Algeria. Thus, there is a small-mindedness, racism, and bigotry in evidence in the film, embodied by the same man who is the disempowered artisan.

One of Bruno's friends is Léone (Signoret), who runs a restaurant. She too has unfulfilled dreams. As a young woman, she had met a lovely man who had asked her to go to Venezuela, but she had been too frightened to take that chance. "I was stupid," she tells Bruno, as she serves him up a sumptuous boeuf bourguignon. So she stayed, got married, and ran the restaurant (it is instructive that we do not get to see her husband; he is asleep or else not there). Bruno is right when he tells her she has not aged. Indeed, twelve years ago she was wearing more or less the same clothes and had the same hairstyle (the only difference being she now has a light streak of white). She was also doing pretty much the same thing: running her restaurant on a shoestring for her friends and clients, many of whom are Bruno's friends. She is and was the provider of food and warmth, the maternal presence that all these men then and now seem to be so singularly lacking elsewhere. She cannot sing (in one of the flashbacks, she is asked to, but declines and attempts to propose a toast), but she can cook (in that same scene she produces a beautiful cake for all to consume).

This persona of the caring maternal figure at work, in the flesh, so to speak, was a departure for Signoret. Prior to this, she had been a worried/terrified mother in *L'armée des ombres*, but we only know this through hearsay; we never see her being maternal, and its only relevance within the narrative is that it brings about her own death (because she may have talked to protect her daughter). In *L'aveu* she shows her maternal care in that she attempts to protect her children from the abusive and intrusive behavior of the police; otherwise, she is spooning out edicts of good communism to them at the dining table. In her earlier film periods, as we noted, she virtually never occupied the position of mother. On the three occasions when she did, she was cold and undemonstrative to her daughter in the one (*Les sorcières de Salem*), cruel to her son in another (*The Seagull*) and, in the third (*Le jour et l'heure*), very much an absentee mother (although she clearly loves her children, her horrid sister-in-law appears to have more control on their upbringing than her). She is absent even to the point of inadvertently abandoning them when, with her American pilot, she clambers onto the train going to Toulouse.

Bozzuffi wanted to make a film against war.[27] As such, *L'Américain* does take a strong stance against war and the futility of lost lives. Indeed, both the Algerian and the Vietnam conflicts are mentioned, but the stronger political edge of this film is the exposure of the suffocating effect of postwar regeneration on a particular youth class—a youth class that did not go anywhere because it lacked the means in terms of education or money; a youth class for whom lucky breaks were an exception and could go wrong, as occurred for Jacky (played by Marcel Bozzuffi), the brilliant footballer whose career was cut short by an accident. Bozzuffi's film becomes an intriguing study on France's silent generation for whom World War II stole their childhood and the Algerian war their youth.[28] No wonder they need a maternal type in the form of Léone, who is deeply tolerant of their rowdiness and occasionally barbaric ways. Significantly her restaurant, which was painted a bright white in the late 1950s, is currently painted a dark crimson red; where before people ate, laughed, joked, and danced, now they stay up late into the night and gamble, chain-smoke, and drink.

The maternal under some guise or another reappears in most of Signoret's films of the 1970s and 1980s, but it will not always be the "good" mother as in this film. The series of maternal molds into which Signoret casts herself ranges from benevolent through controlling to quite intensely malevolent. But first a brief word about *Comptes à rebours*, Signoret's first thriller in fifteen years. Because Signoret was preparing for *Le chat* when Pigaut approached her with his project, she did not, at first, want to get involved. But there was a second reason. For most of the 1960s she had been making films either for political reasons or for reasons of friendship, and she was getting rather tired of it. Not all of these roles suited her (as we saw with Lise London); sometimes the direction was not that strong. Pigaut, in an interview, even went so far as to say that in taking small roles she lacked the space to give of herself fully.[29] Several earlier experiences of doing small parts really do not support this last opinion; as we saw in *The Deadly Affair*, she does so much with so little. However, when Pigaut goes on to say that small parts can work for her if the role sticks or is made to measure for her, then he has got it right.[30] And with *Comptes à rebours*, once she had read the script, she clearly saw herself in the role of Léa, the wife of Juliani (played by Charles Vanel), a former top man in the criminal underworld.

The story of *Comptes à rebours* is of a double revenge. After a ten-year absence (seven in prison and three on parole), François Nolan (played by Serge Reggiani) returns to Paris determined to avenge his brother's death, which occurred during a robbery. He is convinced that one of the four members of his former gang denounced him to the police, which led to his imprisonment and his brother's death. Also out for revenge is a private eye, Valberg (played by Michel Bouquet), who was shot by Nolan during the robbery. Because Nolan's mentor, Juliani, is now confined to a wheelchair and is mute (a victim of a near fatal shooting), Nolan has to call on Léa to help him set up a meeting with his former gang to see if he can get at the truth. This part she successfully negotiates, but all four deny having betrayed Nolan. He warns them he is seeking revenge. One of the four, Zampalone (played by Marcel Bozzuffi), decides to hire his own hitman to get Nolan first. The hitman, Narcisse (played by Bob Askloff), goes to Léa's house and attempts to extort the whereabouts of Nolan by threatening her husband. Because he cannot speak, the dreadful treatment he is subjected to horrifies Léa, who then is equally a target for his abuse. When he threatens to throw Juliani onto the fire, she cracks and tells him where he can find Nolan. However, Nolan systematically wipes out his former gang and Narcisse in an amazing scene with two-way mirrors. Nolan gets badly cut, but, nonetheless, he goes to free his old friends Léa and Juliani. Léa is so ashamed of what she has done and knows that Juliani will never forgive her. Nolan's wound is getting worse, Léa gives him their old car—an American one (what else?)—and he takes off to the house of his former girlfriend, Madeleine (played by Jeanne Moreau) so that her husband (played by Jean Desailly), a doctor, will patch him up. Nolan subsequently receives a phone call from Valberg telling him that the man who denounced him was the doctor—he had done it so he could get Madeleine for himself. Nolan confronts the doctor, who admits his guilt. Nolan leaves him his gun so that he will do "the decent thing" and takes off with Madeleine. At that point, Valberg steps in and kills the doctor but leaves the evidence so that it will point to Nolan. Nolan is arrested. Valberg is avenged, as, in a peculiar way, is Nolan.

The film, then, is about betrayal and revenge—fairly standard for a thriller. There is, however, no femme fatale. Both Léa and Madeleine are entirely honorable women. This is why Léa is so distraught. The understanding she and Nolan had built up over long years of friendship is suddenly broken by events beyond her control: dishonor and treachery in the male province. In this film, weak but brutal men (most symbolically embodied by Juliani, the dephallicized patriarch) are paired up against strong but vulnerable women. Both women pay a heavy price for sticking with their men (they lose them either through death or rejection). It is striking how similar a trope this is to Signoret's earlier 1950s films in which, as we noted, she consistently did not occupy the femme fatale position, often because her position was one of strength but also because it got usurped and taken over by the *homme fatal.*

Part Two: Resisting invisibility—*Le chat* and *La veuve Coudere*

Signoret made these two films in quick succession with Pierre Granier-Deferre; both were adaptations of Georges Simenon novels (as was her very last film, *L'Étoile du Nord*, 1982, made with the same director). Granier-Deferre was determined to work with Signoret even though the producers of *Le chat* were opposed to her being cast in the role of Clémence opposite Jean Gabin's Julien Bouin.[31] But he got his way. Simenon is well known for his cynical portraits of marriage (the exception being Maigret's in his police series of that same name), and Signoret is a far remove from the stingy, unsexual original character (Mathilde) in Simenon's novel. But, as Granier-Deferre put it, he wanted to round the characters out a bit, make them more moving. He went on: "In a film at least one character has to be likeable. That's why I made the woman a victim who is both aggressive and provoking, a victim of herself before she becomes her husband's."[32] And in his mind the only person who could hold those contradictory characteristics was Signoret. Gabin gave his backing, and Signoret got the part (Durant 1988, 105). Both men were right to hold out for her. The film gained just over a million spectators, who were undoubtedly eager to see the double act of two *monstres sacrés*, Gabin and Signoret. The two are brilliantly matched: it is a real ding-dong of a squabbling match between the two, admirably caught by the photography—there are virtually no two-shots of the couple in the whole film (30 out of 500). The entire film is shot almost exclusively in single shots of the two protagonists, as seen in the following table:

ANALYSIS OF SHOTS IN *LE CHAT*

	CUs	MCUs	MS	LS	Percent of Shots	
Signoret	15	51	150	25	[241][1]	48
Gabin	9	51	131	38	[229]	46
Signoret and Gabin	1	1	18	10	[30]	6

CU = close-up; LS = long shot; MCU = medium close-up; MS = medium shot
1. Numbers in brackets indicate total number of shots.

Signoret plays the drunk who has lost nearly everything: her career, her husband's love, and soon their home of twenty-five years. The couple are to be evicted to make way for the building development going on around them. Clémence retains, however, her pride and her love for Julien, no matter that he has abused both for years—by having mistresses and lately by bringing home a cat on whom he bestows all his love and whom he calls Le Greffier (a slang word for *cat*). After several fights, all instigated over the cat, Clémence eventually commits the *crime passionnel* and shoots the cat dead. Henceforth, Julien refuses to speak to her, communicating simply by flicking tightly folded notes at her (most of which have two simple words upon them, "the cat"). They do everything separately: shopping, cooking, eating. This war of silence continues until Clémence collapses (her heart gives way) and dies, soon after which, having recognized too late that he still loved her, Julien commits suicide.

Signoret's role fit her like a glove. So too did Gabin's, although it represented a shift back to earlier roles in his life—namely, his prewar films of the poetic realist period when he played the proletarian hero.[33] Gabin by the 1970s had become identified with roles that had more to do with crusty right-wing values than anything left of center. In *Le chat*, however, he dons once more his credentials of the 1930s, including the cloth cap (an icon of the working class). Julien's job, before he retired, was that of a print typesetter for the liberal press, he was a good union man, and so on. When he met Clémence, he drove a Harley-Davidson and clearly (if the flashbacks to their early love are anything to go by) was a seductive lover. Since then, he has become taciturn and curmudgeonly, moving around the house like a great lumbering bear. He even growls and grunts at Clémence like a cross bear. For her part, Clémence, whose adult life started out as a trapeze artist and tightrope walker, is a far more exotic affair than Julien. She smokes dark cigarillos. She drinks rum imported from Martinique (usually in a glass but also occasionally out of a bone china teacup). She eats fresh oysters for her lunch, neatly setting them out on her plate with seaweed for decoration. Julien drinks French wine and fries up onions with his steak, which he then unceremoniously plonks onto his plate. When indoors, she dresses as if she were still in the circus, even though a fall from the tightrope many years back ended her career and left her with a limp. Thus, at times she sports a silk Russian-style smock over tights, at others she wears a red satin dress under a leather jerkin and leather wristbands. Before retiring to bed, she dons a red satin Oriental-style dressing gown over her sexy black underwear. Outdoors, however, she is as conventionally and drably dressed as Julien is at all times. Evidently to her mind, there is no need for panache outside. Because her defiance is directed against Julien and his loss of love for her, the only appropriate space for acting this out is indoors in their former love nest. But, as her contrasting dress codes of the sexual and the asexual indicate, her refusal to accept that their love is dead has, to all intents and purposes, led to a splitting of the subject: outside she is ordinary, inside she is extraordinary—literally and figuratively.

Structurally, this film is built around three fights and three attempts (by Clémence) to get rid of the cat. The first fight occurs in the cellar, when Clémence has tried to discredit the cat in Julien's eyes by tearing his carefully wrapped newspapers and pretending the cat did it. Julien believes none of it. She accuses him of loving the cat more than her. He suggests she get a parrot, then she will have something to talk to all day and leave him alone. It is at this point that the sparring match begins: Signoret and Gabin play the scene as if they had rowed like this over many years. It is shot almost entirely in single medium close-ups edited rapidly, adding to the intensity. She screeches at him, "You only love your cat," then starts screaming like a cat: "Meow! Meow! Meow!" (fiercely pronounced as "miaayooo"). He tries to get out of the cellar. They fight on the steps. She screams again, "You old goat, you old goat!" He counters, accusing her of being sloshed (which she probably is). She calms down for a moment, asking him what he wants: "A new life? A new woman?" "Nothing, just a bit of air," he shouts back at her, his face purple with apoplexy, eyes bulging. "What about me?" she asks plaintively. "Oh you, you, you, you, you!" he thunders at her then grunts like an old bear, at which point she screeches again: "Yes, me, me, me!" several times over. The scene ends with her taking a tumble down the cellar steps thanks to the cat, who understandably wants to get out. Like

Le chat/The Cat (1971). The dynamic of a dead marriage: Clémence (Signoret) in circus attire smoking a cigarillo; Julien (Jean Gabin) in background, talking to his cat.

animals, the couple know how trapped they are (symbolically reinforced by being in the cellar). Small wonder that their growling, shrieking anger, which expresses their mutual rage and frustration, is so close to animal sounds. It is a fierce scene, and, occurring as it does only a third of the way through the film, it does not augur well. We know we are in for more, if not worse.

The second fight, some five minutes further into the film, is far more subtle in its tone and practice and ends with Clémence on her own tearing her hair out and grunting in her frustration at her inability to get any kind of communication going with Julien other than through a shouting match. It provides another view of the domestic disharmony in which they fester, another fighting style whereby they chip away at each other in their perverse games. In this mise-en-scène of the debilitating erosion of their relationship, Julien plays the card of first provoking Clémence, then deflating her position of attack. She plays the game of whoever has the last word wins. In the end, he walks out of the house, leaving her steaming on the staircase. The interesting thing is that, although she is occupying the higher ground this time (in the cellar incident, it was Julien who was, for the most part, higher up the cellar stairs), she is the one who is left disempowered—as indeed her heavy trailing up the stairs after he has gone exemplifies.

Clémence now ups the ante and sets about deliberately trying to rid herself of the cat. Her first, cruel but comical attempt aborts. She drags the cat off in a shopping bag to a supermarket and deposits him on the fish counter. The way Signoret spies on him from behind the supermarket shelves is a master stroke of acting, pointing to her ambivalence about what she has done (she likes the cat, and clearly wants to be sure it is alright). Cleverly, the cat finds his way home. The next time, however, she is entirely successful. Her fatal shooting of the cat comes as the end point to the couple's third and final fight. The fight is something of a combination of the two others and comes close on the heels of the last one (fifteen minutes on). Upstairs, in the bedroom in the dark, Clémence softly but persistently asks Julien why he stopped loving her. For growing old? Not having a child? Drinking too much? To all of these he grunts no, of course not. She reminds him he had always had mistresses and she had never been unfaithful to him. The scene starts off calmly enough, her voice reasonable if a bit choked (as if holding back tears). Eventually she snaps the light on and demands to know why it was that, one day, he awoke and started looking at her as an object and began to love a stray cat. "I changed," he bellows and goes off downstairs to find his cat and get some sleep. Up until this point, this scene is shot in a medium two-shot; however, there is no harmony between the two, even though Clémence may be trying (it is always she who asks what went wrong). Instead, the temperature is constantly rising. She follows after him, determined to get an answer. Still in a medium two-shot, she continues to probe him until he tells her with a silent fury (cut to a single medium close-up on him), his face apoplectic and eyes bulging once more, that he no longer loves her. Now begins the fierce standoff. The couple are shot in single medium close-ups in a series of fast edited shots. She says she still loves him; he growls at her that it is grotesque to speak like that at their age and that one day they will be separated forever. Why not now, she flares back at him. Fine, he shouts and gets out his gun. He shoves it into her hand (brief two-shot). Cut to single medium close-up on her face full of horror as he tells her she can now commit suicide and everyone will say she died because her husband cheated on her with a cat. He stomps off upstairs. She stands bewildered, goes to her cupboard, and takes a swig of rum from the bottle. Julien comes back down and leaves the house. She calls pitifully after him, and then she flips. She picks up the gun, then hesitates for a moment, as if pondering shooting herself. Just then the cat meows, also pitifully. Clémence, her eyes now ablaze, turns the gun on him and shoots. She misses. The cat scuttles down into the cellar, pursued by Clémence, where she shoots him dead. It is a terrible moment when she registers all she has lost. Julien comes and silently removes the cat—and equally silently removes himself from the house to go and stay with his former mistress, Nellie (played by Annie Cordy).

Gabin and Signoret's performances in these scenes never enter the realm of pathos. Both actors manage to blend a minimalism of performance style with intense anger and succeed, through their different procedures, in engaging our sympathy even as we remain appalled at their cruelty to each other. Nor are these scenes funny; they are ultimately frightening because the rage the two feel is so palpable. Their pain is rendered matter in the form of their two decrepit bodies shipwrecked on their past and unable to move forward. This is so clearly exemplified in Clémence's case when, after a week, Julien comes back. She is thrilled to see him, believing he has "come back to her" (as in, a lover returns). Totally vulnerable in her openness, she sits up in bed, her eyes alive with hope, her lips moist with desire. To no avail; he shatters her moment of hope by laying his final ultimatum: total silence between them forever.

If Clémence felt a desperate loneliness before, that is nothing compared to the chilling loneliness to come. Signoret conveys the nuance between these two types of loneliness by embodying the former as a complete corporeal experience, and by confining the expression of the latter through her eyes and lips above all. By way of illustration let us take two examples, one for each type. In the buildup to their third and fatal fight, Clémence is standing hunched over the mantelpiece in their bedroom, her arms outstretched, her head bowed, and her back to us; Julien is lying in bed in the foreground. Hers is a position of supreme martyrdom and submission, her back awaiting the flail of her husband's cruel words or evidence of his neglectful indifference to rain upon it. Her whole body tells us how desperate she is, but she is not yet totally alone (hence the relevance of the two-shot). Later, however, when Julien leaves her (for the week), the camera catches Clémence in medium close-up looking out of the window at the demolition of the buildings going on all around her. This time it is her face that conveys the meaning of loneliness. She is framed through the square panes of the window in her total isolation. We can read in her eyes how she perceives the demolition of the old buildings on her street as a metaphor for her own relationship being battered into rubble. The sense of desolation is reinforced by the use of slow motion on her and the demolition ball as it thunders into the walls. We can *hear* her eyes crying. Instructively, in a parallel scene (intercut with this one and also in slow motion) we see Julien in medium shot watching from the outside, but his focus is on the cats playing on the scaffolding. To his imaged sense of loss (cat, buildings) tempered by hope (more cats available) contrasts hers of irreparable loss and despair (nothing left anywhere).

Once Julien has returned and banished her to Coventry, the camera catches Clémence in medium close-up as she winces each time Julien flicks a note at her. Yet such is her pain (by now achieving masochistic proportions), she keeps every single note and stores them in a box under her bed, as if they were *billets doux*, not *billets amers* (bitter sweets). Her last moments alive are shockingly painful. Julien has gone out, having just flicked another nasty note at her. She goes up to bed. She lifts the box out from under her bed, painstakingly opening it up. She then systematically takes each note out, carefully setting them on the bed in categories and muttering over the words to herself as if they meant something other than what they really do. We see Signoret/Clémence's lips moisten as she mouths the words, as if anticipating her lover's kiss. A monumental self-deception, but utterly believable.

Signoret's next film, *La veuve Couderc*, is in some ways a mirror image of *Le chat*. To the urban issues of the latter contrast the rural ones of the former. Both make indirect comments about political issues. *Le chat* exposes the merciless redevelopment of Paris, which meant ripping out small communities and filling the spaces with high-rise apartment blocks of anonymous concrete. Economic growth at any price was the policy pursued by President Georges Pompidou in the early 1970s, even at the cost of individuals (as with the Bouins) and certainly the hearts of local *quartiers* (not for nothing is the local park named after Jean Jaurès, the high-minded socialist of the early 1900s). In *La veuve Couderc*, which is set in 1934, the list of political nods is longer. We begin with a reference to the Stavisky affair, an economic scandal that led to a resurgence of anti-Semitism (clearly attested to in the film by the slogan daubed on the church: "The house of God is not for the Jews"). The threat of fascism is hinted at in various ways, including the presence of the extreme right-wing group the Croix de Feu. Reference is also made to the climate of repression, with the mounted police surrounding the factory on strike (in the 1930s, there were thousands of strikes on a yearly basis that were cruelly dealt with by the forces of the government).

Finally, this film fully evidences how Malthusianism still prevailed in France: modernization and expansion were seen as a bad thing (thus, the widow's plans for progress with her secondhand egg incubator will come to naught).

The two films' respective narratives are "love stories" about the transience of love. In *Le chat*, we witness the agonizing death of a love that has outlived itself; in *La veuve Couderc*, we watch a love affair that ends almost before it begins. In both films Signoret stars opposite a *monstre sacré*: Gabin, "the superb ruin of the past,"[34] in *Le chat* and, in *La veuve Couderc*, Alain Delon, unarguably the most beautiful French male star of his time. Both Gabin and Delon espoused political beliefs that were diametrically opposed to Signoret's; nonetheless, they worked extremely well together, and Delon became one of Signoret's friends.[35] Granier-Deferre spoke of the chemistry generated between Delon and Signoret,[36] Durant (1988, 106) of the effect of her femininity on Gabin.

Signoret's roles are mirror images—Clémence, whose heart is cracking under the weight of her loneliness; the widow Couderc, whose heart is at last, however briefly, to be filled with love. Unlike Clémence, the widow Couderc is physically and sexually extremely active. Where previously she had sexual liaisons with her father-in-law (after her husband's death), she now enjoys a full sexual love affair with her young lodger, Jean (Delon), even if she has to come to terms with sharing him with her young niece, Félicie (played by Octavia Piccolo). She refuses to become a victim to her horrid sister- and brother-in-law, who live opposite her farm (on the other side of the canal), and fights them tooth and nail as they work deviously to strip her of her home and assets. She is the opposite of Clémence in this respect, for whom even cruelty is a sign that at least she is noticed. Too much hurt eventually kills Clémence; too much love emboldens the widow to die alongside her lover in the final shootout.

Signoret's women are certainly stronger than Simenon's originals, undoubtedly because in Simenon, they are more sketches than fleshed out creatures, certainly they are not complex, nor are they in contradiction with themselves. Signoret can hold opposing characteristics in counterpoint, which, as we saw in Chapter Two, is part of what gave her performance style such depth. Thus, in these two films currently under discussion, Signoret was able to demonstrate a range of emotions, all within a matter of seconds, within one glance even—for example, in *La veuve Couderc*, when she makes explicit her desire for Jean: she invites him with her eyes into her bedroom even though she knows she is no longer appetizing (in the way Félicie is). Similarly, in these two films, which are, in part, treatises on the loneliness of the middle-aged woman, Signoret, through counterpointing strength with fragility, shows just how women experience it. Thus, in *Le chat*, she can be very determined to pursue Julien, even though emotionally he has been absent for years; but then almost immediately she can crumble inside and reveal just how much she is suffering in her solitude. The scene in the Jean Jaurès Square is just one example. Here the two sit at about ten meters from each other on separate park benches—they might just as well be ten kilometers apart for all that Julien will acknowledge her presence. Yet Clémence persists in looking over at him, willing him to recognize her as he stays hidden behind his newspaper. A child comes by and drops a spade near Clémence's feet; she picks it up and gestures to return it, but the child is long gone. Clémence holds it dangling in the empty air, unacknowledged and surplus to requirements, just like herself.

The widow Couderc lives her solitude quite differently. It is interesting for example, that, unlike Clémence, there is very little space for the unconscious; thus, she does not have flashbacks to earlier happy times as does Clémence. She is very much stuck in the now, defending herself on all sides: trying to keep the farm going singlehandedly (she never stops working), protecting herself from the continuous abuse of her in-laws. But she also takes risks and reaches out for things that will fortify her, give her hope—not the bottle (as Clémence) but the incubator, the young man. The incubator is a financial risk, the love affair with Jean is risky on several counts. First, as she will learn, he is an escaped murderer. He was imprisoned in 1922 for shooting two dignitaries apparently without reason (when asked by the judge, he merely replied, "I'd had enough"). His age spared him the guillotine. Second, he carries a gun, which the widow discovers and "confiscates." But when Jean asks her if she is afraid of him, she says no. Finally, he is not going to be "faithful" to her in the traditional sense.

It is this last issue that is so hard for her to accept, not the other two. At one point we witness the intensity of her jealousy (after he has slept with Félicie) as she furiously peels potatoes and tells him to leave. He persuades her otherwise by refusing to be intimidated by her (just as she had been unafraid of him over the gun). She allows herself to overcome her jealousy of his sexual relations with Félicie because she realizes he is telling her the truth when he says he wants both of them. With her, he says, he wants not just her but what she stands for, namely, the home that she resembles—that is, what is safe, the familiar, the warmth of love—as well as the sexual. As for Félicie, she is young flesh, which he also desires but which, as he says at one point, "is not important"—not as important as home. Her willingness to accept a compromise situation with Jean (a triangulation of sorts) brings stability into her life and happiness. We see them embraced as they lie asleep together; he tenderly seeks out her hand as he awakens, and she watches over him. He protects her from further abuse from her in-laws, and they are excited about their plans to expand the farm, even if they are pipe dreams. Conversely, his moments with Félicie are just that, snatched moments in the barn or in the tall grass away from her father's controlling ways.

This high-risk strategy of the widow's could entail losing it all, which, of course, she does in the end. Her in-laws finally "kidnap" the father-in-law. Until then he had lived with the widow and enjoyed her bed from time to time. They get him on their side and use him to denounce Jean to the police. The father-in-law denounces in the hopes he can get the widow back for himself. The brother- and sister-in-law do it so they can get the widow out of the way and take back the farm.

When Jean comes on the scene, the old man, feeling spurned by the widow, calls her *garce* (bitch); she looks quite pleased at his insult. As a woman in her fifties, it could be read as rather anachronistic, but it makes the point that the father-in-law is angry at her sense that she is free to play the sexual field.[37] This label pleases her but does not prevent her from using a similar one as a term of abuse toward Félicie. The widow Couderc accuses Félicie of being "a slut" because she sleeps with just about anybody (indeed, she has a baby whose father is unknown). Yet the widow sleeps with her father-in-law (to protect her hold on the farm), and, when Jean turns up, she sets her sights on him (as does Félicie) and seduces him into her bed. Thus, ostensibly, the widow dispenses with her sexual favors in a manner not necessarily dissimilar from Félicie, especially from the old man's point of view. There are, however, differences. Prior to her marriage, the widow informs us, she had been raped by the master of the house where she was a servant and made pregnant by his son (she lost the child). Her husband was a drunk, and no further children were forthcoming. Félicie freely gives herself to whomsoever she desires. She oozes fertility and nubile sexuality, which is, of course, why the widow (well into her middle age, no longer fertile, and thereby a crone) resents her so much and picks on her. Up until meeting Jean, then, the widow had only encountered sexuality as a system of power relations. Either she had been the victim of it or she herself had used her erotics as a powerful tool (with the father-in-law as a means of keeping the farm). Now all changes with Jean, and she enters into an erotics of desire (there are numerous occasions when we see her looking at Jean in a powerfully charged way). In the former practice of the self (erotics as power), the widow privileges the rational over the erotic—logically, she knows she needs to keep the old man happy so that he will side with her against her sister- and brother-in-law. Sex becomes a rational exchange and one of power. In the latter practice of the self (erotics of desire), she allows the irrationality of the biological to lead her through to sexual fulfillment (she even celebrates by buying herself a new satin nightie). As both she and Jean say at one point, "No one would understand." Ultimately, she is not understandable because she embodies a variety of positions in relation to her sexuality that appear to be in contradiction—based as they are on power and desire, reason and unreason—even though, for her, they make sense and are agenced by her according to her needs.

Whereas Félicie's sexuality is seen as "natural" ("She can't help it," her parents say), the widow's is one that threatens and, therefore, is deemed unnatural, grotesque even, as is evidenced by the rough treatment she receives from her in-laws, when they literally throw her out of their house like a sack of garbage and give her a drubbing. The various diegetic audiences register their disapproval, whether it be the in-laws on the other side of the canal or the old women in the village. The scene where the widow washes Jean's clothes at the communal bathing house with two older women and one about her own age illustrates the threat her sexuality poses. She scrubs and washes his clothes with relish and pride as the other women rather sourly look on. In a series of close-ups of the widow we watch her returning their disapproving gaze with an ironic smile and knowing looks, very aware that she is deliberately provoking them. She holds his shirt and then his trousers up for all to view and in so doing proudly declaims her sexual knowledge of the body that inhabits them. In their eyes hers is a transgressive body. She is a widow, but she does not behave like one, apart from her black clothing. She refuses to conform to the norm whereby society consigns women of a certain age to the asexual sphere. Indeed, she breaks a number of taboos. She sleeps with an older relative (her father-in-law) and exploits him to her advantage. She then sleeps with a young man who is half her age—young enough to be her son. Just as bad, in the eyes of the in-laws, she gives Jean her dead husband's clothes to wear around the farm. Although, technically, there is nothing "illegal" about her behavior, her sexual practice (sleeping with the "father" and the "son") is clearly read as virtually incestuous. This sense of outrage that her behavior generates comes down to sex, age, and marital status—three counts on which she transgresses. The widow is in charge of her sexuality, and those around her do not like it.[38] To which she retorts: Tough! She is not made to "pay" for this behavior, however, even though she dies at the end. She has known true happiness for a few weeks—more than she could have hoped for. When, in his initial attempt to escape, Jean leaves her behind, she has to gulp back her tears and her fears for both his safety and her loss. When he returns (he realizes he is surrounded and decides to go back to her: the home, the familiar), she elects to stay and die with her lover. The incubator and her house go up in flames; all is lost, no matter. There is no past to return to, and even if there were, it is no longer what she wants. The rational and the irrational cojoin: "No," she says, when he beseeches her to go, "I won't leave." She asserts her will (erotics as power) and her desire (erotics as desire) to end in the present/presence of love. Jean's last attempt to save her by running out of the house into a hail of bullets, which kills both of them at the same moment, does not lessen her choice; rather, it seals her value to him (as worth dying for).[39]

MIDDLE PASSAGE—1972–1976

Constructions of the maternal: *Les granges brûlées* and *Rude journée pour la reine*

Although *Les granges brûlées* is a thriller and *Rude journée pour la reine* a film that comes under the rubric of political/civic cinema, they are worth examining together, partly because they both have Signoret playing a role based on the maternal and partly because they are antagons as ideological types. To explain the last point first, Jean Chapot's film, *Les granges brûlées*, has no pretensions to political/civic cinema. Indeed, in an interview at the time, Chapot (Monserrat 1983a, 244) stated categorically that he thought French cinema was presently stuck in a film type that was difficult, "cut off from reality, the nation," and which focused on the camera rather than the public. The kind of films he was interested in making represented slice-of-life cinema (he cites by way of reference Karel Reisz's *Saturday Night and Sunday Morning*, 1960) a cinema that, to his mind, would show to later generations what France was like in the 1970s. In this context, he preferred, as a man from the provinces, to make, with *Les granges brûlées*, a film about rural France. One kind of attempt at authenticity, therefore, but which is based in eschewing ideological debates (by not showing them) and which, crucially, seems to believe that a slice-of-life film can be free of political resonances and that "showing what France was like" can be a simple case of representation, a one-to-one correspondence free of problems.[40] Conversely, René Allio's film, *Rude journée pour la reine*, is deeply and intentionally political/civic. Allio wanted to show in this film the different forms of oppression experienced on a daily basis by the proletarian classes. But he also wanted to show the mechanism whereby this is brought about and the extent to which the working classes collude with this oppression. Equally, he wanted to make clear that relations of power were not just on the outside weighing in on the working classes but existed within their own social class. Allio researched extensively into this subject, precisely to have a sense of authenticity when he scripted his scenario and shot this film. Thus, the characters are based on documented interviews with real people, in particular Jeanne (Signoret) and her stepson, Julien (played by Olivier Perrier).[41] Signoret also did her homework on Jeanne and went to observe women like her in the various areas in Paris and its environs.[42]

I shall return to the ideological issues in Allio's film a little later. As to the other point of comparison, the roles based on the maternal, what strikes here are the different outcomes for the two matriarchal figures embodied by Signoret: Rose in *Les granges brûlées* and Jeanne in *Rude journée pour la reine*. Both are represented as mother types who, unquestioningly, keep the social fabric of the family going. Jeanne is the living embodiment of a culture that has feminized altruism: she looks after her extended family, which lives under one small, cramped roof. Her husband, his mother, her father and mother, and her sister all live together, and she serves them all—manifestly, no one ever serves her. Not only does she run the household, she also has a series of cleaning jobs (houses, movie theaters, etc.). Rose, in *Les granges brûlées*, for her part is the matriarch who dominates over her family—again, an extended one—that lives on the farm and comprises her husband, her two adult sons, her daughter, and one daughter-in-law (married to her elder son), and their two children. She too serves her family, more begrudgingly than Jeanne, it has to be said. She feeds them and runs the farm—like Jeanne, we never see her at rest. Finally, in terms of comparison, both women have a disruptive son whose behavior causes their lives to be turned upside down. But it is the way in which they cope with this effect that separates the two maternal types. By way of explaining this point, let us consider the two senarios.

Les granges brûlées is set in the Haut Jura (in eastern France). It is wintertime and bitterly cold; snow abounds. A wealthy young woman is found murdered near a farm called Les Granges Brûlées (The Burned Barns). The investigating judge, Larcher (played by Alain Delon), is convinced that a member of the extended family living at the farm is involved. The two sons, Paul and Louis (played by Bernard Le Coq and Pierre Rousseau, respectively), were out on the night of the murder, and, in the judge's view, their alibis are not very solid. In particular, Paul's behavior is such that he remains Larcher's prime suspect. Rose is the dominating force, and she defends her family tooth and nail against Larcher's insinuating allegations, which at one point devolve upon her husband. However, a kind of admiration develops between the two, and, although they work against each other, they also come to respect each other. Finally, Larcher's suspicions prove groundless. Even so, his probing has uncovered all sorts of family secrets and dynamics that shatter Rose's belief in the family as a united social entity.

Rose was the eldest in her family and but for the war and her mother dying she would have been a teacher. As the eldest, she had to take over the farm. Her husband, Pierre (played by Paul Crauchet), was a Resistance hero, and she admires him for that. Since then, however, he has become passive, and all we see him doing around the place is mending clocks in his workshop—he seems fairly detached from the farm and the work it requires. Rose is spoken of by several people (her husband, the judge, and his immediate superior, among them) as a remarkable woman, as a stalwart of the peasant class, as a classic illustration of a dying breed of people—the small-time landowner peasant. She may be exceptional, but her children are all seeking to leave home. Not one of them wants to take over the farm. Her daughter Françoise (played by Catherine Allégret) is going to leave and become a teacher, thereby fulfilling her mother's own dream. Her elder son, Louis, wants her to sell off the part of the acreage that belongs to her so he can set up his own business. He feels trapped on the farm and trapped by a wife he did not want to marry and their two children. Unbeknown to everyone (at least until the murder, which blew his cover), he has been having an affair with Paul's wife, Monique (played by Miou-Miou).

Rose's younger son, Paul, wants to live and work in town so he can be with his wife, who refuses to live on the farm ("I am not a peasant," she tells Rose). He is so frustrated by his apparent lack of options that he has become an alcoholic. It is noteworthy that his wife wants nothing to do with him, a truth he persists in not recognizing. In his desperation, anything is possible, which is why the judge, somewhat reasonably, suspects him and brings him in for questioning. Rose is also afraid that he may be implicated in the murder, although she would never let on to the judge. This fear is exacerbated when her husband shows her the wad of notes he came across when searching Paul's room for wine bottles. She confronts Paul in a very tense scene where her son's fear is palpable (he actually tells her he is frightened of her). Paul confesses that he was so desperate to leave the farm, he thought nothing of taking the money when he saw it in the car. He promises his mother he never saw the murdered woman and he did not kill her. It is not clear what she believes, except his fear of her. However, she does decide not to divulge this information to the police and hides the money away. Thus, driven by some fierce belief in family (if not her son), she is willing to tamper with and withhold evidence to protect her son—to the point, even, of obstructing the police investigation, all criminal offenses in themselves.

When at last the mystery is resolved and the guilty personages apprehended (two young women on the run), Rose finally hands over the money to the judge. Remarkably, he takes no criminal proceedings against her or her son. The whole scene is conducted mostly in a respectful silence, as if the two acknowledge both the necessity of the investigation and the bitter impact it has had on Rose's family. It is not so much that the investigation broke up the social fabric of the family that she had worked so hard to keep in place. Rather, it exposed its weaknesses that she had been unwilling to recognize. Now, however, that fabric is in tatters. There is nothing left to fight for. That is why she decides to sell the upper acreage (the bit that belongs to her) and give the money to her two sons since it is evident they want nothing to do with the farm. When she tells Paul what she has done, he gestures a thanks toward her, but she brushes him off and wants nothing further to do with him. Her concept of the family, which she so ardently defended, was in the end a chimera. Not only were her children desperate to leave and her two sons intimidated by her, her husband failed to be strong alongside her—indeed, in traditional terms he fails completely as a patriarch, and it is she who occupies his role in relation to trying to control the disruptive son, defend the family, and run the farm efficiently. What gets shattered also is her self-deception: she failed to see that her family had become dysfunctional and that things had moved on from her time, when she behaved as a dutiful daughter. Her view of the family is one that is stuck in the past. Now, in 1970s France, the youth are no longer so keen to stay within the familial social grouping, as had traditionally been the case. Most painful of all, then, for Rose is that she has sacrificed her own ambitions for nothing. The barns are indeed burned.

Jeanne's maternal trajectory in *Rude journée pour la reine* goes in the opposite direction. She is the unglamorous second wife of tyrannical, bullying Albert (played by Jacques Debary). As a defense against the drudgery of the life she leads, her mind wanders off into all types of reveries where she can transform herself into a "queen." All of these fantasies are based on the various products of popular culture that she consumes: popular press, mainstream movies, television, and so on. It is noteworthy that her mother, with whom she enjoys a close relationship, also enjoys these products; indeed, it is she we see reading, not Jeanne, who presumably only has time to briefly scan the papers, look at the movie posters at the theaters where she cleans, and snatch a glance or two at the television. One day, Jeanne's stepson, Julien, turns up asking her to deliver a letter to his girlfriend, Annie (played by Arlette Chosson). Julien has been in prison for a year (for a crime he claims he did not commit); during this time his girlfriend has had their child. Both Julien's father and Annie's parents, the Thouars, (played by Denise Bonal and Pierre Léomy), want nothing to do with him. His father has disowned him, and Annie's parents, in their fight to maintain bourgeois respectability, have forbidden Annie to see him. This they can do because Annie is still a minor. In the letter Julien asks Jeanne to deliver, he begs Annie to come and run away with him and bring their child so that they can be a family together. At first, Jeanne is horrified by this idea of abduction (as she calls it), but eventually she comes around to Julien's way of thinking and helps the two lovers to make their escape. She has to do this in complete secrecy, defying and deceiving her husband in the process—hence the title of the film *Rough Day for the Queen*.

Unlike Rose's son, Paul, who is ungrateful and angrily blames all those around him for his misery, in particular his mother, Julien feels totally able to confide in Jeanne, and it is to her that he runs for help. Unlike Rose, who is certainly prepared to defend her son against the outside world, but is quite brutally honest and critical of him within her four walls, Jeanne defends her stepson both inside the home and outside. In defiance of her husband, she secretly writes to Julien when he is in prison. She protects and nourishes him when he comes to her for help, and, even though she is terrified at the idea of delivering his letter, she will eventually do it. She challenges officialdom and shows herself capable of committing what, in the eyes of the law, is a crime (helping a minor escape parental control). She does not tell her husband any of this. She lies to the police to prevent the runaway plan being defeated (during the night of the getaway, she has to hide Annie and the baby while Julien gets hold of a car). In short, she stands up to the voices of oppression. She stops colluding with societal and legal norms. She becomes an agonistic agent of social change. In Rose's story, the opposite occurs. Extreme events shatter her belief system, and her family disintegrates. In Jeanne's case, extreme events liberate her, give her a vital function and a family to believe in—her stepson's, but also her own since her choices include a change of life for her, even if her economic circumstance do not change. She will no longer live hiding away in her fantasies as a means of escape, but draw upon her own inner resources to give her strength to challenge what is not acceptable.

Signoret plays the matriarch in both films with conviction. As Rose, we can believe she is carrying her own bitter disappointments that lead her to be insensitive to her son's needs for a different life while paradoxically supporting her daughter's plans to become a teacher and work in North Africa. There is a cruel irony in the investigation headquarters being set up at the local *lycée*, a place Rose might have worked in had things been different. This irony does not escape her and is registered on her face as she sits in the corridor waiting to be called into the headmaster/judge's office. She is a fierce matriarch; nothing escapes her. She is far from heartless, but it is as if her emotional being has become frozen. She is bundled up against the bitter cold, but also one suspects against the ice in her own soul that nothing can melt, if her last words to her son Paul are anything to go by when she icily says, "Do what you want, it's none of my business." It is instructive that the rooms in her house, with the exception of the kitchen, are freezing cold (for example, we see her white breath as she speaks in her son's bedroom). Signoret is that dour, closed woman. And although Rose may be deemed remarkable by the men who surround her, she is not necessarily very likable, nor does she strive to be. There are only two moments in the film when we get to meet a more convivial Rose. Both are at large gatherings for a meal—once in town and once at her home. Here she chats, smiles, and kisses friends on the cheek. But these are short-lived moments when her face opens up only to close right down again.

As Jeanne, Signoret is a far more complex persona, not just because we are privy to her inner thoughts—through her various fantasies—but also because we witness her radical change, which takes place in less than twenty-four hours. As Allio succinctly put it, Julien is the catalyst for her breaking out of her bourgeois induced reveries and accessing her own dreams. Allio explained that Julien, through his "simple" but monumental request that she deliver a letter for him, which goes against everything she has been told and taught to do, brings her back to her true self. When Jeanne decides to act, it brings about a profound change in her where she can live her real life more fully, more intensely, and not as a drudge whom everyone pushes around.[43] Until this day, Jeanne has lived her life on two levels: her ordinary life and that of her fantasies. The two worlds are not simply classes apart. They are worlds that, on the surface at least, contradict each other. However, they are worlds Jeanne inhabits, and, because she slips easily from one into the other, it is clear that, rather than opposing each other, the two distinct worlds actually merge in her consciousness (which is why Allio perceived hegemonic culture as a menace). The film makes this clear from the very opening sequence. At this point, Jeanne and her extended family are on an outing to the palace of Versailles. At the mention of the ceremonious respect that was paid to Louis XIV's morning rituals (the *petite levée*/morning awakening, for example), Jeanne flashes into an imaginary awakening of her husband that matches the detailed courtesies meted out to the king. She then slips further into fantasy and imagines a beautiful wedding for her stepson, set in some vague moment of the twentieth century in which her husband is a general. Whatever type of fantasy (and there are five throughout the film), the characters who inhabit them are made up from members of her family, people she cleans for, and Annie's family. In other words, Jeanne does not leave the parameters of the social groupings she moves among, she merely adapts them to her fantasy scenario.

It is important to make this point because Allio, in his explanations about the film, said that he wanted to show through Jeanne how the working class is oppressed by the bourgeois culture it consumes and colludes with.[44] Jeanne's fantasies make it clear, based as they are on common popular culture generic types—fairy tale, soap, cop story, political thriller, costume drama—that her frame of reference is bound within narratives that serve to reflect dominant ideology. However, I would argue that Allio underestimates his own theory and practice here because Jeanne is not entirely a passive victim in these reveries. She gets to play out more than just the fantasy of escape. Her fantasies allow her unconscious to come to the surface. How else to explain that in three of her fantasy moments she has her husband either beaten up, shot dead, or as the

Rude journée pour la reine/Rough Day for the Queen (1973). Jeanne's ordinary extended family life at home (from left to right in picture: Orane Demazis, Alice Reichen, André Valtier, Christiane Rorato, Signoret, Jacques Debary).

corpse in a funeral? Thus, there are issues about representation and consumption practices going on that actually make Allio's work stronger still as a political/civic film because he (perhaps unintentionally) manages to portray something much more complex than he might have intended—a resistance to consumption—and that helps better to explain Jeanne's eventual revolt. Allio argued that popular literature offers innumerable representations of the same ideological message: that of social order, bourgeois hegemony.[45] However, as Serge Daney in his critical essay on this film points out, there is always a danger in assuming that popular culture is an opium of the masses, for it assumes that there is no such thing as working-class taste, let alone a working-class bourgeois taste.[46] It is incorrect also to assume that the working classes do not process culture, bend it to their needs, and recycle it, as Jeanne so evidently does. So, although Allio is correct in showing that it is not just a simple case of bourgeois oppression and that there are levels of oppression elsewhere (as, for example, within Jeanne's own milieu), somehow he failed to notice, within his own scenario, that some of Jeanne's dreams constitute a recycling of and resistance to dominant ideology and that she uses them (however unconsciously) as a release of her anger felt at the continued bullying of her husband.

These fantasies occupy 40 percent of the film time. There are eleven in all, three in the early stages of the film before Julien makes his request, the subsequent eight referring exclusively to Jeanne's dilemma as a result of that request. These are the various fantasies:

PRIOR TO JULIEN'S REQUEST TO DELIVER THE LETTER

Fantasy 1 (length: 1 m. 30 s.)	*Fantasy 2 (3 m. 36 s.)*	*Fantasy 3 (30 s.)*	
The *petite levée* of her husband	*Le beau mariage*—but which reflects the tensions between the two families (Jeanne's and Annie's)	Jeanne and Albert wait outside some fantasized prison for Julien. When he eventually appears, it is as a white knight on a white charger; he gallops off.	
	Reference to Albert/the general's lost job situation		
Historical fantasy	Soap/costume drama	Fairy tale	

AFTER JULIEN'S REQUEST

Fantasy 4 (length: 3 m. 29 s.)	*Fantasy 5 (length: 3 m. 8 s.)*	*Fantasy 6 (length: provide)*	*Fantasy 7 (8 m. 15 s.)*
First attempt to deliver the letter to Annie; she rejects Jeanne and the letter, saying she does not love Julien and the baby is not his. Annie tussles with Jeanne and roughs her up.	Police arrest Jeanne and try to force her to give up the letter. She refuses and is beaten up (one of her torturers is her mother-in-law).	Albert and Jeanne are the emperor and empress of a proto-Austro-Hungarian Empire. The father rejects his son's request to marry Annie, and Jeanne approves her husband's sentiments.	Back to cop story: Jeanne is brought along as a suspect to watch the reconstruction of a murder. Police assume she and Julien are lovers and have killed Annie and the baby. Albert is one of the detectives; in the reconstruction, Julien beats him up.
	Diegetic images and sounds of police brutality and corruption	*Nondiegetic, anachronistic sounds of 1970s workers' strike chants outside*	
Soap	Cop story	Costume drama	Cop story
Fantasy 8 (length: 3 m. 40 s.)	*Fantasy 9 (length 3 m. 10 s.)*	*Fantasy 10 (length: 7 m. 42 s.)*	*Fantasy 11 (length: 2 m. 45 s.)*
Return to the Empire story. Albert welcomes his son back as the prodigal. Jeanne exclaims how kind he is. A huge storm is raging outside.	Continuation of the Empire story. Now Albert is dead, and it is his ceremonial funeral. Jeanne attends, mourning her dead husband. However, Julien is her young lover, and as she stands over the grave grieving, he makes advances on her from the back, which she clearly enjoys.	Albert is the president of the republic. He is addressing a massive crowd from a window about the threat posed by the younger generation. His wife, Jeanne, clearly supports him. When given the chance to act on Julien's behalf (he pushes a gun in her hand), she elects not to. She gives his letter to Madame Thouars, effectively denouncing their escape plan. A gathering of long-haired youths dance away lewdly until a couple (Annie and Julien) hole up into an attic window. From there Julien shoots and kills the president. Jeanne screams out to him that he is a monster.	Return to fantasy 4 (soap), only this time with a reverse to the former outcome. With Jeanne's help, Annie leaves with Julien. Jeanne skips in slow motion, happiness written large on her face. As the threesome approach the car, they play hopscotch (shot in slow motion).
Anachronism: Julien is a 1970s hippy with long hair who has recently returned from Katmandu.	*Anachronistic presence of 1970s media (photographers) and Julien in 1970s clothes with long hair.*		
Costume drama	Costume drama	Political thriller	Soap

Between fantasies 10 and 11 there is a twenty-second scene of Jeanne in a butcher's shop viciously chopping a beef carcass in half. She is actually in the local butcher's shop with her husband buying steak; thus, against whom might her angry chopping be directed, one wonders?

Allio in an interview stated clearly that dreaming per se is not reactionary. What is reactionary is a dream that is the fabrication of mass culture, because such dreams all have the same function: "to make order triumph over family conflict."[47] But Jeanne's dreams are clearly more complex than this, and indeed quite contestatory. Contemporary issues seep in—from workers out on strike and demonstrating in the streets, to police corruption and brutality, to the very reactionary attitude of the bourgeoisie to young men with long hair (a reference is made at one point by Julien as to how difficult it is to get a job if you have long hair).[48] She also projects roles onto her characters that basically sum up her high or low opinion of them. Her rich employers are bullies. One of them has the role of a corrupt investigating judge. Her mother-in-law is a brutal cop, her sister a woman of easy virtue blessed with a spiteful tongue; her father is often a servant, her mother a sweet old lady who emits platitudes. Her stepson becomes a young man of principles, later an anarchist. And as we have already remarked, her husband—always in a position of precarious power—is the victim of several brutal assaults (two by his son and arguably one by her in the butcher's shop). Her dreams evoke her own ambivalence to challenging dominant ideology—she is afraid, yet she wants to help.

There are, then, considerable degrees of truth in these dreams. Both the social context of the times and Jeanne's own family context with its own brand of oppressive hierarchy are violently represented. In her daily life, Jeanne is quite timid, always deferring to her family. There are limited occasions for her to

Rude journée pour la reine/Rough Day for the Queen (1973).
Jeanne (Signoret) in her soap opera fantasy (No. 4).

demonstrate any love she might feel. She exchanges more tender gestures with her parents (her mother in particular) than she ever does with her husband. Yet, in her dreams, she often represents herself behaving lovingly toward her husband and having it reciprocated. They are very physical. They touch, dance, and hug (in fantasies 1, 2, 3, 6, 8, and 10). It is instructive that, in her real life, on the one occasion Albert reaches out to her for sex, she looks bewildered, weary, not massively interested, as if she is a stranger to the idea. And, just as she is about to succumb, she cuts away to a fantasy (number 8, the prodigal son and bountiful father, with the storm), taking us with her. After a postcoital nap, Jeanne awakens and immediately darts off into another fantasy—surely a postcoital revenge fantasy if ever there was one, since it is her husband-the-emperor's funeral (number 9). Not only is her husband dead, but at the procession to the grave, she pushes past Albert's doting and sanctimonious mother. Just as he is being laid to rest, her young lover (Julien) comes behind her and unbuttons the back of her dress, reaching in and giving her all sorts of pleasure. These fantasies with their proto-incest and murderous intentions hardly seem to be the stuff of passive consumption of bourgeois culture on Jeanne's part. Rather, they show her being aware of and resistant to the world she inhabits, or they show how, even when she tries to escape the truth of the world she inhabits, nonetheless, it comes crowding in, violently reminding her that all is not well. Her consciousness (in the Marxist sense) is too honest, too authentic to let her enter a state of disavowal.

Signoret holds the complexities of this characterization, injecting them with, among other things, humor. For example, when she rushes into a chemist's to

Rude journée pour la reine/Rough Day for the Queen (1973). Jeanne (Signoret) attends her "emperor" husband's funeral in her costume drama fantasy (No. 9).

get some sunglasses so the Thouars won't recognize her as she tries to drop the letter off, her whole play with these glasses comically points to her unease in the role of deceiver: she keeps pushing them up onto her forehead, and, then, remembering she is supposed to be in disguise, she pulls them down onto her nose again. Having done that, it is clear she cannot see very well what is going on. Her disguise in effect blinds her to her purpose. Signoret also injects these complexities with ambiguity and ambivalence (timidity vs. assertiveness; nondesiring vs. desiring). Her voice hesitates, she suspends gestures; but then equally she can be quite firm, as, for example, with her sister when she insists that she not cheapen herself with her choice of lover or, again, when she stands up to her mother-in-law for the first time (when she comes home late to make lunch for her expectant family and the mother-in-law complains). Finally, Signoret injects these complexities with courage. She shows how Jeanne has to multitask—cooking, baking, cleaning, shopping, tidying up other people's messes—but how she does it without diminishing others, despite their selfishness, without playing the martyr. She reveals to us a Jeanne who thought she knew the limitations of her life but who is ultimately open enough to let another (Julien) help her discover otherwise. The closing sequence is crucial in this context. Up until that moment, the narrative voice of authenticity had been the sole province of Julien. We hear him several times throughout the film speaking in voiceover, documenting his thoughts based on real experience, as opposed to Jeanne's fantasies based on popular culture (a contrast Allio wished to establish). As the film ends, Julien and Annie have taken off with their child; Jeanne waves goodbye. As she turns to walk home, her voiceover comes on track speaking, for the first time, from her own lived experience. The film ends with her sitting alone in the kitchen as the credits roll.

The Emprisoner Emprisoned: *La chair de l'orchidée* and *Police Python 357*

Patrice Chéreau's first film, *La chair de l'orchidée*, and Alain Corneau's second, *Police Python 357*, are two very distinct types of thrillers. Chéreau's is loosely based on James Hadley Chase's novel *The Flesh of the Orchid*,[49] and Corneau's is based on his own idea about a police detective, Marc Ferrot (played by Yves Montand), who loses his self once he discovers his own violence and thereafter consciously sets about his own self-destruction (Monserrat 1983b, 327). Signoret has a minor but significant role in both films. In the former, she is Lady Vamos, a relic from a former circus troupe, holed up in an old disused theater, the Cinema Italia. She and a former clown live there plus a handful of chickens. In the latter film, she is Thérèse Ganay, the rich wife of a police chief inspector (played by François Périer). She is an invalid confined mostly to her bed and wheelchair, a prisoner of her home, therefore, but one who commands over her husband through her wealth and her intelligence. Both women have momentous decisions to make: Lady Vamos to let her charge escape and Thérèse Ganay to help her husband avoid being arrested for the murder of his mistress. Both are responsible for the plot's outcome. Both break out of their confinement and meet their death.

I have already discussed Corneau's film in some detail in Chapter Two, so the focus here will primarily be on Signoret's role and characterization. Although she is in the film for only twenty-three minutes (19 percent of the film time) and Thérèse is the least mobile of the four main characters, it is she who wields the most control and power over events. In the unraveling of the story, it is she who has the greatest lucidity while the others flounder. It is she who "created" Sylvia (played by Stefania Sandrelli), Ganay's mistress ("I know her," she says, "it is as if I had made her"). She condones his affair with Sylvia because she can no longer be sexually active. Thérèse is a wealthy provincial bourgoise living in Orléans, and it is her money that buys all the accoutrements Ganay is so attached to: a house in the country and in the south of France. It is also her money that allows him to afford an apartment and to buy expensive jewelry for his mistress. So indulgent is Thérèse of her husband, she barely minds that he gave her watch to Sylvia. Ironically, this watch will be given to Ferrot by Sylvia as a token of her love for him, but in her mind it is also a sign that she no longer wants to have anything to do with Ganay. However, the watch will play a double role in the unraveling of the plot. First, Ganay will come across it in Ferrot's jacket pocket and realize who was Sylvia's other lover. Second, it contains a vital clue that will, in the end, lead Ferrot back to Ganay as the murderer.

But this runs ahead of the plot. Although a triangular relationship builds between Sylvia, Ganay, and Ferrot, neither man knows about the other. It is only after Sylvia's murder that Ferrot realizes there is a second man in her life. He is right—Ganay was so riled by Sylvia's act of dismissal that he kills her—only he does not work out, until nearly the end of the film, who that second man is. For his part, Ganay quite innocently puts Ferrot in charge of the murder inquiry, not realizing he was the rival. But, because Ferrot and not Ganay was the last person to be seen with Sylvia, all the evidence and witness accounts point to him as the perpetrator of the crime. Thus, Ferrot finds himself having to act in complete conflict with his normally methodical and irreproachable system of investigation. He systematically destroys evidence and refuses to interview material witnesses. However, he knows he is not the murderer, so he keeps insisting on the fact that there is a second man involved. None of his colleagues believe him, but Thérèse does. She also sees him as a threat because she knows how dedicated to his profession he is, which is why she tells Ganay to take him off the case. Only much later in the film, when Ganay realizes that Ferrot is Sylvia's secret lover (thanks to the watch) does he decide against giving himself up and to incriminate Ferrot. The decision costs him his life—he confronts Ferrot, then tries to shoot him, but Ferrot is quicker with the gun (the famous Python 357), part and parcel of his meticulous and thorough training.

When Ganay first confesses to his wife that he has murdered Sylvia, he tells her he wants to give himself up to the police. Thérèse prevents him. She gently orders him about like a child (and it is surely significant that he eats little pots of yogurt when with her, as opposed to the robust meals of pasta he shares with his mistress). Although Thérèse is virtually immobilized, she has a lot of technology at her fingertips and uses it judiciously, she does not occupy a feminine passive space. Thus, for example, when her husband comes home that fateful night and, contrary to usual practice, does not come in to say goodnight, she obliges him to come in and snaps the lights on with her remote control as if about to subject him to a police interrogation. She senses immediately that something is wrong and surmises that Sylvia has left him. Further questioning, as in a police interrogation, produces the truth: that he lost his temper and killed her. She inquires after all the details, what he did with the weapon (thrown into the Loire River), the jewels (he has brought them home, although in his hurry he has failed to realize the watch is missing).

Once Ferrot has surmised there are two men involved, Thérèse is convinced this will help her husband. More significantly, as long as the identity of Sylvia's lover is unknown, Thérèse insists that her husband say nothing to the police. And she prevents him twice from going in. At this juncture she is technically prepared to let another man be hanged for her husband's crime. But once she realizes that Ferrot is the other man (because of the watch), she becomes far less ruthless. She believes this new development will make it easier for Ganay to get him off the case, which is what she had wanted from the start (knowing him to be extremely clever). Ganay's response is to let the evidence point to Ferrot. Her reply is "But he is innocent," to which Ganay says nothing. The roles have reversed. She becomes more compassionate and he more ruthless. Ferrot has become his sexual rival, and for that he must perish. Having been a mouse all along, Ganay is now so confident his plan will work, he no longer heeds his wife/mother. She listens to his plan in silence and, when he has gone, shakes her head in despair: she (like all knowing mothers) knows it will fail.

Up until this moment of getting tough, Ganay has behaved like a spoiled child whose mother denies him nothing. After Sylvia's murder, he turns into a frightened child, running to his mother for reassurance. Thérèse, in turn, has nurtured and indulged him all along. After the crime she calms him down, soothes him, brings him into her bed, gives him a sleeping tablet—all very mothering gestures. But once Ganay gets entangled with Ferrot (even before they realize he is implicated), the dynamics of their relationship begin to change. It is instructive that at this point her face is completely without makeup—naked and exposed—whereas before she had been elegantly made up and coiffed. She demands that Ganay take Ferrot off the case. He makes it plain he will not. As if realizing the dynamics have changed, she accuses him of liking the thrill of the chase. She is right. The whole affair has become a "man's" thing, a posturing of the male ego where the mother has no place. The trouble is that Ganay's judgment is extremely flawed, precisely because he has chosen—until this moment, when the phallic has become so personalized—to be (s)mothered. He has not been able to assert an adult mind of his own and as a result behaves irrationally, first, in his rather decent attempts to give himself up, and, second, in his less than admirable desire to frame Ferrot. Ferrot, for his part, follows a different trajectory into the irrational. He has to do it all on his own because as an orphan (a detail provided for us by Thérèse, incidentally) he has never had a mother. Thus, he burns not only the material evidence (his shoes, glove, pen, etc.) but also his face (with vitriol): he erases his identity because he cannot see a way out. His self-inflicted injury is a last desperate but hysterical attempt to not be the man he was. How precarious now seems his scrupulous method and precision (as evidenced in the opening sequence, when he cleans his gun and makes his own bullets) and his monastic celibate life (mirrored in his sparsely furnished apartment and steel-framed institutional-like single bed). Mothered or unmothered, in their desperate tussle over the sexual other (Sylvia), both men have reacted hysterically and engineered their "death," real or figurative.

Only after her husband is dead does Thérèse manage to regain some sense of agency once more. This time it is to engineer her own suicide. Arguably, all four characters are on a suicide mission. Sylvia comes across as slightly deranged, certainly a woman who has great difficulty knowing her own mind until it is too late. She plays very aggressively with men, seeks to dominate but also to be rescued. She is an obvious femme fatale who meets with a messy end (head smashed in with an ashtray). The two men are different but equally frenzied creatures who act impulsively, failing to think things through; their demises are a direct result of their irrational behavior. Thérèse, however, calmly thinks everything through, and when it comes to her own end, she knows what she is looking for and why. She cannot live without her husband. She is, as she says, "already dead." But she cannot bring herself to pull the trigger on her pistol in the silence of her home. She decides therefore to "kidnap" Ferrot (an amazing piece of planning that takes tremendous physical effort), then take him to the place where her husband died and get him to help her pull the trigger. Her plan succeeds; she literally forces his hand, but not before she has pulled several strings. As she pleads with Ferrot to help her, pain and distress written all over her face, she tells him the truth about Sylvia's murder and Ganay's death—conveniently overheard by a nearby police colleague, thereby exculpating Ferrot. Everything gets cleaned up. She leaves a tidied situation behind her—just as she sought to do in life, imprisoned as she was within her provincial bourgeois values. No one in the end will talk, everyone's reputation remains intact. However, Ferrot's feminized fainting at the end of the final sequence (when he acts heroically in an armed robbery and then flops to the ground) tells us that all is not well, at least where he is concerned.

Corneau's film unequivocally points to police corruption, to its ability to keep scandals hushed up within the ranks. It attacks the complacency of provincial bourgeois value systems, but not in a caricatural way. Thérèse is a complex woman for whom it is possible to feel some compassion. Ferrot exemplifies the career policeman who is fine at his job until he extends his limited emotional repertoire to take on a lover. Even the rather pathetic Ganay is not without depth, torn as he is between his notions of moral rectitude and sexual desire. Finally, all are guilty of some form of self-deception—be it sexual, moral, or social—only to realize too late that they are ultimately imprisoned by it through their own doing.

Chéreau's *La chair de l'orchidée* is more culturally political than Corneau's sociopolitical/civic film. According to Chéreau, "Lady Vamos [Signoret's role] is an autobiographical character," embodying his sentiments that both the circus and the theater are dying art forms.[50] There she languishes, the old lady of the popular arts, like a freak in a theater that no one visits and as part of a defunct circus that no one is interested in anymore. When we first see Signoret, she resembles a frightful caricature of Marie in *Casque d'Or*. Her mane of hair is down, but now it is black, streaked with gray. Her once beautiful face still maintains the same bone structure, but now the flesh on it is completely bloated. In this peculiar story about money and the attempt by a wicked aunt (played by Edwige Feuillère) to defraud her niece, the heiress Claire (played by Charlotte Rampling), Signoret represents the only kind and generous person who tries to help and dies for her pains. Thus, this last relic of a former style of entertainment, Lady Vamos, takes with her to the grave the memories of those times because she was the only one keeping them alive during her lifetime with her screening (albeit for herself) of little films of the circus in the faded and tattered elegance of the Cinema Italia. She is more than a Miss Haversham, then, given that she stayed alive to embody cultures past and died to save a victim of greed.

Chéreau is a man of the theater, and this is very much in evidence in this film with its stress on ambience and decor. The constant rain makes the exteriors exude a Bergmanesque sense of unease. As for the interiors, all are permeated with an aura of decay. Several critics of the time, though admiring the terrific sense of mise-en-scène, felt it could not carry the film. Although it fascinated, they claimed, the characters failed to interest.[51] I would suggest that it is less that they fail to interest than that there is a coldness and decadence about them that alienates (even Lady Vamos, the warmest of them all, is in decay). Furthermore, the story is so difficult to follow, we are held at considerable distance from the characters. The somewhat surreal nature of the mise-en-scène is matched by the situationist aspect of the narrative, where we dip in and out of these characters for a tiny slice of their psyches rather than their lives—and all of them appear to be on the verge of a mental crisis.

But first, let us lay out the scenario. It is a film of cameos (a contributing factor to the disjointed feel of the film), and the two most striking are Signoret's and Feuillère's. Charlotte Rampling's Claire Wegener feels chaotic and overburdened with representation, both textual and intertextual, and her dysfunctional behavior does not really convince. This is partly a fault of the role itself, where she is represented entirely as a passive victim. She is a woman traumatized by incarceration, treated as insane, subject to sexual abuse, and finally makes her escape by gouging out her rapist's eyes. The other problem with Rampling's characterization comes by association with her role in another film as a prisoner in an equally sadomasochistic context, *The Night Porter* (1974), which had recently been released. There she was visibly an intelligent victim. In Chéreau's film it is as if she were directed to suppress her intelligence. Yet this does not sit well with Rampling's persona. Indeed, her intelligence remains writ large on her face, so she ends up being in contradiction with herself. As we shall see, the only time her intelligence surfaces (is allowed to surface) is in her exchange with Lady Vamos—never with the men.

We are never clear what purpose Bruno Cremer's role as Louis Delage serves other than to act briefly as one of Claire's rescuers. He gets inadvertently caught up in the other plot of the film and witnesses an underworld execution of a police informer (a friend of his he was hiding). The two executioners are the former owners of the circus, the Bérékian brothers (played by Hans-Christian Biech and François Simon), who had an act as knife throwers (hence their transferable skills). The brothers attempt to kill Delage and succeed in wounding him. Claire drives him away, deposits him outside a disused factory, and goes off to get help. She gets kidnapped by the Bérékian brothers, and Delage gets picked up by Claire's wicked aunt. The Bérékian brothers hope to exchange Claire for Delage, and while they set up the deal, they deposit her in the safe care of Lady Vamos, advising her that Claire is none other than "the Orchid's daughter" (hence the title). Claire persuades Lady Vamos first to tell her the story of her parentage: her mother worked at the circus but was kidnapped by the man who was to become her father, the Orchid (so called because he left an orchid at the scene of his crimes). Claire then persuades Lady Vamos to let her go. She takes off to a house in Switzerland, where she has overheard Delage will be taken and which coincidentally is her dead father's house (now part of her inheritance). Claire, Delage, the Bérékian brothers, the aunt (surrounded by all sorts of petty functionaries of her own), and the aunt's pathetic son, all end up in the house, where there is a final showdown. Delage passively gives into his murder; Claire gouges out one of the brother's eyes (thereby setting herself up as a future victim to the surviving brother); the aunt and most of her entourage perish; her son commits suicide. The closing sequence has Claire in a hospital rightfully restored to her inheritance but by no means convincingly sane any-more. The surviving Bérékian brother breaks into her room, only to be con-fronted by Lady Vamos, who had come to visit Claire (the only time she had left her "home" in all those years). He throws a knife, intending to hit Claire, but Lady Vamos gets in the way (or his eyesight fails him), and she gets it instead. He then turns another knife on himself. Claire carries on with her business affairs on the phone, almost as if nothing had happened—or, as her tears indi-cate, has she finally, really, gone mad?

Feuillère's and Signoret's roles and performances are antipodal in this film. These two grandes dames of French cinema finally "confront" each other (remi-niscent of Gabin and Signoret in *Le chat*), although, sadly, they do not meet up—one coup de théâtre Chéreau missed out on. They contrast as performers and, coming from the same era as they do (late 1940s–early 1950s), the compar-ison is interesting in terms of characterization and style, which, despite being evolved, remains familiar. Feuillère (age sixty-seven at the time of the movie), in her fancy fur coat and stylish hat and boots, exudes elegance and beauty; she oozes money and grandeur, and recalls the many roles she once embodied as regal or upper-class personages. Signoret (age fifty-three), on the other hand, in her dowdy raincoat and dull dress underneath, embodies the crust of ages but nods back, despite her ugliness, to the roles of her earlier years, especially those of the tart who manages to hold onto her own set of guiding principles. The decay of the one stands out even more fulsomely when measured against the lasting beauty of the other. However, there is no contest as to which body appeals more through its authentic warmth: the grotesque Lady Vamos is infi-nitely more agreeable to our eyes and ears than the cold, punctilious aunt. Feuil-lère's meticulously preserved figure and face suit her—as does her classy, throaty, upper-class, cut-glass voice—to the role of the calculating aunt. Signo-ret's roundness and smoky voice make her eminently suitable as the compas-sionate, hesitant, and giving Lady Vamos, who, as she tells Claire, was once very beautiful, as indeed we know and are reminded of through the nods to Signo-ret's 1950s star persona. We are reminded of this in a clever piece of acting where Signoret, immediately after this exchange with Claire, wriggles her feet into her shoes and, as she moves off, just slightly sways her hips.[52]

Rampling's performance becomes more interesting when she is playing oppo-site Signoret. With the men she is either a sexual thing or an object to be tossed around, countered by the occasional eye gouging (which, of course, marks her out as crazy). But with Lady Vamos she has a more complex and subtle interac-tion. As soon as they meet up, an interest develops between them. Lady Vamos looks in on her in her room, and the camera focuses on her eye as she expresses her surprise and curiosity: "The Orchid's daughter, hmm." Claire eyes her up once she comes into her space, at first, her look is rather contemptuous, as if to say she is no match for her (sexually or in terms of looks). Lady Vamos repairs her dress and returns it to Claire, who shows off her body to the older, rather decrepit, woman, who in turn shyly averts her eyes. But later, once Lady Vamos invites Claire into her world (the theater) and shows her a film of the circus, Claire becomes gentler and engages in a proper conversation (the only one she has throughout the film, the rest being grabbed, jerky sentences dashed off here and there, ineffectually trying to affirm her identity). She becomes more assert-ive and asks questions. So too does Lady Vamos (this is when her scene with the shoes and the hips occurs). Lady Vamos opens up to Claire, literally opening boxes and showing her the treasures she has kept from the past, including the press clippings about her father, the Orchid. She also bestows gifts on Claire when she asks to be set free. She gives her the box containing all her savings and her lipsticks, arguably the last vestiges of her independence and her woman-hood. These are two Pandora's boxes, perhaps, through which the older woman selflessly passes on to the younger one the secrets of the past as well as the sym-bols of freedom and the feminine. This "mother to daughter" exchange of knowledge now means that at last Claire is in possession of her own subjectivity. Her identity has been revealed/restored to her (she knows her parentage), her femininity/sexuality reclaimed (she is in possession of the "female," in the form of Lady Vamos's box). From this moment on, Claire no longer plays victim. When she meets up with Delage, she tells him to fight. He says it is pointless, but she refuses to take the passive way out. This is not to say that Lady Vamos is Claire's role model; her own eccentricity makes it impossible for her to leave her particular circus cage, and she is emprisoned by her past, from which noth-ing other than death will set her free. But she is the catalyst for Claire, however briefly, to be in charge of her own destiny. Notwithstanding the ambiguity of the closing image (with her on the phone saying she is ready to take over the reins of her business emporium), Claire has encountered, for the first time in her life, a free exchange of compassion, which she, in turn, takes to Delage, who pitifully can do nothing with it (since he has decided to die).

CLOSURE—1977–1982

The Maternal Body and Texts about History: The Inscription of Political and Sexual Culture

In this last cluster of films, Signoret's alignment with the maternal body is one thread that runs through them all, whether she is located as the good mother (*La vie devant soi* and *L'adolescente*), the bad mother (*Guy de Maupassant*), or somewhere in between (*Judith Therpauve*, *Chère inconnue*, and *L'Étoile du Nord*). Within these roles, political and sexual discourses are culturally inscribed onto the maternal body, providing us with texts about history—although they are not, of course, historical texts in and of themselves. Thus, in *La vie devant soi*, Madame Rosa becomes the site of the history of the persecu-tion of Jews and Arabs. As a victim of Auschwitz, a prostitute, and a maternal figure for the Arab boy Momo, she is three times a female body (written upon with her concentration camp number, sexed upon as a prostitute, and, finally, depended upon as Momo's "mother") and as such is a totem to, respectively, political, sexual, and cultural history. *L'adolescente* (Jeanne Moreau, 1978) is a woman's nostalgic reconstruction of rural France just before World War II. It is her memory of that time when she grew into her adolescence, but it is told through a reevocation of her strong attachment to her grandmother, Mamie (Signoret). In her recalling the events of that time, it is as if they are mirrored back to her through her experience of Mamie—processing her history, her view of history, through the maternal body of the grandmother. In *L'Étoile du Nord*, it is World War I that is a backdrop memory to the inner drama that Madame Baron (Signoret) experiences. She broods over her boarders like a mother hen. Indeed, she is nicer to them than to her own family: husband and daughters. The chance arrival of a stranger, Edouard Binet (played by Philippe Noiret), to live with them, bringing with him an exotic past, serves as a catalyst for Madame Baron to process her own past. In her relationship with Edouard, she vacillates between the maternal and the sexual, causing a personal crisis that allows her, at last, to unlock the secrets of her own life, which was ruined by the war. In *Guy de Maupassant*, she plays this famous writer's mother. Curiously, given that in real life Maupassant adored his mother, she is represented here as a rather cruel personage. Certainly, she was authoritarian, but Maupassant (played by Claude Brasseur) believed she was his good genie. When he was short of ideas, he would go to her for help. She was "an Amazon" who read poetry and smoked cigarettes, and he always valued her opinion of his work. She was not a domineering mother, and of her two sons, he was clearly her favorite. To help her son's career, she asked her friend Gustave Flaubert to be his mentor, which was a most precious gift to bestow upon her son. However, in the film she becomes a self-centered egotist—more an hysteric than a woman of great courage, which is how he saw her in real life. Her critical skills become judgmental statements in the film; her gift of Flaubert becomes a poisoned chalice, since she will not let her son free himself of him; she loves her other son, Hervé, not Guy. Finally, it is she who interns him in a madhouse and refuses thereafter to see him even though, in real life, Maupassant left his mother abruptly one evening at dinner, never to see her again, because he knew he was going mad and did not want his mother to witness his decline. The one thing that remains true to life about his mother in the film is that he supported her financially after his father abandoned her, leaving her penniless. Much of what is interesting in Maupassant's life—his pacifism (in the face of the Franco-Prussian War), his frequentation of Jewish society, especially Jewish women (in the face of the climate of the times, which was deeply anti-Semitic and would culminate in the Dreyfus affair), his refusal to be bought by the establishment (he refused the Légion d'honneur)—is missing from the film. What does get prime focus is his gradual degeneration through syphilis into madness, and as a result he remains a tragic but deeply unpleasant figure. Similarly, what gets distorted in relation to the mother is the nature of their relationship. A reading of the film leads us to believe that the failure of his parents' relationship, plus the fact that his mother is a domineering presence, led Maupassant to be incapable of forming a proper relationship of his own and turned him instead into an insatiable sexual predator. The history of one of France's national cultural icons gets reduced to the prurient investigation of his madness induced by his authoritarian mother.[53]

As to the last two films in this general overview, in *Judith Therpauve*, the eponymous heroine's body is reclaimed to serve once more the cause of history but fails. Judith Therpauve (Signoret), now a grandmother and a self-imposed recluse, is winched back into the limelight by former Resistance fighters (now also well into retirement age) to save a newspaper—which they all syndicate—from being bought up by a press baron. The newspaper has a history, as does Judith Therpauve. Both are identified with the Resistance, now some thirty-five years past. In trying to save the paper, the old men are trying to effectuate a rebirth of "their" history. But history cannot be resuscitated, which is why, when the project fails (as it must do), Judith Therpauve sees no other solution than to shoot herself: she is as dead as it is. The maternal is sacrificed to a noble, but lost, cause. Sacrifice similarly affects the maternal in *Chère inconnue/I Sent a Letter to My Love* (Moshe Mizrahi, 1980). Here Louise (Signoret), the sister of an invalided brother, Gilles (played by Jean Rochefort), for whom she has cared for years, indeed for whom she has sacrificed her own happiness (marriage and children), decides to write to a lonely-hearts column to bring some spice into her life. Unfortunately, the only respondent is her brother, but she decides to keep the correspondence exchange going. Eventually it all falls apart, and her brother marries Yvette (played by Delphine Seyrig), their old schoolfriend and neighbor. Like Madame Baron of *L'Étoile du Nord*, Louise vacillates between mother and lover only to lose on both counts. However, the added frisson of incest never gets off the ground, although there are a few tense, potentially sexualized moments. Conversely, the frustration and despair of the "old maid" syndrome is never far from the surface, which is surely why Louise fights with her brother and has spats with Yvette. The aging woman, falsely maternal, sexually unfulfilled, is not a comfortable image, particularly when we see where she lives, stuck out in the wilds of the Britanny coastline.

The Proto-Maternal: *La vie devant soi* and *Chère inconnue*

In these two films, Mizrahi investigates, through the personages embodied by Signoret, two different stages of female old age where facing solitude or death has become a reality. These issues carry with them connotations of the bleak and, according to some critics, the sentimental.[54] However, in as much as they portray aspects of life we do not particularly care to think about, they are in fact quite remarkable films. Madame Rosa in *La vie devant soi* is now in her late seventies and Louise in *Chère inconnue* in her fifties. Both women have given their lives over to caring for others. But they also hang onto these same others because of their need not to be alone with their fears: in Madame Rosa's case, fear of the past; in Louise's case, fear of the future. Madame Rosa is at the crossroads between life and death. It is not death that frightens her. Indeed, she is not afraid of death. What does fill her with dread is that her death might be institutionalized, for she is terrified of being taken off to a hospital to die. In her mind—which slips in and out of a form of dementia where she confuses the present with her terrible past—being packed off to a hospital equates to when she was packed off to Auschwitz. Her fears are about being made to live again the brutalizations of her past, the memory of which is inscribed on her arm in her concentration number 17329.[55] And only Momo, the adolescent boy who lives with her and whom she cares for, can save her from being carted away. As for Louise, sensing that her invalid brother may not have much longer to live and unable to envisage a future alone, she turns to the lonely-hearts column in her local newspaper and places an ad, hoping to find loving companionship.

What is interesting is how these two characterizations do not fall into some kind of soupy sentimentalism thanks to the strength of Signoret's performance, where she mixes toughness with tenderness, despair with desire, anger and irony with humor. She plays these two women as assertive bodies, empowering the crone, not diminishing her. Thus, in Madame Rosa's case, she asserts "the ceaseless metamorphosis of death and renewal,"[56] first, in her own death, which she both celebrates and shares with Momo, and, second, by bringing about (through her death) a new life for Momo (he gets adopted by a professional couple)—hence one reading of the alternative title of the film (*Life before Him*). Louise, for her part, asserts an older woman's right to an erotic body. Both assert love's imperative (one cannot live without love, whatever its form).

In order to play Madame Rosa, Signoret had to put on a great deal of extra weight. The bodily contours were forced into a distended corpulence, letting "everything hang out."[57] Arms, legs, and chin are all overflowed with excess fat. To heighten this sense of volume, director Moshe Mizrahi made Signoret wear dresses that were floral in pattern and a size too small.[58] To top it all, she had the tightest of perms, which only served to exaggerate the puffy roundness of her face. As Madame Rosa, Signoret's body truly moves into the grotesque, in the Bakhtinian sense of the body in excess.[59] It is an ugliness that exposes the history of the body, one that suffered pain, pleasure, and now decrepitude. But it is also a corporeality that celebrates the excessive body with its orifices and protuberances and challenges the audience with its size and smell. For indeed, Madame Rosa can hardly move, and we can feel her weight and smell her body as it strains and grunts to get up the six flights of stairs. We sense her exhaustion when she collapses on the stairs one day. Later in the film, when she gets dressed up for her special picnic offered by the neighbors, we enter into a slightly different relationship with her body. As the young men struggle to lift her down the stairs, the grotesque excessive body truly joins the realm of the carnivalesque. This body has to be lifted, contorted, dropped almost, before it can finally be squeezed around the stairwell and out of the door, legs, arms, and torso all akimbo. The scene is funny and crude at the same time. Madame Rosa laughs and acknowledges the coquettish pleasure of being lifted by the gorgeous young men; we, the spectators, are the ones who feel the discomfiture at the "unniceness" of the ugly body momentarily resexualized and exposed (including viewing her thighs, stockings, and garters, which in the past would have more easily carried erotic connotations). And when, in response to one of the young men's questions about her life, she matter-of-factly tells him what she did for a living but adds that "it's no longer aesthetic to be a tart when you are fifty" (which is when she gave it up and became a babysitter), and again later states bluntly "How ugly I have become," she fully recognizes her present grotesque body, salutes it even.

Momo (played by Samy Ben Youb), her proto-son, whom Madame Rosa has protected for fourteen years, is equally at ease with this grotesque body. At one point he tells the couple who will eventually adopt him that "she is old, ugly, and stupid" but that she cannot do without him and he is there to protect her. It is clear that he cannot do without her either, which is why at the end, when she knows she is about to die, he goes down with her to her "Jewish hole" under the staircase and stays there with her as she dies and remains, thereafter, for another three weeks with his "adoptive mother," as he refers to her, keeping the smell of her corpse at bay with her perfume. After years of his proto-mother safeguarding him (including keeping him from being taken away by his father), it is now his turn to safeguard her memory. He has brought down bits of important memorabilia to this "hole"—including photos of Madame Rosa as a young woman (incidentally, stills of Signoret from *Manèges* and her late-1950s and 1960s films)—to join those already in place to celebrate her life and her Jewishness.

Mizrahi shows, through Signoret's body, what has typically been left in the realm of the unrepresentable. Because Signoret's audience already knows that she gives out nothing if not an aura of authenticity, she makes female aging and death a representable part of life. It is Signoret, the star persona as much as her performance, who makes tolerable the unrepresentable. She accepted (as Signo-

La vie devant soi/Madame Rosa (1977). Madame Rosa (Signoret):
the grotesque body as site of history.

ret herself said) "to go to the very end of things," and not to do it by halves.[60]
So she bulked up further her already bulky form, made her body overflow its
already extended limits. She firmly pushed her body over into the ugly: "I am
fat and ugly and I will use it to play Madame Rosa," she said in an interview.[61]
Madame Rosa's body—and Signoret's performance as that body—becomes a
powerful statement against oblivion.[62] Madame Rosa had once lived in oblivion, as 17329. In old age she could again live that oblivion and loss of identity,
which is why hospitalization terrifies her. But her courage and past actions, her
refusal to compromise even as she is dying, mean she still signifies to those who
live around her. She reminds us also, through example, that people can live har-
moniously together provided they remain tolerant, even when times are hard,
economically, as they were in France in the 1970s. Her environment is Belleville
(in the twentieth arrondissement of Paris), which had become a truly multicul-
tural area long before the rest of Paris, recognizing and integrating an inelucta-
ble effect of postcolonialism. In this film, blacks, Arabs, and Jews live together
and give each other support. And, although criticism could be leveled at this
idealized image of fellowship and understanding, it is worth recalling that Mizrahi is himself a hybrid of Jewish and Arab backgrounds (an Israeli of Moroccan
origins), and that he was certainly making a political point about the forever
fraught Arab-Israeli situation in the Middle East.[63] In the sexual domain, there
is also diversity and support. For twenty-five years Madame Rosa has run a
child care center for the local prostitutes. Now that she is too old, the children
have been placed elsewhere, and she is finding it hard to make ends meet. However, her neighbor and close friend, the transexual Madame Lola (played by

Stella Anicette), a former boxer, often helps out. There is a remarkably touching moment when, after one of Madame Rosa's bad turns, Madame Lola comes and cleans her up (unfazed by the various excrescences of the body) and, at Momo's request, makes her "beautiful" again. The mother mothered.

La vie devant soi was a tremendously successful film in France (two million spectators) and internationally. It won the 1978 Oscar for Best Foreign Film, and Signoret won a César (the French equivalent of the Oscar) for her performance. Clearly, the film struck a chord on the political as well as the personal level. As an American review of the film at the time noted, "In the climate and the country that saw President [Jimmy] Carter acting as a professional referee in the bout between [Menachem] Begin [of Israel] and [Anwar] Sadat [of Egypt], it must have been a natural Oscar contender."[64]

Mizrahi's much darker second film with Signoret, *Chère inconnue*, is as outside politics and history as *La vie devant soi* was within. Along the bleak southern Brittany coast somewhere near Quimper, Louise lives with her invalid brother in virtual isolation, apart from the daily visits from Yvette, the local baker's spinster daughter. This middle-aged threesome were all at school together, Louise the eldest, Yvette the youngest in the class. Their world is closed, claustrophobic, and unendingly the same. It is Louise's reaction against this world that unleashes a change that, for a while, enhances her life but eventually forces her to face her situation realistically. As the film opens, we get a sense of the colluding niceness between the three—everyday the same routine, everyday the same exchange of words, Yvette with her prattle from the village

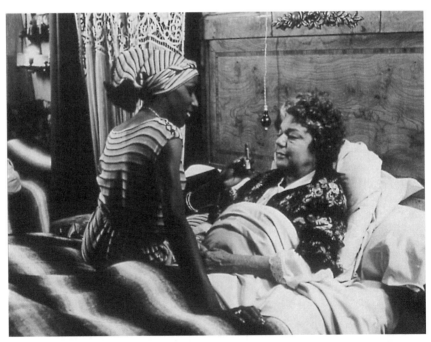

La vie devant soi/Madame Rosa (1977). Madame Rosa (Signoret) embracing difference: the mother mothered (Madame Lola/Stella Anicette).

and the newspapers, Gilles with his banter and sweet talk about his sister, but his irritating and slovenly eating habits. Only Louise occasionally breaks the mold by snapping at the other two, and, at one point, she even fleetingly imagines pushing her brother over a cliff.

In this odd ménage à trois, the primary focus is on the brother-sister relationship. However, it is the shifting dynamics in the latter that will bring about a resolution to the former. Louise, in her frustration at her stuck situation and her fear that her brother might die and leave her all alone, sets out to find some personal happiness only to have it backfire on her. She receives just one response to her lonely-hearts ad, which she had signed Béatrice Deschamps. Of all people, it is from her brother. Undeterred, she decides to keep the illusion going and in the process visibly rejuvenates. She paints her nails, dresses up, has her hair done, and so on. The deception works until Gilles insists on meeting Béatrice. Louise's attempt to bring this about through a proxy goes horribly wrong. Finally, Gilles loses interest and turns his attention to Yvette. Gilles will find happiness in marrying Yvette, leaving Louise very much on the outside, as the closing two-minute sequence of the wedding ceremony makes clear: the camera is far more on Louise in single shot (58 percent of the time) than it is on the happy couple (42 percent).

Let's now unpick this, beginning with the brother-sister relationship. This complex relationship shifts in form. To begin with, rather than resembling a brother-sister dynamic, this twenty-five-year communal life together more closely resembles that of an old established married couple who, though they still love each other, nonetheless live in mutual dependency and torture each other with their cruel barbs. Second, the dynamic has resonances of a mother-son dyad. She has to feed and nurture her brother, who is incapable even of making a pot of coffee. He is a willful slob—his room is a "pigsty," she declares—which obliges her to tidy up for him (much like a mother does for her teenage son). He has no table manners—"Your fingers are not infirm as far as I know," she snorts as he drops food all over his clothes and on the table and floor, where he sits—which means she is constantly cleaning him up and around him like she would a baby.

Two things occur to cause a shift. The first is the prudish and judgmental Yvette's reading out to Gilles and Lousie of a lonely-hearts ad from an elderly widow. "I think it's disgusting," she declares, "like a meat market." The second is the threesome's outing to a fair. The two able-bodied women (at Gilles' insistence) go on the merry-go-round. Also on the merry-go-round are two young lovers kissing and fondling each other (the young man, in particular, is feeling up the young woman's breasts). This couple is seated directly behind Yvette and Louise. Gilles is watching this from his wheelchair. As the merry-go-round gains momentum, the image blurs, merging Yvette, Louise, and the lovers into one. Gilles gets very disturbed, finally succumbing to a malaise. Neither Yvette nor Louise can do anything to help as they are whisked around and around. Once home, Louise expresses her concern that he must not die because he is all she has got. It is immediately following upon that exchange that Louise sits herself down and writes her own lonely-hearts ad. As we shall deduce a bit later, this merry-go-round experience also unleashed things for Gilles, and it is quite probable (if we infer from his own letters to Béatrice) that his malaise was in fact an erection, proving that he is not as infirm as he and the others believed.

The exchange of letters begins. Although Louise knows she is sending these words to her brother, she remains undeterred. Louise/Béatrice expresses her inflamed desire: "I long to be caressed. I want your hands on me, I want to lie against you and feel your warmth," we hear in her voiceover. She also transforms her appearance. She has her hair done, her nails manicured and painted, and she buys a new outfit—not, it is true, the young outfit she would have liked, but a daring (for her) pantsuit nonetheless. She even has to change her true identity—by falsifying her identity card—so she can pick up mail sent to her at a post box office number (since she cannot, for obvious reasons, have mail sent to her own address). Effectively, then, she has entered a proto-incestuous relationship with her brother (of which he remains ignorant until the end of the film, when he accidentally comes across her false ID). They become lovers by correspondence—a "postal liaison," as the still prudish Yvette puts it when she is told about Béatrice at the film's denouement (although she never discovers the true identity of Béatrice, of course). She might be a prude, but she is not incorrect to label it this way, for it is so sexualized.

The point is also that Louise is not a sexual ingénue. Unlike the virginal Yvette, she has had a sexual liaison, albeit many years ago, when she was young. This information is revealed rather cruelly by Gilles in one of the nasty exchanges between the threesome. Tiring of Yvette's incessant prattle, Louise accuses her of being a spinsterish old maid with her legs tightly closed. Gilles counterattacks by blurting out the story about Louise's affair at the end of the war when she became lovers with a black American GI. According to Gilles, this doubly "transgressive" affair (out of wedlock and to a "negro") drove her mother crazy. Her current postal liaison with her brother is, of course, also "trangressive," and there are several indications that Louise is attempting to relive that earlier moment through the present one. The tone of her letters is of a knowing lover. The clothes she wanted to purchase, as she is informed by the surly young saleswoman, are not for women her size or age but for younger women (the woman she once was). But there is no going back in time. This is made clear through the frightful attempt to substitute a younger woman for herself and to send her to Gilles, who, working on the assumption that what was said in the letters was true, makes a strongly sexual advance on the Béatrice he has before him.

The effect of the letters is threefold. First, in writing them, Louise and Gilles affirm each other and their selves as sexual beings, as desirable. As such, the letters act as an unveiling of their suppressed subjectivities. This is, of course, a written, textual affirmation of an idealized image of what they could or want to be—in a word, passionate. In reality, however, this unfulfilled passion takes another form, frustration, which leads them to say terribly cruel things to each other, labeling each other with identities that are monochrome and based on physical perceptions. In one particularly ugly scene they screech these identities at each other: "You're a cripple!" she screams; "You're a lonely old maid," he screams back. A second effect of the letters is that they lead to real ambiguities between brother and sister. It is not just the case of the proto-incestuous postal liaison I am referring to but the fact that the letters unleash a change in the way the two interact. Gilles starts to flatter Louise: "You're completely transformed," he declares as she coquettishly models her new pantsuit. She tells him, "you are so handsome." She puts a locket containing a photograph he sent her around her neck. As the postal liaison continues, the tension of unfulfilled desire rises. At one point, Gilles, in his increasing frustration at not being able to meet up with Béatrice, asks his sister to touch his eyes. She does, and he exclaims: "How soft your hands are!" She goes further and touches his lips. He lets her (for eighteen seconds), then grabs her arm. Finally, the letters bring about an unexpected outcome. They trigger Gilles' desire for Yvette, causing him to leave a desperate "Béatrice" by the wayside and a jealous Louise facing solitude. Once Louise is forced to find a Béatrice for Gilles and his sexual assault on her leads her to flee, no matter how much Béatrice/Louise pleads with him in her letters not to abandon her he does just that. However, Gilles' interest in Yvette had already been sparked before the fatal encounter with Béatrice. He had started getting "frisky" with her after the first exchange of letters, pinching her nipples and her backside. Louise's words of desire found an almost immediate transference onto Yvette. At the beach, when they go on a picnic, he notices that Yvette's pantsuit trousers are split and exclaims with glee: "I can see her buttocks, they're all pink!" Later in that same episode, Louise, who had gone for a stroll, returns to find Yvette cuddled up to her brother, hugging his knees. Her reaction is that of a jealous lover: "What a slut! Don't play the innocent with me, touching up my brother like that, you tart!" As Yvette justly remarks: "My goodness, you're jealous." Interestingly, Yvette, in returning the jacket Gilles had loaned her to hide her split trousers, says (completely unprudishly): "I might dirty it, and anyway you've seen everything, so I've nothing left to hide." The sexual connotations of "dirt" and nudity are perfectly clear. Louise has indeed unleashed a bomb with her postal liaison if it has brought about this kind of transformation. She has, in effect, through the letters, pushed all three out of their dormant sexuality, which, in turn, has brought about fulfilment for all but herself. Her love of theater notwithstanding, her own drama—for it was she who created it—has not turned out as well as she expected. It has, however, found the only outcome that melodrama would allow: the sanctity of marriage having the day over illicit (incestuous) passion.

Signoret plays this complex role with considerable nuance. She can be full of anger (as we have seen above), she can be bold and assertive, but she can also be consumed by nervousness and timidity. The way she enacts her letter scenes are good examples of this. The first time she sits down to write her personal ad, Signoret lets us sense Louise's awkwardness, and she does it in three moves. At the kitchen table, she proceeds to rub her index finger across the virgin page from left to right in a zigzag to the bottom, as if in awe of the page she has to fill (rather like a schoolgirl with an exam). She then hesitates over virtually every word as she reads them out, wondering what is important to say about herself, crossing out words, searching around for words to express her needs, as if to signal how long it has been since she thought in these terms. Finally, she touches her lip as she hesitates over these words, a sensual gesture as much as one of temerity. What she crosses out, of course, is as revealing as what she leaves in: "single woman," "spinster," "refined" are eliminated in favor of "woman with no children, appreciating calm, tenderness, likes walking, theater, would like to meet a kindly gentleman with same inclinations." She rejects words that speak to her condition (as an "old maid") and words also that deter because they hint at an intellect that might intimidate. Of the three, Louise is undoubtedly the one who is bold and intelligent. In her quest for happiness, however, she is prepared to dissimulate sides of herself that men might not find so appealing. In these three incredibly economic moves we glean a great deal of information about Louise.

When Louise receives her first response, again Signoret plays this in three moves. She very slowly unseals the envelope, savoring every push along the seal. She takes out the letter and unfolds it slowly and sensually. She reads it in silence, then exhales a loud "ooh!" and breaks out into laughter. "What a great joke," she exclaims, seeing the irony and humor in it straightaway. The letter is then read out in voiceover (her brother's), and we get the joke. As it gets to the point where her brother talks about Louise, saying "I think she is beautiful, and if I ever loved a woman she would be like Louise," she breaks down in tears. Anticipation, disappointment, irony, and pained and moving sadness are expressed in these three performative moments. They are dense and mostly executed in silence, making them remarkably tense.

Louise's dilemma, so astutely expressed by Signoret, is her lack of a sense of validity within society. Western society tends to validate those who actively promote the social order of things through visible participation in the creation of wealth and heterosexual behavior in the form of marriage and procreation. Louise is out of the loop on all these fronts. But she is bold. Consider for one moment that in the 1970s it was extremely modern as a woman—even daring, if you lived in the provinces, as Louise does—to wear a pantsuit. Louise wants to be noticed, even if Yvette (in her tight sweaters and pearls) ridicules her for it. Consider also how much society takes for granted the unpaid labor of women involved in homemaking, which goes unpaid and certainly unrecognized. Lack of recognition within a social framework can be, as it is for Louise with all her intelligence, extremely demoralizing and devalorizing. How to struggle out of anonymity is a question faced not just by Louise, but by many middle-aged single and childless women who are not gainfully employed. Patriarchal society has no place in its hegemony for the crone with "no purpose." An indication of how difficult and humiliating it is to assert a subjectivity from this position occurs when Louise, having invented a new self (Béatrice), finds herself up against a brick wall when she goes to claim her letters under her new identity. Unless her identity card affirms who she is, she is not that person (namely, a newly sexualized woman). So, to accede to a valorized position (as proactively sexual), she has to forge her "self"—literally efface/deface her existing identity (card) and replace it with another so she can gain access to what she needs (the letters). It is not coincidental that Louise is aggressed and humiliated on several occasions in her endeavor to claim a place as a valid sexual being. There is the incident at the clothes shop when she is insulted by the young saleswoman (who in her insolence chews gum). Then there is the humiliating encounter at the post office when she tries to get her letters and is exposed by the postal clerk (a younger woman again) as just another pathetic older woman, like so many others in the queue, who line up to claim letters either they have written to themselves or will never receive. Finally, there is Yvette's cruel taunt about her pantsuit. Small wonder Louise finds this struggle so exhausting and at one point ends up oversleeping (something she has never done in all her years caring for her brother).

The cruelty of the outcome for Louise—Gilles' marriage to Yvette—is that it returns her, in reduced circumstances, to her former self. It not only sends her back into anonymity, to the status of the "dear unknown" of the title of the film, but, worse still, to less, since Yvette has whisked Gilles away. The relationship of coupledom is over. Unsurprisingly, Louise wears black to the wedding, and although the painted fingernails hint at future possibilities, the darkness of the closure of the film rather militates against any hope. We sense her pain as she is held for a full forty seconds in medium close-up when Gilles turns to her at the ceremony just before the vows are read out, asking her with his eyes for her assent, which she finally gives with a silent small nod. We sense it again when, as the vows are exchanged and Gilles promises to "receive [Yvette] as his wife until death," the camera remains focused on Louise and not the couple. We read the dread of dreary loneliness on her face, a sense of doom reinforced by the church bell gloomily tolling. And in the closing moments of the film, the pathos and poignancy of Louise's solitude is fully underscored as the "Sonatine," which had become identified as Louise's theme and which until now had been played in a major key in the film, now turns to a minor key.

Nostalgia for the maternal: *L'adolescente*

Jeanne Moreau's autobiographical film *L'adolescente* was Signoret's only departure with a woman filmmaker. Moreau was a personal friend, and she wrote the role of Mamie specifically for Signoret. In this role, Signoret plays the young adolescent's paternal grandmother. It is she who gently observes her granddaughter, Marie (played by Laetitia Chaveau), as she struggles into this awkward period of her life, she who explains her periods to her, she who knows the limits of sexual knowledge that should be passed onto her. Although she plays a very central role in the narrative, the actual point of view is that of the older Marie, who is reminiscing about the very last summer vacation spent in the Auvergne with her Mamie before the outbreak of war.

In *L'adolescente*, Marie has come down from Paris with her parents. Her father had left his native Auvergne to seek his fortune in Paris, as so many people did in the 1930s as part of a massive exodus from rural France. In reality, however, he does not fare much better in the city, where, as a butcher, he has long hours to work for his pains. When they arrive at his mother's modest guest house, Marie immediately bonds with her Mamie—quite wisely, as it transpires, since she is almost just as quickly neglected or abandoned by her parents. Her father (played by Jacques Weber) takes off after an argument with his wife: she stops wanting to have sex with him. Her mother (played by Edith Clever) starts an affair with a local doctor (played by Francis Huster), a young Jewish man. Marie meantime struggles with her own emerging sexuality: her periods start, and she has "fallen in love" with the same doctor, only to be gently rebuffed by him. All of these events are woven in some way into her experiencing her Mamie as an idealized maternal figure. Thus, Marie's trajectory into adolescence is viewed through her lens of a maternal relationship shared with Mamie, who helps her to understand what is happening to her body and tries to teach her, through word and example, to be nonjudgmental about other people's sexual comportment, her mother's, among them.

All of this adolescent awakening is set against Marie's awareness of the increasing concern among the villagers about the inevitability of war. And as Mamie closes the door on her guest house, in the final frame of the film, so she closes, for the adolescent Marie (and the audience), a chapter on an era of France's rural history (and, of course, her own). That history is a very select one. Moreover, it is doubly filtered, first, through the older Marie's remembrance of her adolescent self and, second, through the filter of the young Marie's own experience at the time. To be more precise still, these two female bodies (the older and younger Marie) act as a double filter for cultural and political history. The first filter is the contemporary (1939) adolescent Marie, with her perceptions of rural life, sexual behavior, and imminent war as told through the confused experience of her own bodily changes; the second is the mature Marie (of the 1970s), whose voiceover controls the authenticity of those perceptions and gives them order and coherence. The effect of this double filtering is such that that past time is evoked as simultaneously safe and idyllic (as embodied by Marie's grandmother), and dangerous and sexy (as embodied by her mother)— but not in the end perplexing, as it would have been had the subjectivity been solely that of the younger adolescent Marie. This is the "play" of history, to give clarity where formerly there was less, even none. But this is not to say that it does not have a vital function, as what follows will make clear.

The film's narrative involves three generations of women—grandmother, mother, and daughter—and the events that occurred during the summer of 1939 in a small rural village as experienced by the youngest, least experienced and knowledgeable of the three, but related by an older version of that younger woman. What is interesting is the double-edged nature of this reminiscence, which is poignantly nostalgic yet painfully observant of a set of adult hypocrisies, suggesting that the older Marie has not forgotten how much she learned some thirty years ago. Thus, on the one hand, in her nostalgic evocation of this past, the older Marie recreates a world in which she has access to an imaginary maternal (her grandmother) linked to an ideal concept of the nation (rural France) that is uncomplicated, lives by simple rules of right and wrong (where, for example, her father beats up another man to win his wife back), and patri-

L'adolescente (1979). Three generations of women linked by touch, a metaphor for the feminine historical process of sharing knowledge (from left to right: Edith Clever, Signoret, and Laetitia Chaveau).

archs still believe they have the moral right to rule over their children (as in the case of the blind smithy, who will not let his son marry the woman he has made pregnant). But, on the other hand, in her remembrance of all she learned, the older Marie recalls the curiosity she experienced at the time and how she consistently turned to her grandmother, her Mamie, for enlightenment. Ultimately, the nostalgia does not drown out the learning curve, as her separate relationships with her mother and grandmother make clear. For, if the least present for Marie is her mother—who remains some mysterious sexual being, something she is destined to become—nevertheless, Marie investigates this body, watches her every move. She listens through the wall to her parents having sex, and she comes across her mother having an affair (hears the sounds, sees the effects: her mother in disarray). She learns about sex by observing/overhearing her mother, just as she learns about her sexuality by listening to her grandmother.

Within the film's diegesis we are presented with three women embodying the three stages of womanhood, and all with a significant role to play within the narrative as a feminine text—each one passing on knowledge to the next generation in the oldest of traditions, the oral tradition. There is a remarkable shot in the film of the three women being linked through touch: Mamie has her hand on Marie's hat, Marie her fingers on her mother's arm, and her mother's shoulder just touching Mamie's—a metaphor for the feminine historical process of sharing knowledge. Securing that text as women's history is the oral text offered by the nondiegetic voice of the older Marie, in fact, Jeanne Moreau's voice. Securing the filmic text as women's practice and history is Jeanne Moreau the filmmaker.

Moreau's earlier film *Lumière* (1976) was a feminist effort, and she was part of a wave of women filmmakers breaking onto the scene/screen at that time. The 1970s in France, as elsewhere in the West, was a major moment in feminist history, and numerous French filmmakers and stars made films about women's issues.[65] For her part, Signoret was not a feminist, but she was outspoken on women's issues during the 1970s. She supported the Mouvement pour la Libération des Femmes (MLF) on many of its causes, especially those to do with equal rights and abortion rights.[66] She was also a woman who was obsessed by memory, which, of course, is what the film is about—how memory is kept alive by passing on knowledge—which, in this film, appears to be very much the province of women. Signoret herself talked in strong terms of the obligation of forcing memory to stay alive.[67] She called memory nostalgia, as in the title of her autobiography, and nostalgia is, in Freudian terms at least, an aching for what is familiar, for the home, the maternal space—so, again, very much the province of women. Unlike Freud, for whom nostalgia represents a masochistic return to the past, in *L'adolescente* Moreau presents it as a positive space, one of power. Indeed, Signoret also perceived nostalgia as such and, in her later years, chose to revisit the past and to reinscribe a history into her life that she had hitherto glossed over—her own, her Jewishness. Reclaiming a lost familiar, her novel *Adieu Volodia* was part of that process (based in part on her father's life as a Polish Jew who immigrated to France), as was her eventual reconciliation with her cousin Jo Langer from Bratislava.[68]

The Maternal Body as Recycler: *Judith Therpauve* and *L'Étoile du Nord*

By the time of the shooting of *Judith Therpauve*, Signoret had lost most of the weight she had put on for her role as Madame Rosa (shooting was seven months apart). Uncharacteristically, she asked the cinematographer Pierre Lhomme to light her in such a way that she would look younger for this part, as an antidote to the terrible aging she had been subjected to for the Madame Rosa role.[69] Patrice Chéreau's film is done mostly in long and medium shot, so it ends up being quite flattering to her in any event, although Chéreau does not hesitate to use medium close-ups when he wants to reveal a particular aspect of Judith Therpauve's character, such as her surliness, which we easily perceive through her brooding, slightly stormy eyes, and sulky mouth. As a theater director, Chéreau was thrilled at the opportunity offered by the camera "to examine faces and express what is going on inside" and felt this was "especially true when one is lucky enough to direct an actress like Simone Signoret."[70]

The year 1978 was big for Signoret, her success with *La vie devant soi* being matched only by her success with her autobiography.[71] She would not be so lucky with *Judith Therpauve*, with an audience of just under 200,000. But the film, based on Georges Conchon's scenario, certainly appealed to her. Conchon, a former journalist at *France-Soir* (which had once been under the direction of her friend Pierre Lazareff), wrote this story about a regional newspaper that was about to go under. *Judith Therpauve*, Chéreau's second film, was not much liked by the critical press, who clearly expected something more daring from the enfant terrible of theater and opera. Chéreau had just completed a controversial rendering of Wagner's *The Ring* in Bayreuth, and this film fell short, as far as critics were concerned, of his ability to invent, confront, and even shock. The film was accused of being in the tradition of movies from the 1930s and 1950s—that is, deeply conventional both stylistically and thematically.[72] One critic dismissed it as amateurish.[73] Another declared that the plot was weak and that we know from the beginning what the outcome will be, namely, the failure to save the newspaper.[74]

Certainly, in comparison with *La chair de l'orchidée*, *Judith Therpauve* can be located strongly in the realist tradition. But I would argue that it has more in common with Jean Renoir's films of the 1930s and their social realism than the French tradition of quality/*cinéma de papa* of the 1950s. We spend a great deal of time in the places of labor: the press rooms, the printing works; we see men at work; the camera films the actors with an evenness that means they all have their rightful space (as in ensemble acting)—all of which recalls Renoir's *Le crime de Monsieur Lange/The Crime of Monsieur Lange* (1935). But I would also argue that, in its focus on labor relations and its investigations into the different types of hierarchies within a work situation, *Judith Therpauve* moves well beyond the joyful optimism of Renoir's film (where a newspaper becomes a cooperative venture) and must be aligned with the political cinema of its own times. Perhaps the fact that no one comes out of this story a hero—not the workers, not the trade unionists, not the journalists, not even Judith Therpauve, since she both fails in the venture and kills herself—makes the film too bleak in its portrayal of the factionalism that exists in the workplace. Ultimately, no commitment to a single cause—the rescue of the newspaper—is possible because there is no dialogue and, therefore, no potential for negotiations to bring about change. Perhaps Chéreau's film was reflecting too uncomfortable an image in its dispelling the notion (or questioning the myth) of working-class solidarity and the potential for self-governance, to say nothing of his exposing the rigidity with which union leaders are fixed in their ideology, respect hierarchical divisions, and refuse to "cross lines" (namely, trusting the boss), thereby helping save the situation of conflict. Nearly all parties concerned (Judith Therpauve and Jean-Pierre Maurier, her editor, excepted) behave treacherously at some point or another, and their behavior helps the newspaper slide even faster into its inevitable demise. Contextually, the film is speaking to a time, the late 1970s in France, when freedom of the press was a big concern. Robert Hersant, a newspaper magnate, was sweeping up papers into his stable, and the government was not doing anything to curb his greedy takeover practices, which, in the final analysis, were direct threats to journalism's role as the fourth estate. What purpose, after all, does a press that sings with one voice serve? This is an equally uncomfortable question that the film asks as it shows the way in which some parties intentionally and others inadvertently pull toward this disastrous outcome.

Judith Therpauve is a film about the freedom of the press. It is a film about the struggle of the quality press against the threefold effect of television, free newspapers, and newspaper magnates on its political identity. Judith Therpauve herself steps into that fray even though she knows beforehand that she is fighting a losing battle, and it is her interaction with the various constituent elements that tells us how this battle is lost. Chéreau summed up the central importance of his main protagonist when he stated in an interview that this film "poses the problem of freedom of the press, or rather of the survival of a free press not beholden to groups or pressures. But what fascinated me even more in the story . . . was the courageous, desperate struggle of a lone woman who fights with dignity, amid confusion and uncertainty, for what she knows is a lost cause."[75] This ultimately may be the reason why *Judith Therpauve* was dismissed as a failure, because instead of writing a political essay about the freedom of the press, the film is far more about the psychological workings of this middle-aged woman who has been dragged out of her self-imposed retirement and expected to bring about the impossible.[76] It is a political essay, but it is about more than just one idea or one ideal.

Chéreau elected to tell the story through Judith Therpauve, a woman. A hot political topic (freedom of the press, press corruption, hostile takeovers), a topic so identified with a male environment and masculine subjectivity—as exemplified by Alan Pakula's incredibly successful *All the President's Men* (1976), released two years before Chéreau's—is here related through the feminine. And it is not just any feminine subjectivity, but that of a woman whose political credibility lies in the past (the war and the six years of active political life just after it), who is not up to date on the new technologies and who in her heart of hearts believes that the newspaper she once worked so hard for is itself of the past. The complexities lie not in the newspaper's survival or demise so much as in the reasons why she would elect to come out of her shell of solitude and forfeit everything—her house, her shares, her life—to subscribe to a losing cause. Although no one knows it at the beginning of the film, her decision to get involved is in fact suicidal. In this respect *Judith Therpauve*'s plot is not predictable. Moreover, the film's focus, in the end, becomes the investigation of this woman's enigma, far more so than a series of revelations of the evildoings of a press baron and the lengths to which he will go to have his way.

The opening shots of the film, a camera panning and tracking around a large house's interior space that is virtually devoid of furniture and life, tell us a great deal about Judith. This is her home, but it is one that is both huge (one can get lost in it) and semiderelict (the empty rooms). It feels drafty and emits no warmth (Judith has to wear a shawl). As far as we can make out, Judith occupies a minimum of the space. The only two rooms that have any furniture to speak of are her bedroom, which is sparsely furnished, and her husband's study, which by comparison is overstuffed with filled bookshelves, a big desk, and chairs. Her children, accompanied by her grandchildren, visit on a weekly basis, but she resents the intrusion and is irritated by the grandchildren's noise and mess. Her children annoy her with their bickering about money and their attempts to tell her what to do with her house and assets—essentially they want her to sell everything and share the money among them. The grandchildren are a source of chaos in her hermitlike existence. They go up into her attic and empty out her tidily arranged boxes. They chase around the house, screaming at the top of their lungs. Judith locks herself away in her bedroom when they come looking for her. Her response to all of this is to be harsh, brittle, and rejecting. She is unwilling to be disturbed or provoked into behaving either like a mother or a grandmother. Thus, house and inhabitant offer nothing of the maternal. There is no *heimlich*, no familiar nostalgic place of home. As Signoret said of Judith: "She is not that generous. She took no interest in her children (who as a result have ended up being pretty awful), she got involved in politics (after the war) and then shut herself away, selfishly."[77] Before shutting herself away, she was briefly a teacher, but none of this has brought her to empathize with her children, who perhaps act as a constant reminder that her husband never came back from the war—she shared only six years of blissful happiness with him before he died in a concentration camp. She too, as we learn, was arrested and sent to Auschwitz. Her very survival, then, may also be part of the reason why she is so harsh and cold. What we do know is that she is closed in on herself and seemingly has nothing to give.

Judith hates the grasping greed of her children, and if she accepts the challenge of turning the newspaper around, it is in part as an act of defiance against them. She also agrees to do it in memory of her husband and the humanitarian ideals that the paper stood for. In the first instance, then, reasons of the past (her husband) and a desire to break with the present (her family) motivate her decision. These issues, however, quickly recede into the background once she gets to the newspaper's office. Now that she is back, her focus is to fight for the ideal of the fourth estate and against monopolistic practices that have as little regard for journalists as they do readers. Signoret played this woman of newfound purpose to the hilt. Judith takes the job seriously, tries to sort out problems, and becomes forceful when needs be. She also remains stubborn and brusque. She can be brittle, ironic, or sarcastic, but she is always honorable and decent. To save the men from losing their jobs, as the newspaper teeters on the brink of failure, she mortgages her house, but to no avail. When finally she is forced to sell the paper, all the employees save one turn their back on her. All they can see is that she has sold them out. This ignorance on their part comes from their refusal to shift in their relationship to her. A boss is always a boss, and there is no crossing that dividing line.

The only person to cross that line and stand by her is the young man she appoints as the joint chief editor of the paper, Jean-Pierre Maurier (played by Philippe Léotard). It is he who awakens her interest in life, rejuvenates her—but not before an initial tussle, it has to be said. She overhears his insulting comment when she arrives on the first day ("Is that all we've managed to find to save us?") and challenges him on it. Thereafter she quickly brings him around. Indeed, she seems to relish dealing with difficult men. She stands up to the bullying ways of the resident editor in chief, Droz (played by Robert Manuel). She insists on promoting Maurier to a joint editorial post, causing the former to resign (and put the paper at risk, since he will join the competition). She confronts the alcoholic journalist Pierre Damien (played by Marcel Imhoff) with his addiction and tries to help him gain some sense of self-worth. She confounds Lepage (played by Laszlo Szabo), the union leader, by telling him the truth at all times. She stands up to Maurier, but she also listens to him, recognizing that he has a journalist's experience and knowledge of the contemporary newspaper culture, including the new technology, which he explains to her and demonstrates its use. She clearly loves the energy of this young man and responds to him like a mother to a son. Unlike her behavior toward her own family, she approves of his achievements and tells him as much. She takes an interest in his personal life and his own young son. She also reacts like an excited kid in his company. For instance, when he shows her the way the new technology works, her face lights up like a ten-year-old. She has it in her, then, to feel compassion and to touch into a sense of the maternal—but not, as it transpires, with those who are tied to her by blood. When, as the newspaper folds, Maurier is obliged to leave and take a job elsewhere, she generously acknowledges that he will do well wherever he goes, something she is totally incapable of saying to her children, who are jobless failures as far as she is concerned.

The adventure with the newspaper acts to thaw her out as much as draw her out of her shell. It also forces her to confront herself. Whereas before she had lived in splendid egotistical isolation, she is now tested and brought into the line of fire. She gets told off for decisions she has taken without consultation even though they are courageous and in line with her desire to be totally transparent as a manager. She upsets the banks by publishing the names of all the shareholders. She crosses Droz by reinstating an editorial by Maurier that he had cut and replaced with his own. As Lepage tells her, she has humiliated Droz, and this will cause her employees to gang up against her. She has already worked out that Droz is a threat and will sell her and the newspaper down the line, yet she pursues her policy of bringing about changes to the newspaper and staffing positions. She indirectly forces Droz's resignation, which will be the first nail in the newspaper's coffin. She stands up to Lepage when he tries to discredit her in front of the workers by accusing her of holding a gun to their head. They either have to accept wage cuts or face being laid off, is the way he puts it, sticking to ideological interpretations of the facts. But she, having already mortgaged her house to save their jobs, retorts: "No! I won't have that. I have never talked of sacking; even when I could have done so and was told to do it, I wouldn't." Pride and courage impel her along this treacherous route. She fails to heed the warning of the former director of the paper, Hirsch-Balland (played by François Simon), which he gives her on his death bed: "Beware of courage and of pride." But there is more to it than that, more that makes this woman of contradictions even more complex. When, in response to Maurier's question why she came to the aid of the newspaper, she replies: "Because I thought it would give me something to do and help me forget that you always lose in the end." She believed it would help her escape the shadows of her past, free her from the mental mausoleum of her solitude, put an end to her terrible sense of loss, which until losing the newspaper, she had not, as it turns out, properly confronted or dealt with (except to hide away). She came out of her shell, she rediscovered sides of herself that had been lost (the maternal drive, the ability to sacrifice her own interests for those of others), she made herself vulnerable again. The abandonment she is subjected to when she is forced to sell the paper is the last straw. Her suicide is an act of grief (triggered by the loss of the newspaper), a final confrontation with the past and a final reckoning with irreparable loss.

Signoret made *Guy de Maupassant* and *L'Étoile du Nord* in rapid succession (they were shot, respectively, in November and December 1981). She was due to begin filming *L'Étoile du Nord* in May 1980, but illness (recovering from an operation to remove her gallbladder) held it up for over a year. It was to be Signoret's last film. It was not her greatest of this period, although her performance is very intriguing. *L'Étoile du Nord* did well at the box office (1.6 million tickets sold), but the reviews were mixed. Two major criticisms were leveled. First, it was labeled a film in the French tradition of quality (Signoret and her costar, Philippe Noiret, were even dismissed as links to the past, to the prewar cinema of quality).[78] Second, it was criticized for being a poor adaptation of the original Simenon novel *Le locataire*. However, Simenon himself actually approved of Signoret's performances in the three films based on his novels.[79] At the same time, he was not restrictive about adaptations of his novels, leaving the scriptwriters and filmmakers free to do what they wanted.[80] But there are grounds to suggest that the film has less bite than the original, for the following reasons.

In the original novel, the character Edouard (Noiret) is a young Turkish Jew, a con artist, down on his luck and penniless. He has ended up in Belgium in the company of a young dancer, Sylvie (played by Fanny Cottençon), his lover, whom he picked up on his travels in the Near East. He has left Egypt under a cloud. But on the boat to Europe he manages to introduce Sylvie to a rich Egyptian businessman, Nemrod (played by Gamil Ratib), with whom she gets involved. In a fit of rage provoked by jealousy and greed Edouard kills and robs the Egyptian on a train to Paris (the *Etoile du Nord* that travels between Brussels and Paris). When Edouard returns to Belgium, Sylvie tries to help him by hiding him away in her mother's boardinghouse. There he settles into the comfort offered by Sylvie's mother, Madame Baron (Signoret), and a special bond develops between them as he enchants her with his stories of the "exotic" East. He is subsequently arrested, tried, and sentenced to a life of hard labor. But, in her regard for him, Madame Baron travels all the way from Brussels to the west coast of France to the Ile de Ré to see him off to the penal colony in French Guiana.

The major changes concern Noiret's character. The young Turk becomes a middle-aged Frenchman—all reference to his background is lost. Nor are we made aware that he is a con artist. All we do know is that his infatuation with Egypt and his "exotic" protector, Yasmina (played by Liliane Gerace)—a famous Egyptian singer, we are told—blinded him to the fact that he was more of a poodle than a cherished friend. Yasmina on her deathbed left him a ring, which he treasures and believes will bring about his fortune. The film opens in Egypt with the penniless Edouard trying to sell the ring. The police arrest him, but Yasmina's son confirms that the ring is a gift, returns it to him, and pays his voyage back to Europe. It is on this voyage that Edouard meets Sylvie and introduces her to Nemrod. She becomes Nemrod's mistress. But one evening on the train from Marseille to Brussels, Nemrod humiliates Edouard in front of her by suggesting he is a nobody. Sylvie takes pity on Edouard and invites him into her sleeping car. Once in Brussels, she tries to help him out by finding a buyer for his ring. It turns out it is a fake. Edouard, spying on Nemrod in his hotel room, watches him put a big wad of money in his briefcase as he gets ready to go to Paris. He decides to follow him and persuade him to buy the ring. When Nemrod points out that not only is it a fake but intimates how little regard Yasmina and his family had for him, thereby humiliating him once more, he reacts in a fury and kills him. He robs him, returns to Brussels, and ends up at Madame Baron's house.

The rest of the film's narrative proceeds fairly much like the novel with one crucial exception. When Sylvie questions Edouard about the money and the blood on his coat, he claims to have no recollection of how things got there. And he remains an amnesiac until Sylvie, feeling she must protect her mother, confesses to her. Madame Baron, shocked by his deceit, confronts him. He remains in denial until, that night, he has a nightmare, recalls the murder, and also confesses to her. She takes pity on him and tries to help him escape, but it is too late. He is arrested and eventually sent to the penal colony, and in a touching final scene she comes to Ile de Ré to say goodbye.

Three problems ensue from this shift in adaptation. First, the loss of Edouard's original identity deprives the film of the edginess of the original character. The time is 1934; Hitler is in power, and Europe is becoming unsafe for Jews and non-Aryans. On a double count the original Edouard is living in a deeply inhospitable space. This helps to explain why he finds Madame Baron's home so welcoming and is so unwilling to leave (it is like family for him). Second, the amnesia also takes away from the edginess of the original and again weakens the character. Edouard in the film behaves as if there is nothing untoward in the way he is conducting himself. Until the closing moments of the film, there is nothing that helps to explain what made him desperate enough (as in the novel) to commit murder—and even then the humiliation he experiences is rather a poor reason. Third, the great change in age (from mid-twenties to fifties) also works against a convincing role; indeed, it rather infantilizes the older version. The proto-mother/son dyad of the novel, with its ambiguous sexual edge (he does, after all, seduce Madame Baron with his "Arabian tales"), once it is transferred to Signoret/Noiret in the film, ends up diminishing Noiret's character, making him come across as a weak personality and a loser. Although he charms Madame Baron with his incessant babble about Egypt and Yasmina, what strikes is his narcissistic childlike desire to be at the center of attention at all times (as, for example, when it is Monsieur Baron's birthday and he recoups that event into a story of his own about a birthday he once shared with Yasmina). This might be alright in an immature twenty-year-old, but in a fifty-year-old, this pathetic narcissism reduces him, makes him rather sexless, effeminate even. Thus, although he is a vicious murderer (seventeen blows to the head of the victim, as we are told several times), he remains peculiarly contained as a phallic threat and becomes, thereby, safe to be held in a quasi-maternal relationship with Madame Baron and Sylvie, who is as caring and helps him just as much as her mother. We do not get an overriding impression that Edouard had sex with Sylvie on the train. We cut from her attempt to arouse him, by placing his hand on her breast, to them lying in the *couchette* the next day discussing Yasmina's ring, which Sylvie is gazing at. They are resting there—he fully clad in a long-sleeved T-shirt, she in her negligee—more like friends, as they chat amiably away. In the novel there is no question but that they are lovers. Nor does Noiret's fifty-year-old Edouard constitute a real sexual challenge for

Madame Baron, for whom, according to her own pronouncements, sex after a certain age in a woman is unseemly—even though a younger, more enticing man might have shaken that foundation, one suspects.

Yet Edouard walks into Madame Baron's life, and through his talk of the Egyptian light, sex and desire (only the first of which, one suspects, he experienced firsthand) opens up old wounds that had remained unhealed since the outbreak of World War I. It was then that her beloved fiancé, Albert (played by Pierre Forget), was wounded and their dreams of moving to the warmer climes and more exciting promise of Australia were dashed forever. Instead, Albert languishes in a hospital, paralyzed from the waist down and slowly going mad. As a result, she wound up marrying the stolid Monsieur Baron (played by Jean Rougerie), a train guard, and had two daughters, Sylvie and Antoinette, or Toinette (played by Julie Jezequel). To help supplement the family's income, she runs a meticulously clean boardinghouse. She has, we suspect, been careful all her life since those early, heady days with Albert. Signoret conveys this through the precision and carefulness of her gestures: putting money away in a tea caddy, cleaning fish and chopping off their heads, scraping carrots, ironing, sewing.[81] We see her constantly at work—cooking, cleaning, washing up, wiping down— the daily gestures of quotidian life, routinized and safe. Monsieur Edouard (as she calls him) brings not just the unsettling effect of his tales into her life but also the messiness of his own person, as exemplified by her tidying up after him when he carelessly tosses his jacket on the floor.

Mess, like sex, is something she cannot tolerate in her home. But in the end she can control neither. She warns Edouard that no women are allowed in the bedrooms. Yet her daughter Sylvie wanders in and out of his room with impunity. Her younger daughter Toinette is having sex with one of her boarders, Monsieur Valesco (played by Jean-Yves Chatelais), right under her nose, though she remains unaware. She herself spends increasing amounts of time in Edouard's room and is "discovered" there one evening by her husband, sitting on his bed, listening to a record of Yasmina's "exotic" singing. Although she prides herself on running a clean house, it is not, after all, so clean. Sex goes on in it, it harbors criminals, and even she allows herself to be seduced by the sweet talk of a complete stranger. For all that she wants to keep sexuality out of the home, it has a disturbing knack of constantly filtering its way back in.

Let us now examine the various relationships this seemingly "good" mother shares with her family, namely, her two daughters and the three men in her life: her husband, Edouard, and Albert. Madame Baron is distant and frosty with her two daughters, yet she is warm and caring with her lodgers. They are all foreigners and, with the exception of Monsieur Valesco, a Romanian, rather repressed, quiet types (not unlike younger versions of her husband). Her daughters are like the two sides of her own self. Sylvie is the one who "got away" as she had planned but failed to do with Albert. Sylvie has escaped the drudgery of the daily routine, the gray damp streets of Charleroi. Not even Brussels, it is a small mining town 50 kilometers away, where unemployment is rife and working life pretty grim, thanks to the Great Depression. Sylvie has found excitement through travel, being a nightclub dancer, and finding rich men to keep her. She embodies the youthful hedonism of that time, the mid-1930s, when war was rumbling again and young people, when and where they could, grabbed what life had for them in the present. She is not, however, simply a "fast woman," which is how her mother judges her. She is generous and warmhearted. She feels genuinely sorry for Edouard, whom she recognizes as a loser, and helps him. Equally, she is very protective of her mother, even though, as she tells Edouard, "my mother is so hard-hearted and mean."

Sylvie, then, holds up a double mirror to her mother. On the one hand, she reflects the free spirit her mother could have been—and clearly mourns. This is made clear in a conversation Madame Baron has with Edouard about her daughter. She asks him outright: "What do you think of my daughter? Doesn't she take risks?" He answers: "You must trust her." But when he adds "And maybe her life is more interesting than ours," he has surely hit the nail on the head, because Madame Baron immediately replies: "I could have done what she's done. I'd loved to have traveled. I had a fiancé, but the war changed everything." This is why Madame Baron takes Edouard to the hospital where Albert languishes—to prove to herself as much as to Edouard what she had been capable of. As she explains on the journey home, she wanted him to meet Albert so he could know that she too wanted to travel. On the other hand, Sylvie exposes Madame Baron's failings as a mother. When, to protect her mother, she finally has to tell her about Edouard, she begins by declaring: "That Edouard, whom you fuss over and treat so tenderly, is an assassin." Her choice of verbs in French (*cajoler* and *dorloter*) are specifically appropriate in a mother-child relationship (*cajoler* means to have tender and soothing words for a child; *dorloter* literally means to treat a child kindly, tenderly). It is clear that she is telling her mother how much more appropriate it would have been for her to behave in that way toward herself and her sister than toward this total stranger.

As for Toinette, she is the drab sister who stayed behind. Not for her the glamorous clothes and lifestyle of her older sister, whom she clearly envies but also admires. Her clothes are dull and more like a schoolgirl's than a young woman's. She desperately wants to be sexy like her sister, but her mother keeps a tight rein on her. She is obliged to work at home with her mother, helping to run the boardinghouse. At all times she has to do her mother's bidding and is bossed around by her, much like a servant—as indeed the abbreviation of her name indicates. Small wonder she is a snoop, a liar, and a sneak and defies her mother by having sex with Monsieur Valesco, although not openly, like her sister. In comparison to her sister's generous ways, she is hard and cynical, and in relation to her mother, she represents the embittered woman who has not had the life she had hoped for.

At first, Madame Baron seems equally cold to both of them. However, the mise-en-scène of their relationships suggests a nuance. There are only four shots of the threesome together, which already hints at a lack of family cohesion. However, they also tell us more. The four times they are in a three-shot together Madame Baron and Sylvie are standing close to each other and are in the foreground, with Toinette in the background. When Sylvie is telling her mother the truth about Edouard and Toinette comes sneaking in to eavesdrop, she and her mother join ranks together to tell her off and send her to her room. The older daughter and mother have an understanding, a complicity, that is not the province of the younger Toinette. And it is not simply because Sylvie is the stronger, more assertive of the two. Madame Baron ultimately but secretly cares more for her elder daughter, as is evidenced by the way she reacts when, in turn, her two daughters seek to comfort her. After delivering the devastating news about Edouard, Sylvie comes up to her mother from behind and puts her hands tenderly on her shoulders. A few minutes later Toinette executes the precise same gesture, but Madame Baron shrugs her off. She is cruel to and rejecting of the one who most clearly reminds her of herself—but whom, it has to be said, she has made into her own image. For, until Edouard's arrival, Madame Baron also wears drab clothes, is tightly buttoned up (as she impels her daughter to be), and keeps secrets. Toinette is a daily reminder that she has led a life of compromise, that her life has been, if not a lie, then certainly deeply unfulfilling. It is noteworthy that, when Toinette and her mother are talking together (or doing house chores), they are always framed in a two-shot (sixteen altogether); but when Sylvie is interacting with her mother, there is an equal balance of two-shots (eight) and single shots (nine). Toinette and her mother are symbiotically interlocked. As for Sylvie, she has gained her independence from her mother and can experience herself in her own right—hence the single shots of her. It is instructive that these single shots occur during the two scenes when she tells her mother the truth, both times relating to Edouard. The first scene occurs when Madame Baron is clearly put out, jealous even, to discover that Sylvie already knows Edouard and tries to find out (sneakily) if they are lovers. She is furiously scraping carrots as she nudges Sylvie about their liaison. Sylvie, in single shot, is categoric; they are just friends—which, of course, by now they are. The second scene, when Sylvie tells her mother about Edouard's crime, is filmed in alternate single shots of the two women as the shocking nature of what the one is saying is registered on the face of the other.

The daughters hold the mirror up to the mother, represent to her in that reflection her split subject. Her unconscious, repressed self is represented by Sylvie; her conscious, limited self by Toinette. This split subject in turn generates a whole series of further splittings: the ideal image versus reality; free/repressed; "good"/"bad" mother; truthful/dishonest; open/secretive. No wonder she wants to keep them at a distance, given the troubled image they send back to her. Until the closing sequence, she has been unable to find a way to face this divided self. But then she appears to find peace with it: the last image of the film is her looking out to sea untroubled, serene. It is in this context that her menfolk come into play. Edouard is the catalyst for change. He forces Madame Baron to open up: she delivers her secret to him, not to her daughters, we note. He brings about, as a result of his crime, the confrontation with her ideal self (in the form of Sylvie), which forces her to acknowledge the way she is rather than hide behind a wall of rituals and quotidian gestures, so clearly epitomized by the dark charcoal-gray woolen coat she wears to go shopping, all tightly buttoned up, severely corseting her body, leaving no room to breathe. The coat she wears at the end, is loose and flowing and light, as is her tender gesture of goodbye to Edouard.

The three men in her life—her husband (whom she calls either Monsieur Baron or father), Edouard, and Albert—are all desexualized males. Her husband is worn out by life. At home he is continuously at rest, either sleeping because of the shifts he works or sitting in an armchair, reading the newspaper. He has simple needs. When he comes across his wife in Edouard's room listening to his records, and she delivers a tale about the riddle of the Sphinx (the oedipal tale, as it transpires), all he can do is look blank and ask: "When are we eating?" Edouard also rests a lot. He is physically and morally weak. Unable to make decisions for himself, he ties himself to the apron strings of stronger women. He is also rather effeminate and sexless but latches onto women who are sure of their sexual identity: Yasmina, who is lesbian (but also likes men, we are told); Sylvie, who is very clear about her sexuality and is not afraid to flaunt it; and Madame Baron, the maternal force, who keeps the boardinghouse going and who is very clear that, though sex itself is no longer appropriate for her, tenderness certainly is. Albert is confined to bed (to perpetual rest until he dies). Paralyzed from the waist down, he is the least potent of the three men, "castrated" as he is by the effects of war (he even rubs that part of himself to make the point). In a ritualistic manner Madame Baron brings him eclairs every time she comes to see him. He enjoys these poor substitutes, but not before he has brutally mangled their phallic shape. He has languished in this hospital for nearly twenty years, an even worse incarceration than Madame Baron in her boardinghouse.

Edouard serves as a bridge between Albert, her lost dream and Monsieur Baron, her compromise with life once her dream had been shattered ("Thank goodness there was Monsieur Baron," she tells Edouard—as a fail-safe, she seems to imply). Edouard brings her alive again, rekindles feelings and old emotions. Through her fascination with his stories about Egypt, no matter how stock in trade they are, she relives vicariously her former love affair. She dresses smarter, refashions an old dress she has not worn for years, has her hair done (ostensibly for Monsieur Baron's birthday, but only Edouard notices), and experiments with the slippers her daughter brought her from Egypt. She puts Edouard at the head of the table facing opposite her at the other end, typically, the man of the household would sit there, but Monsieur Baron sits to her left

L'Étoile du Nord/The Northern Star (1982). Madame Baron's dinner table sitting arrangements: who is the patriarch? Madame Baron (Signoret) and Edouard (Philippe Noiret) at the two ends of the table, Monsieur Baron (Jean Rougerie) to her left, and her daughter Toinette (Julie Jezequel) to her right.

(as would one of her children), with Toinette to her right. Edouard and Madame Baron talk openly and freely at mealtimes, as if he were the man of the house, and it is no coincidence that the only conversation she has about sex is with him. Provoked by something Edouard tells her ("Yasmina adored young girls"), she inquires into Yasmina's sexuality. Edouard replies by saying that in Egypt there is a more open-minded culture around sexuality, implying that bisexuality is the norm. Slightly shocked by this, Madame Baron asserts her own beliefs that "a man and a woman are made to be a couple; it's a matter of love and harmony." She clearly disapproves of extramarital sex and, at this same meal-time scene, openly discusses Monsieur Valesco's sexual life and behavior with Edouard, much as a mother would with her son's father. She openly criticizes his "rampant" sexuality, the fact that he is always "tarting himself up and then coming home at all hours stinking of perfume," and she complains that he is hardly ever home for meals (even when he is at the table she chastises him, like a child, for eating too fast). In the meantime, her husband is slouched at his chair, saying nothing: hardly the epitome of happy coupledom.

She and Edouard become, metaphorically speaking, the ideal couple she never experienced. Certainly, Monsieur Baron is far from being the patriarch. There is already a hint of this when Monsieur Baron comes upon them in Edouard's room. She is sitting on his bed, and Edouard moves over to stand beside her—the pose is typical of a husband and wife portrait. She narrates (with a little prompting from Edouard) the riddle of the Sphinx, which is about the mis-recognition of one's object of desire (the oedipal story). Which of Madame Bar-

L'Étoile du Nord/The Northern Star (1982). Madame Baron delivers the riddle of the Sphinx—but who is the misrecognized object of her desire?

on's three men is the misrecognized object of her desire, especially when at the end of the film, Edouard gives Madame Baron his only prized object, Yasmina's fake ruby ring? She accepts it, visibly moved, saying she will keep it until he returns, which she knows will never be, thus reenacting her earlier engagement with Albert. The ring itself, however, is so fraught with meanings, all of which are associated with falsehood, forgery, and violence, that it is hard to understand at first why she accepts it. It stands for Yasmina's false token of love to Edouard and the object that triggered his violent attack on Nemrod. Symbolically, it stands for a woman (Yasmina) who is sexually ambiguous and to whom Edouard still remains emotionally attached. Finally, of course, it is a fake.

Two crucial scenes between Madame Baron and Edouard help shift the ring's meaning and make it an acceptable token of exchange—in this instance, of compassionate human love. The first is her showdown with him after Sylvie has told her the truth. He comes into her kitchen with his usual banter about Egypt, and she, having kept her back to him all this while, suddenly turns around and shuts him up. "Now it's finished," she says, fury pouring from her eyes. The scene is shot in medium close-up on her, in a slight low angle, suggesting his point of view. She proceeds to confront him angrily, her face ablaze with the idea of being conned: "I took you in, like into a family. And in exchange you lied to me. You implicated us all, dragged my daughter into a sordid affair. You came here swanning around, being snooty about the others. . . . You don't come here if you are ill or a thief. You can clear off back to your Egypt. I don't want to see you ever again. I don't want to see you ever again!" It is this rejection that brings about Edouard's nightmare, wherein he recalls all the gory details of his murderous attack on Nemrod. By denying him his symbol of security and closing off his maternal space, Madame Baron shocks him into the present, into adulthood, into taking responsibility for his actions and recognizing his own criminal behavior. Hearing him scream out in the night and smash his bedside light (like a child, he cannot sleep without the light on), she comes to his room and comforts him. This scene is the total reversal of the preceding one. Both Edouard and Madame Baron are held in a two-shot medium close-up closing in on a two-shot close-up as she holds him and he tells her what he has done. She caresses and soothes him with her words (the *cajoler* and *dorloter* mentioned before). As with a child having a nightmare, she explains to him that what he has done, the murder, was committed when he was in what psychiatrists call a "second state" (one removed from the self). She knows this, she tells him, because she heard a psychiatrist talking about this condition on the radio. She then whispers to him, as a mother would a child, "We must keep this a secret," after which she tucks him back into bed. Unfortunately, the secret is out. Toinette has told the rest of the boarders, and they decide that, in order to protect Madame Baron, Edouard must go. However, the police have somehow discovered his whereabouts. There is no escape, and he gives himself up.

It is this giving up and the admission of the truth (not keeping anything secret anymore) that releases both Edouard and Madame Baron (she her secret about Albert, he his murder). This explains why Madame Baron is able to accept the ring. It has changed its meaning. It is the last thing Edouard has of his past. He has already given all the rest of his Egyptian memorabilia away to Monsieur Baron, Toinette, and the boarders in the house. In giving the ring to her (just before he tries to escape and subsequently gives himself up) and in her accepting it, both are drawing a line under a past that they never had—a past that was dreamed of by Madame Baron and Edouard.

In terms of Signoret's performativity in this film, we see quite a lot of her back. Partly it points to her fixedness in the domestic sphere—always at the sink or stove. But she also uses it to express certain moods, in particular rejection and distress. There is one very poignant moment, after Sylvie has told on Edouard, when Madame Baron/Signoret sits on her own, huddled over, and we can read through her back the terrible disappointment she feels and the sense of betrayal (after all, she had shared her secret with him). There is the usual fluidity of her gestures—her hands, face, and shoulders working with their usual precision and minimalism to express her thoughts and state of mind. We see her executing the domestic chores with remarkable conviction, especially beheading the fish (in close-up), peeling and scraping vegetables, and wielding a sewing machine. Her face, however, which we see in a fair number of close-ups (twenty-four), is differently ravaged from before. The marks of physical pain are there (from her illness and the operation), as opposed to the swollen marks of alcohol. The lines run deep across her cheeks and forehead and around her mouth. We are confronted with an aging body—with the grand exception of her remarkable legs—that no longer celebrates its self-destruction. The alcoholic body, which Signoret had renounced after her illness, has now morphed into a different body of evidence. It is a raw experience, the flesh speaks of a body that has known both mental and physical pain—the life of a person writ large for all to see.

Chapter Eight

Television Work—1964–1985

IGNORET'S FIRST television appearance was in 1964 in a forty-five-minute documentary she made with the filmmaker and photographer William Klein. Entitled *Aux grands magasins/In the Department Stores*, it was part of the series entitled *Les femmes aussi/Women Too*. The producer, Eliane Victor, launched this groundbreaking series with women as its focus. It was the first of its kind, offering a social reality documentary based on the quotidian, more especially the female quotidian. The department store in question was Le Printemps, and Signoret's function was to interview women who worked there or were shoppers. Although the documentary was shot and then edited, it has a very strong feel of live television. There are several reasons for this sense of the impromptu. First, no one was preselected: people naturally emerged as the ones to be interviewed. Signoret moved around the store waiting to feel the moment. As she said, "We [she and Klein] tried to know the women who went by, without any guideline for choosing, other than chance. One of them would command my attention, coming out of anonymity. On the whole there was a mutual recognition and contact was immediate."[1] Second, in the 1960s, much of television was still live, so the interviewees, by their own admission, were not that much taken by surprise at being invited to speak.[2] Finally, Klein's stylistic approach using a lightweight camera allowed him to seize the images in the raw.

The documentary is remarkable not just because it features women across all classes, but also because of what Signoret manages to elicit from her interviewees and what she reveals about herself. Most significantly, however, all women interviewed stated quite clearly that they wanted more out of life than marriage and children. This extraordinary consensus of female opinion, coming as it does at a time when the focus in social policy was so much on the family and increasing the birth rate for the nation's sake, shows just how skilled Signoret was at bringing out from her interviewees a female consciousness that, ultimately, flies in the face of governmental discourse and practice. Women in France were being given family allocations on an increasing scale for every baby they had—being paid to stay at home and breed, in other words. Also, husbands still had the right to keep their wives from working: in terms of the law governing marital status, the wife was not free to find work elsewhere unless her husband gave his permission for her to do so (this law was not rescinded until 1965).[3]

Signoret explained that she prepared carefully for these interviews, even though, at first, she felt a bit timid about the project, fearing being intrusive.[4] None of that reserve is in evidence in the documentary itself. She questions in a gentle but very direct manner—as, for example, in her interview with the wait-ress in Le Printemps restaurant. She asks this woman, who is unmarried and in her late forties/early fifties, if she would have had a child as a single mother (something we know Signoret did); to which the woman answers, "Yes, I would now, but earlier I would have been terrified." Again, this suggests an increased independence of spirit in women, who by now had experienced twenty years as fully integrated citizens (if not completely emancipated, as the above paragraph makes clear). Signoret interviews both working and upper-class customers; she also interviews an artist. As she remarks: "They all come when they can," point-ing to the nature of the department store as a kind of "femotocracy." Through her own ordinariness and the ordinariness of her questions, Signoret manages to extract some very natural, unaffected answers and to get to the heart of the matter. One customer, for example, talks about her need to buy as a way of staving off being unhappy. Married to a kindly and supportive husband, she is, as she readily admits, a compulsive spender. She feels lonely and empty-brained ever since she left work and got married. She sees going back to work as the only way out of her predicament. What is equally interesting in this documentary is that the questioning does not go just one way. Signoret also gets questions put to her (reflecting the "mutual recognition" she spoke of above) and is com-pletely open in her answers. Thus, in her interview with the artist, a mother of two for whom love and having children have changed her work practice, we also learn, thanks to the artist's questions, that Signoret did not consider that she was a particularly good mother ("An actress cannot be a good mother"), that, contrary to general opinion, she did not sacrifice her career for Montand, and that when she was making a film, she became a monster and nothing else counted but the film and her role.

The documentary ends with Signoret evaluating the experience as it touched her—again, an interesting shift from the standard style of documentary, which purports to go and get the truth "out there." The truth she comes away with for herself is that she is fortunate to feel fulfilled in life. She realizes, she says, that she is not like other women because her life has been built in such a way that she no longer has to do boring things. However, she adds, when it comes down to real problems—work, love, children—then "we are all speaking pretty much in the same way." The sense we get is that the making of the documentary left her with a series of question marks in her own mind as to how she lived her life. At the very end, Klein asks her, "Were you like them before?" "I don't know," is her honest reply. "And now?" he asks. "I don't know," she freely admits. It is not just the series, then, that is ground-breaking, nor the novel and open way in which this particular documentary is handled by Signoret and Klein. What is so refreshingly new is that the *documenteur*/documentarist reveals herself as well—clearly, the process affected some of Signoret's own belief systems.[5]

As a star, Signoret was fairly unique in going into television as early as she did. At that time, most French movie stars preferred not to work in television for fear that its intimacy would kill off their mystery (Vincendeau 2000, 19). It could also be the case that the fact of working and broadcasting live might prove too threatening. In the end, none of Signoret's television work was broadcast live even though the two plays she did in the late 1960s and early 1970s do have that feel, which suggests that each act was recorded in a single shoot. For example, there is a particular instance in Act One of *Un ôtage/The Hostage* (1970; play by Brendan Behan, directed by Marcel Cravenne) when Signoret appears to flub her lines. However, she manages to cover over the mistake by touching her left ear with her right hand so that, as with live theater, our attention is drawn away from her error.

Signoret's choice of work for the small screen has a coherence about it, embedded as it is in the political, whether it be sociopolitical (as with the documentary discussed above), contemporary political issues or those of the past. Of the six programs made for French television, she made three located in the past: a four-part drama about a financial con artist set at the turn of the previous century, *Thérèse Humbert* (1982; written by Jean-Claude Grumberg, directed by Marcel Bluwal); a Bertolt Brecht play, *La femme juive/The Jewish Wife* (1968; directed by Alain Henaut), set in mid-1930s Germany; and a two-part telefilm, *Music Hall* (1986; written by Jean-Claude Grumberg, directed by Marcel Bluwal), set in 1938 Paris. The other three are located in the contemporary: *Aux grands magasins*, *Un ôtage*, and the six-part series *Madame le juge* (1978).

I have not managed to locate and view *Thérèse Humbert* or *La femme juive*, so I will confine myself to a few remarks on these two productions. *La femme juive* was broadcast on TF1 in April 1968. Set in Frankfurt in 1935, it relates the story of a Jewish woman, Judith, married to a man (played by Michel Piccoli) who has become a Nazi sympathizer. He is a doctor and fears losing his job because of his marriage to a Jew. In the end, Judith sacrifices herself and makes the choice to leave him and flee to Holland. The terrible reality of that time is expressed by bringing it down to the level of the individual, as lived by Judith, who is faced with a husband who chooses to compromise his personal life rather than renege on fascist ideology. As we shall see, in her very last appearance, in *Music Hall*, Signoret again embraces this issue when, as Yvonne Pierre, she is obliged to come to terms with and reclaim her hidden Jewish identity.

In *Thérèse Humbert* (broadcast on Antenne 2), Signoret plays the eponymous heroine. The series is based on the true story of this woman who was a notorious con artist and fraudster, and who, for twenty years, managed to hoodwink politicians, financiers, and lawyers into believing that she was the rich inheritor of her American uncle's fortune. Relying only on her say-so and the documents she provided, they backed her business enterprise (selling life insurance annuities) by investing and frequently bailing her out when she hit financial difficulties—all based on the belief that one day she would receive her uncle's inheritance. The extraordinary thing was the length of time she managed to deceive them: almost twenty years, from the 1880s until 1902, when she was finally exposed. Signoret recalled her grandmother telling her about this exceptional woman who cynically borrowed 60 million francs that she knew she could never repay.[6] Thérèse Humbert had truly understood the climate of her times. The 1880s was a period in France when the rigors of probity were being enforced under the austere presidency of Jules Grévy (as we saw with "Jenny de Lacour" in *Les amours célèbres*). Paradoxically, it was also a period when greater opportunism prevailed, which meant, among other things, greater freedom to make money. Freedom was also seen in other areas since, in 1884, freedom of the press and the trade unions was guaranteed. Investment in modernization, including property speculation and development, continued apace. Much of this speculation was built on fraud. So, in certain respects, Humbert was merely practicing what was already happening. Her cleverness was in not getting caught for so long. Undoubtedly, her femininity helped, as men were less apt to confront a woman. But bourgeois respectability also had its part in this collusion with her colossal fraud.

As Signoret said, this period, which included the Dreyfus affair of the 1890s, was one when "France was at its most rich and most poor, most vain, most blinkered, most bigoted."[7] When director Marcel Bluwal, a friend of Signoret's, let it be known he was going to make the televised story of this woman, she put herself forward for the role. Signoret readily admitted that this was out of character, because she normally preferred to be asked, but she was afraid she might be too old if she waited.[8] She was attracted to the part because Thérèse was a woman who had "a side that is deeply vulgar, but at the same time is full of invention, imagination and fast thinking."[9] This was a perfect type for Signoret to play, given her vast experience. As she said, "I like my characters, even when they are bitches."

In Brendan Behan's *Un ôtage*, Signoret stars as Meg, playing opposite Daniel Ivernel as Pat. Set in Dublin in 1958, the narrative is as follows. After an attack by the Irish Republican Army (IRA), the British arrest an eighteen-year-old Irishman and declare he will hang if the guilty parties do not give themselves up. In retaliation, the IRA take a young British soldier, Leslie (played by Hervé Bellon), hostage, saying he will be executed if the British do not set the Irish hostage free. The IRA take Leslie to Meg's boardinghouse, which also serves as a brothel. Teresa (played by Patricia Gozzi), a servant at the boardinghouse who has fallen for the young soldier, escapes and, in the hopes of averting a senseless set of executions, goes and informs the British police where Leslie is. They arrive, but in the exchange of fire, Leslie is the first to be hit. In this play, which is a political satire that mixes tragedy with farce, Behan puts on stage a set of characters who are grotesque, vulgar, or derisory, but some of whom (Meg and Teresa), nonetheless, denounce fanaticism and the inhumanity of war.[10] Behan was against the British, but he was also against the censoriousness of Catholic Ireland with its small-mindedness, bigotry, repressive religiosity, and sexual hypocrisy.

Pat is a relic from the past who dwells on the 1916 Easter Rising against the British government and broods (through his bottle) on the failure of the Irish Republican Brotherhood to secure Ireland for the Irish. Meg is the voice of reason who, though she supports the cause of Irish reunification, challenges Pat's view of Irish heroism by disputing all the stories he tells. A former prostitute, Meg, now runs the boardinghouse. She is unashamed of her past. As she vulgarly asserts in front of the bigoted Salvation Army volunteer Miss Gilchrist (played by Denise Gence): "I'm a tart with a golden heart," she tells Pat, then declares, looking Miss Gilchrist straight in the eye, "You are [no better than] a part-time tart." Moreover, with the exception of the black homosexual Rio Rita (played by Clay Huff), she ridicules all the men for their virile posturings. The only other people to escape her withering tongue are Teresa and the resident prostitutes. She is, however, tolerant of most types, but not bigots like Miss Gilchrist, or snitches like Mulleady (played by Maurice Chevit) aka Princess Grace, the other resident homosexual. She feels sympathy for Leslie as well as for the Irish hostage, both of whom will surely die—two unnecessary victims of a never-ending conflict. As her song makes clear, what is the point of all this bloodshed when "there are no more mothers left [because there are no more sons] to break hearts"?

Signoret plays this role with great energy. When she is on stage, the pace noticeably speeds up. With her quick-fire repartees, she is funny, sharp, and deeply ironic. Signoret, who swore she could not sing, nonetheless, sings in this play. In fact, she gets to sing the most radical of the songs about the horrors of the Anglo-Irish conflict and its decimation of Irish youth ("Qui nous chantera les semaines de Pâques?"/"Who Will Sing Us the Easter Weeks?"). But she also gets to sing it in the most radical of fashions: with the Irish flag draped around her strong shoulders (small wonder this play was banned from mainland Britain). We sense, too, that Meg is more than just her role, that Meg's life consists of more than just running the boardinghouse. Because she is interested or intrigued, she knows every residents' quirky ways. She has a past grounded in reality, unlike Pat and his dreams, and she even finds time to do *petit point*. There is a clever touch in Act One, pointing to other aspects of her authenticity. When the camera moves into close-up on her, we notice that her mascara is smudged over her right eye—evidence of a woman who has had a long and tiring day. Signoret's hair is red and curly—looking very Irish, therefore—and her legs long and slim. However, her face is puffy and her body bloated, pointing, as we know, to another side of her star persona—the woman who drinks and who, at forty-three years of age, is apparently already resigned to the aging process.

When Signoret was first approached by the producer Raymond Thévenin to make the *Madame le juge* series, she balked at the idea: "You want to make me into a Maigret in skirts! Listen, the interesting one in the tragedy is the accused, not the judge. People will get bored after the second episode."[11] Unsurprisingly, given her sentiments about courts and the miscarriage of justice,[12] being a judge was a fairly extreme proposal and as far removed from her political persona as anyone could imagine. "Me, a judge, come on! How could you think it!" was her first reply. Slowly, however, she was brought around. "I've played tarts, cleaning-women, bourgeois-women, so why not the legal gang in a skirt," she said. (The word she used, *basoche*, is a pejorative term for the legal fraternity.)[13] *Madame le juge* was an extremely successful series. First aired in early 1978, it was subsequently rebroadcast five times over a period of twenty years.[14] There are three ostensible reasons for its enduring success. First, the casting of Signoret, seemingly against type, made audiences curious to see how this staunch defender of human rights and spokeswoman for the Left would fare as a judge. Second, the series is an example of successful cross-fertilization between television and cinema; Thévenin invited five distinguished filmmakers and various stars to work on it.[15] Finally, as Signoret herself pointed out, it was refreshingly a series *not* made along the lines of American formulaic TV.[16]

A great persuader for Signoret must have been the character she plays, the things she stands for, and the strongly contemporaneous, even slightly polemical, nature of the different scenarios (property fraud among local politicians, boycotting the World Cup in Argentina, the damaging effects of colonialism, etc.).[17] As Judge Elizabeth Massot, she seeks the truth, looking more for evidence of innocence than guilt. Above all, as she says in the very first episode of the series ("Le dossier Françoise Muller"/"The Françoise Muller File," by Edouard Molinaro): "My job is not to indulge people's masochism, but to try and find out what they have done and why they have done it." Her goal is to fight for justice. In "2 + 2 = 4" (the fifth episode in the series, written by Claude Chabrol), she expresses her wish for a more benign judiciary: "All suspects get condemned before they are tried, and I would have liked to transform this antechamber of madness into a more clement space, where understanding replaces polemics." Her methods are far from conventional. She goes onto the crime scene and endeavors to get to the heart of the matter by going beyond the basic reconstruction of the crime, she digs and probes, acting more like a police detective than a judge. She readily admits that "sometimes, justice does not get done, but that is not its fault," and recognizes that it is the way in which it is treated or interpreted that can lead to the abuse or the miscarriage of justice (as happens in two of her cases). What is also on trial in this series is the justice system itself. Is it viable? Can we trust it? These are questions that constantly trouble Judge Massot's restless mind. For example, in episode 3 ("L'innocent"/"The Innocent," by Nadine Trintignant), a man is gunned down by the police just as he was giving himself up; in episode 6 "L'Autopsie d'un témoignage"/"Autopsy of a Witness," by Philippe Condroyer, a man is arrested based on the testimony of an eyewitness in whom the police put too much trust, and he is nearly sentenced to death for a murder he did not commit.[18]

The series is based in Aix-en-Provence, a very bourgeois town in southeastern France. The length of the series (six episodes, 110 minutes each) gives us time to discover how the judge does her work and also to uncover aspects of her private life. Her character gains in depth, therefore. We learn that she was a lawyer and became a judge after her husband was killed in a car crash in 1968. As such, she was one of the first women to become a *juge d'instruction* (investigating judge)[19]—a rare phenomenon for that time, making her a woman of the vanguard. Elizabeth Massot is modern (she wears pantsuits) and works unconventionally, yet can be quite traditional in some of her views (she wants her son to play proper music and become a student so he can get a decent job). Considerable display is made of her ordinariness within her home environment. Indeed, many of Signoret's own pasttimes cross over here, providing an extra aura of intimacy with both the star persona and the character she plays. She does *petit point*, makes cushion covers, does crossword puzzles, and plays Scrabble on her own.

However, as we know, Signoret is a presence of counterpoints that leak over into her roles, so even within her ordinariness, there are some interesting subtexts that point to the more radical persona that we also know is part of Elizabeth Massot's makeup. Thus, her embroidery work is not "innocent." It is a reproduction from a book, *The Black Book*, given to Signoret by the American author James Baldwin. The book is an illustrated history of the cultural heritage of black Americans. In this book, Signoret came across a photograph of a bedcover that had been stitched by eighteenth-century black women slaves. She decided she wanted to copy it and reproduced it in miniature. But she also decided to bring it into her role as Elizabeth Massot, as well as the book, which we see on her coffee table at one point. The book has a further role to play in that Judge Massot, while leafing through it, comes across the bedcover and suddenly has an illumination about the case she is investigating.[20] It is doubtless symbolic that this book appears in "L'innocent" in which a former Vietnam veteran, Guérin (played by Philippe Léotard), is victimized. He gets set up by his wife, Monique (played by Juliet Berto), to take the rap for a robbery. Judge Massot quickly realizes that Guérin has failed to adapt to civilian life. Scarred as he is by his experience in Vietnam, he is a loose cannon who needs to be carefully handled. Guérin is placed under arrest, but makes his escape and holes up in his house with his two children. He is armed. However, he is really fighting to prove his innocence and to get his wife to come back to him. Judge Massot's moment of revelation as to his innocence comes when looking at *The Black Book*. Convinced that what she has heard from Guérin is the truth, she decides to go in and try to negotiate with him. She almost succeeds but for the impetuous behavior of the police commissioner (played by Pierre Vernier), who scathingly dismisses her endeavors ("These women judges are so theatrical," he exclaims) and orders his men to shoot on sight. His sexism apart, it is he who is rather stupid and hysterical as he barks his orders.

Judge Massot's personal life overlaps with the public in other ways, most significantly through her relationship with her son, Guillaume (played by Didier Haudepin). Massot is represented as a good and decent mother. However, theirs is a difficult relationship. Guillaume tries to assert his independence, and she is not always approving, especially of his slightly hippie approach to life. He wants to be a rock musician, she thinks it is a waste of his talent. He does not want to go to university, she thinks it is essential. He eats Indian food, she does not. The generation struggle is conveyed very well and is often quite funny. But when, at the end of the fourth episode ("Le Feu," written by Philippe Condroyer), Guillaume decides to leave home and set up in his own place, this has a dramatic effect on Judge Massot's judgment in the next case she investigates. In episode 5 ("2 + 2 = 4"), she becomes blind to the evidence and refuses to believe that the adolescent Jean-Michel Draouet (played by Benoît Ferreux) is guilty of murdering his parents (much as she can hardly believe Guillaume's symbolic "matricide" in leaving home). Claude Chabrol, who directed this episode, said he wanted to "insist on the relation between her private life as a judge and her professional life" rather than focus on her job. He also expressed the opinion that "it is impossible to be a judge—either you're made of stone and you understand nothing, or you put yourself in the place of the accused and you cannot judge."[21] This becomes Elizabeth Massot's dilemma.

Undoubtedly, episode 5 is her "crisis of motherhood" moment. Of all the shows in the series, it is the only one that delves into her unconscious—she has seven dreams, all of which center on the suspect Jean-Michel, but which also include her son at times. She first has an imaginary interview with the adolescent and ends up saying, "I would prefer it not be you" (meaning who murdered his parents). If found guilty, he could be sentenced to the guillotine—and this, above all, really bothers her. In a later dream, she fails to listen to him, even though Jean-Pierre keeps insisting he is no longer a child, a clear projection of her own situation with Guillaume. In the next two dreams, she is drunk. In one, she has an exchange with her clerk, Nicolas (played by Jean-Claude Dauphin), in which he tearfully declares that "my mother has abandoned me," to which she responds, "Calm down, you must think things through" (something she is currently unable to do, given her own distress about both her son and Jean-Michel). In the other, she tells Jean-Michel in a drunken state how life has passed her by. He, meantime, is trying to tell her that he committed the crime, at which point she starts to laugh like a madwoman.

This episode is the only one that sends out a discordant note within the series, in that it reveals a deep frailty in the judge. We already know she struggles in her relationship with her son, but her sense of judgment has never been off balance

—certainly not to this extent. Chabrol, well-known for his misogyny, does Judge Massot no favors here as he reveals the unbalanced nature of her mind. Indeed, when Jean-Michel finally confesses his crime, she becomes furious. It is in fact a fairly unpleasant episode in that it represents the main character as potentially mad (madder, perhaps, than the perpetrator of the crime, Chabrol seems to suggest). It may say a lot about Chabrol and his perception of the folly of justice, but the effect is more to demonize the female judge than it does the justice system.

This episode apart, we see Judge Massot at work in a balanced and measured way. We learn about her procedures, particularly her style of investigation.[22] She is precise with words and reminds others to be so as well. She is slow in her interview technique; she allows for pauses as she thinks through what a suspect has told her. She is piercing and finds the vulnerable spot, even though she never brutalizes her suspects. She takes risks because she cannot bear to see someone drowning (as in "L'innocent"). She goes on womanly instinct and mostly gets it right (the exception being "2 + 2 = 4"). And, although she is never arrogant (unlike some of her peers), she is not above taking a lesson in humility (as in "Autopsie d'un témoignage," the last episode), where she learns how difficult it is to be a witness and be sure about what one has seen. In short, she opens the judiciary up and gives it a more humane face.

Judge Massot is tough but fair, decent and fallible—as is justice itself. The series ends with her reconciled with her son and more open to his own ambitions and his music. In a similar gesture of humility, she confesses to her son that, after her own experience of being a witness, she will listen to her witnesses differently but not necessarily believe them, since they are relating their version of events. She adds: "I will never be totally certain ever again, only certain that I can make mistakes. It's me I question, not the justice system."

Equally tough but fair is Yvonne Pierre, a former *chanteuse-réaliste* and now the director of the Eden Theatre music hall. This was Signoret's last role. The very fact that Signoret could muster enough strength to make this telefilm is as strong a testimony to her commitment to acting and honoring her word as it is to her personal courage. By the time of shooting *Music Hall* (summer 1985), she was almost completely blind from retina failure and knew she was dying of cancer. Indeed, during the last few days on the set she was in a great deal of pain, and the day after filming was finished she was rushed to the hospital for an operation.[23] *Music Hall* was broadcast in May 1986, eight months after her death.

The inspiration for the telefilm was the famous prewar music hall L'ABC, founded by Rutty Goldin in 1934 and located on the boulevard Poisonnière near the Rex in Paris. By the early 1930s, the music hall was an anachronism, given that cinema had more or less replaced it in popularity. But this did not discourage Goldin, who, in his determination to fight against the upstart film industry, had signed the likes of Tino Rossi, Georgius, and Allibert to sing in his theater. After the war, Edith Piaf would perform there, as well as Yves Montand and Charles Trénet. Finally, in 1964, L'ABC succumbed and became the Gaumont Richelieu movie theater.[24] Thus, *Music Hall* is about keeping old traditions alive and, arguably, could run into criticisms of retronostalgia. The characters are based on real personages. Yvonne Pierre (Signoret) is a mixture of Yvonne George, Marie Dubas, and Renée Lebas (all *chanteuses-réaliste* in the heyday of the music hall and *café concerts*). Albert Guérin (played by André Dussolier) is loosely based on Maurice Chevalier, and Antoine Gallibert (played by Albert Ripa) on Allibert. However, there is a rawness to the scenario, written by Jean-Claude Grumberg, that prevents it from going down the nostalgia route. The story is far from sentimentalized. Set in 1938, we get a feel of the uncertainty of the times as war looms closer and closer. People are struggling to make a living. Yvonne has to make hard and unpleasant decisions about personnel; for example, she has to fire a woman in the chorus-line who is too old. She is brutally frank about sketches that are "old hat," knowing that she has to move with the times if she is to survive. She will crudely exploit people who can help her—those with money and those with political links in particular.

The arrival at the music hall of a German singing trio, who have escaped to Paris from Vienna, introduces an element of tension close to madness that keeps viewers on edge. Two of the Germans, Paul (played by Daniel Olbrychski) and his sister-in-law, Hannah (played by Laura Morante) are Jews. The other, Rudiger (played by Georges Claisse), is a Communist and a close friend of the other two. None of them can hope to get working papers, and so depend on Yvonne's kindness to survive. All three of them are haunted by the arrest of the fourth member of their group, Paul's brother Edouard (played by Christoph Bantzer), Hannah's husband. He has been taken to Dachau, and the news they receive about him drives them to the brink of insanity. Out of kindness, Yvonne engages them, realizing that they are refugees and surmising that they are Jewish. However, they are so unstable that she eventually has to dismiss them—a tough decision, which she regrets. But when she tries to remedy the situation (by taking them some money to help make ends meet), it is too late. Rudiger has committed suicide, and the other two have disappeared.

Until this moment, even though the reality of what was going on in the world had consistently seeped into her theater, Yvonne had been unwilling to face the truth—namely, the ineluctability of war with Germany, Hitler's fanatical fascism, and anti-Semitism ("I don't give a shit about Hitler," she yells at one of the dress rehearsals when the electricians are too busy talking about him and not getting on with their job). More crucially, she had also been unwilling to face her own truth, her Jewishness—something she had kept hidden from everyone, including herself, until this moment. But the shock of Rudiger's suicide brings her to some kind of Rubicon, and in a clever twist at the end of the telefilm, we see her go to her father's synagogue, where he is a rabbi, to warn him that he must leave France. This is the only means whereby we understand that she too is Jewish. She then returns to her theater, says nothing, but with renewed vigor insists that the show must go on. The show, entitled *Fourtez-nous la paix/ Leave us in Peace*, is bittersweet in its brilliance and is dotted with nationalistic resonances (as the subversive title indicates). It is cheered by the audience as a masterpiece. But Yvonne knows it is her last show, for she too will soon have to disappear.

For her role as Yvonne Pierre, Signoret wears a platinum blond wig. Her face is a deeply powdered white (looking very much like Françoise Rosay in her 1940s films). Her red, sensual lips are thickly painted, as are her fingernails. Her eyelashes are darkly done up with mascara, bringing out the green-blue luminosity of her (now blind) eyes. Her face is striking—a beautiful ugly—as we read her life through the lines etched in her forehead and around her mouth and eyes. She wears different clothes nearly each time she appears, although the color variation is between all white and all black—in keeping with her makeup, as it were. The designs are classic and unostentatious, thus not drawing attention to the body line. However, she certainly makes up for the restraint of her outfits by the extraordinary and most fabulous collection of hats she wears and which do a great deal to enhance her looks—and hint at a playful, carnivalesque body that has not lost its eroticism (as the presence of her lover, Albert, testifies). Signoret's body has lost all its suppleness, and her shoulders are now very rounded and hunched close up around her neck, but she compensates for this greater rigidity of the body by using her arms, gesturing from the elbows through to her hands to fill out her actorly space and give further dimension to her character. She also uses her props to engage her body into that actorly space. Thus, she uses her cigarettes to tap out a musical rhythm, signifying she knows her job and enjoys it. Moreover, we forget her blindness. She moves gracefully around the set as if she were fully sighted. When she takes cigarettes from her pack, we have to look very attentively to see the slightest of fumbles. In order to learn the part, Signoret had to have it read to her so she could memorize it—an extraordinary shift in discipline, which she was mostly successful in pulling off, although, apparently, she did forget some bits.[25] By now, her voice has become very smoky indeed: deep, husky, dusty even.

There is a certain poignant irony to the posters and photographs adorning Yvonne's office recording her former beauty, because this shrine is, in fact, made up of early photographs of Signoret from her films of the 1950s. Yvonne Pierre passing as Simone Signoret—enshrined with her past. Simone Signoret as Yvonne Pierre, looking (if she could but see) at her former self. But the truth is that time has no place for narcissism, and, ever the realist, both women (star and character) have to acknowledge that there is no looking back. As Yvonne says to Gallibert, there is no going back. He tries to persuade her to do a song for the review. She refuses, pointedly acknowledging her age and aging. "I've seen myself," she says. "Do you want me to sing with my back to the audience and the lights out?" She does sing in the end, but only for her friends during the rehearsal as an impromptu break. She chooses a love song: "Moi j'y peux rien, j'ai la tête qui chavire"/"I Can't Help Myself, My Head Is Spinning." They loudly applaud, but the moment, like the song itself, is a poignant one: Yvonne knows that she, just like the tradition she is so desperately trying to save, is a doomed affair. And, as all the beautiful young women dance around in front of her on stage, she surely has visions of her former self (she too started out in the chorus line) and recognizes what is over. She also rids herself of any other illusions. She banishes her lover, Albert, who only sticks with her to get what he can—a nice life, top billing, preferential treatment from the minister of defense (she manages to pull strings so he won't get called up for the army). She has already discovered that he has slept with Hannah. But when she overhears him boasting about it, that is the moment she chooses to kick him out of her house. She banishes him, not for his betrayal of her, but because of his betrayal of Hannah—and, therefore, of all women. Signoret's character, like the woman herself, remains strong and full of integrity to the last.

Conclusion

IMONE SIGNORET'S film career took off in the 1950s, a time when female stars were in the ascendant. After a period of strong masculinization of the industry, especially during the 1930s, French cinema witnessed a relative feminization of its product. This can partly be attributed to the Hollywood effect, with its massive focus on the female star, and the female star body in particular, to promote its industry. But it can also be attributed to the effects of new technology—Cinemascope and color—which brought about certain generic shifts. Comedies and thrillers still prevailed, indeed, predominated, as primarily male-identified genres, often shot in black and white and in standard format. However, a prime generic vehicle for the feminine, the costume drama, was also being made, and on a much grander scale, often as coproductions with Italy. On two counts, therefore, the female body became a more central presence within French cinema. Very few of the female stars of this period could claim to have occupied anything other than a primarily fetishized position, however. Even Jeanne Moreau rarely escaped being the "object" in her films of the 1950s (the notable exceptions being her films with Louis Malle). Even when they are not being fetishized, often the female star (Martine Carol and Micheline Presle, among them) is reduced to rather frivolous roles. Signoret stands out as an exception to this rule.

She also stood out on another count in relation to the French star tradition in that she did not follow the normal route taken by most stars, namely, that of coming from theater (be it classical, melodrama, music hall, or vaudeville) to film. Other notable exceptions include Danielle Darrieux and Michèle Morgan. Most French stars of the 1930s through the 1960s did their training in theater and crossed over to cinema—or indeed, as did most, they maintained a dual practice of working in theater and in film.[1] Signoret's entry into cinema was therefore unconventional and more closely aligned with the later practices of the French New Wave. With her striking good looks and intelligence, she caused herself to be noticed by the intellectuals at the Café de Flore, moved in circles that included film people, and, when trying out for early roles, stood out as different—someone new to work with.[2] As Anne Andreu points out:

> As soon as she appeared in French cinema after the war, it was clear that this woman was going to overthrow the rules of the game. With that look of hers, so clear, so strong, which is more of a challenge than a caress, Simone Signoret, in one blow, makes obsolete all her female contemporaries.[3]

Yves Allégret spoke of how taken he was with her as an actor, unhesitatingly casting her for Dédée and Dora, referring to her as that "flamboyant Simone Signoret."[4]

During her acting career Signoret embodied roles that can only be described as ones that offered the spectator a series of challenging sexualities, feisty femininities, and, later on, a cross section of maternal bodies that had lost none of the former two qualities. In her films she is typically at the center. Even if she is cast in a supporting role, her presence makes things revolve around her. As we saw with *Police Python 357*, where she is on-screen for a total of only twenty-three minutes (18 percent of the time), and *La chair de l'orchidée*, with a total of twelve minutes (10 percent), she is instrumental in turning the plot around. If we compare her to Jean Gabin, the *monstre sacré* to whom she is so often compared, some interesting differences become apparent that help us grasp just how significant her performances were for their time. Unlike Gabin, for whom the "other" (either a woman or a proto-son) was always a projection of his other side, Signoret's is a single individuated space. She reveals all her sides through her own single-minded embodiment. Moreover, she moves easily within male and female spheres, whereas Gabin is typically inserted within a masculine topography (Gauteur and Vincendeau 1993, 177). Signoret does not depend, as do Gabin's characterizations, on a social community for her identity. Indeed, the presence of a masculine social community with which Gabin is so closely identified and which acts as a backdrop to his own persona is very much *not* in evidence in Signoret's films. If there is a social community within the narrative, it will be heterosexual: there are a few exceptions where it is feminine (for example, *Dédée*). Generally speaking, hers is a more integrated social community and, therefore, more egalitarian in terms of representation. This bespeaks a more democratic body, quite distinct from Gabin's more hierarchical masculine body, where he is almost always superior to the women (*Le chat* being a remarkable exception) and often superior to men (in charm if not in terms of economic or physical power).

Where Signoret challenges, then, is in her representation of femininity as self-evident, as a norm. She offers us an "ordinary" femininity in all its complexity. Complex, because she invented a new "modern eroticism."[5] As I have argued, she enacts three types of eroticism: a clean erotics, an erotics of power, and an erotics of desire. She is complex, also, because she is not just astride sexual history but also political and cultural history. We witness, through her embodied roles, a deconstruction of the mythic representations of war, including the Resistance and the Algeria crisis, and the "thirty glorious years" of economic growth in postwar France. Through her we see their real effects: the social imbalances inherent in a system that privileges wealth and the dehumanizing effects of war on the individual psyche. Her roles are heroic, but not in the sense of the excesses inherent in masculine generic types, such as war movies, westerns, and gangster movies. Hers are quiet, unassuming heroics, matched by the silence that surrounds her performances (choosing rather to dialogue with her eyes).[6] Her body has served to break several cultural taboos. To quote but three examples: first, in the 1950s, she broke through the barriers of sexual censorship for example, in *Room at the Top*; second, in her assertion of her ugliness (her 1970s roles), she subverted the Western concept of beauty; and, third, in her almost consistent "failure" to fulfill the oedipal trajectory, she exposed the limitations of the heterosexual imperative.[7] Her costumes throughout her career marked her out as "ordinary," but more than that, in their simple design, it has been possible to equate her lack of frills and furbelows with intelligence,[8] occasionally malicious intelligence (*Manèges*, *Les diaboliques*, and *Games* come to mind). She had an independent power in her own right and broke with the constraints of feminine representation, which dictate that the female is to "be looked at." Furthermore, she defied the concept of the diegetically inscribed masculine gaze: in her films she is eye-catching to both sexes, but it is she who catches their eye, not the other way around.

As a star who was identified mostly with realist films, Signoret traced an incredible line of diversity in performance. Authenticity was always her driving force. By letting the personage enter her skin and invade her, she was able, always, to *be* the different roles with a difference—not repeating herself. Despite the latent or evident misogyny of many of her film texts, she managed to turn them around and assert her single-minded persona as an equal (*Dédée, Les diaboliques, L'armée des ombres*, and *Le chat* are just a few examples). The purpose of much of her embodiments was to drive toward an equality of the sexes, not reassert a series of binary divides based on gender. She strove, then, for a sexual politics that was democratic and unhierarchical. In many of her roles, men or dramatic events, such as war, drew her out of a protective shell and allowed her to occupy a place of great agency alongside her male counterparts. Not even Clémence in her tug-of-war with Julien in *Le chat* emerges a loser: she dies for lack of love, not because she had stopped believing in it. Indeed, in her later roles Signoret shifts from a woman who experiences the difficulties of love—which, nonetheless, empower her—to a woman whose ability to constantly engage in life empowers the crone.

In short, Simone Signoret, actor and star persona, has given us a history of a female body—almost in the form of a palimpsest or, more precisely, a "palimpsex," for the traces of each layer remain for us to observe and decode. Therein lies her power and her tremendous attraction.

Filmography

Release date is indicated first. Production year is given in parentheses after film title if it is different from release date. Under "Cast," only the principal actors are listed.

Unless stated, country of production is France. English title: U.K. and U.S. release title.

Abbreviations: coproduction (coprod.); director (dir.); scenario, adaptation, and dialogue (sc., adapt., and dial.); photography (ph.); music (mus.); decor (dec.); costumes (for costume dramas only: cost.); editor (ed.); producer (prod.); production company (prod. co.); minutes (m.).

WALK-ON/SPEAKING PARTS (1942–1944)

1942   *Le Prince Charmant/Prince Charming* (1941) *dir.* Jean Boyer, *sc. and dial.* Michel Duran, *ph.* Victor Armenise, *mus.* Georges Van Parys, *dec.* Jacques Colombier, *ed.* Louisette Hautecoeur, *prod. co.* CCFC (100 m.)
   Cast: Renée Faure, Lucien Baroux, Robert Arnoux, Sabine André, Germaine Lix, Christian Gérard, Jimmy Gaillard, Louis Florencie, Germaine Godefroid

1942   *Boléro* (1941) *dir.* Jean Boyer, *sc. and dial.* Michel Duran, *ph.* Victor Armenise, *mus.* Georges Van Parys and Maurice Ravel, *dec.* Lucien Aguettand, *ed.* Louisette Hautecoeur, *prod. co.* Pathé-Cinéma (96 m.)
   Cast: Arletty, André Luget, Christian Gérard, Jacques Dumesnil, Louis Salou, Meg Lemmonier, Denise Grey, André Bervil, Guita Karen, Paul Ollivier

1942   *Les visiteurs du soir/Night Visitors dir.* Marcel Carné, *sc. and dial.* Jacques Prévert and Pierre Laroche, *ph.* Roger Hubert, *mus.* Maurice Thiriet and Joseph Kosma, *dec.* Georges Wakhévitch and Alexandre Trauner, *ed.* Henri Rust, *prod.* André Paulvé, *prod co.* Scalera-Discina (123 m.)
   Cast: Arletty, Alain Cuny, Marcel Herrand, Jules Berry, Fernand Ledoux, Pierre Labry, Marie Déa, Gabriel Gabrio, Roger Blin, Jean d'Yd, Roland Pieral (Signoret in small role)

1942   *Le voyageur de Toussaint/The Visitor on All Saints' Day dir.* Louis Daquin, *sc. and dial.* Marcel Aymé (based on Georges Simenon novel), *ph.* André Thomas, *mus.* Jean Weiner and Roger Désormières, *dec.* René Moulaert, *ed.* Suzanne David, *prod. co.* Francinex (102 m.)
   Cast: Gabrielle Dorziat, Jean Desailly, Guillaume de Sax, Jules Berry, Louis Seigner, Serge Reggiani, Roger Karl, Simone Valère, Jacques Castelot

1943   *Adieu Léonard/Goodbye Leonard dir.* Pierre Prévert, *sc. and dial.* Jacques Prévert and Pierre Prévert, *ph.* André Thomas, *mus.* Joseph Kosma and

Charles Trénet, *dec.* May Douy, *ed.* Charles Bretoneiche, *prod.* Jean Gehret, *prod. co.* Essor Cinématographique Français (104 m.)

Cast: Julien Carette, Pierre Brasseur, Charles Trénet, Jean Meyer, Jacqueline Bouvier, Denise Grey, Marcel Perès, Edouard Delmont, Yves Deniaud (Signoret plays a gypsy.)

1944   *L'ange de la nuit/Night Angel* (1942) *dir.* André Berthomieu, *sc. and dial.* André Obey (based on Marcel Lasseaux play *Famine Club*), *ph.* Jean Bachelet, *mus.* Maurice Thiriet and Roger Roger, *dec.* Lucien Aguettand and Raymond Nègre, *ed.* Jeannette Verton, *prod. co.* Pathé (95 m.)

Cast: Jean-Louis Barrault, Henri Vidal, Michèle Alfa, Pierre Larquey, Yves Furet, Gaby Andreu, Manuel Gary, Alice Tissot, Claire Jordan, Albert Morys

1944   *Service de nuit/Night Service* (1943) *dir.* Jean Faurez, *sc.* Randone and Ussellini, *dial.* Nino Frank, *ph.* René Gaveau, *mus.* Roger Désormières, *dec.* René Moulaert, *ed.* Madeleine Bonin, *prod. co.* Francinex (96 m.)

Cast: Jacques Dumesnil, Julien Carette, Lucien Galas, Gaby Morlay, Robert Dhéry, Yves Deniaud, Louis Seigner, Jacqueline Bouvier, Gabrielle Fontan (Signoret is the dancer in the tavern.)

1944   *La mort ne reçoit plus/Death No Longer Awaits* (1943) *dir.* Jean Tarride, *sc.* René Jolivet, *dial.* René Jolivet and Roger Vitrac, *ph.* Fred Langenfeld, *mus.* André Theurer, *dec.* Georges Wakhévitch and Henri Morin, *ed.* Henri Taverna, *prod. co.* CIMEP (100 m.)

Cast: Jacqueline Gautier, Gérard Landry, Jules Berry, Raymond Aymos, Thérèse Dorny, Félix Oudart, Jacques Louvigny, Simone Paris, Georges Lanne (Signoret is Jacques Louvigny's [Firmin] mistress.)

1944   *Béatrice devant le désir/Beatrice's Temptation* (1943) *dir.* Jean de Marguenat, *sc. and dial.* Charles de Perret Chapuis and Jean de Marguenat (based on the Pierre Frondaie novel), *ph.* Fred Langerfeld, *mus.* Georges Van Parys, A. Sablon, and Mario Cazes, *dec.* Georges Wakhévitch and Henri Morin, *ed.* Raymond Louveau, *prod. co.* CIMEP (97 m.)

Cast: Renée Faure, Thérèse Dorny, Fernand Ledoux, Jules Berry, Jacques Berthier, Gérard Landry, Marie Carlot, Robert Pizani, Henri Bonvallet (Signoret plays Liliane Moraccini.)

SMALL ROLES (1945–1946)

1945   *La boîte aux rêves/The House of Dreams* (1943) *dir.* Yves Allégret, *sc.* Viviane Romance, Yves Allégret, and René Lefèvre, *dial.* René Lefèvre, *ph.* Jean-Serge Bourgoin, *mus.* Jean Marion, *dec.* Georges Wakhévitch and Auguste Capelier, *ed.* Jean Sacha, *prod. co.* Scalera Films (99 m.)

Cast: Viviane Romance, René Lefèvre, Henri Guisol, Frank Villard, Henri Bry, Pierre Louis, Robert Pizani, Marguerite Pierry, Gisèle Alcée, Jacques Dyman (Signoret plays Henri Bry's [Pepito] mistress.)

1946   *Le couple idéal/The Ideal Couple* (1945) *dir.* Bernard Roland, *sc.* Pierre Léaud and André Cayatte, *dial.* Michel Duran, *ph.* Claude Renoir, *mus.* Georges Van Parys, *dec.* Robert Dumesnil, *ed.* Marguerite Renoir, *prod. co.* SUF (92 m.)

Cast: Raymond Rouleau, Yves Deniaud, Marcel Vallée, Hélène Perdrière, Denise Grey, Jean Lanier, Philippe Olive, Paul Demange, Jean Sinoel, Annette Poivre, Roger Blin (Signoret plays Annette.)

1946   *Les démons de l'aube/The Dawn Devils* (1945) *dir.* Yves Allégret, *sc.* Maurice Aubergé and Jean Ferry, *dial.* Maurice Aubergé, *ph.* Jean-Serge Bourgoin, *mus.* Arthur Honegger, *dec.* Georges Wakhévitch, *ed.* Jacques Grassi, *prod.* François Carron, *prod. co.* CPLF and Gaumont (100 m.)

Cast: Georges Marchal, André Valmy, Dominique Nohain, Jacqueline Pierreux, Joe Davray, Marcel Ludpovici, Raymond Hermantier, Jacques Dynam, Jean Carmet (Signoret plays Lili, a bartender and prostitute.)

THE EMERGING STAR: MAJOR ROLES (1946–1951)

1946   *Macadam dir.* Marcel Blistène, *sc. and dial.* Jacques Viot, *ph.* Louis Page, *mus.* Jean Weiner and Marguerite Monnot, *dec.* Jean d'Eaubonne, *ed.* Isabelle Elman, *prod.* Eugène Tucherer, *prod. co.* BUP Française and Tucherer (100 m.)

Cast: Simone Signoret (Gisèle), Paul Meurisse (Victor Ménard), Jacques Dacqmine (François), Françoise Rosay (Mme. Rosa), Paul Demange (Marcel), Andrée Clément (Simone), Janette Batti (Mona), Georges Bever (Armand), André Roanne (Marvejoul), Félix Oudart (Léon)

1947   *Fantômas* (1946) *dir.* Jean Sacha, *sc.* Jean-Louis Bouquet, *dial.* Françoise Giroud (based on Marcel Allain novel), *ph.* Paul Coteret, *mus.* Jean Marion, *dec.* Jacques Colombier, *ed.* Monique Kirsanoff, *prod. co.* Latino Consortium Cinema (95 m.)

Cast: Simone Signoret (Hélène), Marcel Herrand (Fantômas), André Le Gall (Fandor), Alexandre Rignault (Inspector Juve), Yves Deniaud (Arthur), Françoise Christophe (Princesse Daniloff), Lucienne Le Marchand (Lady Beltham), Georges Gosset (Burette), René Mary (Germain), Pierre Labry (M. Paul), Paul Faivre (chauffeur), Robert Moor (Professor Cauchard)

1948   *Against the Wind* (UK) (1947) (French release, *Les guerriers dans l'ombre*, 1951) *dir.* Charles Crichton, *sc.* T. E. B. Clark and Michael Petwee, *dial.* P. Vincent Carroll (based on J. Elder Wills story), *ph.* Lionel Banes. *mus.* Leslie Bridgewater, *ed.* Alan Osbiston, *prod.* Michael Balcon, *prod. co.* Ealing Studios (96 m.)

Cast: Simone Signoret (Michèle), Robert Beatty (Father Philip), Jack Warner (Max Cronk), Gisèle Préville (Julie), Paul Dupuis (Jacques Picquart), John Slater (Emile Mayer), Gordon Jackson (Johnnie Duncan), Peter Illing (Andrew), James Robertson Justice (Ackerman), Eugène Deckaers (Marcel Van Hecke)

1948   *Dédée d'Anvers/Dédée* (1947) *dir.* Yves Allégret, *sc.* Jacques Sigurd and Yves Allégret, *dial.* Jacques Sigurd (based on Ashelbé novel), *ph.* Jean-Serge Bourgoin, *mus.* Jacques Besse, *dec.* Georges Wakhévitch, *ed.* Léonide Azar, *prod.* André Paulvé, *prod. co.* Sacha Gordine (100 m.)

Cast: Simone Signoret (Dédée), Bernard Blier (M. René/Coco), Marcel Dalio (Marco), Jane Marken (Germaine), Marcel Pagliero (Francesco), Marcel Dieudonné (drug dealer)

1948   *Impasse des deux anges/Dilemma of the Two Angels*, no UK release, *dir.* Maurice Tourneur, *sc. and dial.* Jean-Paul Le Chanois, *ph.* Claude Renoir, *mus.* Yves Baudrier, *dec.* Jean d'Eaubonne, *ed.* Christian Gaudin, *prod.* Eugène Tucherer, *prod. co.* BUP and Eugène Tucherer (84 min.)

Cast: Simone Signoret (Marianne), Paul Meurisse (Jean), Marcel Herrand (the marquis Antoine de Fontaine), Paul Amiot (the gang leader), Paul Demange (Minus), Jacques Baumer (Jérôme), Danièle Delorme (Anne-Marie), Yolande Laffont (Sophie), François Patrice (Le Gosse), Jacques Castelot (the count), Lucas Gridoux (the impressario)

1948   *Four Days' Leave* (UK) (French title *Suzanne et son marin*, apparently there was no release in France; also known as *Swiss Tour*) *dir.* Leopold Lindtberg, *sc.* Curt Siodmark, Richard Schweitzer, and Leopold Lindtberg, *dial.* Ring Lardner, *ph.* Emile Berna, *mus.* Robert Blum, *ed.* Hermann Haller, *prod.* L. Weschler Lazar, *prod. co.* Preasens Films (98 m.)
   Cast: Simone Signoret (Yvonne), Cornel Wilde (Stanley Robin), Josette Day (Suzanne), John Baragrey (Jack), Richard Erdman (Eddie), Alan Hale Jr. (Jo), Christiane (Martin Madeleine), Liselotte Pulver (a young woman), George Petrie (Sidney), Leopold Biberti (Walter Hochuli) (Film untraceable.)

1950   *Manèges/The Wanton* (1949) *dir.* Yves Allégret, *sc. and dial.* Jacques Sigurd, *ph.* Jean-Serge Bourgoin, *dec.* Auguste Capelier, *ed.* Maurice Serein, *prod.* Emile Nathan, *prod. co.* Films Modernes and Discina (90 m.)
   Cast: Simone Signoret (Dora), Bernard Blier (Robert), Jane Marken (Dora's mother), Frank Villard (François), Jacques Baumer (Louis), Jean Ozenne (Eric), Laure Diana (Hélène), Mona Doll (hospital matron), Gabriel Gobin (Emile)

1950   *Le traqué/Gunman in the Streets* (Fr/USA coprod.) (alternative title, *Time Running Out*, UK) *dir.* Boris Lewin and Frank Tuttle, *sc.* Jacques Companeez and Victor Pahlen, *dial.* André Tabet (H. Kane American adaptation), *ph.* Eugene Schufftan, *mus.* Joe Hajos, *dec.* Paul Bertrand, *eds.* Madeleine Bagiau and Prévin, *prod.* Victor Pahlen, *prod. co.* Sacha Gordine (92 m.)
   Cast: Simone Signoret (Denise Vernon), Dane Clark (Eddy Roback), Fernand Gravey (Inspector Dufresne), Robert Duke (Frank Clinton), Michel André (Max Salva), Albert Dinan (Gaston), Pierre Gay (Mercier), Edmond Ardisson (Mattei) (Film untraceable.)

1950   *La ronde dir.* Max Ophuls, *sc.* Jacques Natanson and Max Ophuls (based on Arthur Schnitzler play), *dial.* Jacques Natanson, *ph.* Christian Matras, *mus.* Oscar Straus, *dec.* Jean d'Eaubonne, *ed.* Léonide Azar, *prod.* Sacha Gordine, *prod. co.* Sacha Gordine (97 m.)
   Cast: Simone Signoret (Léocadie, the prostitute), Anton Walbrook (the narrator), Serge Reggiani (Franz, the soldier), Simone Simon (Marie, the chamber maid), Daniel Gélin (Alfred, the young man), Danielle Darrieux (Emma, the married woman), Fernand Gravey (Charles, her husband), Odettte Joyeux (the shop assistant), Jean-Louis Barrault (Robert, the poet), Isa Miranda (Charlotte, the actress), Gérard Philipe (the count)

1951   *Sans laisser d'adresse/No Fixed Address* (1950) *dir.* Jean-Paul Le Chanois, *sc.* Alex Joffe and Jean-Paul Le Chanois, *dial.* Jean-Paul Le Chanois, *ph.* Marc Froissard, *mus.* Joseph Kosma, *dec.* Serge Piménoff, *ed.* Emma Le Chanoix, *prod.* Raoul Ploquin, *prod. co.* Raoul Ploquin, Hoche Productions and Silver Films (90 m.)
   Cast: Simone Signoret (a journalist), Bernard Blier (Emile Forestier), Danièle Delorme (Thérèse), Julien Carette (a decorator), Pierre Trabaud (Gaston), Gérard Oury (a journalist), Juliette Gréco (herself), Jacques Dynam (a journal-

ist), Pierre Mondy (Forestier's friend), Louis de Funès (a future father), France Roche (Catherine) (Signoret's appearance is extremely brief.)

1951   *Ombre et Lumière/Shadow and Light* (USA) (1950) *dir.* Henri Calef, *sc. and dial.* Solange Térac, *ph.* Yves Bourgoin, *mus.* Joseph Kosma, *dec.* Rino Mondellini, *ed.* Raymond Louveau, *prod. co.* Sigma-Marceau (92 m.)

 Cast: Simone Signoret (Isabelle Leritz), Maria Casarès (Caroline), Jacques Barrois (Jacques Berthier), Jean Marchat (Shurman), Pierre Dux (the doctor)

INTERNATIONAL STARDOM (1952–1983)

1952   *Casque d'Or/Golden Helmet/Golden Marie* (1951) *dir.* Jacques Becker, *sc.* Jacques Becker and Jacques Companeez, *dial.* Jacques Becker, *ph.* Robert Le Febvre, *mus.* Georges Van Parys, *dec.* Jean d'Eaubonne, *cost.* Antoine Mayo, *ed.* Marguerite Renoir, *prods.* Robert Hakim and Raymond Hakim, *prod. co.* Speva Films-Paris Films (96 m.)

 Cast: Simone Signoret (Marie), Serge Reggiani (Manda), Claude Dauphin (Félix Leca), Raymond Bussières (Raymond), William Sabatier (Roland), Gaston Modot (Danard), Paul Azais (Ponsard), Roland Lesaffre (Anatole), Dominique Davray (Julie), Loleh Bellon (Léonie Danard), Odette Barencey (mère Eugénie), Claude Castaing (Fredo), Paul Barge (Inspector Juliani)

1953   *Thérèse Raquin/Adulteress* (USA) *dir.* Marcel Carné, *sc. and dial.* Marcel Carné and Charles Spaak (based on Emile Zola novel), *ph.* Roger Hubert, *mus.* Maurice Thiriet, *dec.* Paul Bertrand, *ed.* Henri Rust, *prods.* Robert Hakim and Raymond Hakim, *prod. co.* Paris Film-Lux (105 m.)

 Cast: Simone Signoret (Thérèse Raquin), Raf Vallone (Laurent), Jacques Duby (Camille Raquin), Roland Lesaffre (the sailor), Sylvie (Camille's mother), Maria-Pia Casilio ([also listed as Anna-Maria Cassillo/Cassilio], Georgette)

1955   *Les diaboliques/The Fiends/The Diabolical Ones/*(alternative title, *Diabolique*) (1954) *dir.* Henri-Georges Clouzot, *sc. and dial.* Henri-Georges Clouzot, René Masson, and Frédéric Grendel (based on Pierre Boileau and Thomas Narcejac novel *Celle qui n'était plus/She Who Was No More*), *ph.* Armand Thirard, *mus.* Georges Van Parys, *dec.* Léon Barsacq, *ed.* Madeleine Gug, *prod.* Henri-Georges Clouzot, *prod. co.* Filmsonor, in association with Vera Films (110 m.)

 Cast: Simone Signoret (Nicole Horner), Vera Clouzot (Christina Delasalle), Paul Meurisse (Michel Delasalle), Charles Vanel (Inspector Fichet), Pierre Larquey (M. Drain, schoolmaster), Jean Brochard (Plantiveau, the gardener), Michel Serrault (M. Raymond, schoolmaster), Yves-Marie Maurin (Moinet, the schoolboy), Jacques Varennes (Prof. Bridoux), Georges Chamarat (Dr. Loisy), Noël Roquevert (M. Herboux), Thérèse Dorny (Mme. Herboux)

1956   *La mort en ce jardin* (Fr/Mex coprod.)/*Evil Eden/Gina/*(alternative title *Death in This Garden*, USA) Eastmancolor, *dir.* Luis Buñuel, *sc.* Luis Buñuel, Raymond Queneau, and Gabriel Arout, *dial.* Raymond Queneau and Gabriel Arout (based on José André Lacour novel), *ph.* Jorge Stahl Jr., *mus.* Paul Misraki, *dec.* Edward Fitzgerald, *ed.* Marguerite Renoir, *prod.* Oscar Dancigers, *prod. co.* Dismage (Paris)/Tepeyac (Mexico) (104 m.)

 Cast: Simone Signoret (Djin), Georges Marchal (Chark), Charles Vanel (Castin), Michèle Girardon (Maria), Michel Piccoli (Father Lisardi), Tito Junco

(Chenco), Raul Ramirez ([also listed as Paul Ramirez], Alvaro), Luis Alceves Castanedas (Alberto), Jorge Martinez de Hoyas (Captain Ferrero)

1957 *Les sorcières de Salem* (Fr/Ger [GDR] coprod.)/*The Witches of Salem*/ (alternative title *The Crucible*, USA) (1956) *dir.* Raymond Rouleau, *sc. and dial.* Jean-Paul Sartre (based on Arthur Miller play *The Crucible*), *ph.* Claude Renoir, *mus.* Georges Auric, *dec.* René Moulaert, *cost.* Lila de Nobili, *ed.* Maguerite Renoir, *prod.* Raymond Borderie, *prod. co.* Films Borderie, CICC, SN, Pathé Cinema (France)/DEFA (German Democratic Republic) (145 m.)

Cast: Simone Signoret (Elizabeth Proctor), Yves Montand (John Proctor), Mylène Demangeot (Abigail Williams), Jean Debucourt (Reverend Parris), Raymond Rouleau (Deputy Governor Hale), Françoise Lugagne (Jane Putnam), Alfred Adam (Thomas Putnam), Jeanne Fusier-Gir (Martha Crey), Miss Darling (Tituba), Yves Brainville (Reverend Hale), Pierre Larquey (Francis Nurse), Michel Piccoli (Putnam's brother), Pascale Petit (Mary Warren), Chantal Gozzi (Fancy Proctor), Alexandre Rignault (John Willard), Jean Gaven (Peter Corey)

1959 *Room at the Top* (UK) (1958) (French release, *Les chemins de la haute ville*, 1959) *dir.* Jack Clayton, *sc. and dial.* Neil Paterson (based on John Braine novel), *ph.* Freddie Francis, *mus.* Mario Nascimbene, *ed.* Ralph Kemplen, *prods.* John Woolf and James Woolf, *prod. co.* Remus Films (117 m.)

Cast: Simone Signoret (Alice Aisgill), Laurence Harvey (Joe Lampton), Heather Sears (Susan Brown), Donald Wolfit (Mr. Brown), Donald Houston (Charles Soames), Hermione Baddeley (Elspeth), Allan Cuthbertson (George Aisgill), Raymond Huntley (Mr. Hoylake), John Westbrook (Jack Wales), Ambrosine Phillpotts (Mrs. Brown), Richard Pasco (Teddy Merrick), Beatrice Varley (Joe's aunt), Delena Kidd (Eva Kent), Ian Hendry (Cyril Kent), April Olrich (Mavis), Mary Peach (June Samson), Prunella Scales (Meg)

1960 *Adua e le compagne*/*Adua and Her Friends* (Italy) (French release, *Adua et ses compagnes*, 1961) *dir.* Antonio Pietrangeli, *sc. and dial.* Ruggiero Maccari, Ettore Scola, Antonio Pietrangeli, and Tullio Pinelli, *ph.* Armando Nannussi, *mus.* Piero Piccioni, *dec.* Luigi Scaccianoce, *ed.* Eraldo Da Roma, *prod.* Moris Ergas, *prod. co.* Zebra Film (120 m., BFI has it as 150 m.)

Cast: Simone Signoret (Adua), Marcello Mastroianni (Piero), Emmanuelle Riva (Mirella), Sandra Milo (Lolita), Gina Rovere (Milly), Claudio Gora (Ercoli)

1961 *Les mauvais coups*/*Naked Autumn*/*Foul Play* (1960) Dyaliscope, *dir.* François Leterrier, *sc.* Roger Vailland and François Leterrier, *dial.* Roger Vailland (based on Vailland novel), *ph.* Jean Badal, *mus.* Maurice Le Roux, *dec.* André Hervée, *ed.* Léonide Azar, *prod.* Jean Thullier, *prod. co.* Editions Cinégraphiques (103 m.)

Cast: Simone Signoret (Roberte), Alexandra Stewart (Hélène), Reginald D. Kernan (Milan), Serge Rousseau (André), Marcel Pagliero (Luigi)

1961 *Les amours célèbres*/*Famous Love Affairs* Eastmancolor, Dyaliscope, *dir.* Michel Boisrond, *sc.* France Roche, *adapt. and dial.* for Signoret's sketch "Jenny de Lacour," Françoise Giroud, *ph.* Robert Lefebvre, *mus.* for Signoret's sketch, Jules Massenet, *dec.* Lila de Nobili, *ed.* Raymond Lamy, *prod.* Gilbert Bokanowski, *prod. co.* Générale Européenne de Films-Unidex, Cosmos Films (130 m., Signoret's sketch, 29 m.)

Cast: for Signoret's sketch "Jenny de Lacour," Simone Signoret (Jenny), Pierre Vaneck (René de La Roche), Antoine Bourseiller (Gaudry), François Maistre (Inspector Massot)

1962   *Term of Trial* (UK) (French release, *Le verdict*, 1963), *dir.* Peter Glenville, *sc. and dial.* Peter Glenville (based on James Barlow novel), *ph.* Ossie Morris, *mus.* Jean-Michel Damase, *ed.* Jim Clark, *prod.* James Woolf, *prod. co.* Romulus Films (130 m.)

Cast: Simone Signoret (Anna Weir), Laurence Olivier (Graham Weir), Sarah Miles (Shirley Taylor), Hugh Griffith (O'Hara, defense lawyer), Terence Stamp (Mitchell), Ray Holder (Thompson), Roland Culver (Trowman), Frank Pettingell (Ferguson), Thora Hird (Mrs. Taylor), Norman Bird (Mr. Taylor), Dudley Foster (Detective Sergeant Kiernan), Newton Blick (prosecutor), Allan Cuthbertson (Sylvan-Jones), Nicholas Hannen (magistrate), Barbara Ferris (Joan), Rosamund Greenwood (Constance), Lloyd Lamble (Inspector Ullyat), Vanda Godsell (Mrs. Thompson), Earl Cameron (Chard)

1963   *Le jour et l'heure* (Fr/It coprod.)/*The Day and the Hour* (1962) Franscope, *dir.* René Clément, *sc.* André Barret, *adapt.* René Clément and Roger Vailland, *dial.* Roger Vailland, *ph.* Henri Decaë, *mus.* Claude Bolling, *dec.* Bernard Evein, *prod. co.* Société Nouvelle des Films Cormoran, CIPRA (Paris)/ Terra-Film, Compagnia Cinematografica Mondiale (Rome) (110 m.)

Cast: Simone Signoret (Thérèse Dutheil), Stuart Whitman (Allen Morley), Geneviève Page (Agathe Dutheil), Michel Piccoli (Antoine), Pierre Dux (Chief Inspector Marboz), Marcel Bozzuffi (Inspector Lerat), Billy Kearns (Pat Riley), Colette Castel (Lucie), Catherine Azoulai (Charlotte)

1963   *Dragées au poivre* (Fr/It coprod.)/*Sweet and Sour* (1962) *dir.* Jacques Baratier, *sc. and dial.* Jacques Baratier, Guy Bedos, Eric Ollivier, *ph.* Henri Decaë, *mus.* Ward Swingle, *lyrics* Bassiak and Jacques Audiberti, *ed.* Nina Baratier, *prod.* Pierre Kalfon, *prod. co.* Films Number One (Paris)/Compania Cinematografica Cervi (Rome) (96 m.)

Cast: Simone Signoret (Geneviève), Guy Bedos (Gérard), Jean-Paul Belmondo (Raymond La Légion), Francis Blanche (Franz), Jean-Marc Bory (reporter), Claude Brasseur (plumber), Françoise Brion (striptease "girl"), Sophie Daumier (Jackie), Sophie Desmarets (the pianist), Anne Doat (journalist), Jacques Dufilho (Monsieur Alphonse), Anna Karina (Ginette), Alexandra Stewart (Anna), Roger Vadim (himself), Monica Vitti (herself), Marina Vlady (radio-taxi operator)

1964   *Ship of Fools* (USA) (French release, *La nef des fous*, 1965) *dir.* Stanley Kramer, *sc. and dial.* Abby Mann (based on Katherine Anne Porter novel), *ph.* Ernest Laszlo, *mus.* Ernest Gold, *dec.* Joseph Kish, *ed.* Robert C. Jones, *prod.* Stanley Kramer, *prod. co.* Stanley Kramer Productions (149 m.)

Cast: Simone Signoret (the countess), Vivien Leigh (Mary Treadwell), Oskar Werner (Dr. Schumann), José Ferrer (Rieber), Lee Marvin (Tenny), Michael Dunn (Glocken), Heinz Ruehmann (Lowenthal), George Segal (David), Elizabeth Ashley (Jenny), José Greco (Pepe), Charles Korvin (Captain Thiele), Lilia Skala (Mrs Hutton), Alf Kjellin (Freytag)

1965   *Compartiment tueurs*/*The Sleeping Car Murder*/*Sleeping Car Murders* (1964) Cinemascope, *dir.* Constantin Costa-Gavras, *sc. and dial* Constantin

Costa-Gavras (based on Sébastien Japrisot novel), *ph*. Jean Tournier, *mus*. Michel Magne, *ed*. Christian Gaudin, *prod*. Julien Derode, *prod. co*. PECF (Paris) (95 m.)

Cast: Simone Signoret (Eliane Darrès), Yves Montand (Inspector Grazzi), Pierre Mondy (Chief Inspector), Catherine Allégret (Bambi), Jacques Perrin (Daniel), Jean-Louis Trintignant (Eric), Michel Piccoli (Cabourg), Claude Mann (Jean-Loup), Charles Denner (Bob), Pascale Robert (Georgette Thomas), Nadine Alari (Mme. Grazzi)

1966 *Paris brûle-t-il?/Is Paris Burning?* (1965) Panavision (final sequence in color) *dir*. René Clément, *sc. and dial*. Gore Vidal, Francis Ford Coppola in collaboration with Jean Aurenche, Pierre Bost, and Claude Brule (based on book by Dominique Lapierre and Larry Collins), *ph*. Marcel Grignon, *ed*. Robert Lawrence, *prod*. Paul Graetz, *prod. co*. Transcontinental/Marianne Productions (original French version 173 m., English version 165 m.)

Cast: Simone Signoret (very small role as a café proprietor); *lead players*: Gert Fröbe (General Dietrich von Choltitz), Orson Welles (Consul Raoul Nordling), Bruno Cremer (Colonel Rol), Alain Delon (Jacques Chaban-Delmas), Pierre Vaneck (Major Roger Gallois), Claude Rich (General Jacques Leclerc), Jean-Pierre Cassel (Lieutenant Henri Karcher), Jean-Paul Belmondo (Morandat), Leslie Caron (Françoise Labé), Marie Versini (Claire), Wolfgang Preiss (Ebernach), Kirk Douglas (General George Patton), Glenn Ford (General Omar Bradley), Claude Dauphin (Lebel), Pierre Dux (Alexander Parodi), Daniel Gélin (Yves Bayet), Michel Piccoli (Edgar Pisani), Charles Boyer (Charles Monod), Anthony Perkins (American GI), Jean-Louis Trintignant (Serge), Sacha Pitoëff (Joliot-Curie), Billy Frick (Adolf Hitler)

1966 *The Deadly Affair* (UK) (French release, *M 15 demande protection*, 1967) Technicolor, *dir*. Sidney Lumet, *sc. and dial*. Paul Dehn (based on John Le Carré novel *Call for the Dead*), *ph*. Freddie Young, *mus*. Quincy Jones (theme song sung by Astrid Gilberto), *ed*. Thelma Connell, *prod*. Sidney Lumet, *prod. co*. Sidney Lumet Productions (107 m., French version 102 m.)

Cast: Simone Signoret (Elsa Fennan), James Mason (Charles Dobbs), Maximilian Schell (Dieter Frey), Harriet Andersson (Anna Dobbs), Harry Andrews (Inspector Mendel), Kenneth Haigh (Bill Appleby), Roy Kinnear (Adam Scarr), Max Adrien (the MI5 adviser), Lynn Redgrave (virgin), Robert Flemyng (Samuel Fennan), Corin Redgrave (theater director), Les White (Harek), members of the Royal Shakespeare Co. in Marlowe's *Edward II* (David Warner as Edward)

1967 *Games* (USA) (French release, *Le Diable à trois*, 1967) Technicolor, Techniscope, *dir*. Curtis Harrington, *sc. and dial*. Gene Kearney (based on story by Curtis Harrington and George Edwards), *ph*. William A. Fraker, *mus*. Samuel Matlovsky, *dec*. Alexander Golitzen and William DeCinces, *ed*. Douglas Stewart, *prod*. George Edwards, *prod. co*. Universal Pictures Company (100 m.)

Cast: Simone Signoret (Lisa Schindler), James Caan (Paul Montgomery), Katharine Ross (Jennifer Montgomery), Don Stroud (Norman), Kent Smith (Harry), Estelle Windwood (Miss Beattie), Marjorie Bennett (Nora), Ian Wolfe (Dr. Edwards), Anthony Eustrel (Winthrop)

1968 *The Seagull* (UK) (French release, *La Mouette*, 1969) Technicolor, *dir*. Sidney Lumet, *sc*. play by Anton Chekhov (transl. and adapt. by Moura Budberg), *ph.* Gerry Fisher, *dec.* Tony Walton, *ed.* Alan Heim, *cost.* Tony Walton, *prod.* Sidney Lumet, *prod. co.* Sidney Lumet Productions (141 m.)

Cast: Simone Signoret (Arkadina), James Mason (Trigorin), Vanessa Redgrave (Nina), David Warner (Kosta/Konstantin), Harry Andrews (Sorin), Kathleen Widdoes (Masha), Denholm Elliott (Dorn), Eileen Herlie (Polina), Ronald Radd (Shamraev), Alfred Lynch (Medvedenko), Frej Lindquist (Yakov), Karen Miller (housemaid)

1969   *L'armée des ombres* (Fr/It coprod.)/*Army in the Shadows* Eastmancolor, *dir.* Jean-Pierre Melville, *sc. and dial.* Jean-Pierre Melville (based on Joseph Kessel novel), *ph.* Pierre Lhomme (maritime and aerial photography, Walter Wottitz), *mus.* Eric Damarsan (also listed as Eric de Marsan), *dec.* Théobald Meurisse, *ed.* Françoise Bonnot, *prod.* Robert Dorfmann, *prod. co.* Films Corona (Nanterre)/Fono Roma (144 m.)

Cast: Simone Signoret (Mathilde), Lino Ventura (Philippe Gerbier), Paul Meurisse (Luc Jardie), Jean-Pierre Cassel (Jean-François), Paul Crauchet (Félix), Christian Barbier (Le Bison), Claude Mann (Le Masque), Serge Reggiani (the barber), Alain Libolt (Dousnat)

1969   *L'Américain/The American* Eastmancolor, *dir.* Marcel Bozzuffi, *sc. and dial.* Marcel Bozzuffi, *ph.* Pierre Willemin, *mus.* Georges Moustaki, *ed.* Marie-Claude Lacambre, *prod.* Claude Lelouch, *prod. co.* Films Ariane, Films 13, Productions Artistes Associés (83 m.)

Cast: Simone Signoret (Léone), Jean-Louis Trintignant (Bruno), Bernard Fresson (Raymond), Marcel Bozzuffi (Jacky), Rufus (Corbeau), Françoise Fabian (woman at the estate agency), Tania Lopert (Hélène), Yves Lefebvre (Morvan), Jacques Perrin (Patrick), Jean Bouise (café proprietor)

1970   *L'aveu* (Fr/It coprod.)/*The Confession* (1969) Eastmancolor, *dir.* Constantin Costa-Gavras, *sc. and dial.* Jorge Semprun (based on book by Artur London and Lise London), *ph.* Raoul Coutard, *dec.* Bernard Evein, *ed.* Françoise Bonnot, *prods.* Robert Dorfmann and Bertrand Javal, *prod. co.* Films Corona (Nanterre), Films Pomereu, (Paris)/Fono Roma/Selenia Cinematografica (Rome) (160 m., USA release 138 m.)

Cast: Simone Signoret (Lise London), Yves Montand (Artur "Gérard" London), Gabriele Ferzetti (Kohoutek), Michel Vitold (Smola), Laszlo Szabo (secret policeman), Jean Bouise (factory foreman)

1971   *Comptes à rebours* (Fr/It coprod.)/*Countdown/Reckonings Against the Grain* (1970) Eastmancolor, *dir.* Roger Pigaut, *sc. and dial.* André Brunelin, *ph.* Jean Tournier and Roger Pigaut, *mus.* Georges Delerue, *dec.* Dominique André, *ed.* Gilbert Natot, *prod.* Eugène Lepicier, *prod. co.* Filmel (Paris)/Cine Azimut (Rome) (103 m.)

Cast: Simone Signoret (Léa), Serge Reggiani (François Nolan), Charles Vanel (Juliani), Jeanne Moreau (Madeleine), Marcel Bozzuffi (Luigi Zampalone/Zampa), Michel Bouquet (Valberg), André Pousse (Gilbert Levasseur), Amidou (Macias), Jean-Marie Bory (Ferrier), Serge Sauvion (Jebel), Jean Desailly (Dr. Saint-Rose), Bob Askloff (Narcisse), Joëlle Bernard (Suzy)

1971   *Le chat* (Fr/It coprod.)/*The Cat* (1970) Eastmancolor, Widescreen, *dir.* Pierre Granier-Deferre, *sc. and adapt.* Pierre Granier-Deferre and Pascal Jardin, *dial.* Pascal Jardin (based on Georges Simenon novel), *ph.* Walter Wottitz, *mus.*

Philippe Sarde, *dec.* Jacques Saulnier, *ed.* Jean Ravel, *prod.* Raymond Danon, *prod. co.* Lira Films, Gafer, Cinétel (Paris)/Ascot Cineraid, Comacico (Rome) (86 m.)

    Cast: Simone Signoret (Clémence Bouin), Jean Gabin (Julien Bouin), Annie Cordy (Nellie)

1971   *La veuve Couderc* (Fr/It coprod.)/*The Widow Couderc* Eastmancolor, *dir.* Pierre Granier-Deferre, *sc. and adapt.* Pierre Granier-Deferre and Pascal Jardin, *dial.* Pascal Jardin (based on Georges Simenon novel), *ph.* Walter Wottitz, *mus.* Philippe Sarde, *dec.* Jacques Saulnier, *ed.* Jean Ravel, *prod.* Raymond Danon, *prod. co.* Lira Films (Paris)/Pegaso Films (Rome) (90 m.)

    Cast: Simone Signoret (the widow Couderc), Alain Delon (Jean), Octavia Piccolo (Félicie), Jean Tissier (the father-in-law), Monique Chaumette (the sister-in-law), Bobby Lapointe (the brother-in-law)

1973   *Les granges brûlées* (Fr/It coprod.)/*The Burned Barns* (1972) Eastmancolor, *dir.* Jean Chapot, *sc. and dial.* Jean Chapot and Sébastien Roulet (based on original idea of Jean Chapot and Frantz-André Burguet), *mus.* Jean-Michel Jarre, *dec.* Pierre Guffroy, *ed.* Hélène Plemmianikov, *prod.* Raymond Danon, *prod. co.* Lira Films (Paris)/Oceania (Rome) (100 m.)

    Cast: Simone Signoret (Rose), Alain Delon (Juge Larcher), Paul Crauchet (Pierre), Bernard Le Coq (Paul), Catherine Allégret (Françoise), Miou-Miou (Monique), Pierre Rousseau (Louis), Béatrice Constantini (Lucile), Jean Bouise (the journalist)

1973   *Rude journée pour la reine* (Fr/Swiss coprod.)/*Rough Day for the Queen* Eastmancolor, *dir.* René Allio, *sc. and dial.* René Allio (assisted by Bernard Chartreux, Janine Peyre, Janine Pszonak, Olivier Perrier, and André Viola), *ph.* Denys Clerval, *mus.* Philippe Artuys (song "Arrêtez les aiguilles"/"Stop the Clocks" sung by Berthe Sylva), *dec.* Christine Laurent and François Darne, *cost. (for Signoret)* Marc Bohan (Dior), Karinska, Jean-Charles Brosseaux (hats), *ed.* Sylvie Blanc, *prod.* Yves Gasser and René Allio, *prod. co.* Polsim Productions, ORTF (Paris)/Citel Films S.A. (Geneva) (90 m.)

    Cast: Simone Signoret (Jeanne), Jacques Debary (Albert), Olivier Perrier (Julien), Orane Demazis (Catherine), Christiane Rorato (Mathilde), Alice Reichen (Rose), André Valtier (Charles), Michel Peyrelon (Georges), Arlette Chosson (Annie Thouars), Denise Bonal (Armande Thouars), Pierre Leomy (M. Thouars), Domique Degoetje (Mme. Flatters), Gabriel Cattand (M. Flatters), Thomas Vincent (the Flatters' son)

1975   *La chair de l'orchidée* (Fr/It/Ger [RFA] coprod.)/*The Flesh of the Orchid* (1974) Eastmancolor, *dir.* Patrice Chéreau, *sc. and dial.* Jean-Claude Carrière and Patrice Chéreau (based on James Hadley Chase novel), *ph.* Pierre Lhomme, *mus.* Fiorenzo Carpi, *dec.* Richard Peduzzi, *ed.* Pierre Gilette, *prod.* Vincent Malle Productions, *prod. co.* Paris Cannes Production, Meric Films, Astrophore Films, ORTF (Paris)/TIT Film Production (Munich)/Oceania Productions (Rome) (115 m.)

    Cast: Simone Signoret (Lady Vamos), Charlotte Rampling (Claire Wegener), Bruno Cremer (Louis Delage), Edwige Feuillère (Mme. Bastier-Wegener), Hugues Quester (Marcucci), Hans-Christian Biech (Gyula Bérékian), François Simon (Joszef Bérékian), Eve Francis (Delage's mother), Robert Baillard (gardener), Gianpiero Fortebraccio (Mme. Bastier-Wegener's son)

1976   *Police Python 357* (Fr/It/Ger [RFA] coprod.) (1975) Eastmancolor, *dir.* Alain Corneau, *sc.* Daniel Boulanger and Alain Corneau, *dial.* Daniel Boulanger, *ph.* Etienne Becker, *mus.* Georges Delerue, *ed.* Marie-Josèphe Yoyotte, *prod.* Albina Du Boisrouvray, *prod. co.* Albina Productions, Films La Boétie (Paris)/TIT Film Production (Munich)/Rizzole Editore (Italy) (125 m.)

   Cast: Simone Signoret (Thérèse Ganay), Yves Montand (Marc Ferrot), François Périer (M. Ganay), Mathieu Carrière (Inspector Ménard), Vadim Glowna (Inspector Abadie), Stefania Sandrelli (Sylvia Leopardi)

1977   *La vie devant soi/Madame Rosa* (alternative title USA *Life before Him*) Eastmancolor, *dir.* Moshe Mizrahi, *sc., adapt., and dial.* Moshe Mizrahi (based on Emile Ajar/Romain Gary novel), *ph.* Nestor Almendros, *mus.* Philippe Sarde, *dec.* Bernard Evein, *ed.* Sophie Cossein, *prod.* Raymond Danon, *prod. co.* Lira Films (104 m, English press releases give 120 m.)

   Cast: Simone Signoret (Mme. Rosa), Samy Ben Youb (Momo), Claude Dauphin (Dr. Katz), Gabriel Jabbour (M. Hamil), Stella Anicette (Mme. Lola), Machal Bat Adam (Mme. Nadine), Constantin Costa-Gavras (Ramon), Mohammed Zineth (Kadir), Geneviève Fontanel (Maryse), Elio Bencoil (Moïse), Vincent Hua (Michel), Bernard Eliazord (Banania), Math Samba (Walloumba), El Kébir (Mimoun), Ibrahim Seck (N'Da Ameder), Théo Legitimus (M. Boro)

1978   *Judith Therpauve* Eastmancolor, *dir.* Patrice Chéreau, *sc. and dial.* Patrice Chéreau and Georges Conchon (based on Georges Conchon original story), *ph.* Pierre Lhomme, *dec.* Richard Peduzzi, Françoise Bonnot, *prod. co.* Gaumont-Buffalo Films (127 m.)

   Cast: Simone Signoret (Judith Therpauve), Philippe Léotard (Jean-Pierre Maurier), Marcel Imhoff (Pierre Damien), François Simon (Hirsch-Balland), Robert Manuel (Droz), Laszlo Szabo (Lepage), Marie-Paul André (Jeanne), Daniel Lecourtois (Desfraizeaux), Jean Rougeul (Genty), Alain David (Louis), Bernard Donnadieu (Laindreaux), Daniel Schmidt (Jean Therpauve), Anne Delbée (Gisèle), Laurence Bourdil (Marianne)

1979   *L'adolescente* (Fr/Ger [RFA] coprod.) (1978) Eastmancolor, *dir.* Jeanne Moreau, *sc. and dial.* Henriette Jelinek and Jeanne Moreau (based on original story by Jeanne Moreau), *ph.* Pierre Gautard, *mus.* Philippe Sarde, *dec.* Noëlle Galland, *ed.* Albert Jurgenson and Colette Leloup, *prod.* Philippe Dussart, *prod. co.* Philippe Dussart and Carthago Films (Paris)/Janus Film (Frankfurt) (90 m.)

   Cast: Simone Signoret (Mamie), Laetitia Chaveau (Marie), Edith Clever (Marie's mother, Eva), Jacques Weber (Marie's father, Jean), Francis Huster (Alexandre, the doctor), Roger Blin (the blacksmith), Jean-François Balmer (the carpenter), Hughes Quester (the blacksmith's son, Fred), Charles Millot (the mayor), Juliette Brac (Mélanie), Isabelle Sadoyan (mayor's wife, Louise), Bérangère Bonvoisin (the mayor's daughter, Thérèse), Hélène Vallière (the witch, Augusta), Michel Blanc (M. Bertin)

1980   *Chère inconnue/I Sent a Letter to My Love* (1979) Eastmancolor, *dir.* Moshe Mizrahi, *sc. and adapt.* Moshe Mizrahi and Gérard Brach, *dial.* Gérard Brach (based on Berenice Rubens novel), *ph.* Ghislain Cloquet, *mus.* Philippe Sarde, *dec.* Bernard Evein, *ed.* Françoise Bonnot, *prods.* Lise Fayolle and Giorgio Silvagni, *prod. co.* Cinéproduction and FR3 (96 m.)

Cast: Simone Signoret (Louise Martin), Delphine Seyrig (Yvette Le Goff), Jean Rochefort (Gilles Martin), Dominique Labourier (the theater director), Geneviève Fontanel (Elisabeth, an actor employed to play Béatrice), Jean Obé (Hugues), Madeleine Ozeray (Mme. Thomas), Gilette Barbier (Mme. Guillaume), Marion Loran (the post office clerk), Florence Haziot (the salesperson)

1982   *Guy de Maupassant* (1981) Fujicolor, *dir.* Michel Drach, *sc.* Michel Drach and Philippe Madral, *dial.* Philippe Madral, *ph.* Philippe Rousselot, *mus.* Georges Delerue, *dec.* Jean-Pierre Kohut-Svelko and Antoine Roman, *cost.* Yvonne Sassinot, *ed.* Geneviève Winding, *prod.* Michel Drach, *prod. co.* Port Royal Films, Gaumont, and FR3 (131 m.)

Cast: Simone Signoret (Laure de Maupassant), Claude Brasseur (Guy de Maupassant), Jean Carmet (his valet, François Tassart), Daniel Gélin (Maupassant's father), Miou-Miou (Gisèle d'Estoc), Véronique Genest (Maupassant's first love), Anne-Marie Philipe (Comtesse Potocka), Louis Navarre (Flaubert), William Sabatier (Dr. Blanche), Jacques Disses (Dr. Meuriot), Anne Deleuze (Princese Polignac), Catherine Frot (Mouche), Dorothée Jemma (Comtesse Funk)

1982   *L'Etoile du Nord/The Northern Star/The North Star* (1981) Fujicolor, *dir.* Pierre Granier-Deferre, *sc. and adapt.* Jean Aurenche, Michel Grisolia, and Pierre Granier-Deferre, *dial.* Jean Aurenche and Michel Grisolia (based on Georges Simenon novel *Le locataire/The Lodger*), *ph.* Pierre-William Glenn, *mus.* Philippe Sarde, *dec.* Dominique André, *cost.* Catherine Leterrier, *prod.* Alan Sarde, *prod. co.* Sara Films and Antenne 2 (124 m.)

Cast: Simone Signoret (Mme. Baron), Philippe Noiret (Edouard Binet), Fanny Cottençon (Sylvie), Julie Jezequel (Antoinette), Jean Rougerie (M. Baron), Jean-Pierre Klein (Moïse), Jean-Yves Chatelais (M. Valesco), Koniency (Domb), Liliane Gerace (Yasmina), Gamil Ratib (Nemrod Loktoum), Jean Dautremay (the engineer), Pierre Forget (Albert)

Audience Figures for Signoret's Major Films Released in France

Title	Production Year	Director	Release Date	Audience Figures
Les démons de l'aube	1945	Yves Allégret	9 April 1946	2,411,166
Macadam	1946	Marcel Blistène	27 Nov. 1946	2,742,018
Fantômas	1946	Jean Sacha	18 Sept. 1947	2,380,672
Dédée d'Anvers	1947	Yves Allégret	3 Sept. 1948	3,077,336
Impasse des deux anges	1948	Maurice Tourneur	3 Nov. 1948	1,324,304
Manèges	1949	Yves Allégret	25 Jan. 1950	1,508,026
La ronde	1950	Max Ophuls	27 Sept. 1950	1,509,922
Ombre et lumière	1950	Henri Calef	27 June 1951	996,292
Casque d'or	1951	Jacques Becker	16 April 1952	1,917,248
Thérèse Raquin	1953	Marcel Carné	6 Nov. 1953	2,364,260
Les diaboliques	1954	H.-G. Clouzot	20 Jan. 1955	3,674,380
La mort en ce jardin	1956	Luis Buñuel	21 Sept. 1956	1,536,292
Les sorcières de Salem	1956	Raymond Rouleau	26 April 1957	1,686,749
Les mauvais coups	1960	François Leterrier	17 May 1961	81,481*
Les amours célèbres	1961	Michel Boisrond	3 Nov. 1961	2,024,604
Le jour et l'heure	1962	René Clément	5 April 1963	1,130,212
Compartiment tueurs	1964	C. Costa-Gavras	17 Nov. 1965	1,079,154
L'armée des ombres	1969	J.-P. Melville	12 Sept. 1969	1,401,822
L'Américain	1969	Marcel Bozzuffi	17 Oct. 1969	53,080*
L'aveu	1969	C. Costa-Gavras	29 April 1970	2,140,297
Comptes à rebours	1970	Roger Pigaut	15 Feb. 1971	1,125,489
Le chat	1970	P. Granier-Deferre	1 March 1971	1,035,709
La veuve Couderc	1971	P. Granier-Deferre	13 Oct. 1971	2,008,203
Les granges brûlées	1972	Jean Chapot	30 Jan. 1973	NA
Rude journée pour la reine	1973	René Allio	6 Dec. 1973	76,214
La chair de l'orchidée	1974	Patrice Chéreau	29 Jan. 1975	552,107
Police Python 357	1975	Alain Corneau	31 March 1976	1,464,582
La vie devant soi	1977	Moshe Mizrahi	2 Nov. 1977	1,997,455
Judith Therpauve	1978	Patrice Chéreau	6 Oct. 1978	190,313
L'adolescente	1978	Jeanne Moreau	24 Jan. 1979	437,875
Chère inconnue	1979	Moshe Mizrahi	9 April 1980	511,601
Guy de Maupassant	1981	Michel Drach	14 April 1982	109,892
L'Étoile du Nord	1981	P. Granier-Deferre	31 March 1982	1,645,275

*Includes figures for Paris theaters only.
NA not available
Source: Simsi, Simon. Ciné-passions: 7ème art et industrie de 1945 à 2000. Paris: Edition Dixit, 2001.
Figures for British and American film releases could not be traced.

Other Work

1968   *La femme juive* Play by Bertholt Brecht, director Alain Henaut; shown on Antenne 2

1970   *Un ôtage/The Hostage* Play by Brendan Behan, director Marcel Cravenne; shown on Antenne 2

1978   *Madame le Juge* Six-part series, various directors: Edouard Molinaro, Nadine Trintignant, Claude Chabrol, Claude Barma, Philippe Condroyer; shown on Antenne 2. (Produced 1976–1977.)

1983   *Thérèse Humbert* Four-part drama by Jean-Claude Grumberg, director Marcel Bluwal; shown on Antenne 2 (Produced 1982.)

1986   *Music Hall* Two-part telefilm by Jean-Claude Grumberg, director Marcel Bluwal; shown on France 3(Produced 1985.)

Signoret as Author

   La nostalgie n'est plus ce qu'elle était. Paris: Editions du Seuil, 1975.

   Le lendemain elle était souriante. Paris: Editions du Seuil, 1979.

   Adieu Volodia. Paris: Arthème Fayard, 1985.

Signoret as Translator

1962   *Les petits renards/Little Foxes* (play by Lillian Hellman)

1967   *Fièvre/Fever* (novel by Peter Feibelmann)

1981   *Une saison à Bratislava/Convictions: Memories of a Life Shared with a Good Communist* (personal memoir of Jo Langer)

Notes

Unless otherwise indicated, in the following notes, newspaper/magazine citations with no page reference are press releases found at the Bibliothèque de l'Arsenal, Paris (BAP). BFI = British Film Institute.

Chapter One: Signoret, a Life—Chronotopes or Topographies of Space and Time

1. For more information on Mikhail Bakhtin and his term *chronotope*, consult Lynne Pearce's excellent book *Reading Dialogics* (London and New York: Edward Arnold, 1994).

2. It is possible that Sartre gets a bit of a send-up in Yves Allégret's *La boîte aux rêves* (1943), which is based on characters frequenting the Café de Flore and figures Signoret in a small role.

3. Even in 1941, 1,400 francs was not a huge amount. When Signoret did bit parts for movies, she was paid between 170 and 200 francs a day. A way to read these figures today is to say that, by 1943, a kilo of butter cost a fifth of that salary of 1400 francs.

4. Signoret records this whole part of her life in *La nostalgie n'est plus ce qu'elle était* (1978, 36–50, 58).

5. Signoret declared in her 1961 television interview with John Freeman (in the *Face to Face* series), "I *was the father* of our family."

6. Apparently Signoret was one of Jacques Prévert's muses (*Libération*, 1 October 1985, 4).

7. Undoubtedly her newly adopted name was also linked (albeit incorrectly) with the famous actor Gabriel Signoret. As Signoret herself admits (1978, 61), "I played, quite hypocritically, with the label 'relative of the great Gabriel Signoret? . . . an uncle; just as my grandmother had done before me. . . .'"

8. Louis Daquin wanted to engage her for the lead female role in *Les voyageurs de la Toussaint* (1942), but when he discovered she did not have a COIC card, he withdrew his offer. He did, however, give her a small bit part (Signoret 1978, 65).

9. For example, the Prévert brothers wrote *Adieu Léonard* (Pierre Prévert, 1943) for their Café de Flore friends (Signoret has a small part in it, as a gypsy).

10. Sartre, quoted in Vian (1997, 117).

11. Ibid. Sartre conveniently forgets that the Flore abounded with actors, painters and the like. He apparently held court upstairs most often, so may well not have mingled with the other cultural embodiments!

12. See her interview in *Cinémonde*, 11 June 1963, 12.

13. At the beginning of her relationship with Montand, Signoret found herself back, very briefly, in Neuilly, where Montand had an apartment.

14. Apart, that is, from a very brief sojourn back to Neuilly with Montand in his apartment, when they first became lovers.

15. A television documentary, *Le sens de l'histoire: La délation sous l'occupation* (1998), by André Halimi, gave a very clear picture of this period of horror for those who were constantly at risk of being denounced, arrested, shot, or deported.

16. Signoret, quoted in *Libération*, 1 October 1985, 2. Elsewhere (Durant 1988, 25) she recalled how she felt that she missed out on a part of her life—the transition from

young girl to young woman: "That whole spate of time where a young girl discovers her womanhood, that did not happen for me."

17. Interview in *Cinémonde*, 26 November 1963, 5.

18. From a radio interview with Jacques Chancel, *Radioscopie* (recorded 11 November 1976 and broadcast in 1977). In this interview, Signoret also spoke of this time as a period that was reduced to simple, basic binaries: things were black and white.

19. Skirts became shorter (practical for bicycle riding), and shoes were made of composite materials. Some shoes even had lightbulbs in them so that you could see at night. For more affluent travelers, *vélo-taxis* were made by cutting cars in half and attaching them to bicycles.

20. Signoret is quoted in Durant (1988, 25) as saying: "I have never really known how to groom myself properly. Because of the war . . . I wore boy's shirts and trousers. Those who wore beautiful dresses had obtained them through the black market. The rest of us just dressed up to keep the cold out." In 1962, she still confessed to being badly dressed (interview in *Cinémonde*, 16 January 1962, 6).

21. *Cinémonde*, 18 May 1948, 16.

22. One could add that this predates the 1950s Situationists by a few years.

23. Signoret had been coached at the renowned cours Sicard (directed by Solange Sicard). However, she was destined never to become a stage actor of any repute, primarily because her voice projection was weak.

24. Gélin recalled (1977, 179, 245) that Signoret remained a true friend to him, in particular when he became a drug addict. She took him to his first detox center. Later, when she was with Montand, they both came to visit him in Bellevue, a detox center.

25. See Hamon and Rotman (1990, 294) for further details. It is noteworthy that Montand wanted a large family, something he would never achieve even with his mistress in later life, Carol Amiel, with whom he had one child, a son, Valentin (1987).

26. Later, Signoret was not treated for cancer here but at the Hôpital Paul-Guiraud in Villejuif (Durant 1988, 267).

27. For example, André Breton in *Nadja* (Paris: Gallimard, 1962, 92) describes the Place Dauphine as one of female enticement that is almost sirenlike and whose holding power is soft and seductive but ultimately breaking.

28. As Signoret (1978, 108) put it, "We are fiancés but we're not marrying."

29. André Malraux was minister of culture during this period (therefore, technically he was responsible for the ban). However, a few months earlier, in 1959, he had also been at the Festival de Cannes and awarded Signoret the prize for best actress for her role in *Room at the Top*.

30. Pierre Goldman (1975, 242–243) wrote a book about his trial and recorded with great vividness the impact that Signoret's daily presence had on him: "I saw Simone Signoret. Her presence particularly moved me. I knew she hadn't come because she was motivated by some arbitrary attraction to the judiciary spectacle. . . . I looked at her and she looked at me. Her face was distraught. In looking at her, I thought about the two films of hers that I had liked. *Casque d'Or* . . . [and] *Le jour et l'heure*, which I had seen with my mother in Warsaw. . . . I couldn't look at Simone Signoret without thinking about my mother. In a way she was a symbolic presence during this trial."

31. Signoret (1978, 96) wrote: "The flat had everything going for it: we were both on the Quai des Anciens Orfèvres and the Place Dauphine. It was right, it was normal and moral."

32. Signoret recorded this whole sorry story in *La nostalgie n'est plus ce qu'elle était* (1978, 157, 209–210). See also Hamon and Rotman (1990, 353–364).

33. During the Occupation, *le tout Paris*, including Danielle Darrieux, Vivianne Romance, Suzy Delair, Albert Préjean, Tino Rossi, and Charles Trénet, went to German culture minister Otto Abetz's cocktail parties and played to German audiences.Only Vivianne Romance escaped any censure. Trénet and Rossi were two of Signoret's favorite singers, and before the end of the war she had acted in a film (*La boîte aux rêves*) with Vivianne Romance and Albert Préjean. She had been in a couple of films starring Arletty

who, postwar, was also suspended from work for a while. The point was that collaboration with the enemy seemed to be a very broad injunction used against people, and Signoret chose to judge no one from that difficult period.

34. In 1949, Signoret had signed a four-year contract with Howard Hughes that she was never able to honor.

35. Signoret (1978, 274) later came to see this Oscar as political in nature, based just as much on sympathy as on her talent. Signoret recognized that it was not difficult to read this sudden turnabout on the United States' part (welcoming her and Montand) as a signaling to the world that the McCarthy era was truly at an end. An editorial in *Films in Review* (11, no. 5, May 1960, 312) revealed the following: "A few days after Miss Signoret received an Academy Award it became known that she and her husband were in this country because the State Department had asked the Justice Department to waive the provision in our immigration laws barring Communists and subversives. Signoret and Montand *were* barred under this provision in 1949 and 1957. The Justice Department granted State's request and allowed them in for six months. A spokesman for State declared that the Montands' exclusion was for 'something much more serious' than signing the Stockholm Peace Appeal."

36. For a full record of these activities on behalf of the Rosenbergs and the North Vietnamese and North Korean women, see *Femmes françaises* (28 February 1953 and 21 March 1953). Here is what she is quoted as saying at the Vel d'Hiv rally (held on International Women's Day, 8 March 1953): "Our thoughts go first of all to the Vietnamese and Korean women who know the reality of war! And our thoughts go also to all women (whoever they are) and we say to them: 'Let us hold hands, let us all unite, we have the strength to push back misery, to stop war, to ensure a happy future for our children, to secure LIFE!'" (*Femmes françaises*, 21 March 1953, 14–15.)

37. Maurice Larkin gives a detailed analysis of the industrial growth of France postwar and makes particular reference to these two car models in *France Since the Popular Front* (Oxford: Clarendon Press, 1988, 131, 185).

38. Hayward (1993, 25–26).

39. This footage can be seen at the Vidéothèque in Paris: *Eclair Journal* (January–April 1948).

40. Although Balmain did Signoret's wedding outfit.

41. Jacques Becker's film *Falbalas* (1945), starring Raymond Rouleau as a Fath lookalike, gives one a very good feel for the energy of this period of fashion excess. Curiously, it was made a few years before the New Look burst onto the scene, and it was actually shot during the Occupation. One could read it as a film of national defiance (France's courageous fashion industry in the face of adversity, etc.). When it was released, it was dismissed by critics, who disliked what they termed its "superficially frivolous nature."

42. Giroud, quoted in Chapsal (1986, 10).

43. Sartre, quoted in Chapsal (1986, 11).

44. The department store Bon Marché was the first to solicit prêt-à-porter for its shop, in 1952, when it asked the couturier Marcelle Chaumont to supply the clothes. Such was the prestige in which haute couture was held, that the Chambre de Commerce insisted that Chaumont change her name. so she worked for Bon Marché under the pseudonym Juliette Verneuil. Interestingly, some ten years later, Signoret would make a television documentary about consumers and saleswomen in another of Paris's major department stores, Le Printemps (*Aux grands magasins*, William Klein, 1964).

45. Balmain again shows his modernity where women are concerned with his ready-to-wear sportswear collections.

46. Susan Buck-Morss, "The City as Dreamworld and Catastrophe," *October 73* (1968).

47. Interestingly, no Golden Lion was awarded that year.

48. She was nominated for an Oscar in 1966 for her role in Stanley Kramer's *Ship of Fools* (1965).

49. In an interview given in 1960 (quoted at length in Monserrat 1983a, 127), Signoret talked of the freedom of choice offered to her by her financial circumstances ("We are two and we have enough money"). She reiterated this in two interviews with *Cinémonde* (17 April 1962, 6; and 11 November 1969, 13). See also the long interview in *Elle* (11 June 1973, BAP), where she once again spoke of her economic situation that allowed her to be free of the obligation to work.

50. See what Jacques Becker himself said about the reception of *Casque d'Or* in an interview with *Cahiers du cinéma* (vol. 6, no. 32, February 1954, 14). See also *Cahiers du cinéma*'s own review of the film, which provides a synopsis of such critics as Georges Sadoul and Claude Mauriac's negative reaction to this film (vol. 3, no. 13, June 1952, 71).

51. See Hayward (1995, 59).

52. In her time, stars were used to sell fanzines and other magazines. Martine Carol and Brigitte Bardot were always on the front covers. But Signoret was on record as not wanting that sort of exposure. See Devarrieux (1981, 11).

53. *Cinémonde* of the 1950s is a mine of information on Martine Carol and her trajectory.

54. See, for example, *Cinémonde* (14 September 1948, 17), which comments on the intelligence she brings to her role in *Dédée d'Anvers*.

55. Columbia Studios press release, 1962 (BFI press cuttings).

56. Even to the extent of making her out to be the Evita Peron of the seventh art (see Josselin 1995, 75–76).

57. Columbia Studios press release, (BFI press cuttings).

58. It is worth noting that Signoret did all she could to dissuade Montand from going, believing that the tour would be professional suicide for him in France (Hamon and Rotman 1990, 355–356).

59. See, for example, the front-page photographs in *L'Humanité dimanche*, (6 January 1957.

60. See Devarrieux (1981, 12).

61. Signoret, interviewed by *Cinémonde* (10 April 1958, 18), listed her "shortcomings" as the following: "aggressiveness; too talkative; hiding my deep-seated shyness and modesty behind everything that is its opposite, which gives the most incorrect impression of who I really am!"

62. During the 1950s, many *Cinémonde* issues ran "competitions" between top-rated stars, mostly women. These competitions revealed vital statistics, including weight.

63. *Cinémonde*, 2 June 1959, 15.

64. *Cinémonde*, 1 January 1959, 19. This was a complaint it would repeat fairly often (see, for example, 10 January 1961, 20; 29 September 1964, 28). In a later issue (8 January 1969, 40), it continued this campaign by remarking how much Signoret is valued in the United States, where she was considered France's best female actor.

65. *Cinémonde*, 12 April 1960, 14–17.

66. See Devarrieux (1981, 15).

67. *Cinémonde*, 26 April 1960, 45 ("No! I'm no angel").

68. In *Cinémonde*'s annual roundup on stars and rising actors (12 January 1960, 15).

69. *Cinémonde*, 30 March 1960.

70. *Cinémonde*, 5 January 1965.

71. Quote taken from footage of Signoret accepting the Oscar from Rock Hudson (in the French television series *Destinées: Simone Signoret—Histoire d'une passion*, TF1, 17 February 1989).

72. Signoret, quoted in Durant (1988, 84).

73. *Cinémonde*, 12 April 1960, 14.

74. *Cinémonde*, 17 January 1967, 34.

75. *Cinémonde*, 17 January 1967, 34; and 21 July 1967, 17.

76. See *Cinémonde*, 4 October 1960. The cover declares: "It is written: Marilyn can do nothing against Montand Signoret." Interesting how Marilyn is the one who is portrayed as the force to blame, not Montand.

77. Eve Ruggieri gave a full account of this terribly painful moment in Signoret's life in her twelve-part television series on Signoret and Montand, "Simone Signoret et Yves Montand" (Antenne 2, 3–20 December 1991).

78. See *Cinémonde*, 14 June 1960, 4. Later, in an interview in *Cinémonde* (26 November 1963), Signoret admitted that when making *Adua*, her own life was chaotic.

79. As Josselin (1995, 95) says, "It was common knowledge that Simone suffered as a result of Montand's infidelities. But to say, as some have, that Montand was responsible for her physical decline and alcoholism, nothing is less certain." Curiously, two years after this momentous event, Signoret declared in a *Cinémonde* interview (17 April 1962, 4) that infidelities on a man's part were less serious than a woman's (not very feminist in sentiment). Yet, in 1952, when at the height of her in-lovedness with Montand, her views on jealousy were solicited for a television program, she stated then that "jealousy was a terrible feeling to have but that you experience it when you feel someone is trying to steal the person you love away from you" (*Jouons le jeu—No. 7: La Jalousie*, André Gillois interview with Simone Signoret). Yves Montand, in a documentary on his career, admitted that Signoret was "torn apart" by the affair (Antenne 2, 9 November 1991).

80. Signoret, quoted in Monserrat (1983a, 164).

81. *Queen*, 11 May 1966.

82. *The Evening Standard*, 4 November 1977 (BFI press cuttings). Interestingly, *Cinémonde* (29 September 1965, 27) was already talking in these terms about Signoret in 1965 (when she starred in *Ship of Fools*): "Signoret, bruised, like an over-ripe peach, tasty with a bitter taste of autumn fruit."

83. Signoret, quoted in Monserrat (1983a, 23).

84. Signoret, quoted in Monserrat (1983a, 270).

85. "I'm fat and ugly and I'm going to use it to play Mme Rosa." Quoted in Monserrat (1983a, 271).

86. Something, incidentally, she was unable to do in 1964, when she was cast to play the old woman Bouboulina in *Zorba the Greek* (Cacoyannis). See David (1992, 150).

87. The two interviews are in *Elle* (11 June 1973, BAP) and *Tribune de Genève* (28 February 1983, BAP).

88. Signoret, quoted in *Tribune de Genève* (28 February 1983, press release on *Granges brûlées* (BAP).

89. Signoret, quoted in *Tribune de Genève* (28 February 1983, press release on *Granges brûlées* (BAP).

90. *Libération*, 1 October 1985, 2.

91. In 1985, when on television to discuss her novel *Adieu Volodia*, Signoret seized the opportunity to talk about the shelving of this film, which exposed a particularly unsavory act of "betrayal" of one group of Resistance fighters, the Main-d'oeuvre immigrée, by another, led by the French Communist party.

92. *Libération*, 1 October 1985, 2. She also referred to them as "*coups au coeur*" (affairs of the heart) (*Regard Magazine sur Simone Signoret* 6 September 1993: 46). Among other acts of this order, she marched in protest against the political regimes in Argentina (1980 and 1981), Czechoslovakia (1981), and Poland (1981 and 1985).

93. However, when Jack Lang, the minister of culture under François Mitterrand, proposed that she be put forward for the Légion d'Honneur, she flatly refused.

94. Devarrieux (1981, 14). In a sense, Signoret was continuing a practice learned some thirty years earlier at the Flore during the Occupation, when she experienced the mutual support given by artists to each other, including those in the film world.

95. *Libération*, 9 December 1976 (BAP).

96. *Le Parisien*, 9 November 1976 (BAP).

97. *France Catholique*, 3 December 1976; *Libération*, 9 December 1976 (BAP).

98. Signoret had always feared a long illness and protracted pain (interview in *Cinémonde*, 11 June 1963, 12), which is why, she said, she lived in the present.

99. *Elle*, 11 June 1973 (BAP).

100. *La Tribune de Genève*, 28 February 1973 (BAP).

101. *France-Soir*, 5 November 1976 (BAP).

102. See part 11 of Eve Ruggieri's twelve-part televised series on Signoret and Montand, *Eve raconte* (*Antenne 2*, 3–20 December 1991). This series can be viewed at the INA-thèque at the Bibliothèque National de France.

103. Letter quoted in Hamon and Rotman (1990, 556–558). Purely anecdotally, years earlier and just before he had met Signoret, in an open letter written for *Cinémonde* (20 January 1949, 3), Montand had described his dream lover: she would not knit, and she would make him lots of babies. Signoret loved to knit and was unable to have his children.

104. Ibid., 558.

105. Her last public appearance was as host of the Césars ceremony (the French equivalent of the Oscars) in March 1985. She could see nothing, and Montand was beside her to help read out the names.

Chapter Two: The Actorly Body and the Body Political

1. For example, Curtis Harrington was adamant that he had to have Signoret for *Games* (*Cinémonde*, 27 December 1966, 31). Sidney Lumet, after making *The Deadly Affair* with her, was impatient to work with her again in *The Seagull* (*Cinémonde*, 11 November 1969, 12). Pierre Granier-Deferre was very clear that he wanted Signoret for the role of Clémence in *Le chat*, so much so that he completely changed the original character (*Cinémonde*, December 1970, 31).

2. Georges Baume, writing in *Cinémonde* (2 April 1954, 19); his term is *"sainement érotique."*

3. *Paris-Presse*, 7 September 1948, quoted in Durant (1988, 55).

4. Durant (1988, 53).

5. In an interview with Claude Fléouter, in *Le Monde* (23 November 1973, BAP) she declared: "I have never been what they call a star, even less a *monstre sacré.*"

6. In an interview with *Cinémonde* (11 June 1963, 12) she readily agreed with Yves Montand when he said that apart from her acting, she remained very undisciplined. She already admitted to this aspect of her character in a series of articles on her career published in *Heures claires des femmes françaises* in the late 1950s (see, in particular, 14 December 1957, 10).

7. Only once did she turn up late to the studios, for *Adua e le compagne*, in an attempt to break her contract (this was during the immediate aftermath of the Montand/Monroe affair).

8. In an interview with *Télérama* (31 March 1982, 25), Signoret said of the director, "My only automatism as an actor is to look at the director and judge, from his expression, whether I have been any good. . . . He is the father, the master."

9. She did, however, have considerable input into her dialogue for *Police Python 357*. For more details, see page 49.

10. Interview with Moshe Mizrahi in *Continental Films Review*, 27 (July 1980): 8–9.

11. In an interview with *Télérama* (31 March 1982, 25), Signoret talked about her attachment to these later roles because the women she played had depth and roots but, she added, "The difficulty is not to play them all the same, to not caricature one's self."

12. See, for example, *Cinémonde*, 30 October 1951, 21; and 23 April 1952, 27.

13. See, for example, *Cinémonde*, 23 October 1953, 5.

14. Numerous references are made to her lionlike qualities: "lion's head" (*France-Soir*, 1 June 1969, BAP), "lioness with blue eyes" (*Paris-Presse*, 9 May 1970, BAP).

15. In an interview with *Femmes françaises* (21 July 1951, 13), she categorically stated that she had played "the complete range of fallen women" and that "with all my might I am seeking to get out of these roles." In *Films and Filming* (8 June 1962, 12), however, she stated that the films she was the most satisfied with were *Room at the Top* and *Manèges*. In that same interview, she also said that the worst film she ever made was *La mort en ce jardin* (11).

16. In a radio interview with Jacques Chancel in *Radioscopie* (11 November 1976), she said, "We take ourselves for the other."

17. In an interview with *Le Monde* (23 November 1973, BAP), she related to Claude Fléouter how, for several weeks, she watched all the other "Jeannes" going to work or to the Samaritaine or a supermarket in Aubervilliers with their huge shopping bags and raincoats. In a separate interview with Mary Blume (*Herald Tribune*, 22 November 1973, BAP), she explains why she will not speak about a role while she is doing it because "it might ruin something while I'm living her life."

18. Interview in *Le journal du dimanche*, 25 November 1973 (BAP).

19. Interview with Michel Delain in *L'Express*, 16 July 1973 (BAP).

20. Interview with Mary Blume in *Herald Tribune*, 22 November 1973 (BAP).

21. In an interview in *Cinémonde* (11 June 1963, 13), she listed *Casque d'Or*, *Dédée d'Anvers*, and *Le jour et l'heure*, as her favorite films. In an interview with *France-Soir* (4 May 1973, BAP), she declared, "*Casque d'Or* is the only film in my career that I felt was a masterpiece."

22. Interview with Nicole Jolivet in *France-Soir* (BAP).

23. The French critics were not alone in this view. See also the British journals *Today's Cinema*, 3 October 1950, 9, and *Monthly Film Bulletin* 19 (October 1952): 138.

24. Respectively, *Cinémonde*, 9 April 1946, 19; 28 October 1947, 13; 14 September 1948, 17; and 2 November 1948, 7).

25. For a more detailed analysis of this idea of masculinity in crisis, see Leahy and Hayward (2000, 77–88).

26. For a very interesting discussion of this idea, see Janet Bergman-Carton's study *The Woman of Ideas in French Art: 1830–1848* (New Haven and London: Yale University Press, 1995).

27. This is not a new phenomenon. In France, before the war, women of all classes—because they were financially bereft of means either because they could find no work or, as their husbands' chattel and goods, had no rights and therefore depended on their husband for any source of income—had to turn to prostitution to support themselves or to obtain independent means of support.

28. The four exceptions to the role of tart are *Fantômas*, *Against the Wind*, *Ombre et Lumière*, and *Les sorcières de Salem*.

29. Instructively, in the full script she tells the count that it was she who chose him (this part was edited out in the final cut). See *L'avant-scène du cinéma* 25 (April 1963): 41.

30. *Cinémonde* (20 September 1956, 15), speaking about her role as Djin in *La mort en ce jardin*, referred to her as a "troubling and sensual prostitute."

31. Emmanuelle Riva, who costarred in this film, made this point (see *Cinémonde*, 6 May 1961, 2).

32. See, for example, *Cinémonde*, 10 January 1961, 9; and 13 October 1964, 18.

33. In an article in *Cinémonde* (16 August 1960, 4), Dominique Chantal informed her readers that "for the first time in her life, Simone Signoret has declared that her work comes first."

34. John Trevelyan, then secretary of the BBFC, quoted in Aldgate (1995, 33).

35. Quoted in Aldgate (1995, 47).

36. Trevelyan, quoted in Aldgate (1995, 33).

37. *Motion Picture Herald*, 11 April 1959, 219.

38. Trevelyan quoted, in Aldgate (1995, 33).

39. Penelope Huston, "Room at the Top?," *Sight and Sound*, 2(2) (1959): 56.

40. Maurice Elvey, "*Room at the Top*," *Film and TV Technician*, 25(171) (1959): 60.

41. Review of *Room at the Top*, *The Daily Cinema*, 21 January 1959, 8.

42. *Variety*, 5 May 1965, n.p.

43. For more details on the homoeroticism in these two films, see Hayward (2001, 107–124).

44. Review in *The Daily Telegraph*, 5 February 1967, 14.

45. When *Room at the Top* was released in the United States and Signoret had received her Oscar, several reviews referred to her seeming plumpness. Thus, *Films in Review* found her "plumper than she looks in her movies" and "not very tall and by no means thin" (*Films in Review* 11(5) (May 1960): 265.

46. *Films in Review* 10(5) (May 1949): 303.

47. *Télérama*, (31 March 1982): "Mme Signoret is the third sex."

48. See Hayward (1993, 37, 246–274) for more details on this period.

49. See the article in *Jeune cinéma* 114 (November 1978): 51, which develops all these points.

50. Chéreau, quoted in *Télérama*, 11 October 1978, 111.

51. In the story, the widow Couderc is supposed to be forty years old; Signoret was fifty. She wore a black dress for the role. Signoret herself said of the dynamic between herself and Alain Delon: "When Alain saw my clothes I could see he was afraid. Alain said 'You're going to look like that?' I knew he was thinking, what will people think of me, sleeping with that old bag? It took him a few hours, but it finally worked out and the result had a sort of quasi-maternal tenderness. If I'd wanted to play it younger, it would have been a story of an old tart after a young man." Interview with Mary Blume, *Herald Tribune*, 22 November 1973, BAP.

52. Maryse Degallaix, "La Veuve Couderc," *Image et Son* 286 (1974): 122–126. Degallaix offers a very fine reading of the film's reactionary message.

53. Ibid.

54. Corneau in an interview said, "Simone Signoret has extraordinary skills as a dialogue writer. The character Thérèse, 'the immobile god' of the film, owes a great deal to her." Quoted in Monserrat (1983b, 328).

55. Corneau, quoted in Monserrat (1983b, 330).

56. Corneau, quoted in Monserrat (1983b, 328).

57. As indeed the review in *Film Society Review* [2(5) (January 1971): 34] makes clear.

58. Michael Sragow's review of *L'aveu/The Confession* in *Film Society Review* 6(5) (January 1971): 35.

59. Granier-Deferre justified his radical departure from Simenon's novel (starting with updating it from the 1930s to the 1970s), in an interview with *Les nouvelles littéraires* (6 May 1971) and quoted at length in Monserrat (1983a, 212–214). In particular, he felt he had to change the character of the woman quite considerably because, as she stood, she was the weak part of the plot.

60. Jean-Michel Gravier's review of *La vie devant soi*, in *Lumière du cinéma* (November 1977): 5.

61. *Cinémonde* referred to her as a *monstre sacré* as early as 1968 (20 February 1968, 29). She is compared to Gabin in *Elle* in the October 1970 issue (BAP).

62. See Stam (1989, 160–165) for a more detailed analysis of Bakhtin's view of the body as non-hierarchical and Stam's proposal of a new kind of cultural politics that can emanate from this view.

Chapter Three: Signoret's Theater Work

1. Pierre Macabru, *Paris-Presse-L'Intransigeant*, 6 December (BAP).

2. G. Guilleminault thought her too voluptuous (*L'Aurore*, 5 November 1962, BAP). Pierre Macabru, in *Paris-Presse-L'Intransigeant* (ibid.), 6 December found her "ungainly and stiff"; the critic for *Arts* 12 December 1962, BAP) reported she was "ungainly and buxom."

3. Signoret, interviewed by François Caviglioli in *Combat*, 30 November 1962 (BAP).

4. Interview with Signoret in *New York Herald Tribune*, 8 October 1966 (BAP).

5. Ibid.

6. Quoted by Pierre Fabre in *Carrefour*, 26 October 1966 (BAP).

7. Interview with Jacqueline Cartier in *France-Soir*, 30 August 1966 (BAP).

8. Interview with Signoret in *New York Herald Tribune*, 8 October 1966 (BAP).

9. So Signoret said in an interview with *Le nouvel observateur*, 7 September 1966 (BAP).

10. The British press reviews of *Macbeth* were systematically recorded by Pierre Fabre in his article for *Carrefour*, 26 October 1966 (BAP).

11. According to Signoret, this is what happened; quoted in an interview with *La Tribune de Genève*, 9 November 1966 (BAP). Details of the Royal Court Theatre's struggle financially can be found in the Neville Blond Archives, housed in the University of Leeds Special Archives Section.

12. Both *Le Monde* (18 December 1954, 12) and *Le Figaro* (18/19 December 1954, 14) use this term.

13. *Le Monde*, 18 December 1954, 12.

14. *L'Humanité*, 18 December 1954, 2.

15. Ibid.

16. Ibid.

17. *Le Figaro*, 18/19 December, 14.

18. *Le Monde*, 18 December 1954, 12.

19. Jean Gandrey-Réty, in *Lettres françaises* (25 December 1954, BAP), speaks of Signoret's "interior sensitivity." Gabriel Marcel, in *Les nouvelles littéraires* (30 December 1954, BAP), speaks of her "contained interiority"; and Georges Lerminier, in *Le Parisien* (20 December 1954, BAP), pays tribute to the density of her acting and her self-effacement.

20. This was a quality Signoret managed to maintain over the whole period of the play's run at the Sarah Bernhardt if these two critics, writing a year apart, are to be believed. Morvan Lebesque, in *Carrefour* (22 December 1954, BAP), talks of her restraint, and Jean Vigneron, in *La Croix* (31 December 1955, BAP), draws attention to her discretion and self-effacement.

21. Marcel, *Les Nouvelles littéraires*.

22. *Dimanche Matin* (12 December 1954, BAP), Guy Verdot in *Franc Tireur* (18/19 December 1954, BAP), and *Libération* (21 December 1954, BAP) all concurred that Signoret had not made the shift from the discontinuity of cinema to the continuity of theater. Jean Gandrey-Réty, in *Lettres françaises* (25 December 1954, BAP), took the opposite view.

23. Thierry Maulnier, in *Combat*, 23 December 1954 (BAP).

24. Verdot, *Franc Tireur*.

25. *Dimanche Matin*, 16 December 1954 (BAP). Once again, Gandrey-Réty in *Lettres françaises* takes the opposite view.

26. Maulnier, for example, in *Combat*, saw it as "a vigourous play, cleverly and solidly constructed." And *Le Figaro* (30 March 1955, BAP), celebrating its one hundreth performance, talked of the staging as "strong stuff."

27. *Lettres françaises* (20 January 1955, BAP), went into Rouleau's style in some detail. Only one critic, B. de Garambe, writing for *Rivarol* (23 December 1954, BAP), found the staging heavy and slow. Nor did he like the scenery, which he thought at times suffocated the actors.

28. In Monserrat (1983a, 267–268) Signoret went into great detail about this inhabiting. In a radio interview with Jacques Chancel (*Radioscopie*, 11 November 1976), she spoke of how you end up "thinking of yourself as that other person."

29. Interview with Claude Fléouter, in *Le Monde*, 23 November 1973 (BAP): "It's like a seed that grows inside me."

30. Interview with Janine Pradeau, in *Femmes d'aujourd'hui*, (12 December 1973, 91): "It's the period of incubation. That is to say that it is 'growing.'"

31. Signoret interview with Guy de Bellaval, in *Tribune de Genève*, 12 December 1967 (BAP): "People are there and judge you immediately, whereas in the cinema they see a finished film which gives them an assembly of the best shots."

32. Monserrat (1983a, 102) strongly defends Signoret's performance, saying that she was not fully understood by the so-called specialist critics. Her performance was full of intensity, she says, adding that at least with Signoret, we at long last know the meaning of the expression "loaded silence."

33. Signoret, in an interview with *Le Figaro littéraire*, 7 April 1969 (BAP): "The only point in going on stage and suffering as one does is because the game is worth the candle. That was true for *Les sorcières de Salem*. [Even] the relative failure with Shakespeare."

Chapter Four: Postwar Films—1946–1951

1. See Burch and Sellier (1996, 224–227). In this section of their book, they focus on the way in which women were scapegoated in this postwar *réalisme noir* cinema. Their argument is convincing but should not exclude this further reading. The female body is typically the arena of censorship, and there is therefore a logic to using it in this way when censorship is so rife.

2. Interview with Calef, in *Cinématographie française*, 18 November 1950, 7.

3. Burch and Sellier (1996, 217–237) develop this analysis in considerable depth.

4. Isabelle's agent (played by Jean Marchat) is well aware of this duality, and the struggle between the two sides of Isabelle's personality. For example, he says: "Isabelle Leritz will always triumph over Isabelle Moreux."

5. One critic in *Ce Soir* (18 March 1951) went so far as to call *Against the Wind* a "a soap opera." Both *Ce Soir* and *Le Figaro* (28 August 1951) found the story too far-fetched, even though it was based on real facts. This film is now of great documentary interest because it actually shows what type of sabotage techniques were used. Presumably, the French did not like the British touching upon their own myths (even though this film was specifically about the Belgian Resistance, not the French).

6. The special effects in *Fantômas* were particularly commented upon as a highlight of the film (*Cinématographie française*, 27 September 1947, 3).

7. Françoise Giroud scripted this film, which could explain the very strong role Signoret has as Fantômas's disruptive daughter.

8. Signoret was in many respects like Anna Magnani in this regard, as acknowledged by *Télérama* (6 November 1976, BAP).

9. If we were to include in the two-shot close-ups in, *Dédée*, this figure would rise by another 5 percent.

Chapter Five: Trajectory to International Stardom—1952–1959

1. See, for example, Jacqueline Michel in *Le Parisien Libéré*, 6 June 1959 (BAP).

2. It is also the case, as Vincendeau in Gauteur and Vincendeau (1993, 124) points out, that male leads in French cinema, particularly major stars like Jean Gabin, could be more in close-up than their female counterparts.

3. See, for example, *Cinématographie française* (19 September 1953, 14) and *Film français* (18 September 1953, 8).

4. At the time of the film's release, Jacques Doniol-Valcroze (1953, 42) refers to Lesaffre's characterization as "a malevolent angel."

5. Carné (1979, 327) reports in his autobiography that Signoret apparently refused to make *Thérèse Raquin* with this radical introduction of Roland Lesaffre as the agent of fate. As we can see, she did eventually agree to the changes. Carné does not paint a particularly generous picture of Signoret's attitude toward him when working on this film.

6. For a more detailed discussion of the homophobic mood of the 1950s, see Dyer (2000, 127–138). It is true that one or two films with lesbian-based narratives did get made, but they were more about schoolgirl crushes than adult same-sex relationships (see Jacqueline Audrey's *Olivia*, 1950).

7. There is a sketch of the type of dress Signoret wears in *Les diaboliques* in the French Communist party's women's weekly *Heures claires des femmes françaises*

(4 November 1954, 14). Called a sort of passe-partout, its qualities are extolled by the weekly because it is functional, smart, and inexpensive.

8. See Dudley Andrew's article on this film, (Andrew 2000).

9. Signoret's 1972 interview with Nicole Jolivet quoted in *Simone Signoret* (1982, 9).

10. See Vincendeau (1993, 124).

11. For details, see *La femme en 1900: les Années 1900 par carte-postale* (Paris: Editions Serge Zeyons/Larousse, 1994, 170–171).

12. Amélie Hélie's husband, André Nardin (who survived her), attempted to prevent the release of the film *Casque d'Or* because he claimed it was prejudicial to her memory, but the court threw the case out (*Cinématographie française*, 15 March 1952, 5; and 5 April 1952, 13). Curiously, given how Becker had softened her image from the original, we might be surprised by this show of uxorial devotion.

13. See interview with Jacques Becker by Jacques Rivette and François Truffaut in *Cahiers du cinéma* 6(32) (February 1954): 8.

14. See Gilberto Guillermo, "Jacques Becker: Two Films," *Sight and Sound* (Summer 1969): 143.

15. Becker, quoted in Lindsay Anderson's review, "The Current Cinema: *Casque d'Or (Golden Marie)*," *Sight and Sound* 22 (October/December 1952): 75.

16. Ibid.

17. See Durant (1988, 62–65) for details. Originally, the film was going to be made by Julien Duvivier in 1939, starring Jean Gabin. When Gabin went to the United States during the war, Hollywood thought it might make the film. Those plans came to nothing. Postwar, Henri-Georges Clouzot and then Yves Allégret (Signoret's then husband) thought about making it. Finally, Becker got the green light.

18. Signoret commented on its contemporaneity and also on the fact that it was a film ahead of its time. See her interview with Jolivet quoted in *Simone Signoret*, op. cit.

19. For more details on this song and a longer reading of this film against the political climate of its times, see Andrew (2000, 112–125). It is worth noting that this film was read by some critics as an attack on the working class (see Périsset 1988, 46).

20. See Andrée Lehmann (1965, 7).

21. In 1954, the PCF's women's weekly *Heures Claires des Femmes Françaises* (4 November 1954, 14) spoke very favorably of the utilitarian nature of this dress, which was in vogue that year.

22. Derek Prowse, review of *Les Diaboliques*, *Sight and Sound* 25(3) (Winter 1955/1956): 149.

23. See, for example, ibid. See also a review in *Variety* (23 February 1955, n.p.), and Pierre Theberge, "Chéri fais-moi peur/Darling Frighten Me," *Objectif* (2[17], October 1962, 37–38).

24. See Noël Herpe, "Les films criminels de Clouzot: le mauvais demiurge," *Positif* 419 (January 1996): 103–105.

25. See his interview in *Cahiers du cinéma* 32 (February 1954): 13.

26. Becker tells us how this scene was cut from several copies by the Censure Commission (it was deemed too brutal and inappropriate) and how he had to remonstrate to get it reinstated (ibid., 14).

27. One critic (Ninode 1967, 133) compared Buñuel's visceral use of color in this part of the film to Goya's paintings.

Chapter Six: Working the International Scene—1960–1968

1. Henri Vinneuil, review of *Ship of Fools*, *Spectacle du Monde*, November 1965, BAP.

2. Olivier Delville, review of *Ship of Fools*, *Le Soir*, 8 October 1965, BAP.

3. See Eve Ruggieri's fifth episode in her twelve-part television series on Signoret and Yves Montand, *Eve raconte* (Antenne 2, 9 December 1991).

4. A copy of this documentary is located in the Bibliothèque Nationale de Paris.

5. Signoret has a five-minute appearance in *Dragées au poivre*. This sketch film is a spoof on cinéma vérité and pokes fun at a number of New Wave tropes (such as a camera in a baby carriage being pulled along by a piece of rope). It also does candid camera–type scenes. Signoret's brief appearance begins with a keyhole shot on her that then cuts away to a lingering shot of her legs. She is dressed in a negligee, and her face is heavily made up as an aging coquette—rather grotesquely contrasting with her beautiful, young-looking legs.

6. *Les amours célèbres* was not particularly liked by critics. The general feeling was that it was only Signoret's performance that saved it. See, for example, comments from *Heures claires des femmes françaises*, 2 December 1961, 9: ("The whole thing is a rather monstrous muddle. . . . Simone Signoret . . . saves *Jenny de Lacour* which, without her, would be no more than a bleak melodrama"); and *Variety*, 15 November 1961, n.p. ("Color is well used [but things are kept on] a theatrical almost comic-strip level.").

7. This darkness contrasts with the other three sketches, all of which are shot in bright pastel colors.

8. According to Jorge Semprun, *Compartiment tueurs* was almost not made, because the killer was a policeman—the CNC approved the project, but the Police Prefecture in Paris forbade it being made in Paris *Film Society Review* 6(5) (January 1971): 45.

9. See the interview by Henri Rode, "At Last Signoret Wept for Joy," *Cinémonde*, 12 April 1960, 16.

10. *Cinémonde* (30 November 1960, 4) quoted Roger Vailland as the title to the article on *Les mauvais coups*: "Roger Vailland admits: Simone Signoret frightens me."

11. See, for example, the review in *La cinématographie française*, 10 June 1961, 102.

12. Reginald Kernan was an American whom Signoret and Leterrier spotted in Saint-Germain-des-Prés. They decided he was the type they needed. He was in fact a doctor who had "dropped out" and come to Paris.

13. See the review in *Motion Picture Herald*, 27 November 1963, 938.

14. The raven (in French, *le corbeau*) refers metaphorically to an unscrupulous man, a writer of poison pen letters, or a denunciator. Henri-Georges Clouzot made a film during the Occupation years by that title (*Le corbeau*, 1943). It did not endear him to any political side.

15. In an interview with *Paris-Presse* (9 May 1980, BAP), Signoret said: "You know, Roberte's role in *Les mauvais coups* was one of the most difficult in my career."

16. Jean de Baroncelli, for one, in his review of *Le jour et l'heure* (*Le Monde*, 11 April 1963, BAP).

17. René Clément, quoted in an article on *Le jour et l'heure*: "For Signoret this man is lost." (*Cinémonde*, 19 June 1963, 12).

18. The policeman-torturer Inspector Lerat (!) is played by Signoret's friend Marcel Bozzuffi.

19. A quick glance of the distribution of shots makes it clear that there are two major focuses: Thérèse and her love relationship with Allen:

	Thérèse	*Allen*	*Thérèse and Allen*	*Total*
Close-up	12	13	21	66:26:76
Medium close-up	54	13	55	
Medium shot	48	30	43	58:36:63
Long shot	10	6	20	

20. Maurice Périsset cites Signoret in *Simone Signoret* (1988, 78).

21. Review of *Term of Trial*, *Monthly Film Bulletin* 299(9) (September 1962): 138.

22. See reviews in *Monthly Film Bulletin*, ibid.; *Le Monde*, 28 April 1963, BAP; and *Les lettres françaises*, 2 May 1963, BAP.

23. In *Cinémonde* (13 February 1962, 11), Signoret spoke of how determined she was to play opposite Olivier.

24. Signoret in an interview with *Cinémonde*, ibid. This is not quite accurate because she does actually slap Manda in *Casque d'Or* and Milan in *Les mauvais coups*.

25. See Signoret (1978, 100–101).

26. Signoret, quoted in Henri Chapier, "Les samedis du cinéma/Saturday nights at the cinema," *Combat*, 23 October 1965, BAP.

27. In fairness to Signoret, later in her autobiography she lists Kramer and this film among her acknowledgments (Signoret 1978, 314).

28. In her autobiography, Signoret (1978, 300) spoke movingly of time spent with Leigh having candlelight dinners when she tried to recapture all that she had lost (her health, her fame, Laurence Olivier).

29. Respectively, in *Gone with the Wind* and *A Streetcar Named Desire*.

30. François Truffaut made the film *Fahrenheit 451* in 1967.

31. Signoret in her autobiography thanks Sidney Lumet for this film (Signoret 1978, 314).

32. *Variety* (1 February 1967, 6) supplies this information.

33. Huston, quoted in *The Spectator*, 10 February 1967 (BFI press cuttings, n.p.).

34. Something the French Communist newspaper *L'Humanité* (17 June 1967, BAP) was quick to point out, adding that although the dialogue, when appropriate, was "prudently anti-communist," the film itself was "not really a cold war film, but a tale about betrayal."

35. I am reminded here of the case of the suburban widow Melita Norwood, who was exposed as a spy for the KGB (see *The Observer*, 12 September 1999, 1, and *The Guardian*, 14 September 1999, 3–5). Norwood was an agent for forty years passing details of Britain's nuclear weapons' program to the Soviet Union. Her reasons are not dissimilar to those put forward by Elsa. In a statement issued by Norwood she said: "I did what I did not to make money, but to help prevent the defeat of a new system, which had, at great cost, given ordinary people food which they could afford, education and a health service."

36. Penelope Huston (*The Spectator*, 10 February 1967, n.p.) argued that Signoret "makes the pouring of a cup of Nescafé look like a gesture of frozen despair."

37. Christopher Marlowe's *Edward II* is not the only intertextual reference. Earlier in the film, Mendel visits the theater frequented by Elsa for her spy drops. He comes upon *Macbeth* in rehearsal. As we know, Signoret was about to embark on her own (somewhat disastrous) version of this play that would be performed in October 1966 (shooting for *The Deadly Affair* began in March 1966).

38. Signoret, interviewed in *France-Soir* (24 November 1966, BAP): "I found it difficult to be in my role."

39. According to *Cinémonde* (27 December 1966, 31), during filming, Curtis Harrington was so pleased with her interpretation he kept shouting out: "Simone, you are sensational; without your presence, your magnetism, I would never have been able to make my film!"

40. Apparently Lumet was impatient to work with Signoret again (*Cinémonde*, 11 November 1969, 14).

41. Critics of the time found *The Seagull* too long and too heavy. See, for example, the reviews in *France-Soir* (25 October 1969, BAP), *Le Figaro* (24 October 1969, BAP), and *Sight and Sound* 38(4) (Autumn 1969).

42. Signoret gave these details in an interview with *Cinémonde*, 1847 (December 1970): 31.

43. *Le Figaro*, 24 October 1969, BAP.

44. *Le Parisien*, 29 October 1969, BAP.

45. *Motion Picture Herald*, 1 January 1970, BAP.

46. Signoret, quoted in *Cinémonde* (11 November 1969, 14). The article is entitled "Why Ever Did Simone Signoret Want to Become the Odious Arkadina in *The Seagull*?"

47. See interview with Signoret in *Cinémonde*, 11 November 1969, 14.

48. See *Films and Filming* 14(10) (July 1968): 28.

49. Other winners include Alfred Hitchcock, Vincent Price, Boris Karloff, and Peter Lorre (*L'Aurore*, 13 December, BAP).

50. Henry Chapier, in his review "*Games*: An Unhealthy Forgery," *Combat*, 30 November 1967, 9.

51. Ibid.

Chapter Seven: The *monstre sacré* Returns to the French Screen—1969–1982

1. See interview with Signoret in French (1982, 52–53).

2. Interview with Melville in *Cinéma 69* 140 (November 1969): 124.

3. Ibid.

4. Ibid.

5. Signoret (1978, 365–366) recorded how Melville managed to obtain this response from her (which is quite different from Mathilde's in the novel; there she has a blank expression that no one can read). Signoret was not getting the effect Melville wanted, but when he said to her "They are going to kill her, but nothing proves that she spoke," she understood the ambiguity of this moment and was able to respond with that combination of "surprise, terror and incomprehension."

6. Within this set of unstable positionings mention should also be made of the subliminal homoerotic relationship between Gerbier and Jardie. Jardie is the only person for whom Gerbier expresses any emotions whatsoever.

7. See Bonnell (1989, 20, 246).

8. See *Cahiers du cinéma* 216 (October 1969): 63 and *Positif* 110 (November 1969): 71.

9. MOI (Main-d'Oeuvre Immigrée) was a Resistance group made up primarily of Jewish refugees who had come to France either in the 1920s (to escape Stalin's anti-Semitic pogroms in the Soviet Union) or the 1930s (to escape Hitler's anti-Semitic laws and persecution). According to *Les terroristes à la retraite*, a 1983 documentary by Mosco on the activities of the MOI during the Occupation, this cell was betrayed by the Communists toward the end of the war. Although there is some lack of clarity on this, the claim in the film, at least, is that the Communists, desperate to take power after the war, did not wish to share any governance with foreigners, more specifically Jews. In this regard their position very much reflects a Stalinian ideological line. As mentioned in Chapter One, it was thanks to Signoret, who did the voiceover for the film, that the telefilm, which had been closeted under pressure from Georges Marchais, secretary general of the French Communist party, was finally screened in 1985.

10. These purges have much in common with earlier ones and all are linked to Joseph Stalin. The first were the Moscow trials of 1936 and 1938. In these purges, the accusations leveled at the victims were very similar to those faced by the Prague fourteen, namely, that the state was threatened by the plotting of Trotskyites and Zionists. As early as 1924 (the year of Lenin's death), Stalin had declared his vision of building socialism in one country—his own and eventually "his" satellites. This vision did not embrace the classical Marxist version, the one adopted by Leon Trotsky, of a socialism that would be aided by the proletarian revolution in Western Europe. By 1928, Trotsky was in exile and branded as "cosmopolitan" and "Zionist" for his internationalist brand of socialism. These are terms Stalin and his acolytes were later to use liberally to purge people who threatened his ideological program of one socialist order and which we hear incessantly uttered in the film (along with Trotskyite) as accusations leveled against London and his coaccused. In 1948, the Communist party came to power in Czechoslovakia, and the nation became closely allied with the Soviet Union. In 1949, under Stalin's immediate instigation, the Czech government was "cleansed," and better Communists were put in their place, including Artur London. This cleansing was in direct response to Yugoslavian President Josip Broz Tito's refusal to align as one of the Soviet Union's satellites. So, in

effect, Titoism (of which these fourteen were also accused) was almost synonymous with Trotskyism.

11. Yet the circumstances of the Rajk trial were identical both to the earlier Moscow trials (about which London was troubled, but which he condoned) and, as it turned out, his own (something he later comes to recognize). See London's own account of these positions in his book *L'aveu* (1968, 31, 78, 93, 96).

12. Costa-Gavras had just released *Z*, starring Montand. It was a strong attack on the repressive junta regime in Greece, Gavras's natal country (as a Communist, Gavras had been forced to flee and live in France in exile). By the late 1960s, Gavras had established a reputation as a maker of civic cinema that reached a wide audience. For his part, Jorge Semprun was a "lapsed" Spanish Communist in exile in France.

13. See Montand's official biography (Hamon and Rotman 1990, 513–518).

14. See Monserrat (1983b, 246).

15. Montand, quoted in Hamon and Rotman (1990, 518): "*L'Aveu* is my act of rupture with the generous sentimentalism of the left's blindness towards its own crimes." It is also, he says, an act of "expiation," an "internal cleansing." In an interview with the *New York Times* (cited in *Film Society Review* 6(5), January 1971, 42), he is quoted as saying: "For the time-being socialism doesn't exist anywhere in the world."

16. Signoret, quoted in Durant (1988, 102).

17. The full account of the letter is to be found in London and London (1968, 476–477).

18. Signoret (1978, 330–340) went into considerable detail in her autobiography as to why she eventually felt with Montand that they had to make the film. London had been rehabilitated in 1967 then, in 1969, stripped of his citizenry and subjected to scrutiny once more. She insisted that the film was "anti-Stalinian" (331) and said categorically that "they" (Gavras, Montand, Semprun, and herself) had no intention of causing any harm to the PCF.

19. See Lise London and Costa-Gavras discussing Signoret's reticence in Hamon and Rotman (1990, 513–514).

20. Durant (1988, 103) quotes Signoret: "How would my absence have been interpreted? People would have believed that I had 'dropped' Montand. The Russians would have said I behaved well, the Americans that I was hard-hearted." Interestingly, ten years later Montand and Signoret would find themselves protesting against another Prague trial, this time that of Czech author Vaclav Havel, who was sent to prison for four-and-a-half-years (see *Ciné revue*, 21 February 1980, 14). Twenty years later, Montand (along with Costa-Gavras, Jorge Semprun, and Lise London) would watch *L'aveu* with Havel, then the first elected president of the Czech Republic (Hamon and Rotman 1990, 521).

21. In the tenth of her twelve-part television program on Signoret and Montand, the television presenter Eve Ruggieri of *Eve raconte* makes this point: "*L'aveu* was for [Signoret] a kind of revelation," henceforth she "activated her indignation in the name of human rights. She was everywhere where her voice was needed to speak out in the name of freedom," (*Simone Signoret et Yves Montand: Eve raconte*, Antenne 2, 3–20 December 1991, locatable at the Inathèque, Paris).

22. According to the book, Lise London was in fact far less accommodating about the place they were supposed to be removed to. At first, they were taken to a decent enough apartment (London 1968, 237), but later they were downgraded and were to be taken, not to a shared apartment, but to one without any means of cooking. She refused to be moved there (256–257).

23. To do an overview of critical reaction would take a great deal of space. But by way of a synopsis, *Cahiers du cinéma* 244 (October 1970): 48 saw it as reductionist and a film masquerading as an authentic political/civic film. *Positif* 119 (September 1970): 60–61 felt audiences were manipulated to like London, whereas he was an orthodox Communist and had previously been on the other side; along with *Cahiers*, it felt the film lacked a political edge. In a similar way, *Image et son* 240 (June/July 1970): 116–118 and *CinémAction* 33 (1985): 14 felt it was more a political spectacle film than a political/civic

film. *L'Humanité* (quoted in *Film Society Review* 6(5) January 1971, 42) accused the film of making a Communist book into an anti-Communist film; along with *Positif*, it felt it was devoid of history and context.

24. As illustrations of this perverse logic, I would cite the following examples. First, perfectly good Communists are forced into confessions that are not true through a combination of torture and the interrogators' artful and manipulative play with syllogisms, such as "To confess is superior to an autocritique; giving an autocritique proves you are a good Communist. Thus, a confession is real proof of your Communist credentials." Second, London's main interrogator, Kohoutek (played by Gabriele Ferzetti), was formerly, under the ancient regime and during the Nazi occupation, responsible for the repression of Communists and now finds himself working for the Communist party yet still accusing Communists, albeit from the other end of the telescope. Finally, the inescapability of the party's objectivity which states that "the past is judged in the light of the truths established by the party today" (words uttered by Kohoutek).

25. Signoret remarks come from the documentary Chris Marker did about the making of *L'aveu, On vous a parlé de Prague?/Have They Told You about Prague?* (1970).

26. Ibid.

27. Bozzuffi, interviewed by *Jeune cinéma* 43 (January 1970): 17.

28. Ibid.

29. Pigaut, in an interview with *Image et son* 250 (May 1970): 106.

30. Ibid.

31. Durant (1988, 106).

32. Granier-Deferre, quoted in Monserrat (1983a, 212).

33. Numerous critics of the time made this point. Noël Simsolo in *Image et son* (25, June/July 1971, 116–117) was particularly scathing in his attack on Gabin and his image creation (very little was said about Signoret). His role as Julien, Simsolo argued, was a complete u-turn on former roles and a playing out of a nostalgia for "who he was," knowing it would appeal to audiences.

34. See *Positif* 131 (October 1971): 68.

35. See Durant (1988, 109).

36. Granier-Deferre: "He with his juvenile, slightly mad side and she with her mischievous eyes full of affection, they managed to seduce each other" (quoted in Durant 1988, 109). Signoret (1978, 364) also mentioned how, although their politics were diametrically opposed, she loved playing opposite Delon and Gabin.

37. An intertextual point is that Signoret in her role as the widow is being labeled in a way not heard of since her 1950s films, when that was one of the types she played.

38. I do not need to make the point that if the roles were reversed and we were talking about an older man/younger woman scenario, then the notion of quasi-incest would not even be mooted. Interestingly, Maryse Degallaix in her lengthy review of this film made this point but used it (along with a few other criticisms) to dismiss the film as reactionary (*Image et son* 289, September 1974, 122–126).

39. It is instructive that, compared with *Le chat*, Signoret and Delon are in two-shots nearly three times more often than Signoret and Gabin (thirty in *Le chat*; eighty-four in *La veuve Couderc*).

40. This may explain why, in this stormy period of political/civic films to which Chapot makes reference, rather than select a "difficult" film, the CNC had considered entering his film as its official entry in international film festivals (in the end, it did not, and the film seems to have sunk very quickly). See *Le film français* 15 June 1923, 1973, 14. The CNC certainly was not interested in funding Allio's film; he got no *avance sur recettes* (see Guy Gauthier's interview with Allio in *Avant-scène du cinéma* 143/4 (January/February 1974): 9.

41. See the extensive details on this film and its preparation in the special issue of *Avant-scène du cinéma* 143/144 (January/February 1974): 3–69. Allio based his two lead characters in part on documented testimonies about their own lives of two working-class people—Janine Pszonak for Jeanne and André Viola for Julien. Most of Julien's voice-

overs are in fact Viola's words, and Jeanne's closing voiceover is a direct citation from Pszonak.

42. Signoret, quoted in *Avant-scène du cinéma*, ibid., (9): "I went and watched all those other Jeannes with their raincoats and shopping bags either going into the Samaritaine or a supermarket in Aubervilliers."

43. See Allio's long article on this film, "Fonction critique: 1," in *Cahiers du cinéma* 249 (February/March 1974): 22–26.

44. Ibid.

45. *Avant-scène du cinéma* 143/144 (January/February 1974): 8.

46. See Serge Daney's response to René Allio's article in the same *Cahiers du cinéma* issue cited ibid.

47. Allio, in *Avant-scène du cinéma* 143/144 (January/February 1974): 8.

48. Philippe Condroyer made a film about this precise issue, *La coupe à dix francs* (1974). It was based on a true story about a young apprentice carpenter who had long hair and was constantly humiliated and taunted by those around him. His boss orders him to get his hair cut, but he refuses, preferring to commit suicide instead.

49. Chase's prequel to this novel, *No Orchids for Miss Blandish*, had already been twice filmed: *No Orchids for Miss Blandish* (St. John L. Clowes, 1948) and *The Grissom Gang* (Robert Aldrich, 1971).

50. Interview with Chéreau by Henry Welsh in *Jeune cinéma* 85 (March 1975): 11.

51. See, for example, *Ecran 75* (34, 1975, 74–75) and *Positif* (168, April 1975, 57–58).

52. Josselin (1995, 105–106) spoke with Signoret about this move. She told him it took her ages to get it the way she wanted.

53. For an interesting biography of Guy de Maupassant, see Paul Morand *La vie de Guy de Maupassant* (Paris: Editions Pygmalion/Gérard Watelet, 1998).

54. See, for example, the review of *La vie devant soi* in *Screen International*, 21 April 1979, 58, which states that, but for Signoret's "hard-edged performance . . . sentiment teeters on the edge of sentimentality." *Films Illustrated* (8(39), May 1979, 350) argued that, well intentioned though it might be, it is a "button-pushing weepie." For its part, *Jeune cinéma* (127, June 1980, 45) was not overwhelmed by *Chère inconnue*, and *Positif* (231, May 1980, 72) found it a tremendous waste of talent (meaning Simone Signoret's, Delphine Seyrig's, and Jean Rochefort's, and not Moshe Mizrahi's).

55. Signoret (1979, 9–15) spoke very movingly about how this number was arrived at and its debt to her makeup person, Maud Begon, with whom she worked on most of her films from the 1960s onward. Begon had been a victim of the German concentration camps.

56. Robert Stam (1989, 160) goes into detail on Bakhtin's notions of the grotesque female body and death as "a shared collective human reality" and "as a way of refusing to project male fear of death onto the imago of woman, . . . of scapegoating women for a universal process."

57. As so pointedly put by the review in *Film Illustrated* 8(39) (May 1979): 350.

58. David (1992, 173).

59. Stam (1989, 93–94) lists thirteen various distinct concepts of Bakhtin's notion of the carnival. In this context of Madame Rosa I am drawing on the fourth concept: "a corporeal semiotic celebrating the grotesque, excessive body and the 'orifices' and 'protuberances' of the 'lower bodily stratum'" (93).

60. Signoret, quoted in Sandre (1981, 60).

61. Signoret, quoted in Monserrat (1983a, 271).

62. Arguably, this is another way in which Signoret's performance changes the tenor of the novel of the same name, which, as already noted in Chapter Two, was so much more focused on Momo's experience. The original novel, written by Romain Gary (under the pseudonym of Emile Ajar) and published in 1975, won many literary prizes, including the Prix Goncourt. Signoret had been approached by several directors (Claude Berri and Costa-Gavras, among them) who wanted to make the film and was at first reticent to do

it because she felt it too closely resembled another novel, *Fever*, by the American author Peter Feibelmann, which she had translated and hoped to get film rights for. She was eventually persuaded by Mizrahi to do the film, but later in 1981, when she discovered that Gary was the author of the novel and that he had known Feibelmann personally, she was very sad that her first instincts about the novel had probably been the right ones (Durant 1988, 119–122). Gary, a war hero and a friend of de Gaulle's, had been involved with Jean Seberg during the 1960s. By all accounts theirs was a very tumultuous relationship, particularly on a psychological level, where he was quite cruel to her and enjoyed causing her pain (see Geneuil 1995, 69 and 80). Although it came to an end, they never lost sight of each other (even if it was in psychologically damaging ways for Seberg). In 1979, they committed suicide within four months of each other.

63. In 1979, U.S. President Jimmy Carter would broker a peace treaty between Presidents Anwar Sadat of Egypt and Prime Minister Menachem Begin of Israel.

64. *Film Illustrated* 8(39) (May 1979): 350.

65. For a good overview of women's cinema in France during the 1970s, see Audé (1981).

66. See Hayward (2001, 107).

67. She is quoted in *Libération* (1 October 1985, 7), in a memorial issue upon her death, as saying: "My personal obsession is memory—nostalgia—that has not been shared. There I am a terrorist. When an event has been lived at the same time as me, I find it very difficult to accept that it has not been recorded, like me."

68. When she had been originally approached by Jo Langer during her visit to Czechoslovakia in 1957, Signoret had brushed her off. Langer wanted to enlist Signoret's help for her husband, who had been arrested during the Stalin-motivated Slansky purges in Czechoslovakia (the ones that are at the basis of *L'aveu*). She believed that if Signoret said something to the authorities about Oskar Langer, it would help set him free. He was sentenced to twenty-two years' hard labor, but his wife was convinced of his innocence. He was later freed and rehabilitated but died shortly thereafter. Jo Langer wrote up the story in a book entitled *Convictions: Memories of a Life Shared with a Good Communist*, which Signoret would translate into French in 1981, some eight years after her formal reunion with her cousin (David 1992, 102–111). See also Signoret's account of this story (Signoret 1978, 189–196). For further details on Langer's book and Signoret's motivation behind translating it into French, see the preface to her translated edition, *Une saison à Bratislava*, written by Jo Langer, and presented and translated by Simone Signoret (Paris: Editions du Seuil, 1981, 7–19).

69. Claude Roy, in his obituary on Simone Signoret, supplies us with this anecdote (*Nouvel Observateur*, 4 October 1985, 5).

70. Chéreau, quoted in *Today's Cinema* 78(239) 111.

71. By 1982 Signoret's autobiography had sold nearly a million copies (Monserrat 1983a, 248), and the first run of *Adieu Volodia* was 126,000 (*Le Monde*, 2 October 1985, BAP).

72. See, for example, *Jeune cinéma* 114 (November 1978): 50, and *Cahiers du cinéma* 295 (December 1978): 47.

73. Jean-Claude Biette, in *Cahiers du cinéma* 295 (December 1978): 48.

74. Alain Rémond, in *Télérama*, 11 October 1978, 105.

75. Chéreau, quoted in *Today's Cinema*, op. cit.

76. Jacques Siclier (quoted in Monserrat 1983a, 255–256) and Jean-Pierre Jeancolas (*Positif* 213, December 1978, 65) were the only two French critics who were astute enough to make this distinction when reviewing the film at the time of its release.

77. Signoret interviewed by Gilbert Salachas and quoted in *Télérama*, 11 October 1978, 113.

78. See, for example, Jacques Fieschi in *Cinématographe* 77 (April 1982): 48: "'Quality' France has come back to power." See also the review in *Positif* 256 (June 1982): 70: "Signoret . . . and, indeed, Noiret embody a 'tradition' of French cinema that harks back to the pre-war period. . . ."

79. Signoret, quoted in an interview, by André Buytaers, for *Les Amis du Film* (308, January 1982, 11): "I have made three films based on Simenon's novels and he has let me know . . . that he was delighted with my playing his characters."

80. Signoret had already made this point in her autobiography (Signoret 1978, 363).

81. Durant (1988, 128–129) gives us a very interesting anecdote on how Signoret thought through the details of her costume, so her role would have that edge of authenticity.

Chapter Eight: Television Work—1964–1985

1. See Belle Laurence's interview with Signoret about the making of this program in *L'Humanité*, 1 October 1964, BAP.

2. Ibid.

3. See Andrée Lehmann (1965, 7).

4. Ibid.

5. Agnès Varda uses the term *documenteur* to refer to the inevitable process of truth-bending that occurs when making a documentary (*menteur* meaning liar).

6. Signoret related this in an interview with *Télérama*, 9 November 1983, 38.

7. Ibid.

8. Ibid.

9. Ibid.

10. *Télé 7 jours* (6 October 1970, BAP) gives an excellent overview of Behan's play and its context.

11. Signoret, interviewed by Michel Guibert in *L'Express*, 5 July 1976, BAP.

12. As, for example, her experience of the Pierre Goldman case (see Chapter One).

13. Ibid.

14. *Madame le juge* was rebroadcast in 1983, 1986, 1989, 1991, and 1998.

15. The range of filmmmakers was astute, going from the popular Edouard Molinaro and Claude Barma, to Claude Chabrol and the more radical Philippe Condroyer and Nadine Trintignant. Among the stars were Juliet Berto, Michel Blanc, Nathalie Delon, Marie Dubois, Anna Karina, Philippe Léotard, Maurice Ronet, and Georges Wilson.

16. Signoret, quoted in *Télérama*, 11 March 1978, BAP.

17. Signoret fell out with Lino Ventura over the World Cup boycott. He went to Argentina, and she did not forgive him (Josselin 1995, 109–110).

18. This part of the story bears a strong resemblance to the Pierre Goldman case (see Chapter One). Goldman was found guilty of murdering two pharmacists and the attempted murder of a policeman on fairly circumstantial evidence. A woman's eyewitness account was introduced in the trial even though she had seen a photograph of Goldman in the papers prior to identifying him as the perpetrator of the crime. The police were desperate to get a result and had to have a suspect. Goldman fit their profile: he was a foreigner, dark-skinned, and a lefty. In the end, the trial was both political and racist (see Goldman 1975, 141–241).

19. Although, strictly speaking *juge d'instruction* translates as "examining magistrate," the English equivalent does not really have the same breadth of power as the French judge, so I have used the term investigating judge.

20. Durant (1988, 260).

21. Claude Chabrol, quoted in "TV: Madame le juge Simone Signoret," *L'Express*, 7 June 1976, BAP.

22. Two women *juges d'instruction* (Madames Watrelot and Fiabrini) were interviewed by *Télé 7 jours* (18 March 1978, 125, BAP) and asked to comment on Judge Massot in terms of their real jobs. They felt the character was too familiar with those she investigated and moved around a lot, more like a police detective than an investigating judge, who mostly coordinates police work and deals with the written dossiers. But on the plus side they felt that using a woman judge for the series humanized the justice system and would help to break its hard-line image. Intriguingly, they pointed out that the

main problem for women judges comes down to the fact that 80 percent of the criminals are men who try to seduce women judges. So the thing to avoid is falling into that trap— arguably something Judge Massot fails to do in "2 + 2 = 4."

23. *Télé 7 jours*, 15 May 1986, 106–107, BAP.

24. All these details can be gleaned from the article by Martine Bourbillon on *Music Hall* in *Télé 7 jours*, 22 May 1986, BAP.

25. So we are informed by Geneviève Cost in her article on *Music Hall* in *Télé 7 jours*, 15 May 1986, 106, BAP.

Conclusion

1. See Vincendeau (2000, 1–41) for more details on the French star system and Vincendeau (2000, 2–10) for details on the theater/cinema interface.

2. There is an intriguing short piece of film where Signoret is trying out for the role of Léontine in Jean Boyer's *Le Prince Charmant* (incidentally, her first casting). Compared to the four other young women trying out for the role, she stands out. Her tone of voice is modulated (as opposed to the others, who play it all in one tone); her performance style is strong, quite phatic (if a little forced at times). But in comparison with the other candidates she is a striking presence. She looks as if she is actively enjoying the task at hand (as opposed to the others, who are all rather anxious). As early as this first trial you can sense the strength of her persona. (The film trial rushes can be found at the CNC.)

3. Anne Andreu, obituary for Simone Signoret, *L'Evénement du jeudi*, 3 October 1985, 5.

4. See "In the Shadows of the Stars: Their Eminence Grise," *Cinémonde*, 24 October 1957, 14–15, where Allégret speaks of the impact of Signoret on his own filmmaking career.

5. In *Simone Signoret* (1982), the writer notes the following: "Long before Bardot, she invented a modern eroticism by displaying another way to seduce, another way to 'be in the world.' Insolent, violent, provocative. And so much the better if she subjugates the world with her beauty."

6. Dora Doll (who appears in *Music Hall*) makes this observation about Signoret's silent dialogue with the eyes in her obituary for the star (*Libération*, 1 October 1985, 7).

7. There is something quite interesting about her evoking the myth of Oedipus in her very last film (as Madame Baron relating the riddle of the Sphinx to Monsieur Baron) since so many of her roles can be read, within dominant ideology, as a similar "failed" trajectory.

8. See Warwick and Cavallaro (1998, 82).

Bibliography

Aldgate, Tony. *Censorship and the British Society: British Cinema and Theatre 1955–1965.* Oxford: Clarendon Press, 1995.

Allégret, Catherine. *Les souvenirs et les regrets aussi. . . .* Paris: Editions Fixot, 1994.

Andrew, Dudley. "Casque d'Or, Casquettes, a Cask of Ageing Wine: Jacques Becker's *Casque d'Or* (1952)." In *French Film: Texts and Contexts,* edited by Susan Hayward and Ginette Vincendeau, 112–126. London and New York: Routledge, 2000.

Aubron, Hervé. "Resistance à l'histoire: à propos de *L'armée des ombres.*" *Vertigo* 16 (1997): 147–151.

Audé, Françoise. *Ciné-modèles, cinéma d'elles: situation des femmes dans le cinéma français 1956–1979.* Lausanne: L'Age d'Homme, 1981.

Bakhtin, Mikhail. *The Dialogic Imagination.* Translated by Michael Holquist; edited by Caryl Emerson and Michael Holquist. Austin: University of Texas Press, 1981.

Bazin, André. "Trahisons." *Cahiers du cinéma* 27 (October, 1953): 23–24.

Benmussa, Simone. "Le geste quotidien et ses transpositions." In *Le corps en jeu,* edited by Odette Aslan, 151–153. Paris: CNRS, 1993.

Bonnell, René. *La vingt-cinquième image: une économie de l'audiovisuel.* Paris: Gallimard/FEMIS, 1989.

Bruzzi, Stella. *Undressing Cinema: Clothing and Identity in the Movies.* London and New York: Routledge, 1997.

Burch, Noël, and Geneviève Sellier. *La drôle de guerre des sexes du cinéma français: 1930–1956.* Paris: Editions Nathan, 1996.

Carné, Marcel. *La vie à belles dents.* Paris: Editions Jean Vuarnet, 1979.

Chapsal, Madeleine. *L'elégance des années 50.* Paris: Herscher, 1986.

Davis, Catherine. *Simone Signoret.* Translated by Sally Sampson. London: Bloomsbury, 1992.

Davarrieux, Claire. *Les acteurs au travail* (Série Bibliothèque du cinéma). Renens, Switzerland: Hatier, 1981.

De Vorges, D. *Le maquillage, cinéma, télévision, théâtre.* Paris: Editions Dujarrie, 1986.

Doane, Mary Anne. "Film and the Masquerade: Theorising the Female Spectator," *Screen* 23, no. 3/4 (1982): 74–87.

Doniol-Valcroze, Jacques. "'La marin de la Malchance,' a review of *Thérèse Raquin.*" *Cahiers du cinéma* 29 (December 1953): 41–42.

Doniol-Valcroze, Jacques. "Déshabillage d'une petite-bourgeoisie sentimentale." *Cahiers du cinéma* 6, no. 31 (January 1954): 2–14.

Durant, Philippe. *Simone Signoret: une vie.* Lausanne: Edition Favre, 1988.

Dyer, Richard. *Stars.* London: British Film Institute Publishing, 1980.

Dyer, Richard. *Heavenly Bodies: Film Stars and Society.* London and New York: Routledge, 1986.

Dyer, Richard. "No Place for Homosexuality: Marcel Carné's *L'Air de Paris* (1954)." In *French Film: Texts and Contexts,* edited by Susan Hayward and Ginette Vincendeau, 127–141. London and New York: Routledge.

French, Don. *Les têtes de l'art.* Paris: Grasset, 1982.

Gauteur, Claude, and Ginette Vincendeau. *Jean Gabin: anatomie d'un mythe.* Paris: Nathan, 1993.

Gélin, Daniel. *Deux ou trois vies qui sont les miennes.* Paris: Julliard, 1977.

Geneuil, Guy-Pierre. *Jean Seberg, ma star assassinée.* Paris: Edition 1, 1995.

Goldman, Pierre. *Souvenirs d'un Juif polonais né en France.* Paris: Editions du Seuil, 1975.

Hamon, Hervé, and Patrick Rotman. *Tu vois, je n'ai pas oublié.* Paris: Editions du Seuil/Fayard, 1990.

Hayward, Susan. *French National Cinema.* London and New York: Routledge, 1993.

Hayward, Susan. "Simone Signoret 1921–1985: The Star as Sign—The Sign as Scar." In *Women and Representation* (WIF Occasional Papers), edited by Diane Knight and Judith Still, 57–74. Nottingham: University of Nottingham Press, 1995.

Hayward, Susan. "Setting the Agenders: Simone Signoret and the Pre-Feminist Star Body." In *Gender and French Cinema,* edited by Alex Hughes and James Williams, 107–124. Oxford: Berg, 2001.

Hayward, Susan, and Ginette Vincendeau. *French Film: Texts and Contexts,* 2nd ed. London and New York: Routledge, 2000.

Josselin, Jean-François. *Simone: deux ou trois choses que je sais d'elle.* Paris: Grasset, 1995.

Kessel, Joseph. *L'armée des ombres.* Paris: Librarie Plon, 1963.

Kramer, Stanley, with Thomas M. Coffey. *A Mad Mad Mad Mad World: A life in Hollywood.* London: Arum Press, 1997.

Leahy, Sarah, and Susan Hayward. "The Tainted Woman: Simone Signoret, Site of Pathology or Agent of Retribution?" In *Heroines without Heroes: Reconstructing Female and National Identities in European Cinema 1945–51,* edited by Ulrike Sieglohr. London and New York: Cassell, 2001.

Lehmann, Andrée. *Le rôle de la femme au milieu du vingtième siècle,* 3rd ed. Paris: Edition de la Ligue Française pour le Droit des Femmes, 1965.

London, Artur, and Lise London. *L'aveu.* Paris: Gallimard, 1968.

Monserrat, Joëlle. *Simone Signoret.* Paris: Editions PAC, 1983a.

Monserrat, Joëlle. *Yves Montand.* Paris: Editions PAC, 1983b.

Ninode, B. *"La mort en ce jardin." Image et Son* 205 (1967): 127–138.

Perez, Michel. *Les films de Carné.* Paris: Ramsay, 1986.

Périsset, Maurice. *Simone Signoret.* Paris: Editions J'ai lu, 1988.

Ross, Kristin. *Fast Cars, Clean Bodies: Decolonialisation and the Reordering of French Culture.* Cambridge, Mass., and London: MIT Press, 1995.

Sandre, Didier. *Simone Signoret.* Paris: Solar, 1981.

Signoret, Simone. *La nostalgie n'est plus ce qu'elle était.* Paris: Editions de Seuil, 1978. First published in 1975.

Signoret, Simone. *Le lendemain elle était souriante.* Paris: Editions du Seuil, 1979.

Signoret, Simone. *Adieu Volodia.* Paris: Livre de Poche, 1988. First published 1985.

Simenon, Georges. *Le chat.* Paris: Presses de la Cité, 1967.

Simone Signoret. Paris: Fondation Gar pour le Cinéma, 1982.

Stam, Robert. *Subversive Pleasures: Bakhtin, Cultural Criticism, and Film.* Baltimore and London: Johns Hopkins University Press, 1989.

Turk, Edward Baron. *Child of Paradise: Marcel Carné and the Golden Age of French Cinema.* Cambridge, Mass., and London: Harvard University Press, 1989.

Vailland, Roger. *Drôle de jeu.* Paris: Buchet-Chastel, 1945.

Vian, Boris. *Manuel de Saint-Germain-des-Prés.* Paris: Pauvert, 1997.

Vincendeau, Ginette. *Stars and Stardom in French Cinema.* London and New York: Continuum, 2000.

Warwick, Alexandra, and Dani Cavallaro. *Fashioning the Frame: Boundaries, Dress and Body.* Oxford and New York: Berg, 1998.

Willett, Cynthia. *Maternal Ethics and Other Slave Moralities.* London and New York: Routledge, 1995.

Zola, Emile. *Thérèse Raquin.* Paris: Livre de Poche, 1953. (Originally published in 1867.)

Index